Charlotte M Reed
1105 Monroe St NE
Minneapolis, MN 55413

THE DIPLOMACY OF MIGRATION

A volume in the series

The United States in the World

Edited by Mark Philip Bradley, David C. Engerman, Amy S. Greenberg, and Paul A. Kramer

A list of titles in this series is available at www.cornellpress.cornell.edu.

THE DIPLOMACY OF MIGRATION

Transnational Lives and the Making of U.S.-Chinese Relations in the Cold War

Meredith Oyen

Cornell University Press
Ithaca and London

First published 2015 by Cornell University Press

Printed in the United States of America

Library of Congress Cataloging-in-Publication Data

Oyen, Meredith, 1978– author.
   The diplomacy of migration : transnational lives and the making of U.S.-Chinese relations in the Cold War / Meredith Oyen.
       pages cm. — (The United States in the world)
   Includes bibliographical references and index.
   ISBN 978-1-5017-0014-9 (cloth : alk. paper)
   1. United States—Foreign relations—China.   2. China—Foreign relations—United States.   3. United States—Emigration and immigration—Government policy.   4. China—Emigration and immigration.   5. Chinese—United States.   6. Cold War.   I. Title.
   E183.8.C5O94   2015
   327.73051—dc23   2015010603

Cornell University Press strives to use environmentally responsible suppliers and materials to the fullest extent possible in the publishing of its books. Such materials include vegetable-based, low-VOC inks and acid-free papers that are recycled, totally chlorine-free, or partly composed of nonwood fibers. For further information, visit our website at www.cornellpress.cornell.edu.

Cloth printing   10 9 8 7 6 5 4 3 2 1

In memory of
黃裕雯
and
Nancy Bernkopf Tucker

Contents

Acknowledgments

Nancy Bernkopf Tucker patiently guided me through a thousand different iterations of this project with both good humor and tough questions. My only regret is that she never got to see the final version. I hope it lives up to her famously high standards, though any failures in this respect are mine alone.

As with any such project long in the making, this work has benefited immeasurably from the help and support of a great variety of individuals, institutions, and organizations. My Chinese language training was funded in part by Americorps and the NSEP Boren Fellowship Program. My numerous research trips were funded with help from the Fulbright Program, the Georgetown University Graduate School and Graduate Student Organization, the Johns Hopkins–Nanjing University Center for Chinese and American Studies, and the University of Maryland, Baltimore County. Everywhere I went, archivists and librarians went above and beyond to help researchers, especially at the Roosevelt, Truman, Eisenhower, Kennedy, Johnson, and Nixon presidential libraries; the National Archives at Kew in England and its U.S. counterpart in Maryland and Washington, D.C.; Academia Sinica, Academia Historica, the Kuomintang Archive, and the Ministry of Foreign Affairs Archive of the Republic of China; and the

Ministry of Foreign Affairs Archive of the People's Republic of China, the Number Two Historical Archive, and in particular, the Guangdong Provincial Archive.

During my repeated visits to Taipei, my dear friend Yuwen Huang also went far outside the usual bounds of friendship to help me figure out how to get into archives when I was first starting out, organize photocopies, mail materials, double-check translations, and take me out for spicy hot pot and Taiwan Beer.

Friends, colleagues, and strangers helped me out by reading drafts in various stages of completion. In particular, my Georgetown classmates Sarah Snyder and Tao Wang helped me at every stage of the project. I am also indebted to Carol Benedict, Gordon H. Chang, Joseph McCartin, and David Painter for reading the manuscript and offering helpful advice and letters of support. More recently, I am thankful for advice and comments from Erez Manela, Sayuri Guthrie-Shimizu, David Atkinson, Stephen Philips, and Kate Brown. I am particularly grateful to Warren Cohen for giving me so much of his time, insight, and friendship.

As this book neared completion, it benefited greatly from the support and advice of Michael McGandy, David Engerman, Paul Kramer, and anonymous reviewers who offered guidance, as well as from additional funding from the UMBC Dresher Center.

Finally, this project would not be complete without the ever-optimistic encouragement of my parents, Duane and Ann Oyen, as well as the emotional support and slightly improbable self-help theories of Matthew Beers.

THE DIPLOMACY OF MIGRATION

Introduction

The Floating Population and Foreign Policy

On February 25, 1943, the RMS *Empress of Scotland* sailed into New York Harbor. The ocean liner had been pressed into wartime service, its luxurious accommodations refitted to ferry fresh troops to the front lines in Europe and North Africa. The urgencies of war usually forced a quick turnaround in port for the ship's 480-man crew, but this call to New York proved much longer than the usual visit. Upon arrival, 177 of its sailors deserted, all of them Chinese.[1]

For decades, a tradition of misapplying the United States' Chinese Exclusion Acts barred Chinese seamen from taking shore leave in U.S. ports. This procedure was often advocated by the Immigration and Naturalization Service (INS) and went unchallenged by the mostly British-owned shipping companies employing Chinese sailors, largely because the British companies were made financially liable for any errant Chinese migrants who managed to slip into the country via a visit to one of its ports. In August 1942, State Department officials more concerned about the appearance of anti-Chinese discrimination than the actual fact of it forged a deal with Chinese consular officials and British shipping authorities to allow Chinese to take shore leave on a trial basis. The agreement required that the local Chinese consul come aboard and warn the seamen against deserting, for the sake of the war, for the sake of the motherland, and for the sake of their own honor.

Desertions skyrocketed. It was not that Chinese sailors working Allied merchant ships were unconcerned about the war, China, or their own reputation. Instead, they were protesting inequality. Unfortunately, they chose to do so in a way that managed to threaten the entire Allied war effort in Europe. There were five thousand Chinese sailors in the Allied Merchant Marine—only about 5 percent of the total manpower—but Chinese desertions tended to follow the pattern of the crew of the *Empress of Scotland*. Instead of deserting one at a time like most other nationalities, Chinese seamen deserted in groups, which crippled the ability of a ship to leave port or join its scheduled convoys, needed for protection against the German U-boats patrolling the high seas. Using this critical moment to make their demands for equal wages, better treatment, and access to shore leave, Chinese sailors brought their concerns to the attention of shipping officials on either side of the Atlantic. Their militancy forced the Chinese government to take action as well, and the result was a series of negotiations between China and Britain, and China and the United States, aimed at pushing back against the legacies of European imperialism in Asia and Chinese exclusion in the Americas.

The fact that the desertions from the *Empress of Scotland* occurred after these agreements revealed just how racially charged the questions of Chinese labor and Chinese desertions remained. British officials and ship officers struggled to overcome what one Chinese editorialist called "the Singapore mentality," or the assumption that all Chinese laborers were "coolies"—often code for cheap, expendable, and inherently unwilling to work.[2] U.S. officials had their own problems, centered on the State Department's wartime view of China as a necessary, if somewhat inept, ally and the INS view of all arriving Chinese as both illegal and undesirable immigrants. American officials tasked with managing the desertion problem struggled between promoting the new official narrative of an equal partner in Asia and the legacies of long-standing exclusions. World War II became a watershed in reshaping how American officials interacted with China, as opposed to the Chinese, forcing a reckoning of the two perspectives. The *Empress of Scotland* did finally depart after several weeks' delay and a raid on Chinatown in which some seamen were arrested and even impressed back into service. And, of course, the *Empress* was only one ship; an average of fifteen arrived in port every month from late 1942 to mid 1944, and a full 20 percent of the Chinese seamen arriving on them deserted.

The scramble to address the complaints of Chinese seamen and stop their desertions during the war reveals something important about the relationship between human migration, foreign policy, and national security. The seamen's concerns were not the primary occupation of wartime policy makers arguing over opening a second front and managing the postwar world; but when enough problems added up, they consumed the time and attention of the officials tasked with keeping the war effort going. In the process, American, British, and Chinese officials learned that even in a time of war, traditionally "secondary" issues like migration policy and management can achieve primary importance. Moreover, it was not enough for the United States or Britain to have good relations with Chinese leaders: they needed better relations with the Chinese people as well.

The Diplomacy of Migration between China and the United States

Developing better U.S.-China and U.S.-Chinese relations was not an easy task during World War II, because a long history of inequality overshadowed both relationships. In 1784, the *Empress of China* set sail from the port of New York, inaugurating a century of rapidly expanding ties and a growing exchange of people. Americans moved to China to seek their fortunes and spread their gospels, while Chinese moved to the United States to get rich or at least to get paid. Early treaties protected the sojourners of either state, but the traffic was always lopsided—there were more Chinese bound for the United States than Americans for China. Because the United States grew in world influence as China faced increasing encroachments upon its sovereignty, the relationship became increasingly uneven as well, opening the door for the United States to seek and obtain extraterritoriality (exemption from local laws) for its citizens in China even while passing an act to exclude Chinese laborers from the United States, as well as tolerating discrimination and injustices visited upon Chinese sojourners. Even after the formal repeal of both extraterritoriality and exclusion during the war, the specter of inequality and exclusion lingered over Chinese migration in the twentieth century.

Despite this lingering inequality—indeed, because of it—the decades between the 1940s and the early 1970s are of particular interest for historians of both Chinese migration and U.S.-China relations. For migration historians, the years from 1943 to the immigration act passed in 1965 are marred by this "de facto exclusion." Race-based standards for quota immigration continued to keep large numbers of Chinese (and other Asians) from immigrating to the United States, though as this book and others demonstrate, there were many other means by which contact, travel, and new migration occurred. For diplomatic historians, the years from 1949 to 1972 were the "great aberration": the period in which there was limited formal diplomatic contact between the United States and mainland China and a great deal of ongoing conflict.[3] Nixon's trip to China in 1972 marked the beginning of the end of the U.S.-led exclusion of the People's Republic of China (PRC) from the international system, though it also began the exclusion of Nationalist China. Combining these two periodizations, the years in between 1943 and 1972 are notable for something else: they are the years of formal alliance between the United States and Nationalist China. During this period from World War II until Nixon landed in Shanghai, the Nationalists faced constant threats to their very existence. First the Japanese, then the Chinese Communists, then the growing loss of recognition caused that government to move from one crisis to the next. After 1949, its relationship with its greatest patron, the United States, determined its very survival. And its human resources during these dark years were limited to the population under its immediate control and the Chinese living overseas. It is not remarkable that managing migration became a vital part of Nationalist Chinese diplomacy; it would have been more remarkable if it had not.

This book identifies and explains the role that "migration diplomacy"—the process of using migration policy for diplomatic ends—played in managing the larger, complex relations between the United States and its Chinese ally and Chinese enemy from the formation of the Cold War during World War II until the start of its denouement in Asia.[4] Throughout the existing literature on U.S.-Chinese relations and Chinese Americans, many points of reference for this history are scattered about, among them the wartime imperative of the repeal of exclusion, the early Cold War suspicions of Communist infiltrators as immigrants, and the use of repatriation of nationals as an excuse to restart direct communications. More than just showing how foreign policy affected migration, this book demonstrates that policy makers used migration policy to benefit foreign policy.

Three patterns in migration diplomacy emerged in this period. First, migration policy and practice became a direct tool of foreign policy, used to signal positive and negative developments in the bilateral relationships, as well as potential changes in the offing. How migrants were selected and treated, what policies were involved and how they were carried out, and whether visas were issued were all at one point or another employed to send a larger message beyond the migration they facilitated. Through two hot wars and the height of the Cold War, Nationalist China used migration policy to seek equality and legitimacy for its government. The United States used migration policies to placate Nationalist China when it could not fulfill other promises; and starting in the mid-1950s, American officials also used migration diplomacy to explore and eventually transform their country's relationship with the People's Republic of China. The PRC, meanwhile, used aid to migrants in the United States as a proxy for diplomatic recognition for as long as it was withheld.

Second, beyond this direct use of migration policy, migration diplomacy was employed more indirectly by both the United States and China as a form of public diplomacy. The United States used new measures to bolster its prestige in Asia and internationally, while the Republic of China (ROC) used migration policy to build an overseas network ready to support its position. The PRC also joined in, using family networks to seek support, both emotional and material, from Chinese Americans. Third and finally, migration diplomacy served a more complex purpose in attempting to remake the Chinese American community in ways that both the U.S. and ROC governments sought. The United States employed strict screening measures to recruit and permit only the "best" immigrants to integrate into American domestic life. At the same time, the Republic of China implemented broad-based screening techniques to ensure emigrants would both support their government in the face of Communist opposition and raise Americans' opinions of the Chinese as immigrants. Both projects contributed to an idealized understanding of Chinese Americans as part of a "model minority" in the late 1970s and early 1980s.

Exploring all three forms of migration diplomacy in these years makes clear the connections between varied forms of migration and the larger international history of the period. Quite naturally, historians tend to treat immigration as an issue distinct from cultural diplomacy, like programs to promote student and scholarly exchanges. Historians often view the former as the purview of social historians and the latter as something connected to public diplomacy. Deportation is considered apart from repatriation. Refugees are in a category of their own, with sometimes limited connections to voluntary exiles. But the post-exclusion, mid-century history of Chinese migrations demonstrates that building walls between these categories can cut off useful avenues of analysis. Thousands of Chinese students arrived in the United States in the late 1940s. After 1949, some simply returned to China, others were detained in the United States and found themselves the subject of ambassadorial talks in Geneva, and of course, many settled in the United States under refugee laws to raise the next generation of Chinese Americans. Immigrants, exiles, deportees, refugees, defectors, and dissidents all shared the experience of being Chinese in the United States, and the uncertainty in the international arena ensured that many individuals held more than one of these labels at one point or another in their migratory lives.[5] From a foreign relations perspective, the distinctions between them fade dramatically: the question becomes instead what role they play in building up or tearing down diplomatic ties.

Beyond policy-level concerns, studying migrants in this era helps to reveal the lived experience of the Cold War: how uncertainty on the international level trickled down to affect people's everyday lives.[6] The subject here is not how Chinese American communities developed and flourished, faced down discrimination, or adapted to American life. Instead, I explore migrant lives at times when they became an issue in U.S. relations with China. Migrants became pawns of unruly governments at times, yes. But they also created their own brand of "people's diplomacy" that affected how the governments understood each other and signaled changing goals and ideals, while permitting the migrants themselves to navigate Cold War politics to their own benefit. The American Cold War national security state proved frequently at odds with the ideological idea of the "leader of the free world," and the migrants who found themselves caught up in that bureaucracy had a front-row seat to its greatest failures, as well as its greatest successes.

Migration diplomacy did not rise to the level of primary security concerns like nuclear policy or shifting Cold War alliances. Instead, its value is found in its subordinate status. During the war-torn decades from the end of Chinese immigration exclusion until the advent of Nationalist China's international exclusion, the perception of these issues as secondary turned negotiations over migrations and manipulations of migration policy into safe ways for the United States and both Chinas to pursue larger diplomatic goals. Leaders and policy makers in all three governments shared a common experience of recognizing that low risk did not mean no risk, however, and persistent problems managing migration issues could affect both prestige and national security. Low risk critically also did not translate to unimportant, as migration diplomacy often had quite a lot to contribute to the success of foreign policy overtures. That missteps on any one such issue did not carry the threat of catastrophic results, however, made migration a useful venue for trying out new policy approaches, reacting to changing events, or making symbolic gestures.

The contingent nature of migration policy proved less ideal for migrants themselves. No amount of policy planning, of congressional debates, of bureaucratic organization, or daily paper pushing could force individual migrants to act in ways against their own interests. As a result, migrants created the policy positions as much as they were affected by them. Individuals became the subject of high-level debate, acted as go-betweens when formal ties failed, campaigned for their own hoped-for results, and protested ill-treatment and poor governance. In some respects they were the wild cards that made lofty policy plans succeed or fail, but they were also the reason these plans had be formed in the first place.

The Diplomacy of Migration provides an analysis of migration diplomacy in the period from 1943 to 1972. We already have some understanding of this dynamic for both the exclusion era and the post–Cold War era. Michael Hunt's landmark work, *The Making of a Special Relationship*, ensured that no future monograph on the Open Door or the turn-of-the-century relationship would leave out the disputes over exclusion policy and the right to consular protections while abroad.[7] Though the open door for American goods and closed door for Chinese nationals summarized an inherently unequal relationship that persisted until the Second World War, the unique ties between the two countries relied on migrants who were not excluded, such as merchants, diplomats, and students and scholars, making their own contributions to increasing mutual understanding.[8] Moreover, migration historians have viewed the exclusion era as a dynamic era of ongoing, even expanding transnational ties between the two countries. The literature on the prewar era highlights migration as a process that joins the United States and China together; forges links between them by way of families, friendship, and funds; and re-creates itself with each new wave of travelers.[9] In the period after rapprochement, studies once again embrace the idea of migrants effecting change in foreign policy, starting with the late 1970s or 1980s, when the Fulbright program restarts, consular offices are reopened, and a new age of cooperation brings more travelers, immigrants, and students to each other's shores.[10]

The relationship between migration and foreign relations histories in the period after the official end of exclusion but before rapprochement is somewhat less clearly defined in the literature. In diplomatic history, the U.S.-China relationship grew increasingly complicated when the wartime alliance gave way to decades of Cold War competition and a divided China.

High-stakes political and security concerns reigned as China experienced a civil war, established a Communist government, and faced off against the United States and United Nations in Korea. Continued U.S. support for the Nationalist government after it moved to Taiwan drove a wedge between Washington and Beijing, curtailing any chance of even economic reconciliation in the midst of ideological conflict. Scholarly treatments of these tumultuous years are both rich and varied, analyzing both particular incidents and long-standing disputes.[11] With exclusion repealed, direct contact between the United States and the Chinese mainland limited, and nuclear war threatening, migration policies and issues tend to fall out of the diplomatic history narrative. That said, more broadly the field of American foreign relations has experienced an international and transnational turn that has proved increasingly mindful of the contributions of private "citizen diplomats," transnational networks and organizations, and public diplomacy in shaping high-level policy.[12]

Postwar and Cold War Chinese migration histories have also embraced transnational approaches. Historians such as K. Scott Wong, Xiaojian Zhao, and Mae Ngai argue that international events and conflicts have had a profound effect on Chinese American lives and migrations. Meanwhile, scholars Cindy I-Fen Cheng, Madeline Hsu, and Ellen D. Wu have turned increasingly to the influence of Cold War politics and preferences on creating and shaping the idea that Asian Americans served as a "model minority" in the United States.[13] Recognition that international affairs can have profound effects on migrants has also come from beyond Chinese America, as historians such as Donna Gabaccia, Eiichiro Azuma, and Carl Bon Tempo note that both migration policy and migrant experiences are shaped by and even occasionally help shape diplomatic goals.[14]

The Diplomacy of Migration aims to bridge the excellent work on this period in both fields by demonstrating the political use of migration policy and how migrants responded. To do so, this book is divided into three parts. Each of the eight chapters considers a core migration policy or related policies in its particular context, then unpacks the policy's efficacy in achieving associated geopolitical goals, as well as how migrants experienced it. As a diplomatic history of migration policy, revealing state-to-state communication, conflict, and collusion over migration issues is important, but the lived experience of the policies, not to mention the ability of migrants to have disproportionate impact on foreign relations (as the defecting Chinese seamen at the start of this chapter demonstrate), means that the experience as subjects of policies is important as well.

Together, the three chapters in the first part of the book explain the role of migration policies in fighting World War II and contributing to the advance of the Cold War in Asia. They also establish what was at stake for the United States, Nationalist China, and the migrants themselves, as many of the migrations begun in this short decade became the subjects of contention in the period that followed. Chapter 1 revisits the well-known story of the repeal of Chinese exclusion, but in so doing explains the mechanism through which the United States and Nationalist China would attempt to negotiate migration policy for shared political benefit, but to the detriment of the population of migrants most affected by it. Chapter 2 explains the roots of the Nationalists' faith in their diaspora as a major component of any political or military victory, focusing on how Chinese officials sought to help Chinese migrants and Chinese Americans mobilize men and money to fight the war in Asia. Nationalist "citizen services" in the name of the war effort form a clear example of the use of migration policy to negotiate equality for the Chinese state. Chapter 3 details the reopening of transportation leading to repatriation and new migration during the Chinese Civil War. Because of the existential threat to the Nationalist state, Chinese officials made use of these migrations to solidify the Republic of China's place as a member of the United Nations and as an ally of the United States, experimenting with greater control over who goes abroad and what they do there in the process. The United States, meanwhile, struggled to balance between the political pressure to support the Republic of China and the popular reluctance to accept Chinese migrants, a schism that would only deepen when the security concerns of the Cold War hardened.

Part 2 of the book demonstrates how Chinese migrants acted as "cold warriors"—influencing international relations both voluntarily and involuntarily. Chapter 4 picks up the story of new immigration begun in chapter 3, plus the dilemma of deportation in the context of closed borders to explain how the Cold War made it necessary for some migration policies simultaneously to serve national security imperatives and promote national prestige. Chinese in the United States both fell victim to fears of Communist infiltration and supported "free China," and in each case struggled with Nationalist Chinese efforts to use their experiences to maintain standing in American eyes. Chapter 5 focuses on how migrants link domestic and foreign policies, explaining how traditional Chinese family remittances became a battleground between the two Chinas. The money trail was vital but difficult to control, and as a result, policy experiments here had tragic consequences. In chapter 6, the push of refugees into Hong Kong created a dilemma for the United States and Nationalist China, both of which politically wanted to be seen as offering assistance but preferred to accept few refugees for permanent residence. This chapter demonstrates that definitions such as "immigrant" or "refugee" mattered and were contingent on Cold War policy aims.

The third and final part of the book explains how migration policy became a means of easing the Cold War in Asia. Chapter 7 demonstrates how the repatriation of detained nationals in the 1950s became both the excuse for the United States and Communist China to open direct communications and a means for both Chinese governments to negotiate legitimacy. As "Cold War hostages," Chinese scholars detained in the United States and Americans imprisoned in China had political significance that made the terms of their repatriations heavily contested. Chapter 8 looks at "visa diplomacy" and immigration policy changes in the 1960s, exploring how the wild card of Taiwan independence activists in the United States helped to break down the cooperation between the United States and its Nationalist allies. And finally, the book's conclusion surveys changes in travel policy in the lead-up to the Nixon trip to China, demonstrating that migration both signaled changing American and Communist Chinese attitudes and offered a low-risk way to explore them.

A Note on Language

I have used the transliterations of Chinese names available in the documents. American, British, and even sometimes Chinese documents often provide a name and a great deal of information about an individual using the former Wade-Giles or other past transliteration systems without also providing the characters. For private citizens, this means the characters or pinyin transliterations are not always available. Where they are, however, I have tried to provide both transliterations. In a few other cases, as with Chiang Kai-shek (Jiang Jieshi in pinyin), Soong Mei-ling (Song Meiling), and the Kuomintang or KMT (the Nationalist Party, *Guomindang* in pinyin), I have opted to use the most common and recognizable transliteration, even at the expense of total consistency. Except where explicitly noted, all translations from Chinese are my own.

Part I

Migration Diplomacy at War

Chapter 1

Unequal Allies

Renegotiating Exclusions

Soong May-ling (Song Meiling), wife of Chiang Kai-shek and arguably the most famous Chinese migrant to the United States in the twentieth century, made an official visit to Washington in 1943. Soong spent a decade in her youth studying in the United States, graduating from Wellesley College in 1917, and after Chiang died she returned to a family estate in New York for much of her remaining years. Over the course of the twentieth century, she traveled to the United States as a student, an official, and as an immigrant. The official purpose of her wartime visit was to seek medical care, though she had a long-standing invitation from Eleanor Roosevelt to visit the White House and took advantage of the opportunity to advocate for greater U.S. support of China's struggle against Japan. The president apparently made a great effort not to allow himself to be taken in by her infamous charm, but Congress was generally not so careful.[1] As one *Time* magazine reporter gushed after her appearance there:

She was with the Senate, but over and above them. In her soul was the hot iron that six years of war, decades of civil warfare and politics can ram into a person, but it had left her rather purged of crass humanness than seared by the flame. . . . She was straight, almost as slender as a reed in a

long, black trailing Chinese silken gown that fitted with more than clerical
precision around her throat. Senators, as she walked to the rostrum, caught
glimpses of well-turned, beautifully flashing legs as the split sides of the
gown opened to the knee as she walked along.[2]

Both beautiful and formidable even while being objectified, Soong made a
strong case for more equal standing between the United States and China
in their joint execution of the war. She appealed publicly and privately for
more aid to China, but she also pushed behind the scenes for the repeal of
the Chinese Exclusion Acts, which insisted that however desirable she was
to the men of Congress, being a Chinese woman made her officially an
undesirable immigrant.

By the time Madame Chiang Kai-shek (as she was known) arrived in
Washington, the American public proved as well conditioned to think posi-
tively about their largest ally in Asia as they had been to think negatively
about Chinese once they arrived in U.S. ports as immigrants. When the
United States finally entered World War II in December 1941, China had
already been fighting the Japanese for four and a half years. Aid had arrived
from a variety of sources: Germany and the Soviet Union first, and by mid-
1941, from the United States and Britain. Private citizens in the United
States joined fund-raisers and campaigns for United China Relief, proudly
celebrating that nation as the "first to fight" the Axis powers.[3] Egged on
by the triumphant coverage from Henry Luce's *Time* and *Life* magazines,
the American perception of the Chinese nation underwent a radical shift
toward the positive during a short time early in the war.[4]

Popular support notwithstanding, official American support for China
consistently fell short of Chiang Kai-shek's expectations. For all the fanfare
and celebration of Claire Chennault's volunteer "Flying Tigers" air force
and their daring supply runs over the Himalayas, the relationship between
"the Generalissimo" (Chiang Kai-shek) and the American representative
in China, General Joseph Stilwell, remained tense and difficult. American
diplomats in China complained that the Chinese leader appeared more
interested in saving his resources for the postwar fight against the growing Communist movement than in making an immediate effort against
the Japanese. According to U.S. Navy Group member John Lacey, by the
end of the war American diplomats in China were "rather down on the
Chiang government." Noting the combination of rampant inflation and
unchecked corruption, he added, "None of us felt very kindly toward the
Soong clan, including Madame Chiang Kai-shek."[5] Meanwhile, Chinese

officials frequently complained about the Allied powers' tendency to place Europe first on the wartime agenda. The Cairo Conference, which brought Chiang together with Roosevelt and Winston Churchill, illustrated this complicated dynamic by simultaneously offering reassurances to Chiang while reinforcing China's status as a secondary power, not important enough to merit inclusion in the regular talks that included Soviet leader Joseph Stalin.[6] Frustrated with being treated as a junior partner, Chinese officials made frequent appeals for a revised Allied policy, additional lend-lease aid, and more support overall. Meanwhile, British and American officials used a variety of means to placate them—without fundamentally changing their own strategies.[7] Migration policy became a useful forum for this, as a symbolic gesture toward equality that did not require a shift in wartime strategy. Repealing the intertwined policies of extraterritoriality in China and exclusion in the United States that the Chinese had long opposed became a way to give an inch and ignore the mile.

Extraterritoriality and exclusion had been closely linked from their very inception.[8] The fact that they could exist in combination became one of the most striking reminders of the weakness of the Chinese government and the inequality experienced by the Chinese people: the privileged position of Americans and Europeans in China could not help but stand in stark contrast to the often brutal treatment of Chinese in the United States. The government of the Republic of China took the opportunity created by World War II to try to make recognition of the equality of the Allies a contingency of victory, pushing carefully but consistently for the repeal of both measures. Chinese equality was not an outcome of the war, however, because the motivations of the United States behind these measures remained rooted in its own security. U.S. officials needed the Chinese to keep fighting, so these largely symbolic victories became a way to promote morale and undermine Japanese propaganda. These differing goals meant separate visions for what the postwar relationship would look like, highlighting the weaknesses in Sino-American cooperation.

The U.S. decision to repeal Chinese exclusion in 1943 has long been understood by scholars of U.S.-Chinese relations and Asian-American history as a measure pushed forward by the exigencies of war and the requirements of foreign policy. Differing accounts of the repeal have considered the role of the Roosevelt administration in pursuing repeal and managing the domestic fallout, the efforts of Chinese Americans to speak on their own behalf in changing the law, the place of repeal in the larger context of the push for civil rights and racial equality in the United States, and the extraterritorial control exercised over Chinese immigrants by a powerful but distant Chinese government.[9] However, there is an even larger context in the period from 1942 to 1946 within which the repeal decisions took place: the end of extraterritoriality, the revision of shore leave provisions for Chinese sailors, and the reconsideration of Asian exclusion as a broader topic. In most accounts, the Chinese government, perhaps only with the exception of Soong May-ling and the occasional renegade consul, often takes on the role of observer in the changing U.S. policy; but when the four-year period is taken into account, a much more profound pattern of influence emerges, one that is consistent with the Chinese government's stated aims in its overseas Chinese policies. These low-level migration issues combined, via active participation on the part of both Americans and Chinese, to revise the two nations' alliance during the war, with profound implications for the postwar period.

The Allied War Effort Grapples with Equality in 1942

The elevation of the Republic of China from a government struggling to maintain control over its vast claimed territory to one of the four "great powers" of the world can be credited in large part to the postwar vision of Franklin Roosevelt.[10] Maintaining the fiction of being "equal allies" required some effort, however, and it led to some changes in U.S. policies on migration issues. In 1942, the first full year of U.S. involvement in the war, three issues emerged as low-stakes, high-reward: the long-promised end to the U.S. system of extraterritorial control, the idea of offering shore leave to Chinese sailors, and the idea of doing something—anything—about the Chinese Exclusion Laws.

Extraterritoriality came to the table first, at least in part because it was the longest time coming. The extraterritoriality system was a lingering effect of the unequal treaties signed between China and the United Kingdom, the United States, and other foreign powers in the wake of the Opium War that lasted from 1839 to 1842. The Anglo-Chinese Treaty of Nanjing established the idea in 1842, and the United States claimed it under the most-favored-nation clause written into the Treaty of Wangxia signed by the United States and China in 1844. The system ensured that foreign nationals living in China would not be subject to Chinese laws and could not be sued or brought to trial in Chinese courts; instead, when the need arose, they would make use of courts set up by their own governments or be sent home to be dealt with there. Such policies were long justified in the West by the claim that the Chinese court system was not yet developed enough to make fair determinations according to the standards of international law. Although the British and American governments defended the system's continuance this way, the existence of extraterritoriality and its attending implication of Chinese inferiority created a cauldron of resentment for the Chinese government and people in the first half of the twentieth century.[11]

Extraterritoriality in China had been the subject of international discussion ever since Germany and Austria lost their rights to it upon their defeat in the First World War. Chinese officials raised the issue at the peace talks at Versailles, but their appeal was largely ignored. The subject was discussed again at the Washington Conference in 1921–22; and then over the course of the 1920s, China signed new treaties of friendship and commerce with a number of European nations, each of which included a provision for the abrogation of extraterritorial rights. On January 1, 1930, both the United States and Britain agreed to the idea of abrogating extraterritorial rights, though they sought to do so gradually over the coming years.[12] Other nations followed suit, and by the time China joined the Allies, only Britain, the United States, Japan, France, Italy, Brazil, Norway, Sweden, and the Netherlands maintained extraterritorial rights in China.[13]

In March 1942, circumstances warranted a revised look at the extraterritorial claims. As scholar Wesley R. Fishel argued, at this point the United States and Britain both had significantly more to gain by abolishing extraterritoriality than they had in keeping it: aside from offering an olive branch to the struggling Chinese, it seemed unlikely that such colonial-era privileges would survive the war.[14] Moreover, leaders in the Chinese government continued to express dissatisfaction with the U.S. and British conduct of the war, especially the priority given the war in Europe and the low level of material support given the Chinese resistance against Japan.[15] Given sinking morale and heavy losses, speculation abounded that China might consider a separate peace with Japan, motivating U.S. officials to look for ways to keep China in the war that would not divert additional resources away from Europe.[16] Still, there were skeptics: Walter Adams of the State Department noted that expressing too much or the wrong kind of appreciation for China's war effort might result in feelings that "spill over the level of appropriateness and good taste to the detriment both of the interest of China and of the US." As an example, Adams noted a recent loan that the Chinese thought ought to have been a gift in recognition of "compensation which was due to China for its past and present resistance to Japan and for what the Chinese regard as our past and present shortcomings."[17] The existence of extraterritoriality was an anachronism, and one that did not coincide with wartime rhetoric of the "four freedoms" and equality for all, as the Japanese propaganda machinery had been energetically reminding all of Asia; but the timing of its relinquishment would set the tone for future bilateral relations and needed to be considered carefully.

But extraterritoriality was not the only reminder of China's inequality, nor was it the only target of Japanese propaganda. There was a disconnect between the maintenance of both exclusion and extraterritoriality policies simultaneously and the U.S. ideal of China as an "equal" ally, as suggested by the Chinese News Service: "On the one hand, persons of the Chinese race, whether Chinese citizens or not, are not allowed to enter the United States on the same quota basis as those of the Caucasian and Negro races. On the other hand, citizens of the United States may enter China freely and, once in China, are not under the jurisdiction of the Chinese Government. Obviously the American Government does not treat the Chinese on the same footing as the Chinese Government treats Americans."[18] According-ing to historian Him Mark Lai, while discussing extraterritoriality treaty revisions, Chinese ambassador Wei Daoming told U.S. Secretary of State Cordell Hull that "the citizens of the United States and China when in each other's countries should experience the same treatment, but because the American exclusion acts exist, in reality Chinese in the U.S. are subject to unequal treatment; this law should be changed to eliminate the dis-crimination against my people."[19] The Nationalist government missed few opportunities to link the two issues.

The fallout from the Anglo-American failure to see the Chinese as fully equal impacted the war effort in other ways—for example, the issue of shore leave for Chinese sailors. In April 1942, a skirmish between the white leadership and the Chinese crew of the SS *Silverash* while it was docked at the port of New York left one Chinese seaman dead and the captain in jail. The roots of the conflict were poor treatment and low wages afforded Chinese sailors by the British merchant shipping companies, as well as the ban on shore leave enforced by U.S. immigration authorities.[20] In June, the American Civil Liberties Union picked up the issue of Chinese shore leave, arguing that immigration authorities had improperly used the Chinese Exclusion Laws to prevent Chinese sailors from exercising this privilege granted to every other group.[21] The Immigration and Naturaliza-tion Service (INS), by contrast, argued that Chinese seamen notoriously deserted in especially high numbers each time they entered a port, so the shore leave ban was a reflection of their behavior, not their race. In reality, their behavior could not be separated from their race or ethnicity: British ship captains and sailors mistreated them because they were Chinese, they tried to desert because they were mistreated, and then the United States denied them leave because of their desertions. Because "the Axis is seeking for material to create the impression in the Far East that the 'four freedoms' are meaningless and that the United States is racially prejudiced against all Oriental peoples," the fact that "Chinese crews on one basis or another are denied over long periods the right to land even for shore leave and . . . [that] practical discrimination against Chinese crews does exist on a wide scale" could be considered a liability.[22] So throughout the summer of 1942, talk was bubbling up favoring change on all three fronts: extraterritoriality, shore leave, and exclusion.[23]

The shore leave question was the most urgent. Frequent desertions by sailors of all nationalities from Allied merchant shipping had put the entire Atlantic supply operation in jeopardy, but the Chinese desertions proved uniquely challenging because they rarely happened one at a time: groups of Chinese sailors deserted together—even occasionally the entirety of the Chinese staff aboard a vessel (which could mean, for example, the loss of an entire engine crew). The desertions can be read a number of ways, though the motivation seemed inevitably to start with unequal treatment for Chinese (and other non-European) sailors, including unequal wages and benefits as well as racism expressed by on-board leadership.[24] In the context of the other negotiations ongoing at the time, the solution proposed in the summer of 1942 can be read as a cooperative one: the United States would grant shore leave, the British would improve Chinese seamen's contracts, and the Chinese would send a consular officer to each crew to warn against desertions. Historian Peter Kwong has interpreted this procedure as insulting to the Chinese seamen, noting quite rightly that the impetus for this change came from the activism of the men themselves. Chinese sailors won their right to shore leave via work stoppages, strikes, and protests for better treatment, in cooperation with unions. The officials granting the compromise solution were largely reacting to the situation created by the seamen.[25] Despite activism on the part of the seamen, however, there was no shore leave without the cooperation of their government, and even that was intended on a trial basis.[26]

While the shore leave experiments continued with decidedly mixed success, serious efforts to relinquish extraterritoriality began anew in August. By that time, there had been a "trend of public opinion in this country favoring relinquishment of American extraterritorial and related rights in China."[27] Likewise, recent comments from Chiang Kai-shek and his wife supporting changes on extraterritoriality showed that China was "adopting a more activist attitude with reference to China's foreign political relations."[28] The combination helped U.S. officials overcome their reluctance to act before the war was over. Additionally, the United States had been embarrassed by a court case involving two American citizens and a trial for manslaughter in China. Boatner Carney, a notoriously hot-tempered former Army Air Force man who became a civil employee of Major General Claire Chennault's China Air Task Force, got into a bar brawl in April 1942 in Yunnan, China. During the brawl, he shot and killed an army man. Because of extraterritoriality, there was no way to charge him with a crime. He could not be charged with murder in the Chinese courts, and the American court in China had been in an area now under Japanese occupation. Eventually the Americans flew in a U.S. civilian judge, and Chennault spoke on Carney's behalf. After his return to the United States, Carney was pardoned via a Senate petition. According to one account of the incident, there had been some concern that if Carney was not tried before extraterritoriality was abolished, he could be tried and convicted by Chinese courts, but the failure to try him at all would have led to an outcry. Given these circumstances, some Americans thought it wise to give up the right to extraterritoriality before China demanded its termination.[29]

The United States and Britain agreed to take a novel approach to abrogation by creating a brief treaty to deal with intermediate concerns in the wake of the termination, with the promise to negotiate a full agreement at a later date. The two allies worked on the details of the draft treaty together, agreeing to approach the Chinese government simultaneously on October 9, with a full, public announcement of the treaty negotiations scheduled symbolically for October 10, the Republic of China's national day. In response to the U.S. approach, the Chinese ambassador replied that the measure "represented a great step in the happy relations between our two countries."[30] The formal announcement on October 10 included a ceremonial ringing of the Liberty Bell in honor of the Chinese Republic. A message from Chiang Kai-shek to President Roosevelt claimed that "these tributes will do more to uphold the morale of our people in continuing resistance than anything else could possibly do."[31] Britain was less delighted with the outpouring of good feeling: a delay in the communications had left the Chinese government with a sense that the initiative came entirely from the United States, and that Britain was only along for the ride. That, in addition to differences in wartime policies and disappointments with British assistance against Japan, ensured that the measure was a great boon for Sino-American relations and at best only a minor boost for already strained Anglo-Chinese interaction.[32] With the announcement made, the three governments set to work negotiating the exact terms of the brief treaties over the course of the next several months. The agreement on terms was very much a three-way endeavor, as neither the United States nor Britain could reasonably expect advantages not given the other.

In November, the Chinese government responded to the first proposed draft treaty with a series of suggestions. Among the ideas it presented for inclusion was a query about the United States liberalizing its Chinese immigration laws. The autumn had seen a growing interest in the effect of exclusion on the Sino-American relationship. During the shore leave debate, the American Civil Liberties Union had begun research on the issue of Asian exclusion generally, and decided to add the issue to its roster of key campaigns.[33] *Asia and the Americas* and the *New Republic*, along with other magazines, printed articles about U.S. treatment of Chinese immigrants, highlighting not only the bars on entry but also the system of discrimination against long-term residents, limiting their options for where to live or work and subjecting the community to intermittent acts of violence. They also detailed the ways U.S. immigration authorities routinely subjected Chinese arriving legally in the United States for business, travel, or study to harsh interrogation techniques and detained them in facilities like the one on Angel Island in San Francisco Bay, instead of releasing them on bond while considering their cases. Even Chinese Americans returning from abroad were not exempted from such treatment, but were instead regarded as "semi-aliens," as nearly all Chinese entering the country were automatically suspected of illegal entry, regardless of their actual status.[34] The FBI also reported that the extraterritoriality debate had created an expectation of changes in exclusion, noting that "many Chinese feel that most immigration restrictions will be lifted after the war, believing the forfeiture of extraterritoriality indicates that this step will be taken, and plans are being laid to bring to the United States families and friends from China."[35] In late 1942, however, Congress was not yet ready for action. The House Committee on Immigration and Naturalization was already debating a deportation bill intended to deal with the seamen desertion problem by sending those caught jumping ship back to the seamen's pool in Liverpool, England. The Nationalist government opposed the measure—in no small part because the seamen themselves stood solidly against it—but Congress was trying to balance the U.S. relationship with China against the desire for a deterrent against desertion.[36]

Beyond the hope of repealing exclusion and other measures directed at Chinese migrants, the Chinese government also sought to revise its treaty with the United States to state, "Relations between the Republic of China and the United States shall be based on the principles of equality and reciprocity." This was the idea that underlay all the negotiations during the war era, and an important reason why Chinese officials pursued migration issues and overseas Chinese protections in the first place. If there was not an immediate reconsideration of Chinese exclusion, this clause would force it sooner or later.[37] As it turned out, the U.S. response was not immediately sympathetic to either repealing exclusion or confirming the idea of equality, viewing both as a distraction from extraterritoriality. On the subject of immigration, the hope in late 1942 was still to avoid the issue entirely—it could be revisited, perhaps, at some point after the war. On the new draft Article I, equality and reciprocity were the natural basis for relations between all modern countries, so the United States considered the point extraneous, not to mention irrelevant to the matter at hand.[38] The United States similarly rebuffed a further inquiry on the subject of immigration, and it remained adamant that the treaty would deal only with extraterritoriality, with all other issues addressed at a later date.[39] Britain did not have a comparable exclusion act to contend with, but those negotiations became even more bogged down in the discussion over the postwar future of Hong Kong. Like their U.S. counterparts, British negotiators were determined not to include extraneous issues in the extraterritoriality agreement.[40]

The United States and Britain signed the final treaties revoking their extraterritorial rights in China on January 11, 1943. The U.S. Senate ratified it unanimously on February 11. The U.S. press hailed the move as the moment in which China "takes her place as an equal partner in the family of the United Nations," and "the way that the peace can be won in wartime."[41] The Chinese response used similar terms; a published statement from Dr. Wang Chung-hui, secretary-general of the Defense Council, noted that "China has attained international equality and has fulfilled the late Dr. Sun Yat-sen's will regarding the abolition of unequal treaties . . . the greatest cordiality in international as well as people's foreign relations is assured." He also pointed to the voluntary decision on the part of the United States and Britain to relinquish extraterritoriality as proof of success in all further cooperative efforts during the war.[42] In a statement to the Chinese people

Figure 1. Secretary of State Cordell Hull and ROC ambassador Wei Daoming exchange ratifications of the treaty abolishing U.S. extraterritoriality in China. OWI, National Archives.

and armed forces, Chiang Kai-shek spoke on a similar theme, reminding them that "the unequal treaties implanted among us disunity, economic backwardness and social chaos. They taught our people a sense of inferiority which we could not overcome.... Now that the unequal treaties have been abrogated, we are on an equal footing with Great Britain and the United States."[43]

As helpful as the new treaties may have been for boosting morale and suggesting equality among the Allies, their signing was not really a diplomatic victory for the Chinese or a sign of China's changing fortunes within the alliance. Because there had been talk of reconsidering extraterritoriality over the past twenty years, the measure was inevitable and even too long in coming. Additionally, "with Japan controlling most of China, Britain and America were in effect, as the Japanese lost no time in trumpeting, giving up rights they could no longer exercise."[44] In the wake of the announcement, Japan, Italy, and Vichy France surrendered their own extraterritorial rights to the collaborating government headed by Wang Jingwei.[45] Still, the negotiations made clear that China could benefit from promoting the principles of equality and reciprocity and exposing the philosophical weaknesses of anti-Chinese (and anti-Asian) exclusion laws. The relinquishment of extraterritoriality was ultimately one act in a larger movement for greater reciprocity in the treatment of Americans in China and Chinese in America. And as 1943 opened, the debate over exclusion would begin anew.

Excluding an Ally

Repeal of the Chinese exclusion laws when it finally happened was not a unique decision, or even a spontaneous wartime measure; it was inexorably tied to all the other decisions that contributed to the idea of greater parity between the Chinese and American citizenry. Like the changes in policy with regard to extraterritoriality, the final form of the repeal act demonstrated that the gesture was largely symbolic, rather than substantive. That this was the case is clear from the omission of Chinese American voices from the formal repeal campaign, a subject highlighted by many scholars studying repeal. L. Ling-chi Wang suggests that the primary role reserved for Chinese Americans was in proving that Chinese "could and did assimilate to American life." As a result, he explains, "The sole enduring stereotypical image of Chinese Americans was that they were docile, hardworking, and successfully assimilated—an image that was clearly false."[46] K. Scott Wong agrees in part, but notes that Chinese Americans were not forced into this position; they took it on willingly as part of a search for acceptance.[47] Renqiu Yu has detailed the efforts of the New York Chinese-language newspaper the *China Daily News* to mobilize its readership on behalf of the repeal effort, printing sample letters and encouraging petitions of support, but also notes that Congress, the press, and pro-repeal organizations all "virtually ignored the voice of the Chinese Americans themselves."[48] Though scholars have sought to reclaim the role that Chinese Americans have played in pushing forward repeal, they have largely assumed the Chinese government "remained inactive throughout the entire campaign to repeal the exclusion laws in the United States, though some of the Chinese officials did work for the repeal through unofficial channels."[49] This conclusion is based in part on the research of Fred Riggs, who wrote a meticulous study of the campaign for repeal in 1950 that has endured as the primary account of American activism on the subject.[50] A consideration of the full diplomatic record of the repeal campaign from both U.S. and Chinese sources reveals a somewhat different story: the official Chinese pressure for repeal exceeded a few efforts via "unofficial channels," though it certainly fell short of a formal demand. The combination of diplomatic efforts with Chinese American pressure and the well-known efforts of American "China hands," the Roosevelt White House, and other interested parties helped generate the pressure on Congress that forced even the reluctant to reconsider repeal.

In February, the formal visit to Washington of Madame Chiang Kai-shek helped to kick off a year of repeal debates. Congressman Martin Kennedy (D-New York) met with Madame Chiang during her visit and discussed with her the possibility of repealing the exclusion acts; on the night before her big speech, Kennedy had introduced a bill to repeal Chinese exclusion and grant Chinese the right to naturalize.[51] Altogether, in the wake of her visit, nine different proposals for the repeal of Chinese exclusion were brought before Congress. She never publicly requested repeal (though she did urge repeal privately to the House Committee on Immigration), but the increase in support for repeal after her visit is an indication of just how much the "first lady" of China represented a changing image of the Chinese people.[52] As one congressman put it, that February "this House collectively lost its heart to Madame Chiang Kai-shek."[53]

Just before her visit, Congressman John Lesinski (D-Michigan) introduced a bill in Congress to admit the alien Chinese wives of American citizens that provided an opportunity to test the congressional waters on the subject of repeal. Chinese wives who married their husbands before 1924 were permitted to enter under the terms of the 1924 immigration act, but all those who had married since then were not permitted entry—a particular hardship for the Chinese community in America.[54] The effect of the omission was that Chinese Americans held a lesser form of American citizenship than did native-born American nationals of Caucasian ethnic background, as the latter could bring Caucasian wives from Europe into the country freely. It also limited the ability of Chinese Americans to lead what in the 1940s would be considered fully assimilated lives. At the time of the early March hearings, support for repeal was still muted and limited to groups experienced with China or charmed by Madame Chiang Kai-shek, so there was some genuine concern that if the committee were to report out Lesinski's bill, it would be defeated on the floor. That would ultimately end up damaging the war effort, rather than helping it.

The debate over the bill proved an initial airing of some of the issues that would engulf the repeal debate: concerns about the utility of

American anti-Chinese laws for Japanese propaganda, the need to improve relations with China for the sake of the war effort, the importance of encouraging the Chinese people, and the idea that the Chinese American members of the U.S. armed forces would benefit from the passage of the bill. The repeal debate would also highlight equality, while the arguments in favor of the wives bill narrowed in on the importance of preventing miscegenation and protecting the white racial stock. It would be preferable, some argued, to allow Chinese Americans to bring in their wives from China rather than leaving them to marry locally, as there were not enough Chinese women in the United States to marry them all. Creating an opportunity to bring over wives would not open the door for all future generations to bring over wives in mass: once there was a decent family culture established in the existing Chinese community, their children could simply marry each other. In other words, for some the measure was intended to prevent full Chinese integration into American society, even while those advocating repeal claimed Chinese Americans assimilated more readily than other "Asiatics." On a related note, if Chinese wives were not freely admitted, the children that resulted from these trans-Pacific marriages continued to have the right to enter the United States as derivative citizens, so some members of Congress considered it a matter of "wise national policy to encourage the raising of American citizens inside instead of outside the country," thereby ensuring their loyalties stayed with the United States.[55] None of these arguments proved decisive, however, and the bill was voted down in committee.

Despite the defeat of Lesinski's bill, Chinese officials continued to express interest in some form of congressional action on exclusion. In a meeting between Foreign Minister T. V. Soong and Stanley Hornbeck of the U.S. State Department, Hornbeck gleaned that Soong had picked two key issues to focus on pertaining to the postwar world: the execution of a new treaty of commerce on a basis of equality, and issues connected to Chinese migration.[56] Though continuing to work in various ways for repeal, Chinese officials like Soong knew there was a fine distinction to be maintained between having his interest perceived as a gentle promotion of preferred legislation and being accused of blatant interference in a U.S. domestic matter. Nationalist Chinese officials kept the lesson of Japan firmly in mind: when the U.S. Congress had begun its consideration of the 1924 immigration act and its Asian exclusion provisions, the Japanese government made a strong, vocal protest against Japanese inclusion in the restrictions. Many in U.S. government and society perceived this complaint as evidence of Japan intending to "meddle" in the domestic business of the United States. Instead of heeding the threats and warnings Japan issued, Congress had passed the restrictive measure with a strong majority.[57] Chinese officials rightly worried that pressing too hard for changes to U.S. immigration law would backfire, or that, similarly, any attempt to link repeal directly with the creation of the new Sino-American agreement on commerce could have the effect of breaking down treaty negotiations.

Instead, the Chinese opted for a quieter, two-pronged approach. The Chinese Embassy in Washington would express to the U.S. government its hope that it would be possible to end racial prejudice in immigration laws, stressing that given the wartime goals of the Allies, no member of the Allied powers should be singling out a race or country for unequal treatment. At the same time, the Chinese would work on persuading American groups and leaders to write to the government and their local newspapers, expressing their opinions that racial equality was necessary, or urging the passage of any reasonable exclusion repeal bills that come up in Congress. In this way, the press for repeal would be coming from native sources, and China could not be accused of interfering in a "domestic" matter.[58]

While the Chinese government, led by its embassy in Washington, considered its formal role in the campaign for repeal, other Chinese groups made informal pushes for the proposal. In March, the New York Chinese Women's Association sent a letter to Eleanor Roosevelt asking whether relinquishing extraterritoriality meant there would be potential for adjustments to U.S. immigration laws. They suggested that even a limited quota would allow the Chinese finally to be considered equals in immigration matters, the way Chinese and American soldiers were already equals in battle.[59] Meanwhile, the New York Chinese Consolidated Benevolent Association (CCBA), one of the most prominent Chinese organizations in the United States and one with close ties to the Kuomintang (KMT) or Nationalist Party, wrote directly to members of Congress and asked them to support repeal and the creation of a Chinese immigration quota.[60] In mid-May, Bishop Paul Yu Pin, vicar apostolic of Nanjing, appeared before the House Committee on Foreign Affairs to present China's need for additional munitions and help launching an offensive against the Japanese. Although thankful for the decision to end extraterritoriality, he noted that that decision alone would not change the tide of the war in favor of China. While making his request for military support, Yu Pin stated that he did not want his statements to be understood as an attempt to influence U.S. domestic policy, but "the candor which should exist between the peoples of the two democracies whose destinies are linked together in the present war impels the Chinese public unanimously to recommend an amelioration of the Chinese Exclusion Act." Beyond his expressed concerns that the continued existence of the law provided a backbone for Japanese anti-American propaganda, Yu Pin asserted that repeal "will mean much for the Chinese psychology and morale of the Chinese people, which in war is a factor of the utmost importance."[61]

The argument that what happened with repeal mattered to China, and not just Chinese Americans, was reinforced when the Chinese press picked up on the possibility of a repeal measure and wasted no time in reporting it in mainland China. The story here was not simply about whether or not the exclusion laws should be repealed, but also the creation of a Chinese quota, entry for wives of Chinese Americans, naturalization for longtime Chinese residents in the United States, and better treatment for Chinese arrivals. Chinese editorialists in papers like *Da Gong Bao* stressed that Chinese would not be eager to emigrate to America in large numbers. During the war, transportation was limited and immigration impossible. After the war, Chinese officials expected that overseas Chinese would be returning to China from around the world to aid in postwar development, not that large numbers of Chinese would decide to leave.[62] *Da Gong Bao* also reported on each of the bills proposing repeal (and the bill dealing with Chinese wives), and once the House Immigration and Naturalization Committee opened public hearings on the bills, Chinese newspapers published summaries of each day's testimony. They also noted the failure of the bill on Chinese wives to be reported out, a fact that reached Washington and reinforced concerns about the potential backlash for the United States if Congress started discussing repeal of exclusion and failed to come to a positive decision about it.[63] Even outside China or the United States, Chinese migrants favored repeal and stood to benefit from it. According to U.S. consular reports, *Da Gong Bao* also reported "that [the] Act has inflicted sufferings on overseas Chinese in the United States; has inspired even harsher laws in Canada, Latin American and [the] South Seas; that [the] racial issue on which [the] Act was in part based should be buried today; and that it believes [the] United States will not follow Nazi and Japanese ideas of race and color prejudice."[64] Japanese propaganda reported on the *Da Gong Bao* editorials, dismissing the calls for a change on repeal as quixotic given "the hatred Anglo-American nations harbor against Asiatic races."[65] The Japanese appear to have interpreted the editorials as part of a formal Chinese government push for repeal that was destined to fail.

The international interest in the question meant that when the House Committee on Immigration and Naturalization took up the question of repeal in May and June of 1943, State Department officials worried over the outcome. In a meeting with House Speaker Sam Rayburn, Assistant Secretary of State Breckinridge Long explained that "the Department felt very sincerely that it would be unfortunate in the extreme from the point of view of our international relations if a Bill should be reported out by the Committee and an acrimonious debate should occur on the Floor and the Bill failed passage."[66] Long argued further that the bills should not be presented to the House at all if it was not inclined to act favorably, reinforcing that the optics of the move outweighed considerations on the substance of it. Over the course of the next few months, these arguments would be raised several more times by the State Department.

During the lengthy House Committee hearings, the most popular arguments in favor of repeal centered on the idea that doing so would aid the war effort. Riggs observed that the voices speaking in favor of repeal were "commercial interests, religious and idealistic groups, friends of China, Chinese-Americans, and Chinese nationals."[67] Witness after witness appeared before the House and Senate committees on immigration to speak of their personal knowledge that many Chinese nationals were not only aware of, but also deeply offended by the American policy explicitly barring Chinese from entry.[68] Propaganda distributed by Japanese forces in China during the hearings themselves came uncomfortably close to telling the truth, that repeal would not mean "any change in America's attitude of racial discrimination against the people of East Asia for it has been proposed only for the purpose of preventing [the Chinese] from dropping out of the anti-Axis camp."[69] But the exigencies of war were not the only arguments made to Congress in favor of Chinese immigration. Most advocates of repeal suggested that there was a link between America's domestic immigration policy—particularly as it was a policy based on the principle of racial discrimination—and the ability of the United States to promote democracy, equality, and freedom around the world. They argued that there was a strong correlation between Japanese protests against Asian exclusion when it was written into law in 1924 and the subsequent cooling of U.S.-Japanese relations to the breaking point of Pearl Harbor.[70] In addition to these arguments in favor of repeal, some proponents (mostly with religious affiliations) also argued in favor of a principle of social and racial equality, though that argument proved largely ineffective in committee and on the floor. Others combated the long-standing economic arguments against Chinese immigration by touting the economic gains and postwar commercial opportunities to be had from improving U.S.-Chinese relations.[71]

Despite these compelling arguments for repeal, many witnesses visited the committee debate to express their opposition. These were predominantly from "labor, veterans organizations, West Coast interests, and 'patriotic' societies."[72] Two arguments against repeal proved most prominent: fear of mass migration, and concern that wartime was simply the wrong time to make changes to U.S. domestic law. The former can be divided into subgroups by degrees: there were those who were against all immigration from any part of the world, those whose principal concern was that granting even a small quota to China would force open a door for the floods of Chinese that would inevitably follow, and those who were concerned less about the numbers of Chinese entering than they were about the opening of a Chinese quota, setting a precedent that would then have to be repeated for the benefit of other Asians, particularly Koreans and Asian Indians. The latter argument, that the timing of the request to repeal exclusion was inappropriate, can be read as a stalling tactic: its supporters were largely immigration restrictionists who hoped to put off the question until a time when the diplomatic and military arguments in favor would be voided and the exigency of repeal reduced.[73] Chinese Americans also observed that the opposition was led by southern racists concerned about stemming the tide toward racial equality.[74]

Advocates of repeal had to consider the next step as well, as simply repealing Chinese exclusion laws would not automatically allow Chinese to immigrate; they would still be barred under the 1924 immigration law for being Asian. A new, special quota would have to be created for the Chinese. Proponents argued that the size of the quota would not be as important as the fact that a quota existed and that it was necessary to provide some avenue for legal entry to combat illegal entry. There was more debate on the problem of ensuring that the Chinese were kept to their quota and not able to take advantage of other nations' open quotas under the national origins system, which sometimes collided with the effort to place Asians on equal footing with all other nations in terms of immigration.[75] A strict application of the 1924 system for calculating national-origin quotas would result in only 105 to 107 visas being made available to the Chinese nation each year. This might have appeared uncontroversial, but there was a hitch: applying the 1924 quota without alteration would charge Chinese arrivals to the quotas of their countries of residence. In 1943, Chinese officials counted 8,613,179 Chinese living outside of China or America—all of whom could be potential new immigrants, and none of whom would be charged to the carefully limited Chinese national quota. Moreover, nearly 40 percent of those overseas Chinese lived in British territories or colonies, leading to fears that masses of Chinese would be able to enter the United States under the generous British quota of 65,000 visas per year. Immigration from anywhere within the Western Hemisphere was not even subject to the national quota system, so the 90,371 Chinese living in Latin America would also be able to immigrate freely to the United States without reference to the Chinese quota.[76]

None of the possible solutions to this problem were all that appealing. Trying to write a numerical restriction on Chinese into existing immigration law would mean identifying Chinese specifically as receiving their quota under a different system from that of the rest of the world—and it was this sort of Chinese-specific immigration restriction that the repeal of exclusion was meant to eliminate. The solution found was only marginally better and was still built solidly on the principle of racial exclusion. Whereas migrants from the rest of the world would be chargeable to the quota of their country of birth, the Chinese (and other Asian ethnicities, once immigration was opened to them) would have a racial quota, so that all Chinese immigrants from anywhere in the world could be limited to the number of 105 per year. In addition to this quota, the nation of China was assigned a separate quota of one hundred slots each year for Europeans born in China who were otherwise not eligible for entry under any other national quota. In order to ensure that the majority of Chinese immigrants came from the Republic of China itself and not from the diaspora, a further provision dictated that 75 percent of the quota slots were reserved for mainland Chinese.

The effort to put tight limits on Chinese immigration did not end there, though, as Congress added yet another strictly racial provision to the legislation. As noted above, the efforts to pass a bill allowing Chinese American citizens to bring their Chinese wives to the United States died in committee. Rather than revive the measure, the bill repealing exclusion actually ruled out this possibility by stating that wives of American citizens of Chinese ethnicity could enter the United States only under the Chinese quota—thereby limiting their number to the maximum of 105 per year, assuming there was no other Chinese immigration in the course of the year. Foreign wives of other (non-Asian) American citizens were allowed non-quota entry under the existing immigration law.

In all its essentials, instead of ending racial exclusion, the repeal measure simply revised it and codified the unequal citizenship of Chinese Americans. By identifying Chinese in diaspora as being Chinese (by race and culture) first and foremost, and claiming that this "Chineseness" trumped whatever other local citizenship they might have had in their place of residence, the measure served to reemphasize the unassimilable nature of the Chinese and ensure that as far as the U.S. government was concerned, even Chinese Americans were Chinese first, and then Americans. By virtue of its own 1929 citizenship law, this was also the position of the Chinese government, though often not of patriotic Chinese Americans themselves. American policies toward the Chinese—as immigrants to the United States and as residents of foreign countries, followed these lines until the late 1950s.[77]

At the end of the House Committee hearings in June, despite having settled these issues and consolidated a workable plan, the House Committee chose not to report out a bill. Though there was support in the House for the repeal of exclusion laws alone, questions lingered about the other possible provisions for quotas and naturalization. The committee itself was divided on the issues involved, but the decision not to report a bill centered on concerns that nothing could be passed in the House before the summer recess. The committee readily took up the issue again when it reconvened in the fall. In the meantime, a summer of repeal campaigning got under way.[78]

Many of the witnesses who appeared before the House committee supporting repeal and the creation of Chinese quotas, in whatever form, did so at the request of the Citizens' Committee to Repeal Chinese Exclusion. The group formed in May 1943, and it met only six times before it disbanded that October. By the end, it had spent only $5,000 on the entire campaign.[79] The citizens' committee worked in close cooperation with the ACLU to gather funds, witnesses for congressional hearings, influential individuals to write articles and editorials, and petitions of support for the repeal. Despite this, the two groups disagreed on what the final goal should be: the ACLU was in favor of a measure that ended all racial restrictions against Asian immigration, including Japanese, and established an equitable quota system. The citizens' committee became concerned that there would not be enough support for such a measure and chose instead to focus only on Chinese exclusion. In spite of these differences, leadership of both groups worked together in the summer of 1943 to promote national acceptance of repeal.

As L. Ling-chi Wang has demonstrated, both the personnel connected with the citizens' committee and the methods they used to achieve their goals foreshadowed the rise of the China lobby.[80] Ever mindful of the charge that foreign nationals should not appear to be involved in U.S. domestic policy, the citizens' committee limited its membership to American citizens, which included prominent "China hands" and people involved in trade or missions in China. It wanted to make the point that Americans—not Chinese or even Chinese Americans—demanded repeal as the right course of action for America during the war. To that end, it sent letters to influential people and the press, arranged radio programs, and organized a special celebration of China on July 7, the sixth anniversary of the start of the Sino-Japanese war.[81] The citizens' committee took the initiative with wide distribution of a pamphlet titled "Our Chinese Wall." It explained to the American people that "the exclusion of the Chinese from this country is no longer a question of domestic policy. It has become a matter of crucial import between two great nations—China and the United States."[82] The pamphlet listed the injustices visited against the Chinese, including the fact of exclusion; denial of naturalization; humiliating treatment upon arrival at U.S. ports; limited employment opportunities; mistreatment of Chinese seamen, including denial of shore leave; special difficulties for Chinese transiting the United States on their way to other destinations in the hemisphere; the subjection of Chinese in the United States to the draft even while visiting every other possible discrimination against them; and the unfair classification of Chinese as undesirable citizens. These multiple forms of discrimination, all based upon the notion that the Chinese were racially inferior to white Americans, were "an insult to a proud nation with a five-thousand-year-old civilization."[83] But in the end, the citizens' committee subordinated any promotion of real equality for Chinese Americans to the larger goal of promoting and preserving the Sino-American bilateral relationship.

According to scholar Yui Daizaburo, one reason for the success of the repeal movement was its ability to build coalitions with traditional "anti-Asian" organizations, something that he contrasts with the inability of anti-evacuation groups to gain similar support in the early 1942 fight against internment of Japanese Americans.[84] U.S. labor unions such as the American Federation of Labor (AFL) and the Congress of Industrial Organizations (CIO) had played prominent roles in getting exclusion laws passed in 1882, and renewed thereafter. With some prompting from both the citizens' committee and the ACLU, the CIO formally came out in favor of the new

Chinese quota. The AFL supported repeal but no Chinese quota, though some individual union groups within the AFL did support more progressive measures.[85] As early as November 1942, the ACLU began discussion of ways to get Western leadership for the repeal movement.[86]

Throughout the summer of 1943, the citizens' committee and the ACLU were the most visible players working hard for the repeal of exclusion, but that did not make them the only players. The Chinese consulate in Los Angeles, itself well aware of the importance of winning over West Coast opinions, used a variety of unofficial channels to promote repeal. One idea was to focus attention on patriotic organizations and conservative groups like the American Legion and the AFL, with the idea that even if proponents of repeal could not change minds, they might at least lessen the opposition these groups had to Chinese immigration.[87] Similarly, the Chinese consulate in Seattle used every opportunity to thank local groups, like the Seattle Chamber of Commerce, for their support of repeal and suggest that they consider also lending their support to bills that included an immigration quota and provisions for naturalization. Though letters sent from Chinese consulates were framed as merely expressing appreciation, they also subtlety promoted the consulate's agenda. For example, one added, "We earnestly hope that the articulate expression of American public opinion will assure [the repeal and quota bills'] passage since we and you no less than our common enemy are agreed that any obstacle or failure in their enactment at this juncture will be many times worse than no public discussion on the subject at all."[88] This argument stressed the idea that the subject now raised could no longer be dismissed.

The Seattle consulate explained in one report back to the ROC government that the bills under consideration were particularly important not only for how they improved treatment of arriving Chinese, but because they would promote China's international status. The consulate reported it was interested in the matter, and "moreover, for the sake of arousing the American people's attention to this matter, endorses facilitating the passage of the repeal of the exclusion laws," which it would accomplish by requesting that the important West Coast newspapers publish supportive pieces, discuss the issue on radio broadcasts, talk over the issue with important organizations and leaders so they would independently urge its passage, and write telegrams to the House Immigration Committee expressing support.[89] The range of actions undertaken at the consulate level was broad, and it reached far beyond the occasional informal mention of repeal or Soong Mei-ling's offhand remarks. The self-conscious strategy of the Chinese government to avoid being seen as interfering with U.S. domestic policy was hardly the same as disinterest or inaction.

The consulate did not often address the American people directly, but the Chinese consul at Seattle, Dr. Kiang Yi-Seng, did occasionally make public the Chinese government's interest in the issue. In a letter to a local newspaper published in June, he assured the readers that "the Chinese people and press have been watching with keenest interest" and that "our common enemy has thus been able to make immense political capital out of [Chinese exclusion], and because it is true, the Chinese people cannot contradict or defend it." Dr. Kiang went on to assure the American public that the Chinese were not particularly prone to migration, so there was no need for concern about a sudden flood of new immigrants.[90] Though documents are not readily available from all the Chinese consulates in the United States, the reports from Los Angeles and Seattle paint a picture of a quiet but activist approach by the Chinese government.

On occasion, more direct approaches by the Chinese government seemed warranted. During the House hearings, representatives from the Chinese Embassy called on both committee members and officials in the INS, promoting the passage of the bill. Edward Shaughnessy of the INS explained to the committee that at these "unofficial" visits, Chinese officials had assured him that repeal "would be a greater face-saving proposition than the recent relinquishment of our extraterritorial rights which was accompanied with a certain amount of ceremony." Not everyone was inclined to listen kindly. Congressman A. Leonard Allen (D–Louisiana) was also visited, and found it "highly improper for a representative of a foreign government to call upon the representatives."[91] More formally, the Chinese ambassador discussed the issue with representatives of the State Department on several occasions. In May, Ambassador Wei Daoming expressed particular interest in the Kennedy bill (long favored by Chinese groups for being both straightforward and comprehensive) and restated Chinese interest in "recognition, technical at least, of China and the Chinese on a basis of 'equality.'" The conversation served to impress upon the State Department representatives the importance for the sake of the war effort that repeal be passed, "along as liberal lines as may be possible and as expeditiously as may be possible."[92] The Chinese ambassador also called on the secretary of state in June to express Chinese support of the newly revised bills under consideration, noting that "while this arrangement would only permit one hundred Chinese to come in, it would establish a principle which would have a good psychological effect on the people of China."[93] After his visit,

Wei reported back to China that he was optimistic the bill would pass, but he was still looking for ways to support it. If there was another failure to report out the bill, he would visit party leaders in Congress and discuss it with them. Meanwhile, more statements from Madame Chiang Kai-shek might be useful.[94] The Chinese government may have been worried about appearing to be involved in a domestic issue, but it was not so worried that it was willing to sit idly by and wait for the outcome.

Chinese American organizations also continued their efforts to win public and congressional support for repeal. In New York, the Chinese Hand Laundry Alliance (CHLA) and its affiliated newspaper, the *China Daily News*, both encouraged members and readers to write to the chairman of the House Committee of Immigration and Naturalization. They also urged the Chinese Consolidated Benevolent Association to become more involved than it was already. The CCBA ultimately engaged in efforts to organize the Chinese community in the United States to contact congressmen and express their hopes for the measure.[95]

After a summer of campaigning, on October 7 the House immigration committee approved a new bill (HR 3070) proposed by Warren Magnuson (D-Washington), which repealed exclusion, established a Chinese racial quota, and allowed Chinese to naturalize. Getting the bill past the committee was like winning the battle that would ultimately decide the war. President Roosevelt threw his weight behind the bill in a letter to Congress on October 11, saying, "I regard this legislation as important in the cause of winning the war and of establishing a secure peace." He reminded Congress that China had been resisting Japan for years and that it deserved respect, equality, and friendship from the United States. He even called the exclusion act "a historic mistake." The same day, a letter arrived from the State Department also stressing the diplomatic importance of repeal, "as the bill will remove discriminations against the Chinese which have been a source of misunderstanding in the relations between the United States and China for over 60 years."[96] With these statements of support, the act passed in the House on October 21, and moved to the Senate for consideration.

Just as the act passed the House, an editorial appeared in the *Central Daily News*, a Chinese newspaper published in Chongqing, that threatened the Chinese strategy of non-visible intervention. The writer acknowledged the domestic nature of the immigration debate but noted that the outcome of the repeal debate "will affect the international friendship between China and the United States, the collapse of the enemy, and further the permanent peace of East Asia." Most of the article discussed the content of the bill and the author's hopes for early passage, but two particular passages raised ire in the United States. First, the author acknowledged that the quota system as outlined was an improvement over exclusion, but said, "from the standpoint of the people of China, we feel that the complete elimination, if possible, of the restrictions on the number of immigrants would more fully meet our expectations." He then went on to praise those who had promoted passage and recognized that some forces in America were "unduly anxious" about the possibility of a mass migration of cheap Chinese labor, and that this was an important reason for the racial quota. Second, the editorial ended with what could be interpreted as a threat: "Whether or not the two great nations of China and the United States can genuinely, shoulder to shoulder and hand-in-hand, undertake the mission of this great epoch will depend on whether or not the Magnuson Bill can pass the Senate."[97] The U.S. Embassy in Chongqing reported to Washington that Chiang Kai-shek was so angry about the editorial, which he worried would backfire and hurt the chances of repeal passing, that he threatened to court-martial the author.[98] Afraid the editorial would be reprinted in the American press and stir up public opinion against the Chinese, the Chinese government undertook some damage control. Dr. Hollington K. Tong, vice minister of information, contacted the American embassy to say that the article "did not represent the attitude or spirit of the Chinese Government, or the Party, or the Chinese people" and to explain that the Chinese preference was to keep quiet during the debate. Only after the measure had passed would the Chinese government consider putting out an expression of appreciation.[99]

As the Magnuson bill went before the Senate Committee on Immigration, the major arguments for and against the measure were so well established that they only required brief airing. Unlike the House committee, the Senate was looking at a single bill. Major questions, like the difference between a national and a racial quota for the Chinese, had already been settled and written into the bill. The principal arguments in favor of passage centered on diplomatic concerns, such as the strength of Sino-American friendship, promotion of the war effort, combating Japanese propaganda, the detrimental effects of past restrictive immigration polices (with Japan and Pearl Harbor naturally serving as the primary example), and the fact of widespread Chinese knowledge of the bill and its present place in the American legislative process. That both the president and the State Department vocally supported passage was a determining factor in the support the bill received in the Senate.

In preparation for the Senate debate, the State Department reviewed what was at stake in the repeal effort. From the department's perspective, the measure was no longer principally about immigration (if it ever was). Instead, the combination of the war, Japanese propaganda, and the sheer volume of reports on the bill in the Chinese press made passage a military and diplomatic necessity. For State, the only sound argument against repeal was the concern that once the United States began to admit Chinese immigrants again, other Asian allies—Asian Indians and Koreans in particular— would be quick to demand parity. The U.S. Embassy in Bombay noted that India was gearing up for a push to question the "preferred status" of Chinese in America and demand an Indian quota.[100] Still, the department's report found that "special treatment" of the Chinese in this case could be justified by the history of special discriminations against the Chinese; also, the United States could also grant small, racially based quotas to other nations to dispel any potential complaints.

Ultimately, none of the arguments against repealing exclusion and granting the Chinese a quota prevented Congress from going forward with the measure. The measure passed the House on October 21 and the Senate on November 26, 1943, and went to President Roosevelt for his signature; on December 17, Chinese exclusion was formally repealed.[101] The Chinese reaction to the news was understandably positive. The American embassy reported that newspapers and radio broadcasts were claiming that repeal "has reaffirmed Chinese faith in American fair play and friendship."[102] The central press release from the Chinese Ministry of Foreign Affairs stated, "The United States, who in the past has consistently lent her support to China's struggle for freedom and equality, has now set a worthy example in international relations by voluntarily repealing the Chinese Exclusion Act. . . .We believe the seeds sown by this bill will be very fruitful not only in the strengthening of future Sino-American relations but also in establishment of world peace in the post-war world."[103] The emphasis on the future suggested that the Nationalist government hoped for a more equitable future for the Allies, though this bill did not guarantee that. The CCBA in Seattle celebrated the repeal by holding a dinner for Congressman Magnuson, honoring his efforts in working for repeal. In the speeches, Chinese community leaders stressed that an important principle had been upheld by the decision to end exclusion and promised there would be no mass Chinese migration to threaten American goodwill.[104] Chinese community leaders in Honolulu celebrated the news with a drive to have Chinese residents purchase $1 million in U.S. war bonds.[105]

Rhetoric aside, the contribution of repeal to the war effort is easily overstated. Repeal itself stopped far short of true equality for Chinese Americans, and the improvement of morale in China in late 1943 could just as easily be attributed to Chiang Kai-shek's conference in Cairo with Roosevelt and Winston Churchill and its statements of support for the ongoing Chinese efforts against Japan (along with the Cairo Declaration's promises to return territory stolen from China by Japan after the latter's defeat). Repeal was pushed forward by the war, but the war itself required far more concrete support for China than a new immigration measure. What repeal did do was reveal the ways in which the Chinese government could use such low-level issues to test the waters of Sino-American equality, to promote the interests of Chinese in the United States, and to assert rights in the postwar world.

The Legacies of Exclusion and Its Repeal

Wartime efforts to use migration policy and migrants to renegotiate the Sino-American relationship met with a mixed record of success. Superficially, it was all successful, in that the United States announced relinquishment of extraterritoriality, and the Chinese government and press celebrated; shore leave was granted, and Chinese seamen ceased to protest its denial; and exclusion was repealed, allowing Chinese Americans a bright new future. But in each case, that was never more than about half the story. In reality, extraterritoriality might have ended, but the scars of colonialism remained in China. Chinese seamen came to shore but continued to desert in high numbers up until 1944, when a procedure to deport them to the Chinese army in India was agreed upon, just as Atlantic shipping became less dangerous. And repeal opened a small door for limited new immigration and naturalization, but it served as a constant reminder of continued inequality for Chinese in the United States.

That said, one of the arguments against repeal had been that it would provide Chinese an unfair advantage over other Asian populations, and the increasing calls for a revision of U.S. immigration laws aimed at Indian and Filipino migrants seemed to bear this out. Even before Roosevelt signed repeal into law, the American consulate in Bombay reported that Indians had started questioning whether Chinese were being given "preferred" status among all Asians.[106] During the war, Sir Girja Shanka

Bajpai, agent general for India in the United States, complained repeatedly to U.S. officials about the relatively poor treatment of Indian sailors (especially as special projects to assuage Chinese seamen's complaints
expanded), as well as other restrictions, from the application of Alien
Land Laws to Indians in California to the need to reward India's valiant
struggles in the war with a revised law on immigration and naturalization.[107] His first requests came during and on the heels of the repeal
debate, and he continued in early 1944. He stressed to Roosevelt adviser
and assistant secretary of state Adolf Berle that London had an interest in
the issue. Berle wondered if the British were using restrictive U.S. immigration laws to score points in India, even "trying to represent the British Government as having endeavored to safeguard the rights of Indians,
while the United States Government was steadfast in denying them."[108]
Whether or not that strategy could succeed, Berle thought it wise to
get "an Indian parity bill" through Congress while the latter was still in
the mood to grant favors to wartime allies. Even so, Indian officials were
encouraged to avoid making official approaches on the subject, so that,
as with the Chinese, the push for repeal would seem to be coming from
indigenous "American" voices.

Hearings on the proposal to grant a quota to Indian migrants in 1945
echoed the strains of the Chinese hearings, with Roosevelt communicating to Congress, "I regard this legislation as important and desirable, and
I believe that its enactment will help us to win the war and to establish a
secure peace."[109] In 1946 measures passed to repeal exclusions and grant
quotas to both Indian and Filipino migrants, but that too is a mixed record. Other Asian groups were granted immigration rights along the same
unequal lines of the Chinese, which meant racially based quotas, limited
entries, and fewer opportunities for family reunification than European
migrants. In these cases, as with the Chinese, the primary role for Asian
Americans in the passage was in demonstrating an ability to adapt, con-
form, and assimilate to American life. By demonstrating an ability to be
a model minority in the 1940s, it was possible to make a case for their
increased numbers.[110]

Although the end of extraterritoriality, the shore leave ban, and exclusion can and should be viewed as elements of American wartime China
policy, they should also be understood from the standpoint of Chinese
foreign policy and overseas Chinese policy. The Chinese government's
efforts in these eras were fundamentally tied to its goal of achieving parity
for its government in international negotiations, as difficult as this would

be to obtain for the time being. The Chinese government, and the Chinese people, were far from passive recipients of American largesse in granting these measures. And going into the postwar years, the Chinese government would seek to use these new rights to try to mold Chinese American society into a welcomed, positive force of unequivocal support for Nationalist goals and anticommunist campaigns.

Chapter 2

The Diaspora Goes to War

Human Capital and China's Defense

In the early 1940s, when the United States was debating whether to end its exclusionary laws preventing Chinese immigration to the United States, an official of the Republic of China suggested that there would be no danger in doing so because the Chinese as a whole were "not a migratory race."[1] He was appealing to an image of China as a static empire of peasant farmers that captivated American imaginations in the early twentieth century through novels like Pearl Buck's *The Good Earth* or reports from missionaries and merchants returning from the exotic East. He might have thought the claim was the way to soothe fears of a continent overrun by the "yellow peril," or perhaps he believed it himself and thought—as many Chinese officials before him did—that no loyal Chinese, no worthy Chinese citizen, would even consider migrating. During the Second World War, however, there were more than nine million Chinese people living across the globe who could have suggested otherwise.

The Chinese have a long tradition of moving and settling abroad. When the great Ming dynasty voyager Zheng He embarked on his travels through the seas of Southeast Asia in the early fifteenth century, he met Chinese merchants settled in ports all along the way. The advent of European colonialism through Portuguese and Spanish contact and expansion only served to form links that furthered the development of Chinese communities abroad. Chinese colonies in Nanyang, or the "south seas," held on to cultural, linguistic, and familial ties with home villages in the southern Chinese provinces of Guangdong and Fujian, and as mercantile bases, they acted as conduits between local economies and the untapped wealth of continental Asia. Even so, traditional imperial policies considered emigrants tantamount to traitors, a function of tumultuous dynastic change that conflated moving abroad with opposing the empire. The British victory in the Opium Wars forced many changes upon the Qing dynasty, including the establishment of extraterritoriality rights for foreign nationals in China, as well as British colonial control of the port of Hong Kong and the creation of a bustling market in labor recruiters and transport for new outward migration. The Qing dynasty also began to develop a modern consular and embassy system, a step in China's entry into modern international affairs.

Just before the turn of the century, Chinese government officials began what historian Wang Gungwu has termed the "upgrading" of the Chinese migrant. In 1909, one of the final edicts preceding the downfall of the Qing established a nationality law that followed the principle of *jus sanguinis*, so all ethnic Chinese living abroad maintained Chinese citizenship, whether they had ever set foot on the mainland or not, and normalized use of the term *huaqiao* to mean "overseas Chinese" as a distinct subsection of the population. The shift from exclusion to inclusion of Chinese living abroad has been explained as a function of the new nationalism emerging in China, though the roots of that nationalism and how it came to include a cultural definition that was not congruent with China's existing borders is the subject of extensive, and ongoing, debate.[2] As Wang and others have observed, however, China's interest in its diaspora has always been inversely proportionate to its strength as a nation. At times of crisis, Chinese governments turn to the overseas population. Soon Keong Ong argues that "*huaqiao* figured prominently in the minds of Chinese nationalists not because they were the extraterritorial constituents of the Chinese nation or the revelation of China's internal history, but rather because of the financial contributions they could make to the state-building projects of a weakened China."[3] For these purposes, two regions proved of particular importance: Southeast Asia for sheer numbers and North America for relative wealth. After the successful 1911 revolution, the diaspora's financial support remained vital for the struggling nation.[4] Chinese abroad sent funds back to help unify China and regain the young republic as it struggled for unity, and they helped defend against the increasing encroachments of the Japanese. The

Nationalist Party (Kuomintang, or KMT) created an "Overseas Chinese Affairs Bureau" to help it reach overseas communities in 1923. The ROC incorporated protection of the Chinese abroad into the formal government structure in 1926, when it established the Overseas Chinese Affairs Commission (OCAC) to protect the rights, interests, and legal status of Chinese who lived outside China.[5]

From then on there existed a push and pull between foreign governments playing host to large Chinese populations and Nationalist Chinese goals. As it faced greater and greater threats to its stability, the Republic of China made greater attempts to exercise what L. Ling-chi Wang has called "extraterritorial control" over Chinese abroad.[6] This meant trying to negotiate better terms for immigration and resident rights with a reluctant host country, but it also meant strengthening the ties between migrants and the homeland for the sake of maintaining financial support. These two goals frequently worked at odds with each other in the United States, where greater immigrant rights would include access to full citizenship, and full citizenship would eventually break the bond with the homeland. During World War II, the Nationalist government tried to pursue an overseas-Chinese policy that bolstered support for the government and its war effort while maintaining responsiveness to the needs of Chinese migrants. Because the policy was as much a part of countering Chinese Communists as it was opposing the Japanese, it also formed an important component in the origins of the Cold War in Asia. The work of the KMT in the United States and its attempts to influence Chinese communities and through them the United States government developed in the 1950s along lines created during the Second World War.

This chapter examines wartime overseas Chinese policy as it affected Chinese Americans and U.S.-Chinese relations on three fronts: the central goals and philosophy behind the policy, the mobilization of Chinese in the United States and elsewhere in Allied war efforts, and the solicitation of donations and remittances to aid China. These three items share in common a focus on how best to mobilize human and financial resources in the diaspora for the sake of the motherland. Additionally, it will consider how Chinese residents in the United States, including Chinese Americans, negotiated belonging and uncertain citizenship. Taken together, this discussion demonstrates how migrant aid could be a safe, low-risk arena in which to negotiate Chinese equality, from the personal to the national, as well as the extent of bureaucratic confusion facing American officials in crafting a response.

The Overseas Chinese Affairs Commission

Having declared itself the protector and patron of Chinese overseas, the Nationalist Chinese government had strong incentives to maintain productive ties with the diaspora during the war. The support of the Chinese abroad could form the physical and financial foundation for continuing the fight against Japan, while supporting the diaspora in their overseas struggles could win their backing and remind the Allies to treat China as an equal. Because the 1909 Nationality Law defined "overseas Chinese" as anyone with at least one ethnically Chinese parent, residing anywhere in the world regardless of nationality, personal loyalties, or formal ties to China, the overseas Chinese population was vast—close to nine million people in the early 1940s, mostly concentrated in Southeast Asia (See tables 1 and 2).

In the years leading up the war, the OCAC took on a variety of tasks, which then became amplified by the national emergency. These included sending representatives abroad to investigate living and working conditions, developing and improving educational materials and Chinese schools overseas, and soliciting investments in the homeland. Often, an overseas Chinese affairs officer would be attached to ROC consulates abroad to manage the workload on-site. More overt attempts at extraterritorial control, including intelligence operations, recruitment drives for party members, and developing close connections between overseas communities and organizations and the Chinese government, fell to overseas operatives of the KMT.[7] Historian Him Mark Lai observed, "The war gave the KMT an excellent opportunity to expand its influence into all areas of the Chinese American community.... Taking advantage of patriotic feelings, the KMT recruited ambitious and opportunistic people into the party, including many key community leaders from district and clan associations and secret societies."[8] Over the course of the war, connections between the Chinese Consolidated Benevolent Associations in the United States and the KMT in particular grew closer, with the result that these U.S.-based Chinese organizations became reliable voices in favor of the Nationalist government and its policies. Together, the OCAC overt agenda and the KMT covert one ensured the Republic of China an unprecedented degree of access to Chinese abroad.

During the period from 1937 to 1945, the Nationalist government developed a series of policy goals for its overseas Chinese operations. They were equal parts service and supplication. Many were intended to demonstrate Nationalist interest in aiding its migrants, but also to elicit financial support for the war effort. Chinese scholar Xizhe Zhang has identified nine

Table 1. Worldwide overseas Chinese population during World War II

Location	Overseas Chinese population	Percentage of total overseas Chinese population
ASIA	**8,715,733**	**96.05**
French Indochina	461,516	5.30
Burma	183,594	2.22
Thailand	2,500,000	28.68
Malaya (including Singapore)	2,358,335	27.06
Sarawak	86,000	0.99
British North Borneo	47,799	0.55
Dutch East Indies	1,344,809	15.43
Philippines	117,463	1.35
Hong Kong	923,584	10.60
Macau	157,175	1.80
Taiwan	59,692	0.68
Korea	70,270	0.80
Japan	19,801	0.23
Other Asian countries	30,350	0.36
NORTH AMERICA	**173,554**	**1.93**
USA (including Hawaii)	102,554	1.13
Canada	46,000	0.53
Mexico	25,000	0.27
LATIN AMERICA	**45,171**	**0.74**
Cuba	35,000	0.40
Peru	7,930	0.09
Other	22,441	0.25
EUROPE	**62,738**	**0.72**
England	8,000	0.09
France	17,000	0.20
USSR	29,620	0.34
Other European countries	8,118	0.09
OCEANIA	**34,598**	**0.38**
Australia	17,000	0.19
Other Pacific islands	17,568	0.19
AFRICA	**9,064**	**0.11**
TOTAL	**9,040,858**	**99.9**

Source: Qiaowu weiyuanhui songlai "sa er nianji qiaowu tongji," 1943, 18/1677, MOFA, Nanjing.

Table 2. Overseas Chinese populations of a selection of significant host countries, as a percentage of the Chinese population

Location	Overseas Chinese population	Percentage of total overseas Chinese population	Total population	Overseas Chinese as a percentage of total population
French Indochina	461,516	5.30	23,030,000	2.00
Burma	183,594	2.22	14,647,496	1.32
Thailand	2,500,000	28.68	11,506,207	21.73
Malaya (including Singapore)	2,358,335	27.06	5,504,094	42.35
Dutch East Indies	1,344,809	15.43	70,539,000	1.91
Philippines	117,463	1.35	13,600,000	0.86
USA (including Hawaii)	102,554	1.13	132,092,605	0.08

Source: Qiaowu weiyuanhui songlai "sa er nianji qiaowu tongji," 1943, 18/1677, MOFA, Nanjing; U.S. Census (Washington, DC: Government Printing Office, 1940).

distinct policy elements, starting with protecting overseas Chinese rights and interests (including efforts to improve their status in their countries of residence). From there, the OCAC would provide relief for the families of overseas Chinese still in China, including efforts to assist with remittances that were blocked in some way or another by the war while encouraging the overseas Chinese to contribute personally and financially to China's war of resistance and organizing overseas Chinese into groups and organizations that could take on tasks in support of the war. Officials would also work on disseminating propaganda to improve the diaspora opinion of the homeland government and increase support for the Nationalist army and leadership. Keeping the focus on overseas communities, they would help overseas Chinese with self-defense and with joining the defense efforts of local, allied governments; select overseas Chinese representatives to the local government and investigate the status of overseas Chinese around the world; and provide resources to support a Chinese education for overseas Chinese students. Finally, it was hoped that once all these policies to connect migrants to the homeland prevailed, they would need to support returning overseas Chinese, including helping them find work and establishing schools for returning youth in mainland China.[9]

It is worth noting that many of the general overseas Chinese policy statements present a vague and idealized vision for policy. In that way they can be seen as aspirational, but not always attainable. Nonetheless, with these nine goals, the ROC demonstrated its intention to create a network of overseas Chinese around the world working together for China's ultimate victory. It also hoped to ensure that in the postwar years, the Chinese population abroad would be invested in helping China to rebuild and develop. Pursuing the Chinese abroad in this way was a necessary step in promoting the legitimacy and sovereignty of the beleaguered Chinese state, but it was not without diplomatic complications. The treatment of Chinese in the United States had the potential to bolster or weaken the overall relationship between war allies.

Though the U.S. record on the treatment of Chinese was appalling in the 1940s, it was in no way unique. In 1942, the OCAC counted twenty-one countries or territories, mostly in Allied nations in Southeast Asia and the Americas, with harsh or unfairly restrictive laws against Chinese.[10] In the mid-to-late nineteenth century, the traditional countries of immigration in the Americas and Pacific created either formal Chinese exclusion laws or put serious restrictions on Chinese immigration through entrance taxes, visa issuance, or literacy exams. In the Americas and Australia, anti-Chinese and anti-Asian racism drove these policies, fed by stereotypes of the Chinese as "coolies." Every country had its own way of discriminating against Chinese migrants, but the United States often appeared as a leader—the first to enact formal exclusion laws, for example, and the first to repeal them. No matter that each national setting was unique, the Chinese government's response was part of a global policy that prioritized overseas Chinese aid.

The OCAC attempted to combat discrimination on every front, aware that worldwide Chinese faced entrance problems, residence problems, and naturalization problems, then seeking improvements in each field. In most cases, though, the goal was not the elimination of numerical restrictions against Chinese, but the end of discriminatory laws that singled out Chinese for special treatment.[11] For example, in the United States the numerically restrictive quotas of the Immigration Act of 1924 would not come under fire from the Chinese government, but the Chinese Exclusion Laws, which specifically isolated Chinese migrants for special treatment, would. The hope was that China's new position in the world as the center of the Asian resistance to fascism would give the government new bargaining ground for trying to get anti-Chinese laws repealed. If the effort failed, China could always blame it on Western colonial prejudices, so the project was low-risk, high-reward. That appearances trumped accomplishments could be further demonstrated by the fact that the Nationalists proved sensitive to other governments' concerns that Chinese immigrants had unfair economic

advantages over local citizens—either as cheap labor with which local workers could not compete, or as rich, networked merchants with a stranglehold
on the local economy. They did not request that all limits to Chinese immigration be canceled, but that legal discriminations singling out the Chinese
be replaced by policies that applied equally to everyone. OCAC officials
considered proposing that nations eliminate discriminatory laws and enter
into a "Gentlemen's Agreement" with China modeled after Japan's pact with
the United States in 1907–8. Under this model China would promise to
restrict emigration for a certain period of time in exchange for the lifting of
laws prohibiting Chinese immigration outright.[12] It might appear the per-
fect compromise, but the ROC had little success persuading other nations to
adopt it. Though the Chinese government approached many nations at the
same time as it discussed the repeal of Chinese exclusion with the United
States, few altered their laws before the United States did so.

Just as important as the project of getting more desirable laws passed
was the second issue, the residence problem, which included ensuring equal
rights under foreign laws for Chinese choosing to live abroad. Beyond the
United States, Chinese living in Vietnam, Canada, Cuba, Panama, the Dutch
East Indies, and Peru were all required to have residence permits, and these
nations had laws in place that allowed them to deport Chinese who failed to
obtain these permits or whose permits had expired. Most overseas Chinese
host countries also required Chinese to register and used the registration
process to investigate the migrants and weed out undesirables. Though residence permits and registration policies themselves were perhaps not unreasonable, often procedures were in place to make it especially difficult for
Chinese to obtain legal status. U.S. detention and deportation policies were
particularly harsh, but so were those of Malaya, Vietnam, New Zealand,
Canada, Cuba, Guatemala, Panama, and Nicaragua.[13] Protesting against such
policies was a way for the Nationalist government to maintain a link with
its migrants once living abroad.

The third aspect of protecting and improving the legal status of overseas Chinese was the naturalization problem. The lack of a single, international law for determining citizenship meant that some individuals would
have multiple citizenships and others none at all.[14] Anyone who was born
of Chinese parents was a Chinese citizen; but in many countries, like the
United States, laws against immigration included laws preventing naturalization, which created a permanent class of alien residents with fewer rights
and protections from the local government. The United States and England
had nationality laws that combined *jus sanguinis* (citizenship determined by

bloodlines) and *jus soli* (citizenship granted by virtue of place of birth). Children born of American citizens were American citizens, no matter where in the world they were born; but at the same time, anyone born on U.S. soil was also an American citizen. As a result, Chinese born in the United States were automatically dual nationals, as were those born in China of American-citizen fathers. For as long as the United States and China were allies, this situation could lead to some sticky legal cases but no real threat to national security.[15] Nationality questions were even more difficult in Southeast Asia, where colonial governments applied different rules for different populations.

Like all other aspects of protecting the diaspora, the ability of the Chinese government to influence changes in the legal status of overseas Chinese as immigrants, residents, or citizens depended on the strength and influence of the government in world affairs. China had long been weak compared to the United States, but the imperative of the war and the need for overseas Chinese support drove efforts to push for at least nominal improvements in migrant rights. Looking ahead to the postwar world also required significant investments in overseas Chinese issues even when the war made it inconvenient, in the hope that these would pay off later. Chinese officials experienced some guarded success in obtaining the revision of American laws on extraterritoriality, shore leave, and exclusion, but these were not the only issues that plagued Chinese migrants in the early 1940s. The Nationalist government also sought to persuade communities abroad to invest significantly in the Chinese struggle against Japan and in the postwar reconstruction. Two issues required particular effort from Nationalist diplomats. The first was negotiating draft status, to protect migrant manpower for the postwar recovery. The second was to ensure that remittances could get through in order to incentivize continued contributions to the Chinese war effort. During the war, Nationalist China also used its overseas Chinese policy and bureaucracy to extend greater degrees of extraterritorial control over Chinese abroad. The methods it employed to do that were particular to each host country, the United States included, but took place in this larger context where discrimination against Chinese migrants was an international norm.

Chinese Migrants and the Draft

In January 1944, Yang-lung Tong was in serious trouble. He was not only in danger of imminent induction into the U.S. Army, but also faced being brought up on charges for delinquency, failure to keep the local draft board informed of his whereabouts, and fraud. For much of the war, Tong had been benefiting from an evolving series of regulations affecting Chinese and other nationalities who lived temporarily in the United States: students could apply for a certificate of nonresidence, which would make it possible for them to avoid the draft altogether, and recent graduates could engage in technical training of use to their respective homelands (as long as these homelands were allies) and receive deferments from service.[16] The status of Chinese migrants under the Selective Service program was unique even compared to that of other immigrant groups because of the uncertainty of their position before the repeal of Chinese exclusion. In those years, Chinese aliens resident in the United States became subject to all the responsibilities of a citizen without any of the rights. Negotiating a separate status became a double-edged sword, because it reinforced the difference between the Chinese and European immigrants even while it subjected the Chinese to accusations of seeking special treatment. The record of the negotiations between Chinese officials, the Selective Service, the U.S. Department of State, and the War Department reveals the extent to which Chinese migrants could be championed not for their own sake, but as symbolic gestures of a larger pattern of cooperation. The Nationalist government, motivated in part by postwar considerations, fought for Chinese migrant rights. However, it proved willing to sacrifice them when necessary to achieve larger goals. Over the course of the four years that the United States waged war, the Chinese government raised a number of disparate concerns over Chinese military service in the U.S. armed forces, but they all had in common a concern for equal treatment of the Chinese and other, non-Asian, aliens.

Under the Selective Training and Service Act of 1940, every adult man was required to register with the Selective Service, and after the United States went to war, men between eighteen and forty-five could be called to serve. You did not have to be a U.S. citizen to be included in the American draft, something that elicited frequent protests that spanned the globe from Moscow to San Salvador. This policy was not unique to the Second World War. Given its history as an immigrant nation, the United States had a long history of drafting anyone "resident in the United States"—and often defining "resident" without reference to permanent or temporary status. From the Civil War on, any immigrant who intended to become a U.S. citizen had to register, with the "reward" of being able to take an accelerated path to citizenship after serving. During that war, this was expanded again to include any man who had voted in the United States, whether or not he had declared his intent to serve. In World War I, the idea of universal, albeit selective, conscription emerged to ensure "that military service was a personal and non-transferable obligation to the nation-state." The United States drafted aliens from neutral nations in that war—whether they had declared their intention to seek citizenship or not—though, as in the Civil War, this sparked diplomatic protests and questions about whether doing so violated international law. Part of the problem for Woodrow Wilson's administration proved to be balancing public opinion—which did not look kindly on aliens being exempt from service to "stay home and make money" while citizens sacrificed—against diplomatic necessity, when otherwise friendly nations registered violent protest on behalf of their nationals. The compromise measure that emerged gave aliens the right to refuse to serve, but then barred them for life from becoming naturalized citizens. Those who did their duty were entitled to expedited naturalization.[17] The conflation of loyal citizenship with military conscription that occurred in these earlier years had a direct effect on how Chinese and other Asian aliens encountered the process during World War II.[18]

Chinese Americans could, of course, be drafted, and they faced the same system as the rest of the population. Among the alien population, however, draftees could include longtime residents technically prevented from naturalizing by the Exclusion Acts and individuals who entered the United States illegally. At every deportation proceeding for Chinese sailors who jumped ship in the United States, the men were required to demonstrate that they had registered with the Selective Service. In some cases, registration was not only completed but done so with enthusiasm: faced with the choice between either deportation to China or re-shipping on merchant vessels, seamen sometimes tried to volunteer for the U.S. Army, often without success.[19] The most controversial cases, however, involved Chinese students in the United States for a temporary course of study.

The Chinese government first raised concerns about the impact of the draft on Chinese students in early 1942, couching all their complaints in the language of equality.[20] The problem was simple: early in the war, students living temporarily in the United States for the purpose of completing a degree had been called up for induction. It was not only Chinese that faced conscription. During the war, the State Department worked in tandem with the War Department and Selective Service to reassure allied nations making complaints about their exchange students receiving unexpected draft notices, and together they tried to develop procedures for ensuring that students could be made exempt. The greatest numbers of students were from Latin America, something unique to the war (many of these students would have normally studied in Europe but were cut off by the conflict). The United States ended up signing reciprocal draft agreements with a number of nations to address diplomatic complaints about Selective Service rules. By the spring of 1942, the Selective Service required bona fide students to certify that they were continuing in their course of study, and it would in return issue a "certificate of non-residence," which would result in automatic exemption from even the requirement to register.[21]

For students who followed a very traditional path of enrolling, remaining enrolled for four to eight consecutive semesters, and returning home, this basic procedure no doubt worked quite well. As the war dragged on, however, Chinese students increasingly failed to be traditional students. For one thing, many continued their education by engaging in "practical training," often using engineering skills in a corporate setting. Chinese embassy officials defended these breaches of student status because they almost invariably considered this training vital to the Chinese war effort, whether it was engineering or newspaper copy setting. In many cases, the war effort could be conflated with postwar reconstruction, making just about any degree useful to China. Another problem for the Chinese was transport. Upon completing degrees, it proved impossible to return to China. Lend-lease supplies and other war matériel were shipped west across the Pacific on loaded ships with little space available for passengers—it was the eastern voyage to the United States that remained open. As a result, Chinese students continued to come during the war, but often could not leave.[22] Many students also found their sources of financial support cut off by the conflict, necessitating local employment. Moreover, language difficulties and confusion about the regulations meant that many Chinese students missed key deadlines, failing to request the certificate of non-residence within the allotted time frame or to report when called up for induction. This led to a growing number of delinquencies, which caused local draft boards to become increasingly unsympathetic to Chinese cases.

These factors combined to create a critical mass of Chinese students who were not strictly adhering to the rules required to maintain status as non-residents, but whom Chinese officials still preferred to protect from induction. In fact, State Department officials themselves did not necessarily disagree. They tended to see this population of Chinese students in the context of the longer history of scholarly exchanges, not to mention future U.S.-Chinese relations, and made arguments in favor of increasing the numbers of U.S.-educated Chinese in a postwar China.[23] Convincing the Selective Service to exempt these nontraditional students from induction required some doing, however. The short-term solution was to use Dr. Chih Meng, director of the China Institute in America and de facto supervisor of Chinese exchange students, to certify to the draft boards whether a change in course of study was warranted or a work assignment could be counted as "practical training." This came with the caveat that local boards would review his determinations, but could not be forced to accept them.[24]

For U.S. citizens of Chinese ancestry and longtime residents, there was no question about the obligation to register for the Selective Service, but U.S. immigration law ensured that they faced their responsibilities without many of the rights enjoyed by European immigrants. American laws kept most Chinese migrants to the United States from bringing wives, children, or parents to the United States to live with them, but the physical separation did not make Chinese men any less the breadwinners of their families. For those Chinese men called up for induction, they could obtain a 3-A or 3-B classification (often given to American and European immigrant men living with their families) and ultimately deferment if they could prove that they sent $360 a year in remittances to their families in China.

All of this, however, required documentation, something that proved unusually challenging for the Chinese. They had no government-issued marriage or birth certificates to document their family life. Most Chinese immigrants in the United States came from a few counties in Guangdong Province that went in and out of Japanese control during the war, making writing home for proof difficult. Remittances during the war were sent irregularly and via a variety of paths, not all of which left a paper trail. Cui Cunlin, first minister of the Chinese Embassy, suggested that his government contact Chinese "guilds and tongs" in the United States and ask them to vouch for both family relationships and past remittances (he was referring to Chinese native place and surname organizations around which the major Chinatowns had organized). At least some of the people involved likely entered the United States with falsified papers (as "paper sons"), which meant that their guild records, not to mention the family members on file for them with the immigration service, were inevitably incorrect. According to historian K. Scott Wong, individuals who confessed the details of their immigration status during their service were given opportunities to wipe the slate clean and become naturalized, but that solution did not come until after the war, and the need was more immediate.[25] The records of the Bank of China would also come into play as proof of remittances, though the bank was not permitted to send funds to areas under active Japanese occupation.

If attempts at deferment failed and Chinese breadwinners were inducted, they should have been able to obtain the allotments sent by the U.S. Army for familial support, but this too came with problems. Most of the families receiving the allotments were in occupied areas, and providing documentation for the number of family members involved ran into the same roadblocks as deferment requests. Chinese draftees grew increasingly frustrated at their inability to continue to provide for their families, and called upon the Chinese Consolidated Benevolent Association and the Chinese consulates to speak to the U.S. authorities on their behalf. In some cases the draftees did this whether or not they were U.S. citizens: U.S. laws separated them as unequal citizens, forcing them to seek protection from another government.[26]

Interestingly, being back in China when the war broke out did not translate to an exemption from the requirement to register. The long arm of the Selective Service worked through the U.S. consulates—and a variety of other volunteers—to try to account for every American in China. After the Presidential Proclamation of October 26, 1943, that all male citizens between eighteen and sixty-five living outside the United States were required to register, the U.S. consulate in Guilin (in South China) reported a heroic effort to travel to every distant town where U.S. citizens were known to be present, to complete their registrations. There were some three hundred such citizens in all, roughly half of whom were Americans of Chinese ancestry "and against whom the presumption of expatriation has arisen." To this end, given the volatile situation in a region often under Japanese occupation, Father Francis J. O'Neill, a Catholic missionary, spent several weeks in Taishan (Toishan in contemporary documentation), the ancestral home of the majority of Chinese immigrants in the United States. He met with Chinese Americans and registered them—a task he was uniquely suited for, given his facility in the local dialect—and reported that many of the people he registered did not speak or write English. The consul in charge of the project, Arthur Ringwalt, noted (with what reads as exasperation), "Occasionally, it was necessary to appoint as registrars the only two Americans situated in a remote area, in order that each might register the other." Ringwalt lamented the fact that the second phase of the program—the physical examinations so that the potential draftees might be classified—had to be delayed owing to the Japanese reoccupation of parts of the region and the consulate's planned evacuation to Kunming.[27]

Beyond the problem of the Chinese students' exemptions and the Chinese residents' deferments or allotments, there were dozens of other smaller problems that emerged during the war. Inductees complained that they were not given desirable jobs or promoted at the same rates as Caucasian soldiers. The U.S. Navy employed a discriminatory system that kept Chinese sailors out of any position other than mess steward or cabin boy.[28] Chinese immigrants were disproportionately likely to own a small business, and the time between when they were drafted and ordered to report was frequently not long enough to dispose of the business properly. Two Chinese theater troupes traveled to the United States for performances, only to find their visas not extended at the end of their tour (when transport home proved difficult) and enough members drafted to leave the remainder unable to perform. Employees in traditionally nonessential and unofficial, nongovernmental occupations—such as those employed by the Bank of China or Chinese-language newspapers—were considered good candidates for deferment by the Chinese and ideal candidates for induction by the Selective Service. Local draft boards grew so upset by the complicated rules for deferring and exempting Chinese that Lieutenant Colonel S. G. Parker of the Selective Service protested, "Our Local Boards feel as though we have been partial in every respect to the Chinese. We have been accused repeatedly of having treated you in ways we would not treat anyone else. The delinquency is so great that this board feels that this is the last straw. . . . There are criticisms by Italians and other groups that we have unduly favored the Chinese."[29] The idea of the Chinese in the United States in early 1943 being privileged seemed rather remarkable to the Chinese Embassy officials, though they felt forced to concede that delinquency was a clear problem.

According to Cui Cunlin and many of his compatriots, the root of all these problems was inequality in the U.S.-Chinese relationship. There could not be a true reciprocal agreement between China and the United States on the draft because U.S. claims of extraterritoriality in China and Chinese exclusion in the United States automatically ensured inequality. Even after the relinquishment of extraterritoriality, U.S. citizens in China were never subject to the Chinese draft, no matter what their residence status, and the United States had not provided its alien Chinese residents the option to choose to return to their homeland for induction rather than join the U.S. forces, a provision used to address draft disputes with other countries.[30] Delinquency was a problem, but it was hard for the Chinese Embassy to demand compliance when so many open questions—deferments and allotments especially—went unresolved. A March 1943 front-page editorial in the *Minqi Ribao* (Chinese Nationalist daily), one of the largest Chinese-language newspapers in New York, stressed the draft problem as being only one of many injustices to which the U.S. government subjected Chinese students—others being particular scrutiny by the Immigration and Naturalization Service, limited choices for courses of study in universities, being investigated if making any changes in the set study program, and possible deportation upon graduation. The article reminded its readers of the injustice of the American focus on the war in Europe over the struggles of China, and asked the Chinese community why Americans always treated both China and the Chinese unequally.[31] The link between the migrants' rights and the larger issue of how the United States was waging the war was as common as it was telling: the Chinese sense of inequality was felt on many levels.

By mid 1943, the U.S. Department of State and the Chinese Embassy found themselves in the rare position of being largely in agreement on the necessity of, and procedure for, exempting Chinese students from the draft. They even agreed on exemptions for those who had left school for employment. The problem was that the Selective Service was unwilling to play along. The director of the service, Major General Lewis B. Hershey, proved recalcitrant, and the local draft boards not much better. Hershey formed some of his ideas about the citizen soldier in World War I, when he acted as a recruiter for the National Guard and grew infamously frustrated by what he viewed as attempts made by young men to shirk their duty through marriage or questionable claims as conscientious objectors.[32] After joining the personnel section of the War Department in 1936, he worked his way up to director by 1941. Through 1942 he acquiesced to the arrangements negotiated by State and the Chinese Embassy concerning Chinese students, but by April 1943 he changed course, likely because of delinquencies and his well-known intolerance for anything that could even loosely be considered draft dodging. In June, Secretary of State Cordell Hull himself wrote to Hershey, stressing that "the Department regards the education of these Chinese students as distinctly a contribution to China's war effort, since their services are needed in China, where there is a great dearth of professionally trained Chinese."[33] Internal memorandums drafted by officials in the Division of Cultural Relations at State commented, "From the standpoint of the cultural relations policy it would be preferable to lose a few inductees rather than to subject some of these men to undue hardship and to create another issue similar to the Chinese immigration question."[34] This line of reasoning was wisely not employed to persuade General Hershey, but it is quite revealing on its own: it highlights the importance of the educational exchanges to broader postwar planning for U.S.–Chinese relations, even as it reflects a keen awareness that the Chinese exclusion laws remained an impediment to cooperation.

Though Hershey accepted the reasoning that at least some Chinese engaged in training could be legitimately deferred, he remained suspicious of Chinese attempts to evade service. In December, he expressed concern that the Chinese Embassy was attempting to obtain deferments for Chinese with American citizenship and that some of the Chinese who failed to comply with the law "go about flaunting their delinquency." He cited in particular Yang-lung Tong, as cases like his were not only in danger of "creating ill will for the Chinese Government, but . . . they prejudice the consideration of meritorious cases."[35] In late 1944, it emerged that Hershey apparently thought the practical training exemption applied only to Chinese, whereas the State Department intended for it to be universal. That explained some of the complaints from the Selective Service that the Chinese were receiving preferential treatment, if not the reluctance to allow the exemptions to take effect.[36]

For Yang-lung Tong, the negotiations on students, delinquencies, and practical training did not come soon enough, and his record had given his local draft board more than enough grounds to reconsider his case. His case was complicated by the fact that his father, Hollington Tong, was vice minister of information for the Republic of China. Early in his career, the elder Tong had taught a young Chiang Kai-shek, and they became lifelong friends. Hollington Tong visited the United States several times during the war, most notably accompanying Soong Meiling in her early 1943 visit. The elder Tong's prominence made the younger Tong's delinquency uniquely sensitive. In a letter to Hollington, the American consul in Nanjing, Willys Peck, detailed the problem. Yang-lung had begun a course in chemistry and medicine, but later left that for work with the U.S. Steel Export Company. The embassy requested an occupational deferment for him, though the department and later the draft board both felt the work was too far from his academic field to warrant consideration. From there, he failed to respond to an order to report for induction in January 1943, becoming delinquent. Tong later requested deferment again, but in the meantime changed jobs and residences without notifying the draft board. Having violated the Selective Service Law on several counts, by mid-1943 he was subject to arrest, imprisonment, and assorted fines. Peck noted that the senior Tong was a great friend of the United States (and had been educated there himself) but that the draft board and the state Selective Service director were inclined to be harsh with the son. The draft boards consisted of private citizens volunteering their services and often forced to make tough choices when facing frequent requests for deferments. "Since they have to be severe in this way with their friends and neighbors the local boards naturally want to feel convinced that when they grant exemption or deferment to a foreign student who is in paid employment such special consideration is fully deserved." Seeing few other options, Peck gently suggested that Tong arrange for his son to return to China at the earliest possible moment.[37]

Yang-lung's side of his story is a little different. Upon hearing of the letter to his father—and finding himself subject to quickly drawn-up plans to leave the country—he wrote his own letter to Peck to explain himself. His story is filled with misunderstandings and near misses. He explained about a move out of Minneapolis to the suburbs and an arrangement with his landlord to forward his mail that never materialized, a subsequent ulcer that sent him to New York to seek treatment, a telegram to his draft board that they never received, and his father's influence in persuading him to take the job at the steel company.[38] It was a series of missed connections that likely would not have saved your average citizen from arrest, but in Tong's case all was well that ends well: he either decided or gave in to persuasion to leave for China on the next available transport. Though never an easy task, a berth was found on a steamship, and he left the country in July 1944,[39] his Selective Service registration canceled (a requirement to depart the United States) "in the national interest."[40]

Yang-lung Tong received special treatment in the end, but General Hershey's concern that Chinese in general were being privileged by the system makes sense only in contrast to the problems of Japanese Americans. The American ideal of the citizen soldier saw expression in both the Chinese American and Japanese American communities: approximately sixteen thousand Chinese Americans served in the U.S. military, along with around thirty-three thousand Japanese Americans, representing in both cases at least 20 percent of the military-age men in their respective communities.[41] But the attempt to demand responsibilities from individuals not granted equal rights also ran into difficulties in the Japanese community in the United States. Selective Service officials suspected young Japanese Americans—and, more often, their family members—of attempting to use expatriation to dodge the draft. That they were subject to the draft at all was a fairly recent development. The whole Japanese population in the United States, alien and citizen, had been classed 4-C at the start of the war, and only as of February 1943 were Japanese Americans permitted to volunteer for service. In the meantime, from March 1942 on, the West Coast population had been forced from their homes and into temporary internment camps to wait out the war, regardless of citizenship status: the ultimate expression of exclusion. The draft came to these camps late, in January 1944. Those who flat out refused induction were arrested and, as historian Eric Muller has demonstrated, tried to use the federal courts to negotiate their rights as citizens: the right to protest without facing charges of disloyalty.[42] Japanese Americans who were dual nationals were both valuable and problematic for their citizenship. In the larger discussion of their responsibilities or duties toward their country of residence, Japan's claim on them was never far away.

During the war, the status of individuals of Chinese and Japanese ancestry in the United States trended in opposite directions: as historian Yui Daizaburo has termed it, the Chinese sought and won greater inclusion, while the Japanese faced increasing exclusion.[43] And yet both populations experienced great difficulty negotiating their rights and duties as citizens and residents, especially when it came to mandatory military service and the American ideal of the citizen soldier. Both populations served proudly and have been celebrated for their heroics, but the unequal status of being an American of Asian descent, or an immigrant of Asian ancestry, cast a long shadow over their achievements.

Chinatown and China's Wars

The Chinese experience with the Selective Service boards offers a reminder both of the extent to which Chinese in the United States embraced military service to make themselves into citizen soldiers and the degree to which some temporary residents preferred to maintain their allegiances across the Pacific. In both cases they became subject to the Republic of China's continuing efforts to exercise some degree of extraterritorial control over their immediate futures. The reasons for this were simple and laid out in the larger overseas Chinese policies, which promoted ties between the Chinese abroad and the homeland to maintain international support for the war. Some Chinese residents and Chinese Americans would remain permanently attached to the United States, and some would seek a future in rebuilding a postwar China. But until the dust settled, the Nationalists required as many as possible looking out across the waters and determined to support their homeland. There were many means to accomplish this, but two of the most prominent were promoting Chinese education to keep migrants and second-generation Chinese Americans engaged with the homeland, and by soliciting remittances, donations, and other contributions from the diaspora.

Despite many other pressing concerns during the war, education played a role in wartime overseas Chinese policy because it bolstered financial support of the homeland, bolstered positive ideas about China in the diaspora, and improved the image of Chinese abroad in the countries in which they lived. As with protecting Chinese exchange students against the draft, Nationalist officials thought defending the educational needs of Chinese abroad would bolster their loyalty to China, as well as create a population of well-educated, Mandarin-speaking professionals that could help rebuild the nation after the war. To accomplish these goals, the Chinese government often provided schools with subsidies for their operation and textbooks that reflected government positions and principles. They taught cultural pride in a way that helped strengthen the link especially between Chinese born abroad and the "homeland" they had never seen. As historian Stephen Fitzgerald has noted, "From the very beginning, the Kuomintang regarded Chinese education as the key, without that, the overseas Chinese might begin to see their future in their countries of residence."[44] This worked the other way as well: Chinese school curriculum aimed to create educated, vice-free citizens who were welcome in host countries. This way, properly schooled Chinese students could help fight stereotypes of the Chinese used in efforts to restrict Chinese immigration.[45]

In 1943, the KMT sent a representative to the United States and Canada to investigate Chinese schooling, and he reported two problems. First, that U.S. segregation laws prevented some Chinese students from attending white schools, and their educations suffered as a result. Second, few cities outside of major metropolitan centers like New York, San Francisco, and Boston had Chinese schools available. Investigators proposed that after the war, the Republic of China send educators to North America to improve schooling.[46] If their purpose was to ensure as many U.S.-educated Chinese as possible moved to China to rebuild after the war, the KMT had larger problems than that. In a discussion of students and young adults, K. Scott Wong describes how "most Chinese Americans in the 1930s chose to cast their lot with America."[47] In a larger discussion of the impact of the war on Chinese Americans, Wong suggests that despite discrimination and limited opportunities, relatively few members of Chinese communities contemplated moving to China, and in many cases they did not have the language skills even if they had the desire. As a result, KMT education policy was sometimes counterproductive. It encouraged academic success and high achievement to make Chinese Americans well accepted by the mainstream American population, but if that policy worked, it would also sever the emotional and linguistic ties that might lead young professionals to China.

Despite these challenges, the Nationalists had another reason to use education to cultivate support: increasingly they had to compete with the Chinese Communist Party for overseas contributions. Mao Zedong, who had emerged in the late 1930s as a party leader, made statements throughout the war about the importance of joining with the overseas Chinese in a united front against Japan. By doing so, he placed overseas Chinese policy firmly in the context of the fight against fascism, rather than stressing the need for supporting the Chinese Communist Party (CCP) itself.[48] Even so, it did not take long for overseas advocates of the Nationalist Party and proponents of the Chinese Communist Party to splinter into two separate groups, paralleling the failing United Front between their respective armies on the mainland.[49] In 1938, the CCP formed an overseas section, composed of returned overseas Chinese and students, to send representatives to Southeast Asia to explain the positive work the CCP had done in fighting Japan.[50] Over the course of the war, their camp at Yan'an also received a steady stream of overseas Chinese visitors, including Americans, some of whom the CCP sent back to their host countries to report on Communist accomplishments.[51] In 1941, the Yan'an Overseas Chinese United Association held a meeting during which it passed a measure to encourage overseas Chinese to invest in Yan'an and to increase the party's communication with and protection of Chinese abroad. The CCP also had its "Eighth Route Army Office" in Hong Kong, which became another base for efforts to win the hearts and finances of the overseas Chinese by creating propaganda, printing and distributing overseas Chinese publications, and sending representatives to overseas Chinese areas.[52]

With both parties courting the good opinion of Chinese abroad, anyone making a donation could consider whether to send it through official government channels, or whether to send funds directly to the Communist-controlled Eighth Route or New Fourth Armies for their use. As Chinese scholars Ren Guixiang and Chao Hongying have observed, "The open strife and veiled struggle between the Nationalist Party and the Communist Party became an obstacle to financial contributions to the National Salvation Movement. The two parties were both trying to win overseas Chinese contributions, each trying to outwit the other, and thereby used up some of the mutual vigor for resisting Japan."[53] The U.S. FBI also reported small numbers of Chinese in the United States openly supporting the Japanese-backed Wang Jingwei puppet government, likely in the hope of obtaining high positions in the postwar regime.[54]

The KMT also felt threatened by CCP propaganda directed toward the overseas Chinese community, especially where it was in danger of losing vital support. The FBI reported on the KMT gearing up for a big membership drive in American Chinese communities in late 1942, "at the insistence of the Party" back in China. Local party leaders expressed concern that new members would be hard to come by, with everyone so busy with war work.[55] One KMT report expressed concern that the Communists were not just winning the overseas Chinese (particularly progressives and youth), but actually succeeding in driving a wedge between China and her ally, the United States, by influencing public opinion in the United States against China and in China against the United States.[56] The U.S. State Department maintained its support of the Nationalists, but the efforts of the Communists drew admiration from American "China hands" frustrated with Chiang Kai-shek's military strategy and KMT corruption. In 1943, Nationalist Party representatives in the United States met with Chinese citizens there to increase mutual understanding and cooperation.[57] Increasing the overseas Chinese commitment to the Nationalist war effort was consistently the central, most important work for the OCAC, whereas the CCP would not develop a strong overseas Chinese policy of its own until after 1949.[58]

All these contests over overseas Chinese support boiled down to the fact that the Nationalist government needed funds to keep fighting the war. Most of all, it needed loans from Allied governments willing to support their struggle against Japan. But they also needed private donations to charities, defense projects, and refugee relief. The families back home of Chinese abroad needed funds to help keep them afloat as remittances increasingly failed to get through to the Japanese-occupied parts of South China from which Chinese abroad overwhelmingly hailed. Transnational networks helped keep these remittances flowing even when the governments involved could not monitor them. Generally, remitters used international banks to wire funds to Hong Kong. From there, associations in Chinatown, like the Chinese Consolidated Benevolent Association or smaller native place or surname associations that had branches in both Chinatowns and Hong Kong, took charge of the transfers. Sometimes agents, friends, or relatives hand-carried funds on visits to their native villages.[59] The onset of the Pacific war threatened the flow of remittances as these networks broke down and Allied nations tried to prevent funds from falling into Japanese hands.

Chinese in the United States experienced difficulties making sure funds reached their intended parties. After 1938, Japan occupied the city of Guangzhou and the surrounding areas in Guangdong, where most of the families of Chinese Americans lived, cutting off many of the common links for transferring funds to South China. By 1942, concerned Chinese regularly visited the office of the Chinese consulate in San Francisco asking for assistance in sending remittances back to China. The consul tried to find a way to send funds via the Bank of China in New York and the Bank of Guangdong Province for distribution among the families, though even that route involved some danger of interrupted transfers.[60] Because it could not ensure that money reached particular families, the Chinese government proposed that remittances be used by government officials in unoccupied areas as relief funds for struggling overseas Chinese families. Solutions such as these were necessary for maintaining Chinese American support, as the inability to get remittances through had negative impact on the willingness of Chinese in America to make other, desperately needed, financial contributions to the war effort.[61] However, more than a year later, in late 1943, China still struggled to get family funds through. The overseas Chinese in America did not really understand the problems and therefore would not forgive the government for failing to fix them.[62] The OCAC responded with a wide-scale relief program in the "overseas Chinese areas" of South China. For a few specific crises, like the 1943 rice famine in south Guangdong Province near Taishan, the OCAC worked in cooperation with overseas groups like the American Aid China Society and local associations in New York to raise funds for relief.[63] The CCBA in New York sent one million in Chinese yuan (around US$300,000) to aid Cantonese refugees, and the Chicago-based Chinese Emergency Relief Society sent 100,000 yuan (around US$30,000).[64]

Aid programs for overseas Chinese families and returnees were important because Chinese abroad made major contributions to China's defense that extended far beyond family remittances. At the start of the war against Japan, the Chinese government sold 500 million yuan worth of war bonds. The overseas Chinese purchased more than half of these, establishing themselves as the financial foundation for funding the war effort.[65] Within a month after the Marco Polo Bridge incident, overseas Chinese in America formed dozens of relief associations, which were ultimately unified into a single China War Relief Association of America.[66] Over the course of the eight years that the war raged, the various branches of this organization contributed more than US$19 million to fund China's defense. When contributions beyond main China War Relief Association branches are added in, conservative estimates put the total donations from Chinese in America at over US$25 million. When other contributions in the form of air force training and fund-raising, remittances, relief efforts, and even individual direct payments are added, it is possible the figure rose as high as US$56 million.[67] Though these amounts pale in comparison to the estimated $1.6 billion in lend-lease supplies provided to China by the U.S. government during the war, their targeted aid to occupied areas of South China made a difference to hundreds of thousands of people in those regions.[68]

Chinese in the United States, Britain, and Australia assumed a disproportionate share of the financial burden of the war among Chinese abroad. In the years from 1937 to 1940, the average individual monthly contribution of overseas Chinese in the United States and Britain was around US$17, and in Australia, around US$12. The overseas Chinese of Southeast Asia averaged a monthly individual contribution of US$1.86.[69] There were several reasons for the difference being as large as it was. Most obviously, Chinese living in Southeast Asia simply had lower income levels than those in the Americas or Britain. Beyond that, local government policies regarding organizing war relief associations and conducting fund-raising campaigns were more stringent in Southeast Asian countries under colonial rule.[70] The U.S. government did eventually place some restrictions that affected overseas Chinese fund-raising efforts. In 1939, it outlawed the purchase of foreign government war bonds. Chinese organizations adjusted to the new regulation by making "contributions" to the Chinese war bond drive, rather than making formal purchases. After 1941, Chinese in America also purchased U.S. war bonds, a war contribution not included in the figures above.[71]

Fund-raising activities in American Chinatowns were not only useful; they were also social occasions. Common activities included parades and "rice bowl" parties, always featuring the Nationalist Chinese flag. In both cases, Chinese entertainers would venture through the streets of urban Chinese communities, celebrating Nationalist achievements and collecting donations from spectators.[72] For a few years, the best of Chinese and American cultures combined with an annual "Rice Bowl" football game between Chinese American teams formed in San Francisco and Los Angeles. The game was sponsored by Chinese War Relief, and all ticket-sale proceeds went to the war effort.[73] Chinatowns mobilized for war when China did, giving them four years of hard work before the rest of the country entered into the shared effort.

As with all fund-raising campaigns, abuses developed in the various drives for overseas Chinese contributions. The Chinese government observed three major problems: forced (involuntary) contributions, misuse of funds and private corruption by organizers, and factional disputes about where the funds should go.[74] Local Chinatown leadership in major cities like New York, San Francisco, and Chicago set individual "quotas" for giving. In Chicago, the FBI reported that the CCBA required "each Chinese to subscribe at least ten per cent of his earnings to the purchase of United States War bonds, auditing the books of the Chinese businessmen to verify that they have subscribed according to their pledges."[75] In New York, the CCBA declared that each individual would be responsible for giving fifty Chinese silver dollars on each of the Republic of China's first two "National Salvation" bond drives, then spending US$5 on war bonds each month, and making a onetime contribution of US$10 for airplanes and US$3 for ambulances. In each Chinese community, the specific requirements were different, but reneging on this responsibility met with similar "punishments," including denunciation by the local Chinese language newspaper, having the community freeze out one's business, being charged a fine larger than the original contribution would have been, and sometimes even facing physical violence. One sensationalist news story out of Cleveland claimed that "Chinese behind in their relief payments had been forced to answer before a tribunal. Those unable to pay, they said, were beaten and forced to parade through the Chinese district with 'slacker' placards about their necks."[76] In some Canadian Chinatowns, local leaders placed non-contributors on a blacklist of people designated "cold-blooded, unconcerned and apathetic," so the rest of the community would know to ostracize them.[77] The fact of Chinese migrants' physical and linguistic isolation from the rest of American society ensured that U.S. officials were often unaware of these problems unless specific complaints were made.[78] Those who went to the authorities failed to find much support from within the community, so local governments took little action against the organizations establishing the quotas.

Some individuals seized on the wave of overseas Chinese patriotism as a quick way to earn money. There are accounts of Chinese with the resources to travel heading south in the late 1930s and touring the overseas Chinese communities in Southeast Asia, asking for funds at each stop along the way, though the vast majority of this money never found its way back to China. So many of these schemes emerged by 1942 that the Nationalist government declared that anyone planning to go abroad for fund-raising purposes would first face investigation by the KMT's overseas section. Later, the government also appointed four banks to be in charge of receiving (and distributing) donations from the overseas Chinese, so that Chinese abroad would know that any fund-raising efforts not affiliated with one of those banks was likely spurious.[79]

The bottom line was that potential fraud or corruption within the fund-raising efforts had the potential of damaging much-needed overseas Chinese support for Nationalist China's war effort, or worse, overseas support for the Nationalists altogether. The loss of the latter could mean funds filtered to the Chinese Communists or simply left at home. At the same time, dissatisfaction with the U.S. government could likewise undermine support, as the FBI reported was happening in San Francisco by late 1943. There, the intelligence reports suggested, "the attitude . . . toward the war effort continues to be apathetic. Unfounded rumors of racial discrimination against the Chinese in the United States Army are still current in San Francisco's Chinatown. . . . The San Francisco Chinese still feel that China is not getting proper consideration from Great Britain and the United States."[80] FBI observations aside, there was no question that Chinese Americans had mobilized to aid the war effort. But discrimination from the United States could stymie enthusiasm as easily as frustration with the Nationalist government, so keeping funds going proved to be a balancing act between both allies.

Clearly, OCAC policy and Chinese mobilization played an important role in the Chinese government's conduct of both wars, the global one and the civil one. First and foremost, the Nationalist government realized that it could not afford to lose the support of the diaspora. That support translated to funds and remittances desperately needed to keep the war effort going, and it also represented a network of sympathetic people located around the world, ideally positioned to influence their local governments in favor of China. Gaining and keeping overseas Chinese support led the ROC to undertake projects like negotiating better terms for the draft, providing aid to family members left in China, expanding KMT influence, and promoting a Nationalist-friendly Chinese education. All these elements of overseas Chinese policy ended up being a hybrid between diplomacy and nation building: some negotiations proved necessary to protect diaspora interests, but solid connections with the migrants themselves also had to be built and maintained.

One element of this process was the expansion of extraterritorial control in American Chinatowns. The KMT did not govern Chinese in the United States, and certainly there was a growing vocal minority inclined and willing to defy Nationalist control and support the war efforts of the Communist forces. But the wartime efforts to obtain the support of Chinese abroad also meant extending the reach of the state to influence them. In the United States, this led to a somewhat counterproductive policy of simultaneous trying to encourage education while preventing full assimilation. Ironically, it helped set in motion a series of policies that the Nationalists would pursue in the postwar years to shape and improve the American Chinese community and which would result in the KMT having even less influence.

The Nationalist government was not alone in its quest for overseas Chinese support. The Chinese Communist Party increasingly put its own efforts into winning the hearts of the diaspora. The battle between the Nationalist Party and the CCP for the sentimental, physical, and financial support of the overseas Chinese continued through the emerging civil war crisis and then into the 1950s, as the Cold War extended into Asia. In this respect, World War II was the opening act of a long-term drama in which migrants had a role in the way Chinese governments fought for legitimacy, recognition, and equality.

Chapter 3

A Fight on All Fronts

The Chinese Civil War, Restored Migration, and Emigration as National Policy

China endured four years of civil war on the heels of its eight-year struggle against Japan, but these were years of heavy distraction in Washington. The Cold War was breaking out in Europe as the World War II alliance gave way to increasing mutual suspicion between the United States and the Soviet Union, and the doctrine of containment overtook more conciliatory approaches to recognizing Soviet security concerns. The large-scale postwar displaced persons crisis both dominated migration policy and practice and became part of the process by which Cold War politics hardened. Asia in general and China in particular had not yet become encircled by the new conflict, but the success of Mao Zedong's People's Liberation Army ensured that it would only be a matter of time before the new status quo would demand attention. As China's civil war dragged on, President Harry Truman would vacillate on how to react to its likely outcome. Throughout the conflict, the U.S. government preferred that the two sides reach some sort of truce, even as American officials continued to offer aid to Chiang Kai-shek. That aid was too little to affect the Nationalist fortunes in the war itself but more than enough to undermine American chances at accommodation with the victorious Communists in the aftermath. Still, until it became obvious to the American people and the U.S. Congress that Chiang was bound to lose his fight, China remained a low priority in U.S. foreign policy goals.

The Nationalist government spent these years in daily danger of losing its country. Finally, in October 1949, the Communists declared their final victory, and Chiang's forces escaped to the island of Taiwan (Formosa), until recently a Japanese colony, located about a hundred miles off the coast of Fujian Province. Despite the constant distractions of war, diplomacy, and existential crisis, the Nationalists never quite lost sight of the ways in which managing migration policy could help their position. Perhaps the most remarkable characteristic of late 1940s Republic of China migration policy is that it existed at all. However, as the Republic of China came closer and closer to losing the support of mainland Chinese, maintaining the loyalty of the Chinese overseas grew more and more vital. During the civil war years, this project took the form of managing a wide-scale refugee problem, offering diplomatic assistance to displaced persons hoping to return to prewar homes across the world but particularly in Southeast Asia, and managing the post-exclusion migration to the United States in a way that would promote continued and, ideally, increased support from Washington for the Nationalist government. More broadly, from the start of the civil war all the way up until the Republic of China lost its last claims to recognition in the United Nations and by the United States in the 1970s, Nationalist China's foreign policy and overseas Chinese policy would be closely intertwined and dedicated to the major project of seeking and maintaining legitimacy in the eyes of the international community. In contrast, the Chinese Communist Party spent these years making the sometimes awkward shift from a revolutionary party to a governing one, which allowed it more leeway to manipulate migration issues to achieve other ends but also made it less likely to be involved in promoting international migrations.

During the civil war years, from 1945 to 1949, Chinese migrating to the United States, whether returning from a wartime sojourn or arriving for the first time, would get caught up in the varied political priorities of all three governments. This chapter follows these various players—two Chinese governments, an American bureaucracy, and individual Chinese migrants—as they both experienced and helped to create Asia's Cold War and the American response to it. In particular, it considers three migration problems: first, the demobilization from World War II, which took place painfully during the increasing violence of the Chinese Civil War; second, the non-quota migration of war brides, wives, and derivative citizens; and

third, the development of new administrative norms to govern the still limited Chinese immigration to the United States immediately after the repeal
of exclusion. The record of the demobilization and migration negotiations
between the United States and China during the civil war years demonstrates that the United States took advantage of the relatively low-stakes
quality of immigration issues in the context of the emerging Cold War to
seek a new, post-exclusion relationship with Chinese migrants and promote
larger foreign policy goals, including promoting American prestige in postwar Asia and protecting domestic national security in an era of increasing
uncertainty. Meanwhile, these issues rose to greater prominence in Chinese
accounting as they became the means for a flailing Nationalist government
to improve its international image and claims to legitimacy.

Demobilization and the Chinese Civil War

The Chinese Civil War grew so organically out of the end of the Second
World War that it is almost impossible to determine when one stopped and
the other started. As Rana Mitter has shown in *Forgotten Ally*, the root causes
and conflicts in postwar China developed during the eight-year struggle
against Japan.[1] Although the two wars can be hard to separate on their own
terms, the migration issues that came out of them are more distinct. Efforts
to woo and win the support of the overseas Chinese continued through
both conflicts because the nature of the emergency required it. Aiding returned overseas Chinese with repatriation after 1945 became a part of that
effort. Repatriation was a positive thing because it would strengthen the
connection between the Chinese abroad and China after it had been weakened by war. Vast numbers of overseas Chinese suddenly needed support
from their home government, and that provided the ROC with an opportunity to try to secure the loyal support of the diaspora and prevent the
Communists from gaining traction. In this way, repatriation and other efforts on behalf of overseas Chinese families and communities were both humanitarian gestures and a means to bolster government legitimacy, ensuring
that remittances would begin flowing once again.[2] The processes by which
these repatriations were completed proved important in their own right for
the ways in which they linked the Republic of China to international organizations formed to help displaced persons. In the process, both the goal
and the effort of sending home the close to 1.5 million Chinese who fled
to China from Southeast Asia or elsewhere during World War II helped to

solidify Nationalist China's determination to use migration policy to fight the emerging Cold War.

Large masses of refugees displaced by the war proved an international problem by 1945, with tens of millions homeless in Europe and equal numbers in Asia. The international response came through the United Nations, both the alliance established during the war of Allied powers and the subsequent international organization they formed to replace the now-defunct League of Nations. The first iteration of assistance came in the form of the United Nations Relief and Rehabilitation Association, or UNRRA. As Ben Shephard has shown, the European operation of this organization was beset with both bureaucratic difficulties and logistical challenges, but through the good offices of impassioned workers still managed to help untold numbers of individuals displaced by the war and the politics that emerged from it.[3] Like most histories of postwar displaced persons, his does not discuss China, but the UNRRA maintained a massive operation in China from 1945 to 1947 alongside a Chinese government counterpart, the Chinese National Relief and Rehabilitation Association (CNRRA).

In fact, the UNRRA spent more money in China (US$518 million) than anywhere else, but it was an endeavor that was uniquely fraught with difficulties. After eight years of constant warfare, the scale of the physical destruction was matched only by the sheer numbers of displaced refugees. By the time the organization was fully operable in 1946, it also faced rampant, unprecedented inflation and civil war. Supplies had a hard time getting to China, much less getting moved to where they were needed. Widespread wartime corruption in the Nationalist government made similar charges against the CNRRA both unsurprising and unavoidable, though this also increased the wariness of American congressmen to continue to foot the bill.[4] The UNRRA helped two groups in China. The first was displaced overseas Chinese who had fled to the mainland during the Japanese invasions of Southeast Asia and who were now looking to return home. The second was European Jews who escaped the Nazi war machine to one of the only places that would take them: the free port of Shanghai. In both cases, efforts at repatriation were slow going, in part because both groups shared an important thing in common: a distinct lack of identification papers and proof of prior citizenship.[5]

UNRRA was always intended to be a short-term organization, so even as its work reached its peak in 1946, talks began for a new organization to take over and continue repatriation and relief efforts. This new international organization could also expand the work beyond relief and repatriation to resettlement, especially for stateless refugees. The Preparatory Commission of the International Refugee Organization (PCIRO) began in 1947 to persuade governments to sign the constitution of the IRO. The commission needed fifteen to sign on to allow it to come into force.[6] Upon first consideration, the Legislative Yuan (the Republic of China's Congress) refused to join, as the civil war made the fiscal commitment difficult. However, both British and American organizers sought to recruit China in order to have a major power in Asia involved and to counteract the Soviet Union, whose leaders had already expressed skepticism of the project. They made appeals based on China's role as an equal ally in World War II, but they also made a pragmatic argument about the costs. If the IRO promised to include in its program the effort to repatriate overseas Chinese, then the Chinese contributions to the IRO budget could scarcely work out to more than the country would spend returning that group home anyway.[7] When the Legislative Yuan finally passed the IRO, it added some important reservations. The legislators required that the organization complete the overseas Chinese repatriation project, and they arranged for their contributions to that effort to count against their fiscal obligations (which they would also be permitted to pay in installments).[8] Though heralded as an important decision, China's entrance into the IRO reflected a political reality—without assistance from international bodies, the Republic of China likely could not successfully negotiate the return of the overseas Chinese.

The overseas Chinese who needed help to repatriate required it for a variety of reasons. Some certainly ran from an invading army, but others had arrived before 1937 to visit family or conduct business, then found their route home cut off by the war. Chinese expatriates also returned to fight in the army or otherwise contribute to the war effort. The highest numbers came from areas sharing a land border with China—French Indochina, Burma, and Hong Kong—but Chinese managed to return from farther afield as well. No matter how they arrived in China, the principal determinant of the ability of the overseas Chinese to be repatriated was their ability to make a documented claim to prior residence in the country indicated. The UNRRA/IRO and the various Overseas Chinese Affairs Commission branch offices registered overseas Chinese seeking repatriation, helped provide maintenance expenses for the destitute while they waited for permission to return to their prior residences, helped arrange for travel documents and visas, and paid for transport. In June 1946, OCAC in China had registered 204,911 displaced overseas Chinese, about half of which—102,683—were displaced from Hong Kong (many of whom returned on their own immediately after the war). Of those that remained, OCAC estimated that 46,000 could establish legitimate rights of domicile in their countries of origin, which would make them eligible for international aid. About a third of these could afford to pay their own way home. The remainder required assistance.[9]

Early in the repatriation process, UNRRA tried to begin negotiations for returns with each of the Southeast Asian governments, then turn over the efforts to the Chinese Embassy or representatives to finalize the arrangements or continue the talks. Within those talks, one American worker observed, "the Chinese principle that Overseas Chinese are always Chinese [citizens] here worked a disservice to many."[10] Rising nationalism, combined with postwar economic difficulties and concerns about the reach of Chinese government influence through its expatriate community, made the returnees particularly unwelcome in many countries. Most countries declared themselves willing to accept the Chinese residents in principle, but the reality was that strict guidelines prevented many from returning. To facilitate the process of reentry, the organization issued those Chinese meeting the repatriation guidelines set by their former residences a general UNRRA visa as a travel document, intended to save the receiving country from having to conduct independent inspections in China for each traveler. Ultimately, Singapore, Malaya, Burma, British North Borneo, Sarawak, Thailand, and French Indochina accepted the UNRRA visa; Indonesia (then still the Dutch East Indies) and the Philippines refused it. Between September 1, 1946, and July 1, 1947, 20,893 overseas Chinese were repatriated through the efforts of the UNRRA, and another 28,745 Chinese waited for repatriation.[11]

Though certainly the majority of the repatriates were heading to Southeast Asia, those Asian nations were not alone in creating tough standards for Chinese repatriation. Some Chinese petitioned to return to other places, but most European countries were not accepting either new or returning migrants from China, and Central and South American countries were particularly strict and often required documents not easily obtained. Leaving aside new immigration, the United States allowed merchants, students, and teachers to apply for nonimmigrant visas, but also found that it needed to create a procedure to allow long-term residents who had gotten trapped while visiting China during the war to return to the United States. Merchants who entered the United States before 1924 on a "Section Six Certificate" were permitted to become permanent residents (the term referred to the sixth part of the Chinese Exclusion Act of 1882 that required merchants seeking exemption from the law to have certification of their status from the Chinese government). Those who entered after the Immigration Act of 1924, up until the law was revised in 1932, had been granted only temporary status; therefore they did not have a right to reentry if they had left for a visit to China. Some men in this category became stranded in China without means of returning during and after the war. Chinese government officials suggested that the very fact they lacked right of reentry at all was an inequity that required correction. Meanwhile, students and other Chinese temporary residents of the United States grew increasingly concerned about their prospects upon returning to China. The two governments discussed these issues on several occasions, and ultimately the Displaced Persons Act of 1948 allowed certain migrants with temporary resident status but long resident in the United States to apply for a permanent residency.[12]

The Displaced Persons Act shone a bright spotlight on another source of inequity: the different treatment of Europeans and Chinese in China by the United States. Throughout the exclusion years, China technically did have an immigration quota: up to one hundred visas could be granted to residents of China each year, as long as they were not Chinese. After the war, the population of Europeans in China had swelled with the addition of thousands of Jewish refugees to the already existing population of White Russians and other long-resident missionaries and merchants. In its original form, the Displaced Persons Act not only did not account for stranded Chinese, but it failed to allow visas for European refugees in China as well.[13] The "Europe first" wartime strategy also applied to postwar refugees. When Congress revised the bill in 1949, they added new visas and included four thousand reserved for Europeans in China, but they also added language that required displaced persons to swear they were not communists—something that was both a reflection of and a contributing factor to the emerging Cold War.[14]

In addition to returning merchants, other Chinese sought repatriation to the United States. A number of Chinese Americans visiting China in the early 1940s left their papers with the American President Line ocean liner company office in Hong Kong only to discover their documents had been lost when the city fell to the Japanese. American consuls (already deeply suspicious of Chinese visa applications) expressed concerns that large numbers of people claiming to be Chinese Americans could repatriate without proper examinations into their claims to citizenship.[15] Though they frequently questioned whether individuals had a right to return, U.S. officials remained adamant that the Chinese government not pay the return tickets for repatriating Chinese Americans. Chinese documents refer to these Chinese Americans as *Mei ji huaqiao*, or "overseas Chinese with U.S. citizenship," whereas the U.S. government did not see Chinese Americans as "overseas Chinese" at all, but instead as U.S. citizens of Chinese descent.[16] Though subtle, this distinction was an important indication of the different perspectives of the two governments. By the mid-twentieth century, the American policy makers had long formed a habit of treating all matters relating to immigration as purely domestic in nature, but Chinese officials consistently viewed Chinese immigration to the United States through the lens of China's international diaspora and overseas Chinese policy, and therefore its foreign policy. Chinese bureaucrats saw little difference between paying the boat fare for Chinese returning to Seattle or Singapore. In contrast, the United States had no objections to the Chinese or IRO paying passages to Southeast Asia to benefit the international effort to aid displaced persons, yet it maintained that allowing the Chinese to pay passage for American citizens to travel to any American destination was both inappropriate and unnecessary. At stake here was the level of influence the Chinese government could exert over returning American citizens of Chinese descent if they were dependent on ROC financial support. Rather than risk it, the United States paid the boat fares itself.[17] This issue of Nationalist China trying to exert extraterritorial influence over Chinese abroad would become a major sticking point in new postwar immigration as well.

During its years of operation, the IRO succeeded in repatriating 11,122 overseas Chinese to their countries of origin, though the repatriations occurred in fits and starts.[18] Governments were changing both in Southeast Asia and in China. Additionally, the IRO began the long process of shutting down offices by 1951. The fact that the IRO office in China had survived the civil war at all was due in part to the overseas Chinese repatriation program. Even an inexperienced new Chinese government recognized that stopping it would damage overseas Chinese opinions of the new government, and the new government needed loyalty and money from Chinese abroad as much as the old one.[19] As of 1950, the Geneva office wrote to IRO Hong Kong to explain that "our immediate desire in regard to the Overseas Chinese is to discover what programme is feasible within the lifetime of the organization, to plan the active completion of this programme, and to dispose as may be possible at the earliest time of the residual responsibilities which it is obvious through no fault of our own we cannot complete."[20] The project was in fact left unfinished, especially with regard to Chinese hoping to return to Burma, the Philippines, and the Dutch East Indies.[21]

The civil war is remarkably absent from the record of the IRO in China, but it had three distinct effects on the project. First, it hurt the ROC's ability to keep up with its obligation to provide financial support. While still in the PCIRO planning stages, negotiations began for China to commit its funds mostly in local currency or in-kind supplies, but even that grew difficult as the Chinese currency underwent rapid, out-of-control inflation.[22] The second problem was logistical: moving armies and ongoing warfare made access to ports for transport hard, and in more than one case it even resulted in the retreating Nationalist forces temporarily occupying an IRO camp, interfering with the repatriation process.[23] Despite these near daily reminders that the war was under way, Nationalist foreign minister George Yeh fiercely protested a line in an IRO report that suggested the ROC government was not giving IRO its full attention, quite understandably having other things on its mind. Yeh and the rest of the Nationalist establishment took issue with the idea that they were not doing everything in their power to help, as apparently the optics of keeping up with the refugee issue remained important even as the Nationalists lost the mainland.[24] Third, the IRO was tasked with both overseas Chinese repatriations and the resettlement of stateless European refugees in China. This latter project expanded to include not only Jewish refugees but also White Russians, owing to concerns over Communist victory in the civil war.[25] Despite these effects of the civil war on IRO work, what is remarkable is the pragmatism with which both the IRO and the new Communist Chinese officials went about their work after 1949. Though the IRO faced Soviet and Chinese Communist accusations of being a Western imperialist construct doing the United States' bidding, the People's Republic of China did not have substantially more disputes with the IRO than the ROC before it.[26]

In all, the efforts to repatriate stranded overseas Chinese demonstrated several important points about China and its interaction with the world after World War II. First and foremost, Nationalist China was clearly not strong enough internally or internationally to negotiate successfully on behalf of its returning expatriates. Even in the case of repatriating overseas Chinese to closely allied nations like the United States, the project was dependent on American policy, not Chinese intervention. After 1949, Communist China was in no better position. Instead, Chinese commitments helped pay for the upkeep of returned overseas Chinese, and also for their transport within China, but when it came to securing their right of reentry to their countries of origin, the PRC turned to the IRO as well. Despite the mutual nonrecognition between the PRC and the United Nations, the IRO office stayed open in Shanghai working on repatriations (which included both Chinese and, increasingly, stateless Europeans) until 1956.[27] Nationalist China was a weak power increasingly insecure about its international position, but the new Communist government was confident enough to choose the most flexible and least ideological course to effect the desired repatriation policy.

Second, past ROC policy toward the overseas Chinese had a detrimental effect on the repatriation project. Identifying the diaspora as distinctly Chinese, with obvious loyalties to the homeland, caused receiving nations great concern for their own political and economic stability. Whether the overseas Chinese formed a substantial percentage of the population, as was the case in Thailand, or a slight presence, as in the United States, the idea of a resident population completely unassimilated and loyal to another nation (or, at best, to both nations simultaneously) caused nations with Chinese residents concern. The Republic of China's overseas Chinese policy asked for equal treatment, but occasionally sought circumstances that were tantamount to preferred treatment for Chinese residents of Southeast Asia. However, in spite of these obvious disadvantages to ROC foreign policy that came from too much interference in overseas Chinese affairs, diaspora policy was clearly fundamental to the Chinese government's claims to legitimacy as the nation collapsed into civil war. Here the lesson of World War II prevailed over postwar experience, and the overseas Chinese were thought to be, once again, the lifeline for a collapsing government, rather than the diplomatic liability they could become.

The U.S. Approach to Postwar Transpacific Migration

Postwar repatriation was not the only form of Chinese migration encouraged by the Chinese government and questioned by the United States. Repealing exclusion had been a wartime necessity, with little immediate impact, thanks to limited transportation options. Soon after the conflict ended, the limits of the new quota became very clear, and Nationalist Chinese officials found themselves seeking liberalization once more.[28] Chinese scholar Qiu Hanping argued in 1945 that claims of equity and friendship between the United States and China on the international stage were belied by U.S. immigration laws that discriminated not only against new Chinese immigration but also against residents simply because they were Chinese or had married Chinese. Specifically citing the forced division of Chinese families under U.S. immigration laws restricting the entry of wives, he questioned

American claims to being a country guided by Christian teachings and humanitarian ideals.[29] Qiu had a legitimate complaint. New immigration, which would in part address it, would come in three dominant forms: war brides and fiancées (non-quota immigrants), derivative citizen applications (which were also non-quota), and new quota immigrants. Processing all three would prove difficult, because of both the complex bureaucratic requirements involved and the inherent skepticism of U.S. consuls toward Chinese applications.

Applying for any kind of visa to visit the United States required a passport and documentary proof of who you were and why you were going. Consular officials in Guangzhou and Hong Kong were the first hurdle to clear—or the first line of defense, depending on your perspective. For the Chinese, most hopes of entering the United States rested on convincing a local consul that you had a right to go. For American consuls, protecting the country against migrants who had no right to enter or had more nefarious purposes in going meant carefully scrutinizing every application. Applicant and screener often butted heads over documentation, because there was no tradition of government-issued birth or marriage certificates in China. Proving identity often involved long interviews with applicants, their friends, families, and neighbors with consuls (and, after arrival in the United States, INS officials) looking for mistakes as proof of fraud. Receiving the right to travel to the United States did not guarantee entry. U.S. immigration laws allowed immigration officials an extraordinary degree of leeway in excluding undesirable immigrants, so long detentions at Angel Island and repeated interrogations became more the norm than the exception.[30] This process was inherently adversarial at many steps along the way. It pitted potential immigrants against first the consuls and then the INS screeners (and sometimes the U.S. judicial system). But it also ultimately brought the State and Justice Departments in the United States into confrontation, as the bureaucratic infighting over new postwar immigration grew and complicated broader efforts by the United States to use migration policy to bolster foreign policy goals.

After repatriation, entering the United States as a Chinese wife of an American citizen had the potential to be the simplest path to admission. For one thing, wives had not been consistently excluded. The 1924 act had officially excluded Chinese wives of American citizens, and though an amendment to the Immigration Act in 1930 allowed the admission of wives who had married their Chinese American husbands before 1924, those who married after 1924 still had no legal means to enter. Congress had considered a remedy during the debate on repeal of exclusion in 1943, and it debated the subject again in August 1945 during hearings on problems related to deportation. Some of the early debate on this issue argued that equality must be granted for racially restrictive reasons. If left unaltered, the law seemed to encourage miscegenation. With few Chinese women already in the United States and quota-free entry for European wives, Chinese American men would have to look to Caucasian women if they wanted to marry at all. On the other hand, encouraging the admission of Chinese women challenged the project to keep the Chinese American population small. Kenneth Fung of the Chinese American Citizens Alliance (CACA) attended a 1945 Senate committee hearing and attempted to make a moral argument for a revised law, stressing that Chinese Americans who served proudly in the U.S. armed services "are entitled to establish a home, no matter what the numbers are."[31] He also estimated that only around six hundred Chinese Americans would be taking advantage of such a measure.

The War Brides Act of 1945 and the War Fiancées Act of 1946 allowed Chinese women to enter in large numbers for the first time (more than five thousand between 1945 and 1950), and the Chinese Alien Wives of American Citizens Act (Pub. L. 713, 1946) extended the non-quota privilege to all Chinese Americans, even those who had not served in the military.[32] The latter measure was introduced by a California senator (Sheridan Downey, D) and a San Francisco representative (George P. Miller, D). As was evident in the repeal debate, congressional attitudes toward immigration in general and Chinese immigration in particular fell more along regional lines than party ones in the immediate postwar period. Democrats and Republicans alike found ample reasons to support limited quotas, and revisions to the quotas that came in the wake of the war similarly considered constituent service as much as larger political philosophies.

Applying the War Brides and War Fiancées Acts to China involved some unique challenges. The U.S. Army and other officials put up many roadblocks no matter where couples were from or where they were marrying, but Congress had clearly intended both acts to ease procedural difficulties for the tens of thousands of British and Western European women who married U.S. soldiers during the war in Europe. As a result, the bureaucratic procedures put in place did not always match realities on the ground in China. First, not every Chinese American serviceman actually had documentary evidence of his U.S. citizenship. Some could produce a photostatic copy of a "certificate of identity" or a letter from the INS, but without definitively established citizenship, applications for brides were often delayed.[33] Second, far fewer new brides were involved. The acts marked the first opportunity for many long-married couples to be reunited in the United States. Historian Xiaojian Zhao sampled files of new arrivals and estimated that 77 percent of the Chinese "war brides" had been married longer than ten years.[34] Third, though long past the honeymoon stage, few Chinese war brides could muster up all the documentation required by the INS: not only proof of the husband's citizenship, but also proof of marriage, proof of the birth of any children, proof of the husband's service in the U.S. armed services, and an affidavit of support. Documents issued by the U.S. government were usually accepted, but anything else was problematic. With the exception of couples married with a U.S. consul present or by foreign missionaries, few had formal certificates of marriage, and their local counties in China did not issue birth certificates for children.[35] Some Chinese had more than one wife, making the legal determination of who had the right to the visa tricky. Occasionally consuls received letters from jilted first wives arguing against visas for their husband's new bride. Additionally, the birth of sons might be recorded in the family genealogy, but the birth of daughters rarely was. Marriage and birth certificates were sometimes for sale on the black market, making verification an issue. Consular officials at the U.S. Embassy eventually became convinced that the kind of expedited processing the War Brides Act intended might not be possible in China.[36]

Even if everyone agreed on the documentary proof of marriage, cultural clashes emerged when U.S. consular officials and Chinese migrants found themselves to have very different ideas about arranged marriage. The U.S. consul-general in Hong Kong, George D. Hopper, complained to the secretary of state that "many veterans of the Chinese race seem to have tried to use the law simply to secure a wife, rather than bring a girl of their choice to the United States. The apparent shortage of Chinese women in the United States would make this desirable for the veteran, and it is alleged to be in accordance with Chinese custom."[37] A Kentucky lawyer already in his mid-sixties, Hopper apparently differentiated between a Chinese man marrying a woman he had romanced and loved in a grand, Western, and perhaps Hollywood-style tradition and the Chinese idea that any girl recommended by family members and friends, of the right age and from a good background, would make a suitable wife, regardless of whether the pair had met before the wedding.[38] Hopper might also have been influenced by a rash of news stories lamenting the high rates of postwar divorce starting in 1945 and attributed to the impetuous marriages of thousands of wartime couples.[39] Nonetheless, Hopper's concerns likely did not make sense to the couples approaching him for a visa. If asked if their goal was "simply to secure a wife," few of the Chinese American veterans involved would have denied it. After generations in which life in America meant automatic bachelorhood, their marriages simply did not require romantic love as a prerequisite.

Earlier in 1947, Hopper wrote to the State Department asking for clarifications on whether arranged marriages counted as engagements under the law. He noted that "in many cases pending here [the] parties have never met. Engagement [was] arranged by families or third parties in accordance [with] Chinese custom."[40] The first department reply noted that it would be difficult to convince the consul that the couple really intended to marry if they had never met, but it later recanted and noted that failure to meet in advance would not actually disqualify them under the law.[41] Hopper disagreed with the latter answer and suggested that the consuls continue to deny such cases on the grounds that failure to meet showed lack of interest, that "probably their love letters, if any, started when he told her about the new law and good chance of getting to the USA."[42] Other consuls agreed, noting the department could not have been fully aware of what it was saying when it claimed that failure to meet before applying would not disqualify applicants, as "it is nothing more than the old picture-bride scheme in a modern setting. . . . These people are undoubtedly paying some ex-G.I. to get them into the states and certainly cannot be considered as bona fide fiancées or as having entered into a valid agreement to marry. I shall certainly continue to refuse such cases."[43] By the 1940s and 1950s, consular officials in Hong Kong had long been in the habit of scrutinizing most Chinese applicants to enter the United States, not just war brides, and their consuming fears of fraudulent entries cast a long shadow over most visa applications.

News of mounting refusals of such cases soon reached stateside Chinese communities. Congress received a telegram from Lim P. Lee of the Cathay Post of the American Legion in San Francisco complaining of the "undue regulations" placed on fiancées of Chinese American veterans; he noted that most veterans were busy studying under the GI Bill and therefore could not possibly make the long trip back to China to court a woman so that they could get married.[44] Still, Thomas DeWitt Bowman, consul-general in Guangzhou, defended their delays, noting that in addition to lacking documentation and other formalities, the vast majority of fiancée applications from Chinese American servicemen had been filed in the last two months before the deadline for processing such applications. The timing of the deluge of new applications only served to feed his doubts about the legitimacy of the cases.[45]

So why did it matter to the U.S. consuls whether or not the couple had an arranged marriage, as long as the pair really did get married upon arrival? Certainly most of the consuls had spent enough time in Asia to be aware of local marriage traditions, though the men in charge of these consulates were often older, southern gentlemen who, like Hopper, likely held more traditional, romantic views of marriage. Beyond personal biases, there were three explanations. The first was the belief that accepting some "questionable" documents from Chinese fiancées could open the door to other problems, particularly demands that other documents of unknown provenance be accepted for regular immigrant visa applications. The second came from the consistently suspicious I. F. Wixon of the San Francisco branch of the INS, who accused Guangzhou consular officers of accepting bribes to process the women quickly. He also charged that some of the women involved did not marry upon arrival but instead were sold into prostitution.[46] Wixon's claims of bribery and trafficking outraged the accused officials in Hong Kong and Guangzhou, but there was some basis for them in history. The bribery charge in particular was not outlandish—it was not unusual for applicants to offer money when applying for visas, especially when they thought they might be refused; and one member of the Guangzhou consulate was charged with accepting bribes in the 1950s. That was the exception, however, not the rule.[47] The third general concern about war brides was that the expedited processing allowed for in the War Brides Act could lead to security risks. It might allow "a very easy entry into the United States of persons who might prove dangerous to the public interest."[48] Infiltration through immigration would only become a more resounding threat as the postwar years gave way to the Cold War.

All three of these arguments against accepting the hastily arranged Chinese marriages demonstrated the growing adversarial relationship between the consulate, the applicant, and the State Department in making these decisions. Consular officials began to take on an almost embattled tone in defending their absolute unwillingness to grant visas. This attitude is partly evidence of continuity from the exclusion era. After the Chinese Exclusion Act officially closed the door to new Chinese immigration, the only ways for most Chinese to obtain entry to the United States was as a member of the exempted class or by evidence of U.S. citizenship. In the latter case, that could mean birth in the United States or being the child of a natural-born U.S. citizen. The latter claims to citizenship were often fraudulent, though as historian Him Mark Lai has explained, "Since the Chinese regarded these laws as discriminatory and unjust, they felt

justified in taking any measures, legal or otherwise, that would successfully get them into the country."[49] The 1906 earthquake and fire in San
Francisco destroyed the birth records of America's largest Chinatown, so
U.S. officials had no way to negate the many claims that followed to having been born in California. With most men's wives still in China, they
could make the round trip and report the birth of a son or daughter upon
each return to the United States. Each reported birth opened up a new
"slot" for a potential future migrant. At times, new immigrants without
claims to U.S. citizenship borrowed an identity from a relative or paid for
one on the black market. These "paper sons" slowly added up to become
a significant portion of the Chinese community in the United States during the exclusion years. Given the lack of documentation in the United
States and the dearth of formal documentation for births, marriages, and
other family connections in China, U.S. consuls and the INS investigated
and determined claims to citizenship on the basis of long, intense interrogations upon arrival in U.S. ports; these covered about every aspect of a
new arrival's family and home village. When denied entry, Chinese sued
for habeas corpus and frequently won on the basis of a lack of outright
contradictions to their claims.[50]

Though the personnel in the consulates in Guangzhou and Hong
Kong had changed since the heyday of the prewar migration years, a sort
of institutional memory of what the consuls called "rampant document
fraud" caused all Chinese visa applications—including expedited war bride
applications—to be suspect.[51] As a general rule, consuls sought as much
documentation as possible, including family photos, certification from the
village head, and supporting affidavits, and they were on the lookout for
illegal documents, because U.S. birth certificates, U.S. passports, and INS
Forms 430 (reentry permits for Chinese residents traveling outside the
United States during the war) were all apparently available for purchase in
the region. The consul at Guangzhou reported in May 1947 that American
documents were selling in the region for US$400–$1,000 (other reports
indicated that prices were determined by the age of the applicant at a rate
of US$100 per year, so a forty-year-old man would pay US$4,000 for a
passport). An investigation into an immigration agency advertising help
obtaining U.S. visas revealed that in addition to legitimate activities, the
agency advised people without proper documents that U.S. passports were
available for purchase elsewhere. If there was any doubt at all, consuls were
to "err on the side of caution" and refuse to issue travel documents, as "experience teaches that any and all Chinese will do everything in their power

to assist their clansmen into the United States."[52] The idea that some un-known percentage of all derivative citizenship applications was fraudulent was borne out by local birthrates for children of Chinese Americans—80 to 85 percent of reported births were said to be sons. Gordon Burke of the Guangzhou consulate called this "an unnatural situation," though he failed to acknowledge that many families simply didn't report the birth of daughters.[53]

The greatest difficulty in processing applications for derivative citizen-ship, visas, or war brides was obtaining documentary evidence for the claims made. The difficulties with marriage and birth certificates notwithstanding, even just matching up different romanizations of Chinese names when the characters were unknown could be an impossible task.[54] In the mid-1940s, Chinese Americans without proper documentation experienced some suc-cess writing to Congress complaining about long waits and complicated application procedures for bringing over family members. The consuls tried to combat this by simultaneously making clearer statements about what documents were required and attempting to educate Congress about the difficulties with Chinese applications. As Burke noted, "the sooner Senators and members of Congress learn that the Chinese-Americans are endeavor-ing to replace documentary proof of their citizenship and visa status by let-ters from Senators and Congressmen, the sooner such cases will be handled, for with our small staff, the reply to the Senators and Congressmen will only delay their cases."[55] For politicians eager to perform citizen services, this proved a difficult lesson.

Chinese frustrated with the process at the American consulate frequently contacted the Guangdong provincial office of the Overseas Chinese Affairs Commission to ask for assistance. Complaints ranged from the slow speed with which requests were processed to indignation over rejection. The OCAC office was concerned first that individuals with genuine familial ties in the United States not be rejected, and second that individuals apply-ing as spouses or derivative citizens not be incorrectly charged to China's small quota. On several occasions, OCAC asked the Ministry of Foreign Affairs to visit American officials and raise these concerns, in the hope that Chinese government urging would press the United States to improve the process.[56] Consular officers then had complaints coming from the Chinese applicants themselves, from their own department, from members of Con-gress, and from the local Chinese government, but they proved remarkably unbending in their willingness to continue the slow pace of investigation and high rate of refusal.

Applications for derivative citizenship were very closely tied to new visa applications, as sometimes members of the same family filed both simultaneously. Months before he became the U.S. special representative and then ambassador to the Republic of Korea, John J. Muccio drew upon his years in the consular service to summarize the intertwined nature of difficulties with both visa applications and citizen services this way:

> One, all Chinese residents of the U.S.—citizens and aliens alike—originated in one small area within the Canton [Guangzhou] consular district, the natural outlet for which is Canton and Hong Kong. The prime industry of the districts of this area—Toy Shan, Sun Wui, Hoi Ping, Hok Shan, Yan Ping, and Chung Shan—is the propagation of Chinese whose single aim in life is to get to the United States. Secondly, families are so interwoven that each family group generally involves both types of consular functions. Thirdly, expert immigration brokers, steerers, and runners working in this lucrative field are constantly prodding and probing each office for the slightest variation in interpretation of laws and regulations that may bring them any real (offensive) advantage over competitors. . . . The problem today is still one of expeditiously and considerately handling bona fide cases without opening a torrent of fraudulent ones.[57]

While Muccio—a voice of experience—was making this stark division between legitimate and illicit applications, vice consul Fong Chuck differentiated between "types" of Chinese applicants. Chuck was a Chinese American, born in Hawaii, who went on to serve as a teacher in China and translator at the Guangzhou consulate. The first group of Chinese, with whom he clearly identified, were "those born in the United States, who have the American outlook and who have never been to China or if they have been back to China, they have been back only for a short visit." He included in this group Chinese who were brought over while young and raised as Americans. "For all intents and purposes," he explained, "these are real Americans." There was a second group, however. "The other class includes those born in China and who spent their youth in China, who have gone to the United States after their views have been set and therefore still retain the Chinese outlook." They might have a bit of basic English, and their wives are China-born and still in their home villages. "The former class think American, dress American, speak American and have their children raised in the American way, and live and die in America. The latter class still retain their China ways. They are like all immigrants except that they have a claim to American citizenship."[58] Chuck's comments echo the strategy taken by some Chinese Americans during the repeal debate four years earlier, in that he is trying to reinforce the equality and legitimacy of Chinese Americans as Americans at the expense of new immigrants. But his implication, combined with Muccio's, is that not only are many of these applicants fraudulent, but the ones that are legitimate are not actually worthy. What, then, offers the impetus to process these applications quickly?

In the late 1940s, the numbers of all kinds of applications increased. In 1947, eleven thousand Chinese left Hong Kong for the United States, even as another twenty-seven thousand left the United States for South China, with most planning to return to America within the year with their dependents.[59] As the number of both visa and citizen applications increased in Hong Kong and Guangzhou, local officials grew concerned about "pyramiding," meaning that each Chinese man granted entry would become the starting link in an ongoing chain of migration: he could bring over his wife and children, and those children might also marry in China and bring over their own spouses and children, until thousands of new residents were admitted, all completely outside the purposefully minuscule Chinese racial quota. This perceived phenomenon, combined with the long, careful investigations, meant that the consuls in Hong Kong and Guangzhou became both overworked and leery, and Chinese looking to head to the United States under any legal provision were ultimately looking at a long wait that incentivized seeking backdoor routes. By September 1948, consular officials in Guangzhou claimed to have a backlog of three thousand citizenship cases with investigations pending, a grossly oversubscribed quota, and wait times for either of three to five years.[60]

After the long delays in China and Hong Kong, Chinese arrivals were inevitably subjected to long detentions upon arrival in the United States while their files were investigated, sometimes for up to two years without a trial.[61] Such detentions caused great bitterness among the migrants themselves and their families, and in a few cases this had serious consequences—one spouse long detained gave up hope of ever entering the United States and committed suicide in the INS facility. Others suffered from severe depression and developed very antagonistic feelings for the United States.[62] American consular officials in China and immigration officials in the United States often could not see any way around the long delays and harsh interrogations. But the impact reached beyond the immediate experiences of the migrants and helped to build a sense of antagonism and distrust between the people of the United States and China.

Building a Better Chinatown

Individuals in the United States worried over the consequences of U.S. policies toward Chinese migrants, but Republic of China officials also worried about the effect of the quality of their migrants on U.S. perceptions of China. As historian Glen Peterson has noted, Nationalist policy toward emigration "was to control their [emigrants'] political and cultural identities but not their physical mobility."[63] Emigration was not simply legal but often desirable, as long as the right people with the right loyalties were the ones looking to go. This policy imperative had long been in use for selecting and preparing Chinese students to study abroad. The Nationalists managed to secure central control and supervision over study-abroad programs by the late 1920s, formalizing a process for screening applicants and granting "study abroad permits" by 1931.[64] A few years later, students not only had to be approved for their courses of study, but they also had to pass an exam on "party doctrine" to qualify.[65] Though new opportunities to study abroad were limited by wartime transport difficulties, the idea of a strict prescreening system for Chinese students, teachers, and scholars bound for international destinations (most often, for the United States) survived the war and became even more vital during the Chinese Civil War that followed. Though these students were expected to return to China to aid in reconstruction efforts, they represented what historian Hongshan Li has argued was the "strongest tie between the two nations in the second half of the 1940s."[66] The extensive screening process developed over the course of two decades to monitor and select students would act as a model for new regulations governing emigration.

Emigrants were harder to control than students, because their travel was by definition not intended to be temporary, but still Nationalist officials tried to remake Chinese American communities in their preferred image— pro-Nationalist, anticommunist, educated, and accepted—through the use of exit controls. This began with the Nationalist government expressing its own preference for family reunification and priority for the wives and children of long-term residents in the United States out of concern that long-divided families had led Chinese men living alone in the United States to develop "every kind of evil habit."[67] Chinese officials were without question aware of the perceptions of Chinese in the United States that developed during the exclusion era: the all-bachelor population, addicted to opium, worshiping heathen idols, speaking foreign languages, and living temporarily in the United States earning money, then returning to China.[68]

Changing U.S. immigration laws allowed wives and children increasingly to enter as non-quota immigrants. For quota visas, which represented new emigration without necessarily any family ties already in the United States, the Republic of China's Ministry of Foreign Affairs proposed high standards with regard to character, education, and occupation for selecting potential immigrants. Not only would such standards provide a way of narrowing down the number of potential applicants, but they would ensure that only the best candidates entered America after the war. This could help to change the American people's and government's prejudices against Chinese immigrants and residents and, in turn, further the friendship between China and the United States.[69] Moreover, a steady stream of skilled immigrants with excellent personal qualities and abilities truly useful to American society just might induce the U.S. government to increase the meager annual Chinese immigrant quota.[70] Sending not just new immigrants, but the right immigrants, had the potential to reap political dividends for the Chinese relationship with the United States.[71]

Beginning in 1944, the Ministry of Foreign Affairs (MOFA) and the Overseas Chinese Affairs Commission jointly established a full list of qualifications and procedures required by applicants for quota immigration to the United States. Potential immigrants and their families were required to have clean records of conduct in China (or for overseas Chinese, in their countries of residence), a good medical report, a middle school education or above, knowledge of English, a good economic background, the ability to find a guarantor who was a citizen or permanent resident of the United States, and any necessary skills and abilities to support himself in America. The procedure for acquiring a passport (a process that had to be completed before visiting the U.S. consulate to request a visa) involved first applying to the Overseas Chinese Affairs Commission for emigrant status. OCAC would then conduct a thorough investigation into the applicant's background and qualifications. If he passed, he could then apply to MOFA for a passport. According to the regulations, overseas Chinese hoping to re-migrate to the United States from their present countries of residence were not exempted from this process. They, too, were to visit the Chinese consul in their country of residence and make a request to be inspected. OCAC accepted applications starting each January until that year's quota slots were filled, at which point hopeful immigrants were to wait until the following January and then submit applications.[72] The final decision on whether or not to issue a passport rested with MOFA because, as one internal memorandum noted, the consuls abroad would ultimately have the responsibility of protecting the immigrants as overseas Chinese. New immigration always had an effect on Chinese communities overseas, not to mention Chinese relations with the country of residence, and the government had a responsibility to see to it that the effect would not be adverse to local or national interests.[73]

This is, of course, an ideal implementation of the process. The reality proved substantially harder to control. From the start, it proved nearly impossible for the Chinese government to review and clear every case of new quota emigration. Rather predictably, attempts to persuade Chinese already living abroad who did not require new or renewed ROC passports to apply through the Chinese government were often unsuccessful. Being outside China's legal reach, they simply ignored the directive. Even in China, some of the applicants already had legal passports and therefore skipped the OCAC and MOFA investigations into their character. The U.S. consuls did not necessarily cooperate with the policy, as issuing visas also did not always require official passports. In some cases, they even issued alternate travel documents to individuals with other forms of legal identification. Despite the fact that the two countries agreed on the end goals, U.S. consuls often did not comply and wait for applicants to have emigrant passports. Instead, they stood on principle: the U.S. government considered new immigration a wholly domestic matter, so U.S. officials alone could determine who was eligible to immigrate. Obviously, the ROC did not agree.[74] When it emerged that too many of the limited quota slots were given away each year completely outside the knowledge of OCAC and MOFA, the Chinese government created a new regulation. Once an individual was cleared by these offices for immigration, his passport would be stamped with the word "emigrant" (*yimin*). The Chinese government then informed the U.S. consuls that starting in the spring of 1947, only individuals with the stamp could be given immigrant visas to the United States, and that as far as the Chinese government was concerned, only emigrants with both the stamp and a U.S. visa could be counted against China's annual quota.[75]

The U.S. officials posted to China objected to Nationalist Chinese attempts to manage their quota with the new regulations, on the grounds that the investigation procedures interfered with the American ability to select its own immigrants. They worried, first of all, that "the [Chinese] Government is seeking to effect some sort of control over emigration in order to ensure that no dissident elements enter the United States for permanent residence."[76] Anyone who could potentially undermine the position of the ROC government in the United States would, presumably, not be granted a passport for emigration. A second concern was that the regulations "offer some evidence of an intention on the part of the Chinese Government to exercise control over Chinese immigrants into the United States after their admission into the United States for permanent residence."[77] The concern about China exercising extraterritorial control was not new; it was a part of the debates over the draft and exclusion during World War II. Given the demonstrated capacity of the Chinese in America and around the world to support their homeland, ever-closer ties between the Chinese government and Chinese overseas could have been construed to mean that if relations between China and any host government soured, the latter would have to worry about the existence of a potentially destabilizing "fifth column" in the form of the local Chinese population. The United States, a strong and independent nation with a very small Chinese population, was consistently less concerned about political or economic destabilization due to its Chinese population than governments in Southeast Asia, but it was concerned the Chinese Americans still loyal to China and under ROC influence would not become assimilated Americans, leading to social and racial conflicts. Given the demonstrated capacity of many American communities to resist Chinese attempts at assimilation during the exclusion era, this position was ironic.

Finally, the Chinese procedure raised the fundamental question of who should be responsible for selecting immigrants: the sending or the receiving country. Although the United States had some valid concerns about the immigrant investigation process, attempts to oppose the system exposed the murky nature of the issue. In a conversation between MOFA officials and representatives of the U.S. Embassy, J. E. McKenna, speaking for the United States, explained, "The Chinese Government has, of course, the absolute right in granting or refusing to grant passport [*sic*] to any applicant for emigration; but this does not involve the right of choosing applicants for immigration to the United States."[78] McKenna tried to suggest that passports should not be granted until the United States had approved applicants for their visas, but the Chinese side pointed out that in the reverse situation, that of an American moving to China, the applicant would first secure a passport and then request a visa (by the 1950s, the United States would even use passport control to limit travel to mainland China, reinforcing the idea that the United States would come to recognize state limits on migration). Unable to agree on the exact procedures, the process that emerged proved to be a de facto compromise measure. The U.S. consuls considered the absence of an "emigrant" stamp as a reason for refusing a visa if one was needed, but if the United States preferred not to refuse it on these grounds, it did not. Hopeful Chinese emigrants without special contacts or extenuating circumstances therefore increased their chances by submitting to the OCAC-MOFA investigations and obtaining the stamp. This screening was clearly quite rigid; one OCAC monthly report noted that of forty-one complete applications to immigrate to America, twenty qualified to be sent on to MOFA for further selection. Thirteen of these were actually granted "emigrant" passports. In other cases MOFA proved even more selective, at times granting passports to only 10–20 percent of the applicants approved by OCAC.[79] The compromise did not prevent Chinese officials a few years later from wanting to reopen the discussion on whether only visas issued on emigrant passports could be counted against the quota.[80]

Beyond the long-term project of improving American perceptions of its Chinese residents, Chinese policy makers had short-term political concerns. Controlling emigration meant controlling the ideas and leaders that shaped American Chinatowns, which in turn shaped the U.S. view of Nationalist China. As the civil war continued in the late 1940s, Nationalist officials became more concerned about overseas support for their opponents. In the United States, efforts by Nationalist-supporting Chinatown leaders to maintain a united front of support for the Nationalist government grew muddled by the genuine difference of opinion between the upper and lower ranks of big-city Chinatowns. Organizations like the Chinese Consolidated Benevolent Association or the Chinese Six Companies included many KMT members in leadership, many of whom continued to demand that the United States prove its ongoing loyalty to Chiang Kai-shek. But as historians like Renqiu Yu, Him Mark Lai, and Peter Kwong have shown, in the back rooms of laundries and restaurants across New York and San Francisco and other cities, support surged for the Communist movement that might finally undo some of the mismanagement (sometimes corruption) of the Republican era and promote a stronger Chinese state that might finally be able to campaign successfully on behalf of the Chinese abroad.[81] For all the supposed "gains" by the Chinese in the United States during the Second World War, none stood out as marks of true equality, and mistreatment of Chinese nationals both coming and going continued unabated.

Meanwhile, the United States faced blame from Chinese migrants for contributing in a small way to lengthen a civil war that was tearing apart the nation. A handwritten letter to Truman from two Chinese seamen in 1946 chastised the president, "Me and my fellow men condemn every reactionary statesman in the United States who insists on antagonizing the situation in China, You can be sure that your policy will not crush the spirit of the people in China, but you can be sure that it will strengthen it to the peak that it needs to achieve to smash all persistent individuals who are determined to keep my people in slavery."[82] The hand-laundrymen of America's Chinatowns, joined by the merchant sailors, day laborers, and many others, discounted the usefulness of Nationalist control and saw in the Communist Party a new hope. That letter was not an isolated incident. In 1946 Truman received countless letters from Chinese students in the United States asking that the U.S. government not interfere in the civil war, not use American troops to disarm Japan (a U.S. project intended to make sure Communist forces didn't get there first), or make financial commitments to China until the situation became clearer. The volume of letters and their shared message raises questions about an organized campaign, though it certainly could have been a very informal one. They served as a reminder, however, that not every Chinese national in the United States was eager to see the United States take action to help Chiang Kai-shek stay in power.[83]

Prominent San Francisco businessman and, for a time, informal "mayor" of Chinatown Albert Chow also warned of growing discontent among America's Chinese population. He reported back to Dean Acheson about a meeting with the Generalissimo in which Chow claims he "told him that the people in the United States, both the Americans and the overseas Chinese, are not satisfied with his conduct as a leader especially his solicitous attitude toward his relatives, the Soongs and the Kungs. . . . I asked him about the lack of defense of Canton because of the disappointment of the overseas Chinese in its capture." Chow stressed in his communications his own status as an American citizen, but acted as an informal and unofficial citizen diplomat between his country and his ancestral home. As a result, his agenda did not always match that of either government.[84] Despite this dissatisfaction, Chow continued to support the ROC and advocated for American aid in 1950, on the eve of the Korean War. From the other side of the ideological aisle, Chinese students, scholars, and residents cheered the developments that allowed a new, stronger government to take over. Him Mark Lai has documented the ways that Chinese supporters of the Chinese Communist Party in the United States worked throughout the civil war to question KMT propaganda, argue against U.S. government intervention, and present a more positive narrative of the rising new regime.[85]

On October 9, 1949, a fight broke out at a meeting in San Francisco's Chinatown where Chinese residents had gathered to celebrate the news of the Chinese Communist Party victory over the KMT-run government.

After the event was interrupted by the arrival of a handful of Nationalist-supporting youth barging into the room and accusing those present of disloyalty, the two sides came to blows. Emerging from the dust was a Chinatown largely split between elite support for the losing KMT and popular support for the prospect of a new, stronger homeland, whatever its political inclinations. The people involved in the fight had very clear ideas about the future of China, but for everyone else, the lines between the communists and the anticommunists were not drawn all that clearly, and most opted simply to wait and see what happened.

Divided Loyalties

The Chinese Civil War had the potential to change the nature of diaspora contact with the homeland. Chinese living abroad were often dual nationals, entitled to Chinese citizenship by blood and local citizenship through birth or naturalization. Because Chinese abroad had rallied to the Chinese defense during World War II, both sides of the new conflict saw value in courting and winning their loyalties. During the civil war, supporters of the KMT and the CCP emerged within many diaspora communities; and because the United States was heavily engaged in rebuilding Japan and required open markets and noncommunist governments in Southeast Asia, the U.S. government watched the developments in overseas Chinese communities carefully. A CIA report explained that the overseas Chinese, "vitally interested in affairs at home, have split into much the same political factions as exist in China. The existence of strong rival Kuomintang and Chinese Communist organizations in Southeast Asia not only has aggravated native resentment there but also has prevented the overseas Chinese from forming a united front against local pressures."[86] FBI reports concluded that the same divisions existed in Chinese communities in the United States from the early 1940s.[87] The outcome of the civil war naturally had important consequences for U.S. relations with whichever Chinese government proved victorious, though it also meant that for a time the State Department paid extra attention to the Southeast Asian overseas Chinese. The prospect of a large Chinese diaspora in Asia supporting a Communist regime could upset the international balance of power.

The hope of a stronger China appealed to Chinese all over the world. This was an expression of both nationalism and self-interest, as an assertive China could do much more than past governments to protect migrants' interests. In the United States, support for the Chinese Communist Party took the form of Marxist study groups and an Overseas Chinese League for Peace and Democracy founded in New York in 1947. As scholar Him Mark Lai has shown, however, the repressive anticommunist culture of the United States in the 1950s stifled the development of a well-organized Chinese American Left.[88] A late 1948 cable from the Chinese Communist Party's Workers Committee to several overseas Chinese communities reminded the diaspora that all Chinese hoped for the same thing: an independent, free, democratic, unified, strong, and prosperous China. It explained, however, that Nationalist China's cooperation with American and British imperialists placed this hoped-for future in jeopardy, selling out the country for their own purposes.[89]

Though losing the war at home, the Nationalist Chinese government continued to fight in the diaspora through programs designed to win loyalties. Chinese schools in Asia and the Americas not only taught students Chinese language and history, but also gave them a sense of racial pride and patriotism.[90] Cooperation in the repatriation programs developed through UNRRA and the International Refugee Organization was another way to try to maintain ties with Chinese abroad and promote gratitude (and financial contributions) to the struggling state. Promoting not just new emigration, but the right kind of emigration, coupled with a degree of extraterritorial control over Chinese communities abroad, was another important way the Nationalists tried to achieve this goal. A 1947 broadcast to overseas Chinese commended the diaspora on its sacrifices and struggles during the war and outlined the efforts MOFA was making on their behalf. It called upon the overseas Chinese to remember their place in China's foreign affairs—as representatives of China, they were to press for greater understanding between the homeland and their places of residence. The address warned the overseas Chinese not to believe the rumors spread by the Communists or their sympathizers, but to believe in Nationalist China, and, if possible, to continue to invest their faith and finances in it.[91]

When the Nationalists lost their civil war, instead of collapsing and becoming engulfed by the new Communist state, they fled to the island of Taiwan. For the next two decades, the United States walked a tightrope maintaining diplomatic relations and support for Nationalist China as the legitimate government of China, while attempting first to isolate and then to live with the new Communist government of China. Migration policy became one way to fight this new Cold War, just as it had been employed in the hot wars of World War II and the civil war that had just ended.

Part II

Migrant Cold Warriors

Chapter 4

Chinese Migrants as Cold Warriors

Immigration and Deportation in the 1950s

The fracturing of China into two rival governments pursuing differing policies in the name of finally winning their civil war while fighting the Cold War wreaked havoc on political goals but also complicated individual lives. Chinese migrants found themselves caught between opposing governments as the new, Communist China and the United States endeavored to isolate each other from allies and competitors. Migrants also sometimes became pawns in Nationalist China's efforts to retain its place in the international arena. The Truman White House initially adopted the wait-and-see approach with respect to China in late 1949, but the rise of the pro-KMT China lobby, fed by the release of the "white paper" documents that led to accusations against Truman of doing nothing while China fell to communism, created an anticommunist constituency demanding that Truman continue to support Chiang Kai-shek. Truman and his secretary of state, Dean Acheson, were so convinced the KMT on Taiwan would collapse that they tried to ride out the storm, look for signs of discontent among the native Taiwanese, and bear the growing criticism from the right.[1]

The outbreak of the Korean War in June 1950 ended the uncertainty in Chiang's favor by preserving international recognition of the ROC as the government of China and making anticommunism a contingency of American aid. After the war broke out, Truman opted to "neutralize" the Taiwan Strait by sending in the U.S. Seventh Fleet to prevent a new outbreak of China's civil war. Doing so froze the civil war in place, ensuring that there would remain two governments still claiming legitimacy as the government of China for the foreseeable future. Truman's action also solidified Nationalist China's standing as an American ally and helped preserve the ROC claim to China's seat in the United Nations and on the UN Security Council. When the People's Republic of China entered the Korean War against the UN, it only reinforced its exclusion. With the ROC preserved, American occupying powers in Japan also ensured that Japanese officials retained their diplomatic relations with Taipei, and most of the Western bloc did as well. The one early exception was Britain, which recognized the PRC early in 1950 out of concern for Hong Kong.[2]

Beyond propping up the international position of Nationalist China, the Korean War also set in place the Asian theater of the international Cold War. Washington and Beijing came down on opposite sides not only in Korea but in Vietnam as well. They competed against each other for status and support in Southeast Asia, both among the local governments and the overseas Chinese. Throughout the 1950s, the secret to obtaining American aid in Asia was expressing fear of Communist expansion, and "no government learned to manipulate the system more expertly than Chiang Kai-shek's Nationalist regime."[3] The United States supported Nationalist China with economic, military, and political aid, even while leading the effort to isolate Beijing by imposing an economic embargo, curtailing Communist Chinese involvement in international politics, and soliciting, even coercing, the assistance of the surrounding Asian states. This policy meant there would be limited direct contact between Beijing and Washington until 1955, and between people from the Chinese mainland and the United States for much of the decade. In September 1954, the start of the Communist Chinese attack on Nationalist-held islands in the Taiwan Strait seemed designed to force an end to American support for the Republic of China, but instead this first Taiwan Strait crisis drove Washington and Taipei closer together. A second crisis in the strait in 1958 would further fan the flames of regional tensions.[4] Mutual distrust alongside fundamentally irreconcilable views toward Nationalist China would keep the United States and the People's Republic of China from normalizing relations or pursuing even lesser forms of cooperation.

The rapidly changing political landscape in Asia had an almost immediate effect on migration policy. In the early Cold War, two major issues came to dominate foreign relations thinking, both of which spilled over into migration: the first was the paramount importance of national security, including aiding allies and ensuring safety from forces seeking to undermine the nation from within. The second was international image. For both Communist China and Nationalist China, this translated to recognition and legitimacy internationally for their respective claims to govern China. For the United States, this could be seen in prestige and perceived leadership in the region.

In Asia, the Cold War was fought on multiple fronts, from battlefields to propaganda. As a result, all three governments used migration policies as tools in these battles. The United States adjusted its laws to consider the potential costs of immigration to U.S. national security. Anticommunism became a precondition to immigration, as well as an expectation for current residents, to the detriment of some liberal sections of the Chinese American community. Nationalist China continued efforts to exercise control over who emigrated, to mold what Chinese communities abroad believed and supported, and to assert authority over migrants being repatriated, forcibly or otherwise. The People's Republic of China stood ready to exploit missteps in both these efforts for domestic gain as it consolidated its revolution and sought regional support. In the months and years that followed the American and Communist Chinese armies meeting in Korea, migration policies proved a safer front for governments pursuing security and prestige even as the geopolitical strife continued to heat up. Chinese migrants caught in the crossfire, meanwhile, sought not only to avoid falling victim to Cold War politics, but occasionally to benefit from them as well.

Balancing Security and Prestige

Migration, or more accurately, free migration, became a major battleground of the Cold War. It was built into the dichotomy between the "free world," where migration was nominally uncontrolled and emigration a right rather than a privilege, and the Communist bloc, where citizens' lives were closely monitored and movements restricted. According to Matthew A. Light, "The most striking features of Soviet policy were the minimization both of emigration and of immigration, severe limits on foreign travel by Soviet citizens, and the systematic bureaucratic control of internal migration."[5] Western observers balked at these controls, though efforts to advocate freedom of emigration from the Communist "second world" was not matched with any willingness to accept free immigration to the Western "first world." Instead, politicized efforts determined who entered and when. For the United States, historian Mae Ngai has argued, "the Cold War overdetermined both international and domestic politics; it invaded debate on nearly every issue and prompted opposing sides to each assume the posture of anti-communism."[6] The American debate on accepting new migration hinged on which principle should win out in immigration policy: protecting national security by carefully selecting and screening the limited numbers of new arrivals, or promoting foreign policy goals with a more liberal entrance policy that welcomed even groups long shunned in restrictive laws. In the early 1950s, national security won.

Going into the 1950s, Asian immigration was still quite limited by statute. The Chinese had seen their exclusion repealed in word, if not strictly in practice, and World War II allies India and the Philippines had benefited soon after. These Asian migrations followed a racial formula in place of the national-origins formula used in Europe, a compromise first forged in the repeal of Chinese exclusion and then copied in subsequent measures. And other Asian nations were still restricted. Any hopes of liberalization were checked by a unique combination of racial concerns and anticommunism. The former created a debate between a more open quota policy for Asia and a continuation of limited, racially based quotas. The latter received reinforcement in 1950, when the Internal Security Act revised immigration laws to provide tighter controls over aliens in the United States. Moreover, the unique rules in place for Asian migrations served as a reminder that the exclusion era was over in name only: the practices that U.S. immigration officials had developed in the exclusion era continued to cast shadows over post-exclusion migration.

In 1952, Congress considered two bills to revise U.S. immigration laws that took different approaches to the issue of how to balance security and prestige. The bill proposed by Senator Pat McCarran (D-Nevada) and Representative Francis Walter (D-Pennsylvania) limited immigration on a national security prerogative. It applied the compromises of the repeal of Chinese exclusion to all Asian immigrants, allowing them a quota, but an explicitly racial quota.[7] This bill had support from Asian American ethnic groups (most notably the Japanese American Citizens League) on the strength of its plan to eliminate racial tests for naturalization and the belief that it was the best option a conservative Congress in the midst of a red scare would be willing to pass. The competing bill proposed by Senators Hubert Humphrey (D-Minnesota) and Herbert Lehman (D-New York) focused much more on immigration as an extension of U.S. foreign policy, proposing greater immigration quotas for American allies and allowing for the pooling of unused quotas each year to allow additional immigration from countries with small quotas. As Senator Lehman put it, "Each country of Asia must be recognized as a member of the world community. We cannot solicit their friendship and at the same time deny them a quota under our immigration laws."[8] The two sides disagreed over whether to frame immigration law in such a way as to prevent subversion by communist-leaning immigrants, which would require tight guidelines for exclusion and deportation as in McCarran's bill, or to promote American prestige abroad, which would require more open laws with fewer race-based provisions, as in the Humphrey bill.

At the end of the debate, the McCarran version won the most congressional support, though not the support of the president. Truman, in a private letter, framed the measure as almost an accident, saying he went to Congress in the wake of the displaced person crisis asking for three hundred thousand more refugees, "and all I got was this terrible McCarran Bill."[9] Truman made a strong public case for the importance of immigration to foreign policy in his veto message, complaining that the bill would "perpetuate injustices of long standing against many other nations of the world, hamper the efforts we are making to rally the men of East and West alike to the cause of freedom, and intensify the repressive and inhumane aspects of our immigration procedures."[10] Unconvinced, Congress easily voted to override his veto. Security won out over foreign policy. As it took effect, McCarran's bill also created a new organization within the State Department, the Bureau of Security and Consular Affairs (SCA), which, as historian Carl J. Bon Tempo has shown, was intended to be a security apparatus reinforcing the restrictionist intent of the bill even when the Immigration and Naturalization Service failed to do so.[11]

In the aftermath of his defeat, Truman ordered a special commission to investigate the weaknesses of the law and suggest possible legislative remedies. Chinese Americans testified about the inability of Chinese to appeal for judicial review from outside the country (so if the consuls denied an application for derivative citizenship, there would be no way to get the decision reviewed), concerns that the act limited opportunities for discretionary relief for people like deserting seamen, and expressed hope that future revisions might allow migrants to naturalize when under an outstanding order of deportation.[12] From Hong Kong, the organization Aid Refugee Chinese Intellectuals asked for measures to admit Chinese as refugees and provisions to force a more lenient approach by the consuls. All these complaints had to do with the history of how Chinese experienced U.S. immigration law, and the idea that past mistreatment could be codified into the new law demonstrated just how limited the World War II gains really were. In its final report, the special commission speculated that long-term Chinese resentment of racist American immigration laws helped to create the anti-foreign and anti-imperialist rhetoric of Communist China. Japanese propaganda used U.S. immigration laws to great effect in World War II, and the Communists would now do so in the Cold War, and indeed already were doing so in the ongoing conflict in Korea.[13] Of course, even though liberal critics complained about how restrictive, racially based quotas damaged U.S. credibility and prestige, none offered solutions that would open wide the door to Asian immigrants.[14] Just as in the discussion over the repeal of Chinese exclusion a decade earlier, lawmakers sought only the appearance of equality, not true parity.

U.S. policy toward Chinese migration did not change much as a result of the McCarran-Walter Act, and surprisingly, neither did Chinese government policy, even though there were now two Chinese governments. Immediately after the Communist victory, the new People's Republic of China did not give priority to emigration or overseas Chinese issues. In the first months after "liberation," the new government set few national regulations on the movement of people. Thousands of refugees fled the uncertainty of China for Hong Kong, and many of the men attached to the army of the Republic of China followed (or were taken by) Chiang Kai-shek to Taiwan. Allowing such people to leave could be interpreted as removing potential sources of future instability, but a continued exodus would look bad for the new government. As the Communists solidified control, the chaos eased, and the PRC established a formal policy of making it difficult to leave the mainland but easy to return.[15] Travel documents, exit permits, and even opportunities to slip over the border became much harder to find. Although it made exit difficult, the PRC kept its borders just porous enough to allow the easy return of overseas Chinese to invest, work, study, or be with family. Between 1949 and 1952, reception centers in Guangdong Province received more than fifty thousand Chinese returnees.[16] Eventually acknowledging that tight exit controls created difficulties for families whose survival depended on travel between overseas family networks, the PRC liberalized the law in 1955 to allow overseas

Figure 2. Travelers passing through the Lo Wu checkpoint between the People's Republic of China and Hong Kong were carefully screened by Chinese border police. United States Information Service–Hong Kong, National Archives and Records Administration.

Chinese and their family members to travel more freely.[17] The government stood to benefit from having a steady stream of migrants thinking well of it and bringing their opinions abroad. The fact that migration in and out of the mainland tended to be temporary helps to explain the relative disinterest with which the People's Republic treated transpacific migration in the early years, though as the decade wore on the Communist government became more concerned with migrant remittances, refugees, and repatriations.

Meanwhile, Chinese migration continued to be overseen and monitored by the Nationalist government, despite its relocation to Taiwan. After 1949, the ROC continued the postwar policy of investigating and approving all potential emigrants before granting them a passport. Remarkably, the Nationalists did not announce the first minor changes to their system for vetting prospective immigrants to the United States until 1953—six years after the original program began operation. When they came, the changes appeared minor, given the earth-shattering events and reversals suffered by the Nationalist government in the meantime. The revised rules eliminated requirements that some emigrants found impossible to fulfill after 1949, such as the need to provide high school transcripts and health certifications from particular hospitals.[18] Additionally, the government offices, now in Taipei, obviously could no longer perform the kinds of thorough investigations that they did while still on the mainland. The government did continue to require some investigation and apply the strict selection process equally to all Chinese, whether or not they lived under Nationalist jurisdiction in Taiwan. Ironically, it became just as difficult for Chinese abroad to gain entrance to Taiwan as the United States, as security concerns post-1949 were by no means limited to those championed by Americans. As frustrating as the requirements proved to be for potential emigrants, they allowed the Nationalists to maintain the illusion of control over the transnational communities that linked their government to that of the United States. As in the late 1940s, officials continued to believe that selecting only the most desirable emigrants would help improve U.S. opinions of China and the Chinese.

False Identities and True Loyalties

Having set into law the idea that immigration policy intended to screen out more than allow in, the United States and Nationalist China both made careful investigations of potential arrivals to American shores. Chinese had long entered the county under false identities to circumvent restrictive immigration laws, but the Cold War created new urgency to knowing the true identity and ideology of everyone residing within U.S. borders. The conflation of the "paper sons" problem and Cold War concerns solidified in the mid-1950s in the larger context of tension with Communist China and posed a serious problem for Nationalist officials determined to retain support of the Chinese in the United States.

After the Korean Armistice was signed on July 27, 1953, tensions in East Asia did not suddenly disappear. One factor keeping tensions high was Chiang Kai-shek's declared determination to retake the mainland. In theory, Truman placed the Seventh Fleet in the Taiwan Strait at the outbreak of the Korean War to prevent him from doing so. In 1953, Eisenhower shifted its purpose to protecting Taiwan, theoretically "unleashing" Chiang to restart counterattack plans. In the summer of 1954, American and Chinese Communist officials met at the Geneva conference on Korea and Indochina, and American talk about renouncing the use of force created suspicions in both Chinese governments that the United States had begun to consider advocating for "two Chinas"—one on the mainland, and one on Taiwan. Neither Beijing nor Taipei welcomed the idea. On September 3, Communist China launched an attack on the Nationalist-held islands of Jinmen (Quemoy) and Mazu (Matsu). The attack was less an overture to war and more an attempt to establish a claim to Taiwan, as well as to shore up the young Communist revolution, but it had an effect opposite of the one intended. Motivated by Beijing's actions, the United States signed a mutual defense treaty with Nationalist China committing the United States to aid Taiwan if the island itself was threatened, and the later Formosa Resolution promised assistance in defending all the ROC's possessions in the strait.[19]

The crisis would have many repercussions for the region and for migrants, but first there was a short-term problem of what to do with "enemy aliens." Back in 1939, FBI head J. Edgar Hoover had developed an emergency detention program to address potential internal threats during times of war, and "what began as a program within defined limits and based on a sensitivity to legal and congressional considerations, after 1945 evolved into a program wherein the sole consideration was how to insure that individuals deemed by FBI personnel to be 'dangerous' to the national security could be apprehended during a national emergency."[20] The "detention of Communists" program, or DETCOM, tracked potential subversives and established a "Master Arrest Warrant" that would have made arrests easier if they became necessary, though over the course of the several decades that the FBI continued the program, the warrant was never used. The list included thirty-six Chinese aliens, a tiny fraction of the population, but enough to raise questions about Chinese residents' loyalties.

Trying to use the list to detain or deport aliens during the Taiwan Strait crises was problematic, however. The Justice Department began a legal review that was intended to consider the problems with the program. For the Chinese aliens on the list, the key issue was the ongoing question of the legality of arresting aliens not already under orders for deportation.[21] When the legal review ended, the Department of Justice found that it was not legal to arrest aliens not considered deportable, but that "the warrants should not be canceled, pending the review of the cases by the Internal Security Division of the Department, and should an emergency happen tomorrow, we would make the arrests of these 35 persons" (one Chinese immigrant had died since the original list was created). The FBI could therefore temporarily forgo legal rights with regard to aliens, though it continued the search for other statutes that might allow it to detain the Chinese.[22] This sent the FBI on a chase to find either a reason these aliens were already deportable or another reason why they could be arrested. As the crisis continued, the FBI reported that "of the 35, five are under deportation now and [the INS] is trying to get them out of the country."[23] Given how few deportations to China were effected in these years, and the fact that the INS reported no Chinese deportations for subversive or anarchistic action in 1955 (and only one in 1956), it is unlikely that these attempts were successful.[24]

Against this backdrop of tension and geopolitical strife, immigration officials found themselves on a new sort of front line. They were tasked with defending the homeland, in a sense, by not allowing any subversives to enter as migrants. It was not the most dangerous task in those precarious years, but it was by no means insignificant. It took place in the context of Senator Joseph McCarthy's accusations of Communist infiltration of government, the House Un-American Activities Committee's efforts to identify and prosecute Communist sympathizers, and the reality for some in law enforcement that although the red scare might be overwrought, it was not always wrong.[25] As one INS official observed in 1952, "Some of the Chinese now arriving have attended Chinese Communist schools and some show evidence of indoctrination. These persons will be potentially dangerous in the event of outright war with China. Certainly this is no time to relax the control over them as they seek to enter the United States."[26] In the context of the new Cold War, ensuring that Chinese and other new migrants were who they said they were was not simply a matter of law and order or even immigration restrictionism. It could be said to be a matter of national security.

Whether or not potential migrants subjected themselves to Nationalist China's ongoing scrutiny to receive a passport, they would all be subject to American investigations before ever leaving Asia. The U.S. consuls required Chinese born in or having recently visited Communist China (including Chinese in Hong Kong) to undergo extensive security screenings, a provision that applied even to individuals with U.S. government grants for study or speaking tours in the United States. There were so many applicants, however, that these screening appointments were hard to come by. One frustrated Chinese applicant complained that it was easier to set up a meeting with the president of the United States than with the consul general at Hong Kong.[27] There were fears of backlash, of course, that Chinese resentment for the intrusive process would have dangerous results. As early as 1951, consular officials worried that "general injury to American interests are serious, and a matter of concern."[28] The potential damage to U.S. prestige would need attention, but not until the basic security concerns had been addressed.

Security concerns about Chinese migrants in particular came from both ends of the entry process: the consular side that issued visas and the immigration officials who screened entrants at U.S. ports. Chinese who claimed U.S. citizenship faced extensive investigations while still in Asia, then long interrogations and detentions after arrival at either New York or San Francisco. With limited solid proof to demonstrate the truth of marriages, births, or residences in China, arrivals based their claims to derivative citizenship upon the results of interrogations, affidavits, and testimony, all of which could be fabricated, as long as everyone involved was willing and able to stick to the agreed-upon story. A 1953 INS memo complained that "a Chinese approaches the requirement for the submission of documentary evidence much in the manner of a person entering the field of negotiation. He submits as little as possible, knowing that, if more evidence is required, he can then meet the additional requests."[29] As a result, inquiries could take months, even years. While putting the blame for delays on Chinese applicants, the same memo attempts to constrain the varieties of evidence accepted by U.S. officials. For example, proving the right to derivative citizenship required positive proof that the applicant was the child of the American citizen father, that his parents were married at the time of his or her birth, and that the father was in fact a citizen. That the INS accepted a claim to citizenship and allowed the father to enter the United States as such was not considered positive proof. Instead, the INS wanted more documentation like family photos, evidence of continued correspondence, school records, record of birth in a real and recognized village, blood tests, and even radiological examinations. (There was evidence that efforts to use X-rays to estimate age and match the blood type of passport applicants with their purported citizen parents were easily foiled by Hong Kong immigration brokers who ordered their own X-rays and blood tests, then sold identities to match personal characteristics.)[30] Because these accepted forms of evidence were in reality rarely available, both INS officials and consular officers saw only two solutions to the problem: vigorous investigations and free-will confessions.

On the consular side, the most infamous expression of these concerns came in the form of a report cabled to Washington in December 1955, submitted by the American consul general at Hong Kong, Everett Drumright, and likely authored by vice consul Leo Mosher. The report claimed there was a serious threat of Communist spies entering the United States through false identities.[31] It expressed concern for the safety and security of law-abiding Chinese Americans and proposed a system of increased investigations to end the practice of "buying and selling the rights of American citizenship before Communist China is able to bend that system to the service of her purposes alone."[32] A second report from Hong Kong six months later complained that "American Chinese, born in the U.S. and speaking excellent English, have valued U.S. citizenship so lightly as to sell the identity of their real sons in China to imposters for financial gain."[33] The author, Maurice Rice, worried that the United States had no way of knowing just how many ethnically Chinese American citizens still resided in China, an important point for determining both the scope for potential fraud and for protecting U.S. nationals abroad.[34] Both reports demonstrated the extent to which exclusion-era concerns about controlling Chinese migration developed new life in the politically charged atmosphere of the Cold War.

Drumright preferred to reject visas rather than increase investigations, but investigation would expand nonetheless under the State-Justice joint effort to end the practice of Chinese immigrating as "paper sons." When Drumright filed the December 1955 report, he was not a novice on China. He had graduated from the University of Oklahoma at the start of the Great Depression, and took the foreign service exam because he lacked other options. He stayed in country—with one brief exception when he and other diplomatic personnel were traded by the Japanese for their own officials—straight through until 1944, learning Chinese in the process. He also remained solidly anticommunist throughout his tenure in China, something that helped spare him from the Cold War purge of State Department China hands perceived as too ideologically aligned with the Communists. Having watched the Chinese Nationalists struggle energetically in their battle against first the Japanese and then the Communists, he was certainly sympathetic to the Nationalist government and Chinese people. He landed in the Hong Kong consulate in the 1950s after a time in Japan, Korea, and India, as well as on the China desk in Washington. He later explained of his time in Hong Kong, "The main

Figure 3. Everett Drumright began as a Chinese language officer before rising to the rank of consul general in Hong Kong and Macau in 1954. In 1958, he moved to Taipei to become the U.S. ambassador to the Republic of China. State Department, National Archives.

thing that occurred in Hong Kong was the development of a plan to stop the fake emigration that had been going on there for many years. . . . We had about thirty who were investigating these cases that were coming to us. And our investigations in the long run showed a great many of them were fakes. We were rather proud of that program there."[35] Drumright was both committed to Nationalist China (something he would later have an opportunity to prove as ambassador to the Republic of China from 1958 to 1962) and steeped in anticommunist politics. Historian Mae Ngai has noted that his perception of the Chinese was also steeped in exclusion-era-style "racial hostility and suspicion," which caused him to be suspicious of Chinese applicants as "culturally inclined to fraud and perjury."[36] That was true with respect to potential migrants, though it did not characterize his attitude toward the Chinese people as a whole. Essentially, he had the quintessential American attitude of his generation in both State and Justice: the Chinese were a wonderful people, as long as they stayed in China.

Drumright's report reflected both this worldview frequently shared by U.S. consular officers and the fact that it could prove genuinely difficult to decide which cases were worthy of visas or travel documents. In early 1956, the U.S. consulate in Hong Kong reported that it had uncovered evidence of fraud in 85 percent of the passport cases it investigated. In the other 15 percent of the cases, they claimed, consuls suspected fraud but could not prove it.[37] The fact that they assumed all cases to be fraudulent was itself problematic, as it made them inclined to deny even legitimate applications and count them as clear evidence of ongoing fraud. Still, it was undeniable that not all the applicants were who they claimed to be. Investigations might have been the only solution, but they were costly, time-consuming, and required a large staff. The large size of the U.S. consulate in Hong Kong strained relations with the British colonial government as the U.S. staff roster swelled to accommodate all the American "China watchers" and an elaborate propaganda program in Southeast Asia by the U.S. Information Service (USIS), the overseas satellite of the U.S. Information Agency. Adding additional teams of investigators would not be well received.[38] At the same time, the consulate had a backlog of some fourteen hundred cases early in 1956, meaning that wait times for U.S. passports extended into years.

The cases not only increased the workload of the investigators in the U.S. consulate in Hong Kong, but also clogged up the circuit courts, which heard and decided any appeals on decisions regarding U.S. citizenship. Finally, U.S. authorities convened grand juries in New York and San Francisco—two centers of Chinese American life—to help investigate the allegations of fraud. They issued blanket subpoenas for all the records of a number of prominent businesses and Chinese organizations, even without specific suspicions that the records contained evidence of fraud. Even acknowledging the existence of some cases of falsified identities, the grand jury investigations were clearly a violation of the rights of Chinese Americans and Chinese residents.

Historians Mae Ngai and Him Mark Lai have documented the ways the Chinese communities protested these subpoenas, and Xiaojian Zhao has noted that protests also came from abroad.[39] But Nationalist-affiliated Chinese community leaders also explicitly reached out to the government of the Republic of China. In line with its broader efforts to protect and support overseas Chinese (and in so doing, continue to exert extraterritorial control over them to the benefit of the government), Nationalist China lodged a series of protests with the U.S. government over its treatment of Chinese in America. Chinese consuls called the Departments of State and Justice to complain about the disruptions of business, the accusation of illegal activity where no proof existed, and the short notice the courts gave organizations to comply with the subpoenas.[40] Chinese ambassador V. K. Wellington Koo lodged formal complaints with the U.S. government based on the concerns of the New York Chinese Consolidated Benevolent Association. Foreign Minister George Yeh and other high-ranking Taipei leaders were watching the activities of the grand juries and the fraud cases very closely.[41] Harried INS officials dismissed these concerns as undue interference, reminding the Taipei government that as long as the individuals involved claimed to have U.S. citizenship and resided on U.S. soil, they could not seek the protection of any foreign government, even if they had dual nationality. Dual citizenship allowed American officials to ignore the complaints of the Nationalist government, but that did not mean the latter stopped making them.

The so-called "confession program" proved more effective at ending the cycle of Chinese passport fraud than the ongoing investigations. If a family voluntarily confessed illegal entry, and everyone joined the confession, then the INS would try to admit them legally under a variety of existing statutes. For example, a veteran of World War II would be eligible for naturalization, and his spouse could be readmitted as a war bride. Others might have their status adjusted under the Chinese quota or through the available visas under the Refugee Relief Act. Of course, not everyone who confessed was forgiven—the INS ordered some deported to China, though given the difficulties completing deportations in the 1950s, this often meant staying in the United States under "suspension of deportation" without the legal rights of a resident. And, of course, not everyone confessed. Tung Pok

Chin's memoir *Paper Son* poignantly laid out how his political ties with left-leaning organizations made him wary of doing so.[42]

Although eliminating potential sources of false identities was important to the American perception of security during the Cold War, doing so was not without costs. The greatest costs were borne by the Chinese community in America, which faced down a new wave of "yellow peril" thinking in government and society and delayed their acceptance as equal citizens.[43] The "peril" onus was particularly strongly felt among the Chinese American Left, and the documentary film *The Chinatown Files* offers some evidence of this through interviews with members of left-leaning organizations like the Chinese Hand Laundry Association and Ming Qing.[44] But there was additional international fallout from the discovery of a Chinese "immigration racket." Communist Chinese officials followed the investigations, casting them in racial terms as another example of "white America" pursuing a new program of exclusion against the Chinese, particularly pro-PRC Chinese.[45] The effect of the confession program in the People's Republic of China was to create even greater suspicion that the U.S. government regularly mistreated Chinese overseas, a complaint that was not without merit but which hindered ongoing negotiations over migrant repatriations. In March 1957, a PRC government newsletter on overseas Chinese affairs reported on how the United States convicted Liu Chengji, a businessman, longtime contributor to the New York economy, and a hero of World War I, for aiding in passport fraud, and sentenced him to twenty years in jail and a fine of $40,000.[46] Another report recounted the story of Li Shou, who entered the United States as a paper son in 1929, then returned to China three times, each time reporting the birth of additional children. With the slots he opened, additional "family members" entered the United States in 1939 and 1947. Finally, in 1952, U.S. authorities held for investigation the passport application of one of the members of his paper family, implicating all of them. Li Shou attempted to flee to Mexico to escape harsh treatment by U.S. officials, but he was discovered, returned to the United States, and then imprisoned with a four-year sentence. He killed himself in jail.[47] These stories served multiple purposes: they placed American officials in a bad light by highlighting persecution of even contributing members of society, argued that racism and inequality for Chinese were inherent in the American system, and demonstrated the agony of emigration to the so-called "free world."

In addition to the overseas implications, once the story of the "smuggled Chinese" broke in the popular American press it also raised public relations problems at home. The *New York Daily News* ran a four-part series in the spring of 1956 on "a traffic which has become one of America's top problems in the war against Communism." It explored all the sensational details of how "the government of [PRC premier Zhou Enlai] is buying up many of these immigration slots," because it was "an almost foolproof way of getting a thoroughly indoctrinated young Communist into America." The series shed doubt on the entire Chinese community, from new applicants for passports all the way up to interpreters long resident in the United States and employed by the U.S. government. Though the articles ultimately acknowledged the role of anti-Chinese-immigration discrimination in creating the perceived need for falsified documents, they stressed that four-fifths of the Chinese community entered illegally, and that the persistent ties between American Chinatowns and relatives in China had the potential to compromise the entire community.[48] Several scholars of Chinese America have suggested that the leaders of the New York and San Francisco Chinatowns actually used immigration policy and the fraud investigations to cleanse their communities' ranks of those they suspected of being "disloyal" by selecting out PRC supporters (and sometimes personal enemies) and, if possible, reporting them to the INS as illegal immigrants.[49] The entire process created a pool of individuals in the United States and abroad with a history of bad experiences with U.S. immigration officials and few reasons to look kindly upon the U.S. government.

Deportation and Forced Expulsion

The precarious balance between security and international prestige made vital by the Cold War also overflowed into deportation policy. Between 1949 and 1959, U.S. INS annual reports count a total of 650 Chinese nationals deported from the United States (destinations would have included China, Hong Kong, and Taiwan). By contrast, the Alien Address program reported that at any given time during the decade, there were anywhere from 31,305 to 42,514 legal Chinese aliens residing in the country. Despite the McCarthyist claims of a "Red Chinese plot" to infiltrate the United States through Chinese immigration, only 3 of the 650 deported were expelled as a result of suspicion of subversive or anarchistic activity.[50] All the persistent concerns about the allegiances of Chinese aliens notwithstanding, only a minute number were actually forcibly removed from the country. What these numbers do not reveal are the failed attempts at deportation, the nature of the investigations, and the diplomatic issues that prevented Chinese deportation from being more common than it ultimately was.

This indicated, of course, that deporting even non-subversives proved deeply problematic. In 1951, the INS detained a group of ten Chinese seamen after they deserted their ships while on shore leave. This was a fairly notorious problem. Chinese seamen's desertions in World War II had nearly brought the Allies' Atlantic convoys to a halt, but the seamen's reasons for deserting (shipboard mistreatment, unequal wage scales, and, admittedly, a desire to immigrate but no way to get a visa) had not fundamentally changed in the period since the war ended. Between 1949 and 1960, an average of 144 Chinese seamen each year deserted from ships docked in U.S. ports, and by entering without an immigrant visa, they could be detained and deported if caught.[51] INS officers arrested the ten deserters in 1951 and held them at Ellis Island, the former immigration screening center now turned detention center, while considering how to deport them back to their homeland, mainland China. During the proceedings, the ROC ambassador in the United States wrote to the secretary of state, "In view of the large number of Chinese people who have been and are being summarily executed or liquidated daily for no apparent reasons according to the civilized concepts of law and justice, the Ambassador wishes to request that the case of these ten Chinese seamen be reconsidered on humanitarian grounds." The ambassador added that these seamen would be particularly vulnerable in Communist China because the posts they abandoned were with Western shipping companies, operating under democratic principles.[52] He made his appeal by reminding the INS of the many contributions Chinese seamen made to the Allied effort in World War II, though U.S. officials likely did not remember their efforts nearly so fondly. The State Department responded that it would be happy to reconsider the deportations ... if the ROC would let the seamen go to Taiwan instead.[53] The ROC demurred as it did with most deportation cases, so the choice remained between sentencing the men to potential persecution via deportation, or allowing them to remain in the United States indefinitely with no legal status.

Even if unwilling to accept the seamen themselves, the ROC had good reason to make the public appeal on their behalf. The arrest and subsequent deportation of Chinese citizens periodically made newspaper headlines in both the United States and Taiwan, so the appeal made by the Nationalist government "on humanitarian grounds" simultaneously painted the Republic of China in the best possible light and the People's Republic in the worst. It showed that the ROC was standing up for its citizens, protecting them, and reinforced the idea of the Communist Chinese government as the enemy of free people. This in turn could aid the ROC with its most vital diplomatic goal of the decade: the ongoing drive to prevent international recognition of the People's Republic, including in the United Nations. Over and over again the ROC would use these situations to make a positive point in its public diplomacy.

Though the United States often chose to defer to its own anticommunist propaganda and concede to ROC demands for leniency, the reality of the situation was that the INS likely could not have deported Chinese migrants to the mainland even if it tried. In 1950, the INS reported, "deportations to China proper have practically ceased, the last group having been deported through Hong Kong to the Cantonese area at the close of fiscal year 1949 [June 30, 1949]. The British Crown colony of Hong Kong, early in 1950, decreed that they would accept as deportees only bona fide citizens of Hong Kong. The same situation exists in Formosa [Taiwan]."[54] The following year's report (for the year ending June 30, 1951, months before the exchange of notes about the seamen) explained that the low number of deportations to China was a result of being unable to acquire legal travel documents for destinations on the mainland.[55] Without documents indicating the PRC's willingness to accept U.S. deportees, Hong Kong would never allow them to transit, because the odds were too high that instead of crossing into China, they would simply join the local Chinese population.

In 1955, the INS experienced a record number of orders for deportation to Communist-controlled nations that could not be executed: 10,967 in all.[56] Given the anticommunist rhetoric of U.S. foreign policy during the decade, almost anyone who did not want to be deported would claim fear of persecution if returned behind the iron curtain. Moreover, aliens sometimes appealed their orders for deportation to higher courts, forcing the U.S. judicial system to navigate a minefield of foreign policy questions. In 1953, after the United States had completed complicated arrangements with the British government for filtering deportees to the PRC through Hong Kong, all fifty-five Chinese aliens in the first group to be deported applied for stays because of the "threat of physical persecution" that awaited them in China. After that impressive action, INS officials suspected that "practically all of the Chinese will claim 'physical persecution' when arrangements for their deportation are completed."[57]

This placed the United States in an awkward situation that pitted its immigration law, itself rooted in national security concerns, against a foreign policy tied to promoting the U.S. international image and credibility. If it did not expel those deemed deportable, the nation would be left with a number of unwanted and undesirable aliens, perhaps even aliens with Communist sympathies, and it would seem to "reward" illegal entry. On the other hand, if the United States declared the threat of persecution to be negligible and deported the Chinese to the PRC anyway, it impugned its own reports about the cruelty and illegitimacy of the Chinese Communist regime. Deporting to the mainland would open a door for anti–American propaganda, as "it [was] entirely possible that [the deportees] would at least temporarily receive somewhat favorable treatment as part of an effort to exploit them propaganda-wise as worthy proletarians who as deportees are the innocent victims of American oppressive and discriminatory treatment of persons of the Chinese race."[58] By the mid-1950s, the PRC, the ROC, and the United States were already in the midst of a massive propaganda war in Asia, and the United States grew increasingly concerned about how both immigration and deportation polices could damage its image. The more the deportees appealed their deportation orders with public pleas against returning to Communist China, the more difficult the situation became for U.S. public diplomacy.

The U.S. solution to the problem was to highlight the Nationalist claim to be the one, true government of all China and request that it demonstrate that role by accepting all Chinese deportees in place of the PRC. The problem was that few if any Chinese in the United States had any personal ties to Taiwan, so quite aside from the ROC's reluctance to take them, almost none wanted to go. INS files reported that the ROC consul received communications from leaders of the Chinese community suggesting that the U.S. government forgo the difficulties involved in deportation and simply allow the deportees to remain in the United States.[59] U.S. Cold War refugee policy made that legally possible, if not necessarily simple. Barring that, some migrants claimed they could not return to their homes on the mainland because the PRC was not a country—or at least not one recognized by the government undertaking the deportation proceedings.[60] Others took that a step further and argued their new deportation orders to the ROC were illegal because Taiwan was not a country. The District of Columbia District Court agreed that ambiguous language in Department of State documents (designed to avoid accusations of a "two Chinas" policy) made deportations to the Republic of China legally questionable.[61]

The State Department accepted many deportees' claims that they would face persecution if returned to the mainland, but it found dealing with claims of persecution if returned to Nationalist China more perplexing. Dr. K.C. Wu was the governor of Taiwan from 1949 to 1953, when he was purged and accepted voluntary exile to the United States. He called the Nationalist regime in Taiwan tyrannical and dangerous to dissenters, supporting the claims of those requesting stays of deportation. After one defendant claimed he feared persecution if forced to go to Taiwan, the Ninth Circuit Court of Appeals referred the case to Congress, saying it could be that "[Congress] will not credit Dr. Wu's allegations or will refuse to act upon them against a friendly nation."[62] In this case, the foreign policy implications of deportation, damaging relations with an ally, were so clear that the court sought guidance from the governmental body with the authority to address it. Further complications ensued when migrants claimed they would be persecuted under either Chinese government. Eventually, even the safety of deportees in Hong Kong would be open to doubt.[63]

Subversive or not, security threat or otherwise, Cold War concerns clearly interfered in the ability of INS officials to carry out what used to be relatively routine deportations. Interestingly, this was not always limited to deportations to Communist countries or claims of persecutions. Sometimes it came down to the question of who could speak for the overseas Chinese. Quite beyond what the United States wanted or needed, the ROC for its own security and economic reasons did not accept deportees who did not have relatives in Taiwan or who had not originally come from the island. As a result, the very few individuals who were actually legal residents of either Hong Kong or Taiwan before their misadventure on American shores could sometimes be deported, and the rest were a problem.[64] U.S. officials eventually hit upon a solution of sorts: making the issuing or extension of visas dependent on holding a reentry permit for the country or territory departed (usually Hong Kong or Taiwan). The PRC, of course, would never comply with such a measure, and the policy became a bureaucratic nightmare for State Department officials tasked with issuing visas in Hong Kong under the Refugee Relief Act of 1953. Later, the deportation measure would also inhibit repatriation talks with Beijing, as the law required Chinese students in the United States to hold reentry visas to be able to extend their visas. Some exchange students avoided the issue by simply abandoning their studies and returning to China. The rest had to figure out how to get reentry permits from the ROC—despite having no connections to the government or Taiwan—to stay long enough to graduate before leaving for the mainland.[65]

That accusation of mistreatment proved frustrating to U.S. officials, but without reentry permits, it was frequently impossible to complete deportations at all, even in cases that didn't directly involve the PRC or ROC as destinations. This led to one of the more bizarre injections of Cold War politics into U.S. deportation policy—by 1954, the United States followed the ROC policy of recognizing all Chinese anywhere in the world as legal citizens of the ROC. This created a challenging requirement that ethnically Chinese sailors from Singapore (all legal citizens of the majority-Chinese colony) hold Nationalist Chinese passports in order to be granted entry to the United States. The policy was less about promoting the ROC's controversial claims to be the sole government authority over the "overseas Chinese," though, and more about Singapore's repeated failure to accept deportees even when they held local passports. Nonetheless, British colonial authorities were astounded at the suggestion, with one official commenting privately, "I cannot believe that the U.S. Immigration authorities seriously expect a British subject of Chinese race born at Singapore or Hong Kong to hold a Chinese Nationalist passport; there must be some misunderstanding. They might just as well maintain that British subjects of Italian name and race—and there are many in Soho—must travel on Italian passports." The official reply to the United States pointed out that Chinese from Britain's Southeast Asian colonies were not necessarily eligible for passports from either Chinese government, "nor do we welcome any notion which would encourage them to strengthen their ties with China or would retard their integration in the life of the Colony where they are established."[66] Individuals within the British Colonial Office realized, however, that for as long as they did not accept even legitimate deportees, it was difficult to argue with the United States over passports. Singapore ultimately began accepting some deportees, though the whole problem led some in the British government to question the very idea of having Chinese sailors in their crews at all, as "in particular, Chinese seamen are a very sore subject with the U.S. Immigration Service."[67]

As with its immigration and repatriation policy, the United States increasingly used its deportation regulations to serve its foreign policy and national security interests. Attempts to use deportation as a deterrent against illegal immigration failed in the Cold War climate that made it quite difficult to send anyone to a Communist country involuntarily. Sometimes, however, deporting aliens to friendly countries was just as tricky. Governments like those of the ROC, Hong Kong, and Singapore were no less sensitive to the threat of subversion and infiltration via immigrants or deportees than was the United States, and that meant that all three often refused to accept even legitimate nationals. The ROC claimed to be the one true government of China, though, and that provided the United States with occasional leverage for forcing through a deportation. When the United States was determined to send Chinese back home, the ROC would step up to accept them only if the alternative was sending them back to the PRC, something it viewed as an implicit acknowledgment of that government. When there was no insistence, they demurred and preferred to have the Chinese in question remain in the United States. With so many different factors beyond the execution of the letter of the immigration law at stake, deportation cases sometimes took years to settle, as was the case with George K. Jue.

The Deportation Case of George K. Jue

George K. Jue (Zhou Jiajing) entered the United States in 1919 at the age of eight as the son of a merchant, one of the few classes of Chinese permitted to enter and live in the United States during the exclusion era.[68] In the years that followed, he built his own Chinatown restaurant (the "Lamps of China"), led the Chinese Chamber of Commerce, and became active in rallying the Chinese in the United States to support the Nationalist government in the war against Japan. He traveled to Asia periodically, and in 1950 he reentered the United States via Honolulu. At that time, he allegedly assisted fifty Chinese in obtaining visas fraudulently using fake ROC passports, ostensibly to visit the Chicago World's Fair, but in fact to immigrate. His indictment claimed he conspired to obtain the false documents with former U.S. vice consul in Hong Kong John Wayne Williams, who was convicted on bribery charges and testified against Jue.[69] In his parole interview, Jue's version of his offense is a little different. He claimed to have helped write character letters for individuals traveling to the World's Fair, some of whom failed to return and instead enrolled in American universities.[70]

INS officials discovered the forged documents and prosecuted Jue late in 1953. In February 1954, Jue was found guilty of conspiracy to defraud the United States and sentenced to one year and one day in jail, though district court judge Oliver D. Hamlin recommended against eventual deportation.[71] After Jue served his time, INS unexpectedly challenged the advice of the court and ordered his return to China. In spite of his long residence in the United States, Jue's Chinese citizenship was not in question— he had renewed his ROC passport at the consulate in San Francisco on

October 2, 1950.[72] For the next year, Jue, his lawyer, and congressional supporters scrambled to stop his deportation via the only legal avenue left to him: a private bill passed by Congress.

Private bills for a variety of constituent services had existed almost from the beginning of Congress, but as immigration policies became increasingly strict after the quota laws were enacted in 1924, and again when the McCarran-Walter Act reinforced the quotas without allowing for large numbers of World War II refugees, the number of such bills introduced each year swelled. It became quite common to use Congress as an immigration court of last resort—more than a thousand such cases were cleared each year. So when Jue's last chance at staying his deportation came and went, his lawyer went to the House and Senate Judiciary Committees looking for a bill "for the relief of George K. Jue." He found support from Congressman John J. Rhodes (R-Arizona) and Senator Barry Goldwater (R-Arizona).

When Jue's case went up, however, he discovered that Congressman Francis Walter (R-Pennsylvania)—famous for giving his name to the McCarran-Walter Act and highly influential in Congress on matters related to immigration—wholeheartedly opposed its approval.[73] Roy Howard, owner of the Scripps-Howard newspaper chain, speculated to Jue at one point that Walter's interest most likely stemmed not from personal knowledge of Jue, but from "resentment of the fact that, as you know, sometime back there were quite a number of cases involving the smuggling of Chinese into the United States."[74] Chinese "fraud" cases and "rackets" plastered the papers in the mid-1950s, and a 1956 article in the *New York Times* explicitly put the Jue case in the context of two other "passport rings" engaged in bringing Chinese to the United States illegally and led by prominent Chinese who had long resided in the United States.[75] In reality, though, Walter had followed Jue's case from the beginning. The *San Francisco Chronicle* claimed that the eighty-two-year-old Judge Hamlin's recommendation that Jue not be deported inspired Walter to introduce a bill requiring all judges to step down by age seventy. When pressed, Walter explained the stay of deportation had only been intended for aliens who "made a mistake and in whose case deportation would cause suffering and hardship to his family." But to him, at least, Jue's case was different. Walter was quoted saying, "Jue is an habitual criminal who has caused many hardships and heartaches to poor Chinese he deceived, tricked and extorted in obtaining fraudulent papers and brought to this country illegally."[76]

Emanuel Celler (D-New York), chairman of the House Committee on the Judiciary, planned a hearing in June 1955 to discuss the merits of the Jue case, though as he explained to Congressman Rhodes, "Frankly, we are somewhat disturbed about this case."[77] The various bills' sponsors all argued that Jue's anticommunist activities both made his deportation to China dangerous and deprived the United States and Nationalist China of an influential Cold War ally. The INS was less convinced of this fact, noting in its investigation of Jue that "representations have been made that Mr. Jue is one of the key figures among Chinese in the vicinity of San Francisco in the fight against Communism. Although investigation has developed that he is a member of the Chinese Anti-Communist league, a member of the Chinese Consolidated Benevolent Association . . . and is considered as sympathetic to its policies, it was not found that he is active in anti-Communist affairs among Chinese and is not known as a leader among Chinese in that movement."[78] Given both the unclear case and Walter's violent opposition, both the Senate and the House failed to act on private bills for Jue in 1955, so Jue was forced to find another route to avoid deportation. His case followed the pattern of other Chinese deportees in claiming that his outspoken anticommunism would mean he would face persecution if returned to mainland China. On February 24, 1956, the United States formally requested that the Republic of China on Taiwan accept Jue for deportation.[79]

Instead of agreeing, the ROC refused to issue the paperwork that would allow Jue to enter Taiwan. The Nationalist government authorities frequently refused to accept any deportees at all, because of what it called the unstable political and economic situation in Taiwan, expressing concern that admitting people with no family on the island would destabilize the already weak state. Moreover, officials there expressed concerned that accepting deportees from the United States would open the floodgates to similar requests from the nations of Southeast Asia. U.S. documents on the Jue case acknowledged these to be legitimate concerns, but they also speculated that someone very influential in the Nationalist government had taken a personal interest in the case and persuaded Foreign Minister George Yeh not to give in and issue the necessary entry permit.[80] At the same time, prominent private citizens campaigned on Jue's behalf, calling his role in the Cold War irreplaceable. Frank Ford of the Scripps-Howard newspaper chain attempted to convince State Department officials that "Jue had done outstanding anti-Communist work. . . . Jue had traveled extensively in the Far East impressing on Chinese groups the firmness of the United States anti-Communist position. He convinced Aw Boon Haw

that his newspapers should choose the side of the free world."[81] Aw Boon
Haw, also known as the "Tiger Balm King," was a Chinese businessman,
philanthropist, and publisher of Chinese-language newspapers in Singapore
and Malaya.

The recorded correspondence of Foreign Minister Yeh with Roy W.
Howard, the Scripps-Howard owner, reveals that the speculations of U.S.
officials were right. Yeh was resisting taking Jue back on purpose. Yeh noted
at one point that he was under a lot of pressure to accept Jue and could
not "resist much longer." He then asked that Howard send advice and information on what was still being done in the United States to prevent
the deportation.[82] The ROC government worked with the privately run
newspaper chain to stall the deportation for as long as possible. Their argument was that the personal, private diplomacy conducted by Jue benefited
both the United States and the Nationalists, and summarily deporting him
meant not only a personal loss for him, but the loss of a Cold War asset for
both countries.

If still determined to carry out the deportation, the U.S. government
had several ways to compel Nationalist China to accept a deportee that did
not involve persuasion or newspaper middlemen. A provision in the 1952
Immigration Act permitted the United States to stop issuing immigration
or travel visas to any country that refused to accept its own citizens as
deportees. If the threat of ending new immigration was not enough, U.S.
officials could stress the importance of accepting deportees to the Nationalists' claim to legitimacy as the true government of China.[83] Another way
to force the issue was to withhold all aid to Taiwan until the Nationalist
government issued Jue's entry permit.[84]

In weighing the possible repercussions of either denying or accepting Jue, Foreign Minister Yeh noted that overseas Chinese newspapers and
communities did not seem to be strongly on Jue's side, so allowing his
deportation might not have an adverse effect on Nationalist efforts to maintain the loyalties of the Chinese diaspora.[85] Agreeing to accept Jue might
also demonstrate to the United States how willing Nationalist China was
to cooperate, whereas continued refusal could do irreparable damage to
ROC-American relations.[86] The U.S. State Department had noted internally that "if Congressional opinion were to become further aroused in this
case, it could generate unfavorable publicity reflecting on the [Nationalists']
position as the sole legitimate Chinese Government."[87] It is unquestionable
that this consideration had also reached Taipei. Eventually, the principle
ultimately proved more important than the person. In 1961, the Nationalist

government finally buckled under all these pressures and agreed to accept Jue, but he immediately filed for a stay of deportation, and this time the U.S. courts granted it.[88]

Jue's stay of deportation expired in 1962, and he once again sought to avoid being sent away. For the Nationalists, the material circumstances had not changed—all the reasons Taipei once had for refusing to issue the entry permit in 1956–57 still held true, as did the reasons why it finally gave in.[89] This time, however, some members of the Chinese community in the United States took a more sympathetic view of the case. One lengthy editorial in *Sanmin Chenbao*, a pro-KMT Chinese-language newspaper in Chicago, argued that the efforts undertaken by Jue and others to help Chinese immigrate illegally via fraudulent paperwork or false statements were a natural outgrowth of the anti-Chinese prejudice built into American immigration laws. The author claimed that if the ROC accepted Jue for deportation to Taiwan, it would demonstrate that it could not and would not protect the overseas Chinese, which raised questions about the legitimacy of the ROC government and the responsibility of Chinese Americans to continue to offer their support for it.[90]

Though Congressman Walter died in 1963, not all opposition to Jue's case died with him. In 1966 the Board of Immigration Appeals granted Jue a suspension of deportation, but "Congress took adverse action," leaving Jue in limbo. He would neither be deported by the INS, nor would permanent resident status be granted to him. There he stayed another twelve years until 1978, when President Jimmy Carter pardoned him. So convoluted had his case become that the pardon did not automatically eliminate his order of deportation. In 1984, Senator Goldwater reintroduced Jue's case with a private bill restoring lawful permanent residence, which permitted Jue finally to become a naturalized citizen in 1987.[91]

The Jue case provides great insight into the diplomatic exchanges and compromises that governed attempts to deport Chinese in the early Cold War. If the United States had held a greater stake in ensuring Jue left the country, it is possible that the entire process would have been over sooner (certainly before the 1960s), because the McCarran-Walter Act had built-in consequences for countries that failed to accept deportations. The Nationalists ultimately gave in to these pressures and issued Jue an entry permit, but in spite of the unequal balance of power between the United States and Nationalist China, the latter could still be remarkably recalcitrant on accepting deportations when it chose to be. The Nationalists, in other words, knew how to use American anticommunism to achieve their own goals.

Nationalist choices in this case appear to have been based on a complicated calculus that involved balancing one claim of legitimacy against another. On one hand, they sought to maintain their claims to legitimacy as the sole government of China through reinforcing their ability to accept Chinese deportees. On the other, they needed to maintain overseas Chinese support by standing up to the United States to protect their citizen from a deportation that would have both personal consequences and implications for Nationalist public diplomacy. And balanced between these two extremes was the belief that Jue could do more for the Nationalists in San Francisco than in Taipei, if only he could be allowed to remain in the United States.

In the transition to Cold War in Asia, policies governing Chinese immigration and deportation could not be divorced from foreign policy aims for either the United States or Nationalist China. Both countries used these policies to promote their respective positions in Asia and within their bilateral relationship. For the United States, security concerns and anticommunism sometimes won out over promoting the American image in Asia, but there were always forces within the U.S. government and the Chinese American community to provide a critique of such policies and laws. More and more, the United States came to realize that even "domestic" issues governing immigration and deportations were linked to the international project of bolstering American prestige in a region deemed strategically important but lacking in substantive reasons to trust the U.S. government. Nationalist China, meanwhile, used immigration policies (and its control over entry to and exit from Taiwan) to demonstrate its legitimacy as the government of China, not to mention to manage its relationship with its more powerful ally. Migration diplomacy became an important weapon in the "Free China" arsenal for showing the world that it still claimed both the loyalty of the Chinese people and the right to govern them.

In 1954, the U.S. consul in Hong Kong noted that U.S. policy governing Chinese migration "imposes a public relations problem here of some magnitude."[92] During the Immigration Commission investigation into the ways that U.S. immigration policy needed to be revised, the litany of Chinese complaints about the law boiled down to a particular issue: that how the State Department interpreted the law through consular officials in Hong Kong, even more than the imperfect law itself, acted as a new "unwritten Chinese exclusion law."[93] The way that the American consular bureaucracy carried out its work in the postwar period revealed that its institutional memory was far too steeped in exclusion-era concerns to be efficient in the post-exclusion era, and that the blind, security-focused rigor of the investigations did far more damage to the U.S. reputation among the Chinese than anyone in the U.S. government had anticipated.

For all the faults of U.S. policy and implementation, however, the Nationalist government had its own inherent contradictions. These included the rigorous, time-consuming investigations into potential emigrants that were intended to build positive demand for future arrivals but ended up stymieing the chances of some migrants to go at all, as well as an overseas Chinese policy that attempted to select the best immigrants based on their ability to assimilate locally into the United States even while continuing to claim them as citizens loyal to the Republic of China. Absolute insistence on the right to speak for Chinese nationals in the United States and elsewhere abroad would become a hallmark of Nationalist overseas Chinese policy, but dependence on this idea also meant that losing this right could undermine national legitimacy.

Chapter 5

Remitting to the Enemy

Transnational Family Finances and Foreign Policy

Decades of Chinese migration, coupled with restrictive immigration laws, had helped to create transnational families. Transnational families maintained transnational financial ties. Established overseas Chinese communities had a long tradition of sending remittances home to families left behind in China, to the extent that in the principal migrant-sending areas in Guangdong and Fujian Provinces, entire villages depended on foreign funds to survive. These "overseas Chinese villages" sent most of their able-bodied young men abroad as part of a long-standing tradition of chain migration. Those left behind then relied almost exclusively on funds sent home for their livelihood.[1] The overseas Chinese had already demonstrated their sheer financial strength to Chinese Communists, Chinese Nationalists, and the United States during World War II, when their remittances, investments, and donations propped up the Chinese economy, funded the war effort, and provided relief to struggling citizens. After 1949, Beijing wanted to see these funds continue, and Taipei wanted to see them stop or get redirected into investments in Taiwan. Both sought the loyalty of Chinese abroad. Achieving these goals meant developing and applying an effective policy toward the overseas Chinese in the United States. Nationalist China had the advantage of access as the recognized government, cooperation with

American officials similarly interested in appealing to the Chinese diaspora for support, as well as party members well placed in major Chinatown organizations. Communist China lacked these things, but it had something else: the other half of transnational Chinese American families.

For Communist China, transnational family connections became both a vital source of foreign exchange and a means of attacking its U.S.-imposed international isolation.[2] With tightened exit controls and few individuals other than refugees traveling from mainland China to the United States in the early 1950s, existing connections between Chinese in the United States and their extended families in South China served as a lifeline for communicating Communist China's interests. Influencing the writing of family letters allowed Beijing to ensure that its messages reached American audiences. One of those messages was to send remittances.

Though a seemingly simple message, it ran into difficulties. Beijing struggled to reconcile the Communist ideology of collectivization with the income generated by tolerating capitalist-supported overseas Chinese communities. Early 1950s efforts at completing land reform directly affected the flow of remittances, as the decision to classify overseas Chinese and their families as landlords or rich peasants led to a sudden collapse of support for the regime within the diaspora. Meanwhile, attempts to use family communications to improve the overseas impression of Communist China failed when accusations emerged that the PRC government was using relatives' letters to blackmail the overseas Chinese and extort money from them. The combination of these experiences demonstrated that in order to win the Chinese abroad, the Communist government had to alter its policies at home.

The United States and Nationalist China, on the other hand, looked to exploit the rift caused by land reform and the extortion rumors to gain support for the Nationalist regime. Explosive press coverage of the extortion scandal led the United States to enforce the Trading with the Enemy Act against Chinese nationals sending money home, most famously by prosecuting the left-leaning Chinese-language newspaper the *China Daily News*. Though the successful prosecution of its editors for violating U.S. law technically achieved both American and Nationalist goals, it exposed the political fault lines in the Chinese American community and led to backlash from Chinese Americans frustrated by their inability to send regular remittances to China. The connections between land reform and remittances, and the "extortion racket" and the *China Daily News*, have been drawn by scholars interested in either overseas Chinese policy or the development of Chinese American identity and civil rights.[3] The bigger picture encompassing these issues as part of larger competing overseas Chinese policies demonstrates how migrants' financial activities formed an important but hard-to-control link between nations.

Beyond their financial roots, the overseas Chinese policies developed by all three governments in the 1950s had another point in common. U.S. State Department attempts to use Chinese Americans to improve the U.S. image in Asia, Nationalist efforts to control Chinatown opinions, and Communist attempts to extort additional remittances all shared an experimental quality. In each case, governments tried out a new policy and quickly discovered that they could not control how migrant communities reacted to it. As a result, the migrants themselves drove policy as much as any bureaucrats.

Overseas Chinese Americans and Public Diplomacy

Chinese migrant remittances and financial investment proved inexorably tied up in questions of loyalty, legitimacy, and political support. In the early Cold War, overseas Chinese policies were a continuation of wartime policies to secure approval and, with approval, funds. The difference was that now there were two viable Chinese governments competing for this support. The competition explicitly singled out two audiences: the vast numbers of overseas Chinese in Southeast Asia, and the relatively financially successful Chinese in North America. It was not only a two-way contest—for a time in the 1950s, officials at the U.S. State Department became very concerned with the prospect of Chinese abroad supporting Communist China and acting as a third column.[4] Chinese nationals in the United States and Chinese Americans played two roles in this contest. First, they were recruited by United States Information Agency (USIA) and State Department projects to act as cultural ambassadors to bring a pro-American message to the Chinese diaspora in Southeast Asia. Second, they became the object of Communist and Nationalist competition for support in North America.

USIA messaging in the 1950s focused on shoring up support for Nationalist China and combating reports of racism against nonwhite residents in the United States. In Asia, this meant not only addressing the burgeoning civil rights movement but also continuing to counter Communist propaganda on unequal treatment for Asian migrants. As with Japanese information campaigns during World War II, these arguments could be devastating to American interests because they were largely true. The United States

Information Service (USIS) experimented with a variety of ways to use Chinese Americans to combat accusations of anti-Asian discrimination in the United States. They employed Chinese Americans at the Voice of America and considered ways to get unattributed radio messages out that could be interpreted as being from one group of overseas Chinese to another.[5] The USIS publication *Free World Magazine* also regularly featured success stories of Chinese American mothers, veterans, and civil servants.[6]

In 1952, USIS brought Jade Snow Wong, whose book *Fifth Chinese Daughter* had just been released in Chinese translation, to Southeast Asia.[7] Her speaking tour was intended to combat Communist propaganda about the status of Asian Americans in the United States, as "the appearance of a Chinese American whose artistic achievements have been recognized by the American public would be a much-needed testimonial to the opportunities our society offers to citizens of so-called 'minority races.'"[8] During Wong's trip across the region, including stops at Bangkok, Hong Kong, Kuala Lumpur, Penang, Rangoon, and Tokyo, some audiences embraced her, while others proved skeptical. Responding to calls for more Asian Americans to join East Asian propaganda tours, a consul in Hong Kong noted, "Although such grantees present some possible pitfalls—local Chinese for example are inclined to view with some disdain their more 'foreignized' Overseas brethren—they still are living refutation of hostile claims that Asians are maltreated in the United States."[9] USIS also contracted with Chinese scholars and artists to visit the United States on their own speaking tours, hoping that these short-term grants would undo misconceptions. Unfortunately, an immigration service predisposed to suspicion of all Chinese entrants as potential illegal immigrants sometimes undid the good work of USIS. One grantee returned home "complain[ing] that he had been 'hounded' by immigration and naturalization officers and that he had been subjected to racial discrimination."[10] State and INS each had its own agenda, and these did not always work together.

Historian Ellen D. Wu has argued that the political dangers to Chinese Americans in the Cold War "meant that both community members and the state found it useful to superimpose an Overseas Chinese identity on ethnic Chinese in the United States."[11] She explains that Chinese in the United States often chose to identify with a larger diaspora supporting the Nationalists when it was useful to signal support of anticommunism, and that the State Department also employed them as overseas Chinese when needed to reach Chinese communities in Singapore, Malaya, or Indonesia. Though there is ample evidence that this is the case, the willingness to connect Chinese Americans with the overseas Chinese on the part of the U.S. government was highly contingent both on concerns over the Nationalists' attempts to exercise extraterritorial control over American Chinatowns and the section of the government bureaucracy in question. State made use of Chinese Americans like Jade Snow Wong to advance a larger overseas Chinese policy in Southeast Asia, but the INS sometimes found that conflating Chinese Americans with overseas Chinese invited undue interest in immigration and deportation cases from Taipei.[12]

The Nationalist government more unambiguously tried to incorporate Chinese Americans into a larger overseas Chinese policy. As Mae Ngai explained, the KMT offered dire warnings of Communist Chinese efforts at influence in American Chinatowns, but "the warning was ironic, for the Kuomintang had . . . pursued an aggressive overseas Chinese policy based on the principle of jus sanguinis—that persons of Chinese blood, regardless of their country of birth, are citizens of China."[13] These projects were overt, as with KMT members engaged in community leadership and activism through organizations like the Chinese Consolidated Benevolent Association, and covert, with unattributed news articles planted in Chinese-language newspapers that were not known as KMT organs.[14] The KMT had opened offices, published newspapers, and recruited members among Chinese in the United States starting even before World War II, and Nationalist leaders also worked with "pro-KMT lobbyists and politicians" to create and build the influence of the China lobby.[15]

Though the Nationalists had the advantage of U.S. recognition, a long history in the United States, and the cooperation of U.S. officials, they lacked an important asset: any kind of access or control over Chinese Americans' families back in the mainland. That was one reason why speaking on behalf of migrants, and attempting to represent their interests in battles against the INS or abuse by other governmental agencies, proved so important to Nationalist officials. These actions were both symbolic of recognition as the true government of China and the most immediate way to secure loyalty from ethnic Chinese facing day-to-day challenges in which cross-strait politics might not have played a direct role.

Rather than simply being manipulated by sensationalist accounts of immigration rackets or public diplomacy campaigns, members of the Chinese American community voiced their own opinions about U.S. laws and policies toward China. In many cases these statements self-consciously identified with the Nationalist government, which historian Cindy I-fen Cheng argues was part of a deliberate effort to enhance the social standing

of the Chinese community in the United States.[16] Many tried to negotiate acceptance in American society by simultaneously declaring their
American citizenship and their unique understanding of East Asian and
Chinese politics. In some cases, community organizations voiced strong
opposition to communism as "the sentiment of the Overseas Chinese in
this country,"[17] or identified themselves more broadly with "the Chinese
people everywhere who are sturgling [*sic*] to win back democracy and
freedom for China."[18] Nor were such efforts unique to the atmosphere
of the 1950s—in 1967, a full-page ad ran in the *New York Times* to remind
the nation that "17,000,000 Overseas Chinese Opposed Admission of Red
China into United Nations."[19] In other cases, as with the Seattle Chinese
Benevolent Association, Chinese American leaders drew upon shared values of common citizenship, explaining that "being Americans, we are all
deeply concerned about the role our country takes in World Affairs. Being of Chinese origin, we are especially concerned over the actions of the
United States in the Far East." That organization's telegram on the subject
of ROC exclusion from the Japanese Treaty Conference reminded the U.S.
Congress that "most of us have some direct contact of one sort or another
with China, either through trade, family ties, or natural interest," but that
"in our contacts with China, we have always stressed the advantages of the
American way of life."[20] Such statements confirmed both the worst fears
and best hopes of immigration committees in Congress. They caused concern because Chinese migrants to the United States, even once they had
assumed the role of U.S. citizens, appeared to retain ties and, potentially,
loyalties to China. They were, however, reassuring in that those loyalties
seemed to be with the "right" China—the Republic of China rather than
the PRC. These communications with Congress represented the opinions
of the Chinatown leadership, which had an interest in presenting its community as completely loyal to U.S. interests and who themselves often had
close ties with Nationalist leaders.[21]

Of course, not all members of Chinese American communities in the
United States accepted or agreed with these self-appointed spokesmen. At
the height of the confession program, members of left-leaning organizations felt disproportionately attacked and scrutinized for their activities,
which included anything from Chinese labor unions to, most famously,
the Chinese Hand Laundry Alliance (CHLA) and its affiliated newspaper,
the *China Daily News*. Some supporters were leftists or communists, of
course, but as Him Mark Lai observed, "The corrupt and repressive KMT
rule undoubtedly played an important role in politicizing and radicalizing

these individuals so that they turned to the CCP as the hope for build-ing a prosperous and strong nation."[22] Scholar Reniqu Yu's study of the Chinese Hand Laundry Alliance agrees, but also suggests that the conflict between the (KMT-supported) Chinese Consolidated Benevolent Associa-tion (CCBA) and the left-leaning CHLA was as much about class as it was politics. The "merchant elites" used the shifting tides of the Cold War to control laboring-class dissenters.[23] And then there were Chinese who sup-ported neither the Nationalists nor the Communists, as Cindy I-Fen Cheng has detailed in the case of the San Francisco newspaper *Chinese World*.[24] In other words, backlash against Nationalist control in China and attempts at extraterritorial control in the United States helped build support for the People's Republic of China.

Even when Chinese dual nationals expressed vocal support of the United States and Nationalist Chinese governments, it was still not without some risk. The United States by this time had a long history of hosting diasporic nationalisms—the Irish, Italians, and early twentieth-century Chinese were all examples—and proved somewhat wary of their potential to complicate both internal security and foreign relations.[25] U.S. laws prevented ethnic Chinese with U.S. citizenship (by virtue of birth or naturalization) from participating in a foreign political party. Because "most loyal and active Kuomintang members in the United States are also American citizens," there were strict limitations on what kinds of actions they could undertake on behalf of the ROC without putting their citizenship and residency sta-tus at risk.[26] One newly naturalized Chinese American attended the ROC National Assembly as a representative and discovered when he returned that the U.S. government responded by stripping him of his U.S. citizenship. Thereafter, the ROC government did not publish name lists of Assembly participants in order to protect future representatives from the United States and Canada.[27] When the ROC tried the other course and encouraged as-similation and integration into local societies, it faced potential backlash from a certain facet of the overseas Chinese population. An editorial in a Chinese American newspaper criticized the ROC government for suggest-ing that in some cases, local citizenship might replace Chinese citizenship, claiming that such a policy demonstrated that the Nationalist government was no longer willing to take responsibility for protecting the rights or interests of the Chinese abroad.[28]

Propaganda, protection, and other overseas Chinese policies directed at Chinese Americans by the United States and Nationalist China ultimately still came down to the same common denominator: the need to deny support, especially financial support, to Communist China. Unfortunately for the Nationalists, the new leadership on the mainland had an important asset on its side, in the other half of transnational families spanning the Pacific—but only if it could figure out how best to use them.

Land Reform and Remittances

In the early 1950s, the overseas Chinese policy of the People's Republic of China took two directions. It had an external policy, centering on the Chinese living abroad, which included the overseas Chinese, ethnic Chinese with or without Chinese citizenship, and the study-abroad students. This policy focused on uniting the diaspora behind the new government and combating the opposing rhetoric of American imperialists and adherents to Chiang Kai-shek. It also worked to encourage remittances and investments and support overseas education.

In addition to the external policy, the PRC had an internal (or domestic) overseas Chinese policy that was directed at four groups: refugees fleeing from overseas areas, returned overseas Chinese, overseas Chinese students returning to attend schools and universities, and the villages or relatives of overseas Chinese. These groups formed the best and most reliable links between the homeland and its citizens abroad. Their letters to and visits with relatives overseas had a profound impact on what members of the diaspora knew and believed about life in China. When these groups suffered mistreatment or perceived prejudice on the mainland, it reverberated abroad by reducing the level of overseas support for the PRC government. Domestic overseas Chinese policies addressed such issues as land reform, the distribution and use of remittances, ease of entry and exit for visits, and assistance for arriving students and destitute refugees. The resources devoted to setting up "service centers" in overseas Chinese areas in Guangdong and Fujian Provinces and to educating these special classes of citizens on new policies demonstrated their importance to the PRC.[29]

These external and internal policies converged in one area of particular importance to the young government: that of overseas remittances. In addition to being the sole source of support for the wives and families of overseas Chinese residing in China, remittances were vitally important to the new nation as a means of acquiring foreign exchange and new investment for development. The exigencies of World War II and Japanese incursions into South China cut off many of the overseas Chinese villages from their

remittances, a situation that caused considerable hardship—even death. After the war, the emergence of the civil war meant that it took some time
for steady remittances to China to stabilize, because many of the funds went
through private sources in Hong Kong rather than through the regular
remitting banks. Scholar Chun-hsi Wu estimated the total overseas remittances to China in 1946 at US$60 million; in 1947, at $80 million; in 1948,
$87 million; and in 1949 reaching a high of $105 million. A 1950 report in
the *People's Daily* (and duplicated in ROC publications) reached the same
average for these years but trends in the opposite direction; it put the numbers at US$130 million in 1946, $80 million in 1947, and $66 million in
1948. Still, by either estimate, postwar remittances soon approached prewar
levels: averaging around US$80 million a year between 1946 and 1949.[30]

The initial excitement caused by the end of the civil war, the stabilizing
Chinese economy and political situation, and the potential emergence of a
strong Chinese homeland caused the amount of money sent to China from
the overseas Chinese to start an undeniable upward trend, at least initially.[31]
According to PRC documents, remittances continued to grow after the
Communist victory in the autumn of 1949, steadily increasing until the
autumn of 1952, when they suddenly fell off. If the total number of remittances received in 1951 equaled 100, they explain, then remittances in
1952 would be equal to 95.3; in 1953 they would be 71; and in 1954, 70.[32]
Determining the exact amounts entering China is nearly impossible; some
of the most credible estimates provide wildly diverse figures (see table 3).
The discrepancies are due to such problems as determining how much
of the money entering Hong Kong from overseas Chinese sources was
ultimately transferred to the mainland, differences between the exchange
rates given by banks and the black market, and the lack of formal transfer
methods. Though the figures vary widely, most do indicate the overall drop
in remittances after 1952 that the PRC documents discuss. Still, regardless
of the actual amounts entering China, the PRC government believed that
remittances had improved after their takeover but then started falling off in
the early 1950s, and that it needed to take action to prevent further decline.

In the immediate aftermath of the civil war, remittances remained
strong, and China began concerted efforts to further increase the funds
sent back.[33] Almost immediately, American observers assigned nefarious
motives to these efforts. As early as 1949, the *New York Times* reported on
a campaign for the purchase of "People's Victory Bonds." The *Times* explained that some groups pooled their funds to buy the bonds, then remit-
ted money through the Bank of China so that the actual purchase took

Table 3. Estimated remittances to China, 1950–1956, a comparison (in millions of U.S. dollars)

Source	1950	1951	1952	1953	1954	1955	1956
U.S. CIA[a]	44.6	133.6	136.4	112.6	116.8	107.0	91.3
Chun-hsi Wu[b]	60	56.81	41.05	45.34	41.22	46.49	45.85
Bank of China HK[c*]		37.8	40.6	33.42	33.25	30.45	25.9
FE Economic Review 1964[d*]	(126.31)	(126.31)	(126.31)	(126.31)	(126.31)	(126.31)	(126.31)
OCAC (Taiwan)[e]	102	63	52	52	70.17	70.17	70.17
Guangdong Archive[e†]	[157]	[157]	[149.06]	[111.3]	[109.7]		

[a] "Communist China's Balance of Payments, 1950–65," May 1, 1966, EO-1996–00177, 42, U.S. Central Intelligence Agency, Freedom of Information Act Documents, www.foia.cia.gov.
[b] Chun-hsi Wu, *Dollars, Dependents and Dogma: Overseas Chinese Remittances to Communist China* (Stanford, CA: Hoover Institution, 1967), 42.
[c] *Gongfei qiaohui de yanjiu* (Taipei: Qiaowu weiyuanhui diqing yanjiu shi, 1969), 14–23.
[d] Frederic Hohler, "Hongkong: Role Reversed," *Far Eastern Economic Review* 46.1 (October 1, 1964): 35–36.
[e] Guonei qiaowu gongzuo ruogan zhengce wenti, Zhong qiaowu dangzu, July 25, 1955, 235/2/9–67, Guangzhou.
[*] Based on a HKD/USD conversion rate of 5.7 and a HKD/GBP exchange rate of 16.0.
[†] Estimated, based on total number for 1950–54 given as 684.06 and statements about how the level of remittances changed during those years.

place on Chinese territory, to get around the fact that selling bonds to benefit a foreign government was illegal in the United States unless previously approved by the Federal Securities Commission. (It had also been illegal for Chinese Americans to buy bonds in support of the ROC government in World War II.) This way, the Chinese in the United States wanting to buy bonds could obey the letter of the law, if not the spirit. The *Times* suggested, however, that the majority of Chinese Americans supported the Chiang Kai-shek regime, so they would report to the American authorities anyone trying to sell or buy the PRC bonds.[34]

In general, two factors affected the level of remittances China received after 1949. First, economic and political conditions in the parts of China where the families of the overseas Chinese lived determined how Chinese with family members abroad communicated with their relatives and what they discussed. Second, economic and political conditions in the host countries affected the willingness of Chinese living abroad to send funds and their ability to get funds out of one country and into another.

Within the PRC, the so-called "domestic overseas Chinese policies," combined with the process of collectivization, were likely important factors causing the diaspora communities to feel unease with the actions of the new government. In particular, the execution of land reform policies in Guangdong Province and other overseas Chinese areas caused resentment and concern. CCP classification of some overseas Chinese landholders as "tyrant landlords," or of "enemy classes," angered citizens abroad who worked long hours in inhospitable environments to acquire their land and houses in China, though such classifications were not universal, and there were considerable differences in how various counties carried out classification. Most controversially, early efforts at collectivization threatened the freedom of use of remittances. Rumors abounded that peasant committees forced families to turn over most, if not all, of the funds they received to aid in developing communes or to invest in local enterprises. The government could appropriate money sent back for weddings and funerals on the grounds that the latter events were "feudalistic" or "counterrevolutionary."[35]

In mid-1951, a meeting report claimed that the vast majority of the overseas Chinese were in fact quite supportive of the land reform project, but that there were a few remaining rich peasants and landlords with overseas ties still being struggled against. The report noted that the local cadres often failed to carry out policies consistently; instead, some were too soft on overseas Chinese landlords, while others were far too harsh.[36] After the autumn of 1951, however, remittances began to fall off, and in February 1952 the Guangdong government reported receiving a large volume of letters from abroad expressing confusion or anger about land reform and demanding answers. In some cases, it seemed the U.S. and ROC governments had been successful in selling their version of what land reform meant and how it affected the overseas Chinese, and one outcome of that success was that the diaspora no longer supported all the PRC government policies.[37] At the same time, it showed a weakness in the execution of land reform policies with regard to the overseas Chinese and a failure to disseminate information properly explaining the policies.

As news about land reform and the potentially disadvantageous effects of the policy on overseas Chinese holdings spread abroad, Guangdong officials grew increasingly concerned about the effect of the policy on the relationship with the overseas Chinese. By the mid 1950s, it was an accepted fact among PRC overseas Chinese committee officials that the execution of land reform, if not the policy itself, in the overseas Chinese areas of Guangdong and Fujian Provinces affected the rate of overseas remittances to the mainland. The major errors included classing the families of overseas Chinese who received remittances but did not own land as landlords, forcing them to invest their remittances in collective projects or to purchase bonds against the national debt, and in some cases holding family members hostage until they wrote to their relations abroad requesting that they send money.[38]

As signs of misunderstandings and problems with land reform emerged in 1952, the importance of the letters increased. Family letters in all their forms were absolutely fundamental to the overseas Chinese propaganda efforts in the newly established PRC. As early as 1950, letters offered a means to reunite families lost to each other through more than a decade of war, as well as a means of taking a census of transnational ties.[39] Letters filled with praise or condemnation for the new regime and its policies influenced the perceptions of the Chinese abroad, and that in turn affected whether they supported the government. Students returning from the United States reinforced the need to get better information about Communist China to Chinese nationals living in the United States. Everyone in China with friends or family in the United States could engage in some measure of personal diplomacy to help relatives abroad understand the true situation in the motherland.[40] Reinforcing the connection between family letters and remittances, the Bank of China (which handled most transfers of funds) set up "Overseas Chinese Letter Writing Bureaus" in south Chinese branches.[41] The overseas Chinese offices in China encouraged those with relatives abroad to write more letters explaining how the local committees managed land reform in their hometowns, and at the same time, the government looked for ways to do a better job answering the letters that poured in from overseas asking for information or clarification.[42] In 1953, Guangdong officials reported receiving 12,480 letters from overseas Chinese asking for investigations or more information, many of which expressed specific concerns over land reform. In the first nine months of 1954, the provincial government received another 10,038 letters. Aside from general requests for information, 372 of the letters asked for specific action with regard to unsettled land reform cases. It became vital for officials to provide satisfactory answers to these letters, celebrating the accomplishments of the program, providing redress for mistakes, and guarding information about some of the more tragic consequences of land reform, such as suicides or property liquidations.[43] Starting in the winter of 1954, the Guangdong government began to revise the class status of the overseas Chinese, changing them from "landlords" to workers or rich peasants. By midyear in 1956, the committees had adjusted the status of 94 percent of the overseas Chinese families in the province originally classified as landlords.[44]

There were inherent contradictions between revising the status of the overseas Chinese and the larger project of class struggle. As scholar Glen D. Peterson has noted, "Looking after the special interests of *qiaojuan* [overseas Chinese families] and *guiqiao* [returned overseas Chinese] frequently meant sacrificing the spirit if not the letter of other, universal policies espoused by the party center."[45] As a result, confusion and contradiction marked the process of collectivization and land reform in the region, and the overseas Chinese families and returned overseas Chinese faced frequent changes in their status and circumstances over the course of the first several decades of Communist rule in China.

The Extortion Rumors and Reality

In addition to having questions about the handling of particular land reform cases, some overseas Chinese accused the government or the peasant committees of using strong-arm tactics to squeeze additional funds out of them. The letter-writing campaign in some cases "had the opposite of its intended effect, heightening suspicions rather than allaying them"[46] as Chinese abroad received family letters that demanded sums of money to ensure their own safety.

A 1952 report from the Southern Bureau of the CCP Central Committee contained samples of letters from Chinese living in Canada and the United States about rumors of extortion and violence they had heard from their families in China. A letter from a Chinese organization in Vancouver, Canada, described how peasant committees had forced some members of their community to send back anywhere from one thousand to ten thousand Hong Kong dollars (US$175–$1,750) and pleaded with the Guangdong authorities in the PRC government to investigate the peasant committees responsible for the extortion. The letter listed seven counties where Chinese Canadians reported incidents: Enping, Kaiping, Taishan, Zhongshan, Heshan, Xiangyu, and Xinhui, all of which were also the principal "sending" villages for Chinese living in the United States.[47] A letter from San Francisco complained that those executing land reform had taken everything—from jewelry to land—from the families of overseas Chinese, calling them landlords and tyrants and forcing them to kneel in glass or human waste, sometimes even "struggling" them to death. Another man from San Francisco expressed concern over reports that the local peasant committees were "settling accounts" with the families of overseas Chinese. Overseas Chinese worked daily from eight in the morning until eight at night in laundries and restaurants, he noted. What "accounts" could there be to settle with them? Now to be fined 10,000 yuan, and then 10,000 more later, continuing on until they were no longer able to pay . . . he wondered if such actions were the work of the new government, or if the government had lost control of the peasant committees. Another letter from California complained that when Chinese Americans unfolded letters from home, they found nothing but tales of extortion and violence, and some became so overwhelmed by the news that they could not work or lost their minds. He asked for investigations, because until the situation improved, the overseas Chinese could take no pride in the Communist victory.[48]

Officials in Beijing discovered the backlash against perceived extortion letters through communications with overseas Chinese, but American and Nationalist Chinese officials largely learned of the problems via the press. The *San Francisco Chronicle* broke the news first, and others followed. Cindy I-Fen Cheng has argued that the mainstream press (particularly the *San Francisco Chronicle* and the *New York Times*) acted as intermediaries informing the general public of the "racket" that dominated the Chinese press, substantially increasing the influence of the latter. However, the two had different ultimate goals: while the mainstream press hoped to paint Communist China in a bad light, the Chinese newspapers and the *Daily World* in particular tried to use the ransom demands to stress both the bankruptcy of the Communist government and the inhumanity of U.S. immigration laws that had created transnational families in the first place.[49]

The United States and Nationalist China, already engaged in Cold War propaganda battles, had no doubts that the ultimate responsibility for the extortions lay with Beijing and wasted no time in condemning the "extortion racket." After December 17, 1950, the United States government made sending money from the United States to the PRC for any reason illegal under the Trading with the Enemy Act—no matter whether the purpose was to buy bonds to support the new government, provide remittances to support family, or pay off a blackmailer. The United States had used this act to great effect during World War II, and the national emergency triggered by the outbreak of the Korean War and the Chinese involvement in it caused President Truman to issue an executive order putting it back into effect. According to news reports, U.S. Treasury Department officials flew out to San Francisco, as well as to other major cities, to visit the Chinese communities and collect evidence on the racket. The Nationalist Chinese government tried to step in, but its solution was to copy the evidence collected by editor Dai-Ming Lee of *Chinese World* and submit it with a protest to the United Nations—as an offshore government, the Nationalists had no way to offer direct protection for transnational families against either Communist cadres or the INS.[50]

A midyear State Department press release in 1951 commended the leaders of the Chinese community in the United States, represented by the Chinese Consolidated Benevolent Association, for offering their full assistance in stopping the flow of money, as "the only way to keep Chinese in this country from being milked dry by blackmail claims is to maintain a united position of refusal to make the demanded remittances." To further this aim, the Treasury Department announced that it would prosecute anyone caught making or facilitating remittances to China.[51] By late 1951, the FBI had investigations under way in most major American cities. Authorities were ostensibly seeking to end the "extortion racket" they claimed was destroying the Chinese American community, but they were also trying to stop the flow of currency to China via illegal remittances and investigate "the activities of any persons in the United States which may be directed at furthering this scheme on behalf of the Chinese Communists." The problem was that most Chinese remained unwilling to report actual threats or the names of people involved in the ransom schemes, and many continued to send regular remittances via Hong Kong. Because most remittances to Hong Kong were not illegal, and many Chinese Americans had relatives there as well as in China, it was not possible to know the amount of extralegal remittances entering China by this route.[52] In December 1951, Chinese Consolidated Benevolent Associations (in San Francisco, known as the Chinese Six Companies) declared that Chinese in the United States were unified against paying the ransoms and would band together. The U.S. Treasury Department cooperated as well: "By special amnesty last week the Treasury forgave violations of the ban to date 'because of the barbarous nature of the Chinese Communist government's (ransom) campaign.'"[53] That declaration came with a warning that, from now on, remittances would be prosecuted as a violation of the Trading with the Enemy Act.

The extortion scandal emerged and died away in a relatively short window of time between early 1950 and late 1952, but it had a widespread effect on overseas Chinese communities.[54] In New York, a laundryman felt forced to send his life savings of $700 to China to rescue his family, only to receive another demand for $1,000 more soon thereafter. Driven insane by worry and helplessness, he tried to stab himself with a knife, and in light of his increasingly erratic behavior, neighbors called the police. In the resulting confrontation the police shot and killed him in self-defense. The story quoted U.S. Treasury Department officials explaining that in just thirty days near the end of 1951, Chinese residents of the New York area sent around $1.5 million to Hong Kong for transfer to China, a third of which amount was "regular normal transactions." Chinese sent the rest of those funds, the story explained, after being blackmailed with the safety and freedom of their relatives in China.[55]

British Colonial Office documents also reference complaints coming from the governments of Canada, Jamaica, and Singapore, all expressing concern about letters allegedly received by their Chinese citizens and residents asking for money lest their relatives be harmed.[56] The U.S. Embassies in Bangkok and Saigon also reported that "Chinese citizens in Thailand and Vietnam are being blackmailed into donating money for the purchase of arms under threat of punitive action against relatives residing inside China."[57] In January 1952, the ROC delegation to the United Nations forwarded a copy of a letter from a large number of prominent Chinese in Singapore calling on the UN to take action to stop the extortion. The delegation claimed their letter was "representative" of notes their officials were receiving from Chinese all over the world. The statement claimed that "adopting the tactics of banditry, [the Communists] are holding our dependents and families on the Chinese mainland as hostages and forcing them, under threat of death, to ask from us urgent remittances of large sums of money to meet the Communists' extortions. We have received countless letters asking for such remittances." They provide, by way of example, the sad tale of Mr. Oong Tsao-Tuen of North Borneo, whose mother was killed by the Communists after he refused to pay a ransom of 80 million RMB. They claimed the PRC "would not spare us from their inhumanity, and would plot our destruction by draining every penny and every drop of blood from us. Such is the terror of Communism! We cannot tolerate it. We beg to the General Assembly for help."[58] Such claims could not be definitively proven, though the accusations were enough to make them a weapon in the fight for diaspora loyalties.

By 1952, U.S. officials reported that remittances to China had fallen off, and they assumed it was because the extortion scheme was "no longer profitable," especially in light of measures taken in the United States and elsewhere to prevent cash transfers to the PRC.[59] Nationalist China publicized its theory that extortions first began when remittances dwindled after collectivization polices declared overseas Chinese to be landlords and gave peasant committees control over most of the funds received by families. As a result, blackmailing overseas Chinese became the only way to ensure that the funds kept coming. The overseas Chinese eventually discovered that sending more and more of their hard-earned money to the Communists did not ensure their families' safety; instead, the ransoms increased. Eventually, they refused to be abused in this manner, and so remittances fell again.[60] The ebb and flow of remittances proved somewhat more complicated than that, though there was some truth to the Nationalists' thesis.

The PRC government had its own ideas about why remittances were falling. It named a combination of factors, such as the policy of certain reactionary governments (like the United States) of restricting remittances, along with misunderstandings about policies like land reform and class status. It also cited a growing unwillingness among the overseas Chinese families in China to write letters appealing for funds. As Western "propaganda" about the "extortion" problem gained steam, letters to relatives abroad could be mistaken for blackmail attempts or cause their family members trouble under local laws for maintaining contact with and sending funds to China.[61] The solution, they thought, was to have family members persist in sending letters to the Chinese abroad explaining the truth behind PRC policies. In spite of currency controls and economic blockades, there was still hope for a resurgence of remittances. Officials in Guangdong noted that in spite of restrictions like the U.S. Trading with the Enemy Act, when Chinese Americans chose to send money to Guangdong, the funds could always get there, whether they went through Canadian or Mexican routes, through Hong Kong relatives or agents, or by other means.[62] The public relations problem created by the existence of extortion on whatever scale, combined with missteps in land reform, had serious financial consequences for the regime, so it was important to try to counter the rumors.

Even though the accusations of extortion faded in late 1952 and early 1953, the blackmail scandal continued to be important fodder for information work in the war to win the hearts, minds, and pocketbooks of the overseas Chinese. To U.S. and ROC officials, the extortion problem was evidence of Chinese Communist duplicity and savagery. At the same time, British monitors of Chinese news sources noted that Beijing publicly claimed the extortion story to have been invented by rogue KMT agents in league with Chiang Kai-shek who wrote letters to family members abroad, forcing them to send remittances and creating misunderstandings about the nature of the PRC government. The British noted that the emergence of this "party line" on the extortions problem "suggests that the Chinese authorities are becoming worried over their loss of popularity among the Overseas Chinese communities, as a result of the latter's growing knowledge of the methods used in land reform and of the outcry caused by the policy of monetary extortion."[63] Documents from the overseas Chinese offices in Guangdong show that there were blackmail cases originating within China, and therefore they were not simply a plot cooked up by enemies of the revolution. But whether the extortion scandal was the result of an experiment in extracting foreign exchange or the byproduct of overzealous peasant committees, the outcome was the same: a loss of some of the initial post-victory surge of prestige for the PRC among overseas Chinese and a steadily declining volume of remittances.

The *China Daily News* Case

Rumors about land reform and extortion easily affected the rate of remittances to China in the early 1950s, but the other side of the coin was how the overseas Chinese "host governments" dealt with the issue of money sent back to China. Many of the countries with significant Chinese populations restricted transfers of remittances after 1950. The United States, the Philippines, and South Vietnam (after 1954) all made sending any amount of money to Communist nations illegal. Singapore, Malaya, Indonesia, Burma, and Thailand limited the amounts of money Chinese could send, to ensure that remittances went for family support, not to aid the new government.[64] Even with such restrictions, overseas Chinese still had ways to send money through Hong Kong or the black market, so such laws may have affected the total value of remittances, but they did not prevent them altogether. The effort to find and prosecute those aiding in the blackmail scheme led the FBI to the country's most prominent left-leaning Chinese language newspaper, the *China Daily News* (*CDN*).

Most of the news about Communist China—good or bad—traveled to and through Chinese American communities via the Chinese-language press. The Chinese press in the United States had long been a conduit for sharing news and ideas between otherwise isolated Chinese communities, much in the way that local gazetteers and magazines in southern China's overseas Chinese counties connected migrants to home.[65] Many newspapers, like the *Chinese Times* in San Francisco or the *Chinese Journal* in New York, had the support of the Nationalist Party or pro-Nationalist organizations, while other papers, such as San Francisco's *Chinese World*, attempted a third way, supporting neither the Nationalists nor the Communists.[66] Rarer was any paper that openly espoused support for the PRC. The left-leaning New York Chinese American newspaper the *China Daily News* attracted the attention of the FBI in mid-1950 for publishing articles recommending the purchase of "Chinese Victory Bonds" to help bolster the new PRC government. The *China Daily News* also stepped up to refute the *New York Times* article about the purchase of the bonds and the need for "reporting to the authorities," explaining that unlike the days during World War II when the ROC forced fund-drives on Chinatown and punished or ostracized anyone who did not contribute, the PRC made its bond drive strictly voluntary. Additionally, sending remittances home and instructing family to purchase the bonds was still not illegal.[67]

Because of the *CDN*'s reputation as a left-leaning newspaper, the FBI kept close watch on the paper's contents and editorial staff. New York laundryman Chin Tung Pok subscribed to the newspaper and occasionally contributed poetry under his real name, Lai Bing Chan (Chin Tung Pok was his "paper son" name, the one he used to enter the country as a derivative citizen). In his memoirs, Chin recalled that his status as a subscriber and suspected contributor earned him frequent visits from FBI agents investigating the newspaper's Communist ties. He claimed the U.S. government opened and inspected his mail from relatives in Hong Kong, listened in on his telephone calls, and searched his trash for signs of Chinese-language materials. Chin himself was not pro-Communist, but he believed the new government led to a better life for the Chinese people than they had enjoyed under any previous government. He also did not believe the paper had direct ties to the PRC, but he preferred it because he felt it was more honest and open about the real state of events in China than any of the KMT-owned newspapers available in Chinatown.[68] The FBI disagreed, and agent Roland G. Kearns reported that in September 1950, a Chinese newspaper in California carried a story that claimed the "[Taishan] District Union Conference of Overseas Chinese, Labor and Women's Organizations resolved to issue a letter of information to Chinese abroad and arrange by letter with the *China Daily News* to set up a special column explaining conditions in the Father-land and the government policy of protecting the overseas Chinese."[69] In other words, the FBI suspected the *CDN* was not simply left-leaning or sympathetic to the Communists, but that it actually was the PRC's mouthpiece in America and a vital source of Communist propaganda.

The newspaper ultimately remained independent—it never fell under the direct control of the PRC—but the fact that the Chinese government had propaganda plans for the paper can be corroborated from other sources. The September 21, 1950, issue of the *Overseas Chinese Bulletin* (*Qiao Xun*, the overseas Chinese affairs internal office newsletter) reported—much as the California newspaper being monitored by the FBI did—that a Taishan association decided that the best way to reach overseas Chinese with propaganda was through individual letter-writing campaigns, books, and frequent letters and columns in the *China Daily News* in New York. The article noted that local officials in Guangdong Province had been receiving letters from individuals in the Americas long subject to U.S. anticommunist propaganda, and they were asking "very strange" questions about whether the CCP had divided their land, would brand them as class enemies if they returned from the United States, and if their families were actually receiving the remittances they sent. As a result, the article contended, using letters and sympathetic newspapers abroad to improve understanding of the new regime would simultaneously improve relations between China and the overseas Chinese and protect a source of income.[70] Years later, PRC organizations continued to use the newspaper as a medium for distributing information. A 1954 self-study of the success rate of placing news articles sympathetic to the Communist regime in overseas Chinese newspapers reported that in February and March 1954, the *China Daily News* picked up eighteen articles put out through the PRC wire service.[71] Newspapers like the *CDN* remained important to the PRC because they allowed it to disseminate its version of news events from mainland China and compete with the far more incendiary accounts offered by KMT-controlled newspapers. That, in turn, could promote positive perceptions about CCP policies, which helped to protect the flow of remittances.

The *CDN*'s consistently anti–Nationalist China editorial policy not only attracted attention from the FBI, but also earned the paper the ire of the KMT-affiliated Chinatown leadership. On December 2, 1950, the CCBA called for a general boycott of the newspaper. Thereafter, the three largest Chinese dailies in New York, the *Chinese Journal*, the *Chinese Nationalist Daily*, and the *China Tribune*, all refused to sell their newspapers at any newsstand selling the *China Daily News*. Anonymous men also threatened the principal advertisers in the *CDN* and forced them to withdraw their commitments.[72] These two actions served to cut off a major source of income for the newspaper, but editor Eugene Moy responded with a broad appeal to the readership to donate funds to keep the paper operational. Chinese from across the Americas responded, and the donations allowed the presses to keep running.

The PRC government followed the campaign against the *CDN*. The *Overseas Chinese Bulletin* quoted at length from one editorialist who stated that the "white Chinese"—a term intended to make a parallel between overseas supporters of the losing Nationalist regime and the White Russians who fled abroad after the Russian Revolution—may try to take down the *CDN*, but of the four major Chinese-language newspapers in New York, only the *CDN* provided real information and not simply rumors and propaganda from the reactionary Nationalist faction. He went on to claim that 99 percent of the Chinese in New York far preferred the *China Daily News* to any other Chinese-language publication.[73] The accuracy of this statement was impossible to prove in light of the boycott, but the financial support from Chinese across the Western Hemisphere undoubtedly came as a surprise to those seeking to shut down the paper.

In April 1952, the effort to silence the *CDN* took a decidedly official turn. According to FBI investigations, between January and August 1951 (after the Treasury Department imposed restrictions on remittances to China), the *CDN* ran advertisements from three Chinese banks offering services for individuals wishing to remit funds to China. According to the report, "the *CDN* conspired with each of these banks to assist in a violation of [the] Trading With the Enemy Act by making available financial facilities to the Chinese residing in the United States to make unlawful remittances to Mainland China." The three banks were the Nanyang Commercial Bank Ltd., Hong Kong; the Bank of China, Overseas Chinese Service, Hong Kong; and the People's Bank of China, Taishan, China.[74] The FBI brought the information to the attorney general, who decided to make an example of the newspaper in court—apparently, the amnesty for private individuals who had sent funds to China did not apply to newspapers that facilitated them. The prosecution delivered a fifty-three-count indictment against the newspaper, which included the *CDN*'s acceptance of payment (totaling less than $330) to run the bank advertisements, along with many counts of aiding remittances to China and charges of being involved in an "international racket of extortion, murder, robbery."[75]

All the charges except those directly linked to the bank advertisements were ultimately dropped, but the potential connection to the extortion cases

cast a shadow over the trial that followed. The *New York Times* made sensational reports of "red extortions," leaving the general public with the impression that Moy was under Beijing's control. One story quoted the U.S. attorney
prosecuting the case as saying, "This cash . . . was often used to buy arms for
Chinese Reds in Korea."[76] In other words, Moy and the *CDN* were complicit
in the deaths of American soldiers. Over the course of the next three years, the
paper and its editor endured a series of trials and appeals. The government had
nothing to support the extortion charges, but the fact that the *CDN* accepted
and ran the bank ads after the prohibition against them was not in dispute.[77]
The government used the trial to determine the extent to which editor Moy
had personal knowledge of the advertisements and their implications.

Moy and two others were found guilty, a foregone conclusion, given
the evidence against them and the general mood of the court. The real
issue was the sentencing. Moy claimed repeatedly that the only reason he
was being prosecuted was that his paper's editorial line diverged from the
foreign policy of the United States. He was, in other words, just one more
victim of a society in which fervent anticommunism imperiled free speech.
The sentencing judge insisted that he had not read translations of any of
the editorials in the *CDN*, nor did he care what the political leanings of
the paper were. What did concern him, he noted, was the issue of extortion
and the role the paper played in facilitating it.

When handing down his verdict in the case and in preparation for the
sentencing, Judge Sylvester J. Ryan asked the government to prepare answers to three questions: he wanted to know if Moy personally profited from
the advertisements, if he personally helped send funds back to China, and
"whether he participated in any extortionate practices which were prac-
ticed upon any residents of Chinese extraction." The attorney representing
the U.S. government answered all three questions negatively, saying there
was no evidence of Moy's being involved in seeking profit, transferring remittances, or attempting extortion. In spite of the government's denial that
there was evidence linking the case to extortion and the defense attorney's
insistence that such rumors had no place in the sentencing, Judge Ryan
claimed the background of the Chinese extortion problem was linked to
the motive Moy and the *CDN* had for running the advertisements:

> Mr. Ross [defense counsel]: If your Honor please, there was no evidence
> in this case, either by news items or any other way, that this newspa-
> per ever had anything to do with any question of ransom or extor-
> tion, and the United States Attorney admitted it.

> The Court: I am not saying that they did, I am not saying that they did. But there is evidence in this case that these ads were all published as part of a general scheme to induce people in China, who had relatives overseas, to send money to them in the form of United States dollars.
>
> Mr. Ross: There is no such charge in this case.
>
> The Court: Whether there is a a [*sic*] charge or not is immaterial when it comes to sentence, because it bears upon their motive, and motives always are important when determining what sentence should be meted out.[78]

With this rationale firmly in place, it was clear the rumors about Chinese blackmail and extortion were so firmly entrenched in American society as to have a decided effect on a case that, by all rights, should have been unrelated. Ryan sentenced Moy to two years in jail, his codefendants to one year each, and charged the newspaper a fine of $25,000.

In 1955, the Supreme Court refused to hear an appeal of the case, although the trial court later cut the jail time for Moy to one year (the fine, however, remained at the maximum). At that time, Judge Ryan made additional comments on how he arrived at his decision for the sentence. He noted:

> I had information that came to me that a large number of Chinese residents of New York and the vicinity, most of whom come from Kuantung [*sic*] and Canton, and who have relatives over there, were subjected to extortion on a very brutal and unconscionable scale. . . .
>
> In order to accomplish this extortion, it was part of the machinery to provide a means whereby these people here in America could transmit money which might serve as ransom for their relatives who had been arrested and fined and who were being persecuted in China, and that these defendants, knowing that—and they must have known of it, being of Chinese origin themselves—deliberately published these articles in this newspaper so that it might afford a means whereby these extortions and persecutions might be carried out.[79]

Judge Ryan explained again that he had no interest in the political leanings of Mr. Moy, but that he felt the man to have "knowingly and willingly made himself a party to this systematic persecution and extortion."[80] So although there was an ongoing investigation and demonstrable persecution of the

CDN for its left-leaning editorial policies, Ryan claims the outcome of the case had more to do with the link between extortion and remittances. Of course, the link between the newspaper and the existing extortion problem might never have been made at all if the paper's editorial policy had been more conciliatory toward the United States and the ROC. The indictment of the newspaper technically came after the U.S. authorities announced that they would begin prosecuting any individual or firm involved in remittances in violation of the Trading with the Enemy Act, offering some political cover against claims of persecution.[81]

Historians largely argue that the entire court case was a witch hunt designed to shut down the Chinese Communist Party's only reliable supporter in the North America news media. Mae Ngai noted three cases of contributors to the *CDN* who were deported or stripped of citizenship during the confession program and documented rumors that members of left-leaning organizations were uniquely persecuted.[82] Renqiu Yu has observed that the men involved in the case considered it more than anything a "part of their struggle against KMT forces." In other words, the *CDN* refused to submit to extraterritorial control and was punished for it. The irony for Yu is that unlike the CCBA or the KMT, the Chinese Hand Laundry Alliance and the *China Daily News* were genuinely democratic organizations.[83] These scholarly arguments are bolstered by the fact that other Chinese were charged with violations of the Trading with the Enemy Act (like bookstore owner Louis F. Phong is San Francisco) but acquitted on all charges.[84] In his statement to the court at his sentencing, Moy himself made this claim explicitly: "It is only because our newspaper's policy differs from the policies of a certain other Chinese language newspaper and because we sometimes disagree with the present foreign policy of the Administration, that the Government agencies began to persecute us in 1951."[85] Politically motivated, the fine levied against it could have been designed to force the newspaper out of business. If that was the idea, however, someone misjudged the strength of existing support for the paper. Throughout its three-year legal battle, the operating expenses and legal fees for the *CDN* (which, given the CCBA-sponsored boycott, was no longer earning money on its publications) were paid through donations from Chinese across the United States, with contributions also coming from elsewhere in North and South America. An eleventh-hour fund drive to raise enough money to pay the fine and keep the newspaper running while Moy served his sentence collected a full $3,000 more than was needed, allowing the newspaper to stay in business.[86]

The funds came from Chinese in various communities around the country after the *CDN* printed an appeal for assistance, but also from leaders of the American Left. Ida Pruitt, who was born and raised in China as the daughter of American missionaries, wrote on behalf of herself and six other self-identified progressives in the United States to urge their friends and acquaintances to contribute to the emergency fund.[87] The ACLU never took up the case, in large part because its initial knowledge of the issue came from newspapers like the *New York Times*, all of which implied that what was at stake was an issue of fraud, not a question of civil liberties. When the news finally came out about Judge Ryan's use of "insider knowledge" of extortion and blackmail in the sentencing, it was clear that there were civil liberties violations. By that time, however, the appeals were over and the *CDN* had already successfully raised the funds to pay the fine.[88]

The conflict in New York between supporters of the KMT and the Communist-sympathizing *CDN*, with remittances at the center, was a microcosm of the larger battle between the two Chinas for the support and assistance of the overseas Chinese in the early years of the Cold War. Communist China needed to find a balance between land reform, overseas Chinese communications, and overseas Chinese remittances. The "extortion racket" that emerged in the early 1950s had some official sanction, but it did more damage to the PRC's prospects for increased remittances than it did good. For its part, Nationalist China tried to shore up support among Chinese overseas and use the tales of extortion to strike at the Communist government's claim to legitimacy. With no political control over the areas that hosted the China side of these transnational families, the Nationalists could have no hope of laying claim to the remittances, but they could and did advocate that less money be sent into Communist hands and more to Taiwan, to bolster the strength of the Nationalist military so that it might one day soon retake the mainland. The U.S. rationale behind prosecuting violators of the Trading with the Enemy Act was to prevent hostile nations like the PRC from gaining access to foreign exchange, which would then be used to purchase arms and to develop its economy. However, there is ample reason to question whether Treasury officials were not manipulated into fighting the KMT's battle to control opinions in American Chinatowns. Although the prosecution of the *China Daily News* case was, strictly speaking from the U.S. government point of view, successful, it carried the danger of being interpreted in China as yet another way in which American officials persecuted Chinese overseas.

Whether in the policing of identity and immigration status, as in the "paper sons racket," or controlling the ability of Chinese to remit funds to the enemy, the early Cold War also demonstrated the growing diversity of American Chinese communities. They included Chinese long resident in the United States and Chinese Americans; increasingly speakers of Mandarin alongside the more traditional Cantonese; an educated elite as well as a laboring class; and supporters of Nationalist China and Communist China, as well as those uninterested in the geopolitical struggle beyond its effect on their own lives. They all became subjects of larger governmental experiments with how to make these transnational families serve the foreign policy goals of the Cold War. Despite this, it was the migrants' choices themselves—in this case, what money to send, and where to send it—that created powerful connections between domestic law and foreign policy.

Chapter 6

Crossing the Bamboo Curtain

Using Refugee Policy to Support Free China

On June 6, 1950, twenty-three-year-old Zhang Shijie helped a Cantonese egg merchant carry his wares across the Lo Wu border crossing into Hong Kong, sneaking past stern British border police and arriving in the colony as a refugee. Around the same time, thirty-two-year-old Hao Cihang paid all the money he had to a guide who helped him over the barbed-wire barrier separating the colony from the Chinese town of Shenzhen. Meanwhile, both eleven-year-old Wang Guoyi and his mother, and fourteen-year-old Qian Dunxi and his cousin, took advantage of the less stringent entrance requirements in Macau and then traveled by boat from the Portuguese colony to the British one. All were part of a larger wave of people, many with personal ties to the KMT, fleeing the PRC shortly after its founding.[1]

Though it had always been porous, during the 1940s and 1950s the border between China's Guangdong Province and the British colony of Hong Kong experienced even greater than usual activity. Migration to and from Hong Kong historically increased during times of conflict, natural disaster, or special holidays, but during the Second World War refugees fled the Japanese-occupied colony only to return in force once the civil war drew to a close. After the initial wave of returning residents in the late forties, worried supporters of the KMT began to trickle into the colony. By 1950, the

Table 4. Population of Hong Kong, 1931–1971

Year	Total population	Increase
1931	840,000	
1941	1,640,000	800,000
1945	750,000	−890,000
1951	2,138,000	1,388,000
1961	3,133,131	995,131
1971	3,950,000	816,869

Source: Edvard Hambro, *The Problem of Chinese Refugees in Hong Kong* (Leiden: A. W. Sijthoff, 1955); National Census of Hong Kong.

stream had turned to a deluge, and the colonial government faced a crisis: there were simply not enough jobs, housing facilities, schools, or hospitals to support such a rapid swelling of residents.[2]

The Cold War transformed what had been a common migration pattern between the British colony on Hong Kong and the people of Guangdong Province into a hotly contested and heavily politicized battle. In 1951, both the government of Hong Kong and the PRC tried to stem the tide of the crossings by placing new controls on the traditionally open border. Hong Kong closed access to anyone traveling without PRC travel documents, and the PRC implemented a system of exit and reentry permits.[3] Some U.S. press reports condemned both measures, citing the humanitarian plight of those left trapped in mainland China without ability to flee and speculating on the harsh punishments meted out to those captured by the Hong Kong police and returned to the mainland.[4] Actually, there was a clearly visible humanitarian crisis, but it was in the colony, where basic services were limited and food supplies scarce.

Refugee policy is traditionally the one area in migration policy that is most readily associated with foreign relations. Refugee movements are both caused by foreign policy choices and can force interventions on humanitarian grounds.[5] Historians have grappled with the roles played by refugee assistance from UN-affiliated offices and nongovernmental organizations in the development and deepening of the Cold War, particularly in Europe.[6] The 1950s and 1960s refugee crisis in Hong Kong represents both a clear example of the interconnectedness of refugee policy and migration policy and a unique set of challenges that demonstrate the difference between Cold War politics in Europe and in Asia. The core question of what makes someone a migrant and what makes him a refugee was present everywhere, but in Hong Kong, the answers provided did not fall along easy "Communist versus free world" lines.

Faced with the difficulties of supporting the growing population, Hong Kong and PRC officials often saw the problem in similar terms: unauthorized border crossings, illegal migration, and scarce resources for supporting a human population both where they landed and in the towns from which they fled. The PRC needed to defuse any assumptions about the migrants fleeing a failing state and prevent the public-relations disaster of having too many more leave, but it also wanted to maintain the open border between Guangdong and Hong Kong that had long been so important to the economic well-being of South China. The government of Hong Kong fought to absorb or remove the new migrants before malcontents could be led to riot, but it wanted to do so without angering the PRC or inviting an international takeover of the colonial government. According to historian Chi-kwan Mark, U.S. involvement and the Cold War politicization of the problem drove Hong Kong officials to the conclusion that integration of refugees into Hong Kong citizens was the solution to the problem that best served the colony's interests.[7]

Outside forces, particularly the United States and Nationalist China, viewed the unfolding situation differently, looking at it through the lens of the Cold War and imprinting political values onto the humanitarian concerns. The ROC hoped to lobby on behalf of Chinese refugees in the international community, using the situation to demonstrate both the morally bankrupt nature of PRC rule and the continued legitimacy of the ROC as the one true government of China. For much of the 1950s, it tried to do all this without doing the one thing that would most alleviate the problem, which was accepting vast numbers of refugees into Taiwan. The United States similarly looked at the refugee crisis as a human tragedy that it could also use to further its public diplomacy goals in Asia. There were many opportunities in the situation in Hong Kong that could bolster American prestige and weaken Communist influence, depending on how well information campaigns could be employed. The crisis in Hong Kong also illustrated the need for the United States to develop a Far Eastern refugee policy that would demonstrate no less concern for the plight of escapees from communism than it showed in Europe, but not challenge racial restrictions on immigration at home.[8] Historian Madeline Hsu has argued that the U.S. policy response to the Chinese refugee problem, ad hoc though it may have been, helped create the impetus for more relaxed immigration laws in the lead-up to the 1965 Immigration Act, as well as establishing a new class of educated and economically secure Chinese migrants who, by entering as families, helped to build a new middle class and stereotypes of successful Asian immigrants as a "model minority."[9] Studying the administration of the immigration act, however, suggests that this outcome may have been more coincidental than intentional.

For all four governments, refugee policy became the most visible area in which migrant lives were made subject to national security and foreign policy goals. Though the human stakes were high, the geopolitical stakes were less so, and solutions to the problem were not obvious. As a result, all four governments engaged in an ad hoc, highly reactive style of policy making that frequently brought them into conflict with one another and in the process broke free of traditional Cold War alignments.

Refugee Life in Hong Kong

However they managed to make their way into Hong Kong, immediately after arrival new migrants like Zhang Shijie, Hao Cihang, Wang Guoyi, and Qian Dunxi slept at the homes of friends or acquaintances if they had them, or on the street if they did not. By mid-1950, it seemed clear to local officials that most of the arrivals would not be immediately returning to the mainland, so a number of private charities began to gather resources to aid the homeless. The Hong Kong government established a few settlement areas. Some of these, like Rennie's Mill, became populated predominantly by Nationalist Party and ROC supporters and former KMT soldiers, adding an element of political tension by their presence in the colony. None of the squatters' camps had permanent housing, as the British governor of Hong Kong at the time, Sir Alexander Grantham, recalled:

> Thousands slept in the streets, jealously guarding their pitches which constituted for them and their families a home. Most of them, though, built themselves a house—if a structure of a few square feet, made of beaten-out kerosene tins, old pieces of discarded match-boarding or old sacking can be called a house. Around them would be hundreds of similar shacks with little or no space between. Many of the squatter areas were as populous as a fair-sized town in England. From a distance they looked quite picturesque, especially those on the hill-sides, with their jumble of buildings. A visit to them, however, soon dispelled sentimentality and revealed the full horror of their squalor.[10]

Quite aside from the daily conditions of the camps, they were also fire haz-
ards, and that persistent threat provided another motivation for government
or charitable action.

After a short time shuffling between makeshift camps, Zhang Shijie was
part of the first group sent to the Rennie's Mill camp.[11] The camp administration provided meal tickets for two meals a day, but only early arrivals
received the tickets. People who came later, like Hao Cihang, had to buy
tickets from another migrant who had found work and no longer relied on
the free meals, or who had come up with another way to eat. Meal tickets
were scarce and valuable, but although the meals they offered included rice
with eel, beans, peanuts, or sardines, sometimes refugees found less desirable items mixed in, such as sand and rat droppings. Without a meal ticket,
one strategy was to trek to Central Hong Kong—a long trip from the
resettlement camps that were not connected to public transportation—and
get discarded bread crusts from Western restaurants, which refugees would
mix with water to make a kind of porridge. Strict curfews and regulations
against cooking, lighting lamps, or using candles made it hard to prepare
food in the camps.[12]

Before late in the 1950s, aid came primarily through private church
organizations, which held services in the camps and provided assistance to
their parishioners. Wang Guoyi recalls that each church group would have
different things to offer at different times, so families divided up and joined
different churches. Although often very helpful and well-intentioned—he
remembered beautiful clothing arriving every Christmas and "relief packages" that would get as much as twenty Hong Kong dollars if refugees opted
to resell them to nonbelievers—occasionally the European and American
churches sent items without reference to the Chinese context. Wang remembered a church receiving a large block of what the Chinese presumed
to be soap, which was immediately cut into pieces and distributed among
the parishioners. His family's attempt to wash clothes with the European
soap was a complete failure, however, as not only did it not produce any
bubbles, but it also made the clothes smell far worse than they did before
washing. Eventually, they brought the defective offering back to the church
and learned that it wasn't soap at all: it was cheese.[13]

Over time, the migrants created community associations, built roads,
started ferry businesses to connect the camps to the city, and established
schools, all with limited assistance from a Hong Kong government concerned that offering aid would only encourage new arrivals. Both Wang
Guoyi and Qian Dunxi attended Rennie's Mill schools, with Wang Guoyi

eventually testing into college in Taiwan. Zhang Shijie became a teacher and later the principal of one of those schools, and he later recalled the tears he cried the first time they raised the blue and white flag of the Kuomintang over the school building. He remembered the camp as a community of people very willing to help each other, as long as no one spoke for the Communists or criticized the Nationalists, which in those parts would have incited a riot.[14] Although many—perhaps most—of the residents of the Rennie's Mill camp hoped to resettle in Taiwan, only those with personal ties, government connections, or military experience actually had the chance to go. The question of what to do with the rest of them drew international concern.

The UN Mandate and the Term "Refugee"

Private aid could take the residents of Hong Kong only so far, so to address the issue of the growing population fully, the colony would need international support. At the center of all debates about international aid was the term "refugee." That these migrants had crossed over an international border was not in question, and the fact that some were fleeing from the possibility of persecution or political violence seemed undeniable. But both timing and motivation influenced how they were classified. Did it matter if they arrived in the colony before October 1, 1949? Was there a difference between those who came for economic as opposed to political reasons, and if so, how could these motives even begin to be determined? After arrival, it generally became impossible to distinguish the newcomers from the rest of the bustling Chinese population, especially from those in the city who were impoverished for other reasons. Strictly humanitarian groups argued that the semantics were unimportant, as long as a crisis existed, but refugee status mattered for both UN involvement and outward migration from Hong Kong.[15]

The UN High Commissioner for Refugees (UNHCR) first wrestled with the plight of the Chinese of Hong Kong in early 1951, and again in early 1952, when Nationalist Chinese representatives raised the issue. Seeking international support for Chinese refugees fit with the ROC's broader policy to represent the interests of overseas Chinese, and claiming the right to speak for them to the UN served as a reminder of the ROC's claim to recognition. The Nationalist representatives argued that the UNHCR and other affiliated organizations expended time and attention on refugees, escapees, and defectors crossing from the Soviet Eastern Bloc into the free countries of Western Europe, but they essentially ignored the anticommunist border crossers in Hong Kong. In their appeal to the United Nations, ROC officials implied that this was because the UN had a racist tendency to place a higher value on European lives than Asian ones. The fact that continuing International Refugee Organization programs to aid Europeans escaping from China in the wake of 1949 did not extend to Chinese escapees seemed to support these claims.[16] Additionally, historian Glen Peterson has argued that the UNHCR had its own interest in considering Hong Kong: the organization did not initially attract support—or, more critically, funding—from the United States, but engaging on an issue of anticommunist refugees in Asia might help it do so.[17]

UN intervention on behalf of refugees in Hong Kong was not simply a matter of expressing interest or even allocating the funds, however. There was a legal concern about whether the Chinese arriving in Hong Kong fell under the UN mandate for refugees, and the resources of the UNHCR were far too scarce to redirect to a swelling population that did not fit the parameters for their use. To be classified as a bona fide refugee by the international organization, migrants had to have fled a genuine fear of persecution in their country of origin and/or be afraid of persecution if they were to return. Additionally, refugees had to be "unable to avail [themselves] of the protection of the government of the country of [their] nationality."[18] With the government of China divided, and both the PRC and ROC claiming to be the only legitimate power, the issue of whether the refugees could seek assistance from their government was unclear. If their government was the PRC, then perhaps they were refugees; if their government was the ROC, in theory they could still appeal to it for support.

To settle this question, in 1953 the UN appointed a commission to travel to Hong Kong and report back on the situation. The United States and the UK both expressed some concern about the mission, worrying about the political implications. The UK Foreign Office preferred that the chief of the survey mission not be an American, lest the entire project become enfolded in the larger U.S. propaganda projects to promote the free world and anticommunism in Asia, something that could cause future problems for the Hong Kong government in its relations with the PRC. On the other hand, having Americans involved might make substantial U.S. aid more forthcoming.[19] The United States preferred private donors to fund the mission, and expressed related concerns that the fact of the survey alone would raise expectations for a solution impossibly high. Instead, the UN should try to determine what obstacles prevented migration out of Hong Kong, and then work on eliminating those obstacles.[20] The UN finally settled on Dr. Edvard Hambro, a Norwegian lawyer and political scientist who was at the time registrar of the International Court of Justice, to lead the survey.

Hambro and his assistants spent three months in Hong Kong in the summer of 1954, and on their return to Geneva they submitted a report detailing the situation in the colony and their opinion of the UN's role in addressing it. Hambro found that in terms of timing and ideology, some genuine political refugees had reached the colony—he estimated around 385,000 out of the 500,000 recent arrivals could be so classified.[21] But the confirmation of fleeing political persecution was only half the issue—the other half was the question of whether the UN was entitled to use its resources to help such refugees. Here, China's divided government created an impossible situation. Because the UN recognized Nationalist China, it saw no reason why "refugees" outside of the Chinese mainland could not appeal to their government for help. But because the refugees were in Hong Kong, which along with the UK recognized Communist China, perhaps they could not appeal to the Nationalist Chinese government to aid them after all. This created a situation steeped in irony: the very countries that preferred, for political purposes, to see the Hong Kong immigrant Chinese as refugees were the ones that legally could not class them as such (the ROC and the United States), whereas the countries that far preferred to treat the Chinese as economic migrants (the UK and Hong Kong) were the ones whose recognition of the PRC gave them refugee status.

Hambro was not responsible for making a final determination, but he suggested that, in his opinion, the "political immigrants" of Hong Kong did not fall under the UN mandate. At the same time, he believed that the dictates of humanitarianism required outside governments and organizations to help with the human crisis in the colony. Although the UN might recognize the ROC as the government with the right to protect the Chinese immigrants, there was no doubt that the ROC had no way of actually doing so in a territory that recognized the PRC.[22] Oddly enough, the one party whose opinions and preferences were not consulted in this process was the government of Hong Kong, which proved less than enthusiastic about the prospect of UN intervention in its internal affairs. Officials there expressed concern that they had no fair or reasonable means to distinguish between refugees and the rest of the population, all of whom struggled to maintain a livelihood in the face of the population boom.[23] Hambro's commission made its report, but the UN did not make any formal effort in Hong Kong until the report went before the General Assembly, which in 1957 finally recommended that efforts be made to raise funds for Hong Kong refugees, even though they did not fall under the UNHCR mandate.[24]

With the new immigrants' legal standing unsettled, Hambro suggested that the crisis, like any other refugee problem, had only three solutions: repatriation, resettlement, or integration. Repatriation was the least likely of the three options. There were no legal controls or government policies (either in Hong Kong or the PRC) preventing any of the refugees from returning to China at any moment. Voluntary repatriation was therefore always an option, just not a popular one. Involuntary repatriation—that is, the deportation of refugees as "illegal immigrants"—was politically untenable in the early to mid-1950s. Refugees had escaped communism, exercising their right under international law to flee persecution. The United Kingdom, the United States, and the ROC had all committed to the idea of nonforcible repatriation in Asia over and over in the 1950s, announcing that POWs in the Korean War would choose their destinations and demanding that nationals locked behind closed borders be sent home at their own will and discretion. For as long as the local government considered new arrivals in Hong Kong refugees and not illegal immigrants, they could count on not being sent back.[25]

Removing repatriation left two options for Hong Kong: resettlement and integration. Hambro's survey of the immigrants found that of the total number of refugees, 0.4 percent were willing to return to China, 52.5 percent hoped to settle permanently in Hong Kong, and 39.8 percent preferred to emigrate. The remaining 7.3 percent claimed indifference.[26] Of the refugees willing to emigrate, 70.4 percent asked to be resettled in Taiwan or on the offshore islands still held by the ROC government. Within the remainder, most preferred the United States or elsewhere in Asia, and some indicated no preference (see table 5).[27] To a certain extent, then, the refugee problem centered on the extent to which the governments in Taiwan and Hong Kong were willing to accept and integrate the refugees. With a significant number indicating a desire to resettle in the United States, and American officials already accepting European refugees by the thousands (not to mention enjoying significantly better resources for absorbing new migrants than either Taiwan or Hong Kong), U.S. refugee policy also inevitably became an issue.

Table 5. Resettlement preferences of postwar Hong Kong immigrants

Preferred destination	Percentage	Number of refugees
Taiwan	52.2	461,970
Offshore islands controlled by the ROC	18.2	161,070
United States	14.2	125,670
East and Southeast Asia	10.4	92,040
Latin America	1.8	15,930
British Commonwealth	0.6	5,310
Other destinations	0.2	1,770
No stated preference	14.1	124,785

Source: Hambro, *Problem of Chinese Refugees*, 153, 186.

The Far East Refugee Program

The U.S. response to the Hong Kong crisis came in two forms: through support for nongovernmental organizations engaged in aid and resettlement work, and by offering a small number of visas for refugees to enter the United States. The two projects were closely related, and as time wore on, the State Department increasingly relied on private organizations to process visa applicants. The relationship proved quite symbiotic, as government aid provided the resources necessary for the organizations to work, and the private groups provided political cover for the United States when the preferred policies were less than popular.

In the early 1950s, American refugee efforts were increasingly pulling away from UN programs and forging their own course. In Europe, the International Rescue Committee became the vanguard for U.S. efforts, especially for aid to scholars and scientists fleeing Eastern Europe. Already engulfed by the European crisis, the committee's executive director David Martin suggested a new organization to focus on Asia. An ad hoc committee created by Ernest Moy (a Chinese American with close ties to the KMT) found Congressman Walter Judd (R-Minnesota), a onetime medical missionary in China with a lifelong interest in Asia, to lead it.[28] It would evolve to become Aid Refugee Chinese Intellectuals Inc. ARCI, as it was called, has received attention from scholars in recent years in part because it was the only nonreligious organization operating in Hong Kong, but even more because of the overlap between its leadership at the pro-Nationalist "China lobby."[29] Unlike the National Lutheran Council, for example, ARCI was so well-connected that it became hard to determine where ARCI stopped and U.S. government actions began.

In Hong Kong, ARCI's decision to focus on intellectuals was largely practical, made out of concern for limited funds, a sense that scholars would adapt less well to life in the squatter camps or jobs involving menial labor, the relative importance of intellectuals to the success of the new Communist government and therefore the necessity of offering them an alternative path, and the fact that many Chinese intellectuals fleeing communism had been trained in American universities.[30] In introducing the new organization to Congress, Judd explained to his fellow congressmen that those Chinese who recognized the moral bankruptcy of the Communist regime "looked to the West for freedom," but that the United States "cannot be proud of the way we received them. . . . They voluntarily exiled themselves into a strange land where they are ignored by the very people who once pleaded for their loyalty and friendship."[31] The new organization relied heavily on a narrative of historical racism to raise funds and promote the importance of its activity to a Cold War audience. Fund-raiser Harold Oram would appeal to every major philanthropic organization in the United States with a caution that their support was needed "to make clear that American philanthropy does not discriminate against Chinese."[32] ARCI also argued that its work, which would come to include helping resettle refugee intellectuals in Taiwan, represented an important project in building up the island's defenses and keeping it in "friendly hands."[33]

The argument that there were clear foreign policy reasons for being seen helping Asian refugees, and not just Europeans, also hit home with people like Edwin Martin, an assistant (and future director) of the Office of Chinese Affairs in the State Department. His arguments and those made by his colleagues at State in favor of U.S. action hit similar notes to those of ARCI: he also expressed concern with U.S. failure to offer aid to the migrants, though less out of humanitarian anxiety and more out of a sense that these individuals would lead the future, democratic China after the expected fall of the Communist regime. For the sake of U.S. relations with that once-and-future China (given the dearth of productive American ties with the contemporary mainland), the United States needed to aid and accept Chinese refugees.[34] On a more immediate level, he and other State officials saw some danger in Chinese refugees in Hong Kong being transformed into "a symbol of the alleged neglect of the United States for refugees and migration problems in the Far East during a period when unprecedented resources were being devoted to the alleviation of similar conditions in Europe and the Near East."[35] Rather than allowing the refugees to be used in a Communist propaganda attack against the United States, the West needed to turn their presence into an advantage. On the most basic level, "there were important political and psychological advantages to be gained for the United States in adopting a program for aiding escapees in Asian areas."[36] Early efforts to help included offering assistance to a select number of especially worthy individuals through the China Area Aid Act, as well as a program through the United States International Information and Education Exchange to employ very highly qualified Chinese refugees in the production and dissemination of its propaganda in the Far East.[37] The ROC government itself and the Free China Relief Program, an organization operating through the ROC government but with extensive U.S. financial support, also arranged for some 147,768 Chinese to resettle in Taiwan from Hong Kong and Macao between 1949 and early 1954. The bulk of these migrants, some 93,176 of them, arrived in 1949 or 1950; the rate of resettlement to Taiwan dropped drastically after that.[38]

In 1952, ARCI began work to help set up programs that fell along similar lines to the recommendations in the Hambro report: limited programs to aid refugees or provide them with a livelihood in Hong Kong, expansive efforts to resettle as many more as possible in Taiwan, and attempts where possible to obtain visas for others to move on to other destinations, including the United States. In anticipation of these efforts, the organization registered more than twenty thousand refugees and their families, beginning with overly expansive definitions of who qualified as an "intellectual"—definitions that would come back to haunt ARCI.[39] Despite an ambitious agenda, ARCI suffered from a perennial lack of funds, and faced an American public inundated with other requests and already suffering from donor fatigue.[40] ARCI continued to raise funds among the American public for as long as its organization was in operation, but eventually a grant via the expansion of the Mutual Security Act to include anticommunist refugees helped to keep ARCI afloat before government funds began quietly taking over operating budgets for the rest of the decade. By the time ARCI ended its work, 92 percent of its budget came from U.S. government sources.[41] The funding sources of ARCI were kept quiet in the colony to allow both the organization and the Hong Kong government some degree of political cover. ARCI's supporters were prominent KMT advocates, but if it also became publicly known as a U.S. government-funded organization, Communist China could demand that Hong Kong allow the PRC reciprocal access to the refugee population.[42]

With at least short-term funding in place and facing thousands of registrants, ARCI's Hong Kong office began efforts to aid them. One ambitious project turned refugees into piece workers of woven bamboo mats and screens then sold in the United States. Under the title "Chinese Refugee Development Organization," it was the only ARCI-originated project to become self-supporting.[43] Other efforts to put refugees to work faced apprehension from the Hong Kong government, so ARCI focused its attention on resettlement. The Republic of China continued to accept several thousand escapees each year, and ARCI proved so central to the process that the temporary housing facility for new arrivals in Taipei was nicknamed "Juddville." But Taiwan would never be the sole solution, as it was already overpopulated, and concerns over security and stability kept its borders fairly consistently closed to new migrants or those without family already on the island. There seemed to be little chance of any of the countries of Southeast Asia taking Chinese refugees, as most had already curtailed Chinese immigration and were struggling to come to terms with the presence of their own large Chinese minority populations.[44] Some were even producing Chinese refugees of their own.

Before 1965, U.S. immigration law had no standing provision for the regular acceptance of refugees.[45] Instead, the decision to take in those fleeing war, disaster, or persecution was made on an ad hoc basis, usually in the form of private bills in Congress, or for large groups through a presidential directive or the initiative of the Senate or House of Representatives in passing legislation like the Displaced Persons Act of 1948. The so-called Escapee Program intended to expand programs for admitting refugees while making use of them in a much more systematic way in information work, tying U.S. refugee policy more explicitly to the Cold War. Still, these early American efforts to aid refugees and displaced persons consistently focused on Europe, or occasionally Europeans in Asia.[46]

In 1953, the Congress passed another Euro-centric program: the Refugee Relief Act (RRA). This time, the law made two hundred thousand non-quota visas available to European refugees and escapees for resettlement in the United States, but thanks in large part to the efforts of Congressman Judd, it also designated an additional five thousand visas for residents of areas under American consular jurisdiction in the Far East. Of these five thousand visas, two thousand were reserved for Chinese with passports endorsed by the government of the Republic of China.[47] Worldwide, the implementation of the RRA proved fraught with administrative difficulties. Historian Carl Bon Tempo has argued that the RRA itself demonstrated a triumph of restrictionism over liberalism, in large part because of how it was implemented through the Security and Consular Affairs (SCA) section of the State Department. (SCA had also been responsible for investigating suspected communists in the State Department and Chinese document fraud before and during the confession program.)[48] As a result, each application for a refugee visa involved a preliminary evaluation, health investigation, and a security investigation. This last requirement was the closest most European refugees ever came to understanding what it was like to be an exclusion-era Chinese immigrant: they were put through an extensive interview process that called on them to account for every aspect of their lives and families.[49] The heart of the security screening was to ensure that migrants were not communists, but the thorough investigations excluded more applicants than they admitted in the first few years of implementation.[50]

Ironically, U.S. visa procedures for Chinese had long been so intrusive and nearly impossible that issuing the RRA visas actually proved slightly easier for U.S. officials than regular immigration visas or certification of derivative citizenship. The newly appointed administrators of the Far East Refugee Program (FERP) descended upon the Hong Kong consulate to carry out their task but quickly ran afoul of long-term consular officers in the U.S. consulate. The bureaucratic infighting that resulted slowed down the efforts to process visas. Halleck Rose, a FERP investigations officer, complained that consular officers automatically assumed "every Chinese seeking to enter the United States is a fraud."[51] He went on to observe that the presumption of guilt meant security investigations were not only intense but frequently heavy-handed enough to drive anyone not already there into the arms of the communists. They were "lurid affairs where every scrap of correspondence in the home is piled into sacks and taken away to be examined in the fraud office. The 'visits' are made with the approval of the Hong Kong police but they have not endeared us to the Chinese community."[52] FERP officials found consular methods distasteful, but that wasn't the only problem. The refugee law and immigration law approached standards of evidence in radically different ways. The two sides were "directly opposed to each other in their objectives. [The FERP officers] are seeking to facilitate the entry into the US of qualified Chinese refugees and the regular program is, in effect, seeking to restrict Chinese immigration to the United States."[53]

With only five thousand visas for all of East Asia, it seemed likely that the visas would be snatched up quickly. In reality, FERP officers struggled to fill the slots. Beyond the security screening, two other requirements slowed the process in Hong Kong. The first was the mandate that all applicants have a certificate of reentry, and the second was that the Nationalist Chinese government endorse the passports of all refugees applying for the two thousand visas earmarked for Chinese. The reentry visa—already emerging as a difficult issue in the deportation and repatriation efforts then under way—required that refugees who were by definition people without a home have a government willing to accept them back. The overladen Hong Kong government proved deeply reluctant to issue such permits, and few refugees in other parts of Asia found them easier to come by. Eventually the British acquiesced to the request, but their reluctance made it all the more important to maintain careful screening procedures to ensure FERP granted visas only to people unlikely to be sent back in the first place.[54]

Even if a refugee passed the Hong Kong government's test to receive a reentry permit and the FERP investigation to receive a visa, to use one of the two thousand visas reserved for the Chinese he still needed an ROC passport. New regulations passed by the Nationalist government in 1954 mandated that refugees have a guarantor in the United States to help with finding a job and housing. Additionally, refugees required proof of refugee status, documents certifying good health, and a report on where the applicant had been and what he had been doing in the last two years. All these items were then reviewed by a committee composed of one representative each from the Ministry of the Interior, the Ministry of Foreign Affairs, the Overseas Chinese Affairs Commission, and the Taiwan Public Security Bureau. Together, they screened the applicants.[55] Some of this material duplicated the requirements of the RRA, but some proved even more extensive. To speed things up, the committee accepted statements of refugee status from ROC consulates, respected overseas Chinese organizations, and nongovernmental organizations like ARCI, but the process proved as cumbersome as the regular immigrant passport procedures. In both cases there were vast numbers of applicants but only a small number of visas available, and in both cases there were complaints about how slowly the process moved and that the ROC spent too much time investigating and selecting the most desirable emigrants from the standpoint of its foreign policy goals in the United States. As with the U.S. immigration quota, the Nationalist government viewed refugee visas as an opportunity to shape American Chinatowns into stronger, better respected, and more welcomed communities that offered unconditional support to the Republic of China. The Chinese consulates in the United States reported that the major Chinese American and overseas Chinese organizations were growing frustrated with the government's excessive caution and sending them appeals for a more streamlined process,[56] but in the meantime most Chinese preferred to apply directly to their local U.S. consulate for admission as a Chinese refugee without a ROC-endorsed passport. RRA procedures might be difficult, but they were still easier than dealing with Taipei.

With the deadline for issuing refugee visas looming, organizations like ARCI stepped in to help potential migrants ease their way through the complicated investigations process. Alongside such organizations as China Institute in America, the Church World Service, the National Lutheran Council, and the War Relief Services of the National Catholic Welfare Conference,[57] ARCI helped to screen applicants before their names went up before consular or ROC officials, leading to a higher success rate. They also negotiated with the ROC to give preferential treatment to ARCI registrants, a program successful enough that the first Chinese refugee family admitted to the United States under the RRA, Paul and Pricilla Liu and their two children, received their visas through ARCI.[58] Part of its success was its conservative approach to the RRA visas. After having initially made the mistake of over-registering and over-promising, ARCI employees worked to select out only the candidates most likely to receive universal approbation and, importantly, who already had extensive contacts in the United States to help ease their transition.[59]

The Refugee Relief Act was due to expire in 1956, so the cutoff date for applications was in June of that year. As of October 1955, ROC documents indicate that only 570 complete applications had been received. Of these, 390 had been processed, and the other 180 were still being investigated. It was therefore very doubtful that all the visas would be used, which only served to increase the interest in ARCI intervention to help move the program along. The U.S. consulate in Hong Kong had already received six thousand applications from individuals without ROC passports, in the process "having gained the not entirely unjustified impression that too much red tape is involved" in applying in Taiwan.[60] American accounting painted an even direr picture: as of February 1956, the United States had issued 1,747 visas for the region, only 280 of which it issued on ROC passports, though it had another 9,000 applications still in the pipeline. The United States encouraged all Chinese refugees to apply for ROC passports, but the rigid screening process in Taipei has scared many away from doing so. U.S. officials recognized that the elaborate investigation process was "designed to give an endorsed passport to the higher caliber Chinese ethnic refugee seeking to migrate to the United States."[61] In other words, the ROC saw the same political opportunity in the refugee program that it did in quota immigration: the chance to improve American perceptions of its government and people through careful selection and screening of emigrants.

Given the difficulties in processing, FERP looked beyond Hong Kong for visa recipients. In the mid-1950s, the INS reported an increase in refugee applications from Chinese facing deportation orders but looking to stay in the United States. This was because in order to receive a stay of deportation under standard immigration law, an immigrant had to prove that he or she faced physical persecution upon arrival in the country of destination, but to qualify for a visa under the RRA, an immigrant or refugee needed only to fear physical persecution in the homeland, not guarantee it. Anyone who opposed communism might reasonably fear persecution upon returning to a Communist country, so some of the Chinese already in the United States used RRA visas to adjust their immigration status.[62] In many cases, students who traveled to the United States on nonimmigrant student visas, often with Nationalist government support, made use of the RRA to adjust their status and remain rather than repatriating back to a mainland now controlled by the Communists.[63] Other visas ended up in the hands of Korean War orphans, victims of natural disasters in Japan, and other East Asian migrants who did not always fit the stereotypical definition of a refugee.

By 1956, Walter Judd reported to Congress that there had been 20,209 applications for the 5,000 visas in Asia, and to date, 3,948 visas had been granted before the deadline.[64] Many of the unused visas from the RRA were reallocated, especially to Japanese agricultural laborers sponsored by large California plantations, something much less in line with the philosophical origins of the act but justified within the INS on the grounds that poverty could breed communism in Japan, too.[65] After the Soviet invasion of Hungary in 1956, the United States responded quickly and accepted more than thirty-eight thousand Hungarian refugees, so to promote U.S. credibility in Asia, stepping up on behalf of Hong Kong refugees was also necessary. In 1957, the Refugee-Escapee Act would act as a reprieve of sorts and allow thousands who applied under the RRA but who could not be processed in time the opportunity to get a visa.[66]

Like the RRA itself, ARCI's record was mixed. The failure of ARCI to live up to its initial promises of solutions and resettlement opened a door for attacks on American commitment to the Chinese people and PRC propaganda about the organization as a possible front for American and ROC spies in Hong Kong.[67] It also faced criticism from the Hong Kong government, which opposed any efforts by government or private organizations (other than the International Red Cross) to help the refugees with anything other than resettlement abroad, and ARCI dabbled on more than one occasion with direct relief. British officials were often concerned about parity, that for each American organization handing out relief in Hong Kong, it would have to permit a PRC organization to operate as well or face backlash in other areas of Anglo-Chinese cooperation.[68] Already the "Berlin of the East," Hong Kong feared that its squatter camps had the potential to turn very quickly into the new Cold War battleground. In terms of stability within the colony, efforts to aid recent escapees from the PRC but not long-destitute residents—some of whom had suffered greatly under Japanese rule—had the potential to cause not simply dissatisfaction, but actual riots.[69]

Watching the drama of the refugee crisis in Hong Kong play out from a more detached perspective, PRC officials tended to be split between calling for the traditional right of entry for Chinese into Hong Kong and saying "good riddance" to the retreating backs of those who fled into the colony.[70] The internal government's overseas Chinese affairs bulletin *Qiao Xun* reported on the U.S. program for offering refugee visas to individuals coming from Communist countries, calling it a scheme to recruit reactionaries, train them, and then re-release them into their original countries to try to topple the governments. That publication also noted that many Chinese in the United States hoped to use the act to bring over family members (not "refugees") from Hong Kong, but that they were growing increasingly frustrated by requirements that they gain ROC government approval to do so. The PRC interpreted the approval process as just one more way for the Chiang Kai-shek government to manipulate the overseas Chinese and blackmail them, and by this point, they had amassed many such examples. The article also claimed that "counterrevolutionary" leaders in American Chinatowns were unhappy about the law because it would allow some Chinese to adjust their status, making it impossible for the KMT-supporting local leaders to exploit these individuals' alien status to force them to follow orders in the future. To the PRC, rumors of a black market for ROC passports in Hong Kong meant there was yet another way for Chinese emigrants to face dangers and personal loss at the hands of the ROC.[71]

Politicizing Refugee Lives

Simply resettling the refugees was one project, but there were larger gains to be made by both advertising assistance programs and using refugee information. The United States combined its aid packages with an information program that promoted its goals in the region. One way the United States joined the two was by formally extending its Escapee Program to Hong

Kong and Taiwan in 1954. The program also served as a clearinghouse for a variety of private organizations doing work among the refugees: ARCI was one of them, of course, but also the National Catholic Welfare Conference, the Church World Service, the Lutheran World Federation, and the ROC's own Free China Relief Association. In addition to resettlement aid, housing projects, and vocational training, the Escapee Program provided funds for interviewing refugees about the real conditions on mainland China, undertaken with the hope that the information gleaned from such discussions would be useful for intelligence and propaganda goals in Asia.

The Escapee Program also provided a means through which to broadcast information about the refugees to the Chinese mainland. Such programs aimed to demonstrate "concrete and factual results of the negative and oppressive aspects of Communism," along with the "knowledge that escape is possible." The broadcasts would also counter PRC propaganda about the United States, "emphasizing the friendship which is held for the captive populations of China by the Free World."[72] Information programs stressing that the majority of refugees preferred resettlement in Taiwan also seemed useful in programs promoting the ROC as an "alternative" to the PRC among the Chinese in both Hong Kong and Southeast Asia, as "the work of the program serves generally to enhance the prestige of the free world among the Chinese population in Hong Kong, particularly through the use of U.S. voluntary agency channels, and to strengthen Sino-American ties in Taiwan and among the overseas Chinese."[73] The one thing the Escapee Program in China did not do was encourage defection—it was still far too easy for Chinese to move across the border, and the resources of Hong Kong were already far too strained.[74]

The information programs developed by the U.S. Information Service (USIS) similarly took advantage of two clear opportunities in the Escapee Program. The first was the chance to receive new and accurate information from recent arrivals from the mainland. American interviewers showed particular interest in two groups of interviewees: intellectuals who could comment on thought reform, state control of information, and indoctrination; and peasants who could report on land reform and rural cooperatives. USIS also sought out specific information on traditional hometowns and villages of Southeast Asian overseas Chinese because it could use that information to demonstrate the problems with sending back remittances, returning to China, or doing anything to support the Communist regime.[75]

Every once in a while, the Hong Kong consulate happened upon a particularly good story for such information work. Lin Hsing-yu studied in the United States on a KMT-sponsored grant and worked for a time in the New York consulate general of the ROC. He described his own politics as "progressive," and he described how while in the United States he began receiving letters from like-minded friends in China telling him "the motherland needs you." In 1952, he returned to China. After a brief period in which party officials feted and welcomed him, the government gave him a job with a low salary, then denied his subsequent requests to change jobs, marry, or visit his family in Guangzhou, then in the midst of land reform. When he finally did visit his parents, he found that they "had been reduced to virtually no land and were living in a small one and one-half room building that was virtually a hovel." While in town, Lin also unwittingly met with old friends now deemed "politically questionable" and as a result found his journey interrupted by eight days of detention and interrogation. On a subsequent visit to Guangzhou, he visited a town on the Hong Kong border, hoping to find a route for escape, but the police immediately suspected him, and he landed back in jail. He made two more attempts to flee in the following years, one by boat and one by bus, but both attempts failed. He finally succeeded with the aid of acquaintances in Hong Kong in March 1955.[76] In interviews in Hong Kong, Lin expressed concern about having his story used by USIS, but he suggested ways to change the identifying details so that his complaints against the PRC could receive wider coverage without implicating him directly (he planned to write and publish a book on his adventure, so Consul General Everett Drumright speculated that he might have been less fearful for his life and more interested in saving the juicier details for a later payoff).[77] After arrival in Hong Kong, he received assistance through ARCI and applied for a visa to return to the United States under the RRA.

The Escapee Program presented a second opportunity for propaganda by providing relief for the refugees in the form of food, housing, clothing, and education that could then be reported upon internationally, demonstrating U.S. concern for Asian refugees from communism and the region as a whole.[78] After a fire in the squatter settlement of Shek Kip Mei, Grantham, the colonial governor, recalled that the United States immediately offered aid for the more than fifty thousand refugees who had lost their homes, an action that he claimed forced the British government into allotting funds for the situation first. Each time a disaster like this occurred, funds and assistance came from both the United States and the PRC, demonstrating that regardless of the status of the refugees, both sides of the Cold War contest thought there were potential public relations gains in humanitarian aid.[79]

今日美國

版出日八十月二年〇五九一　　　　第 九 期

Figure 4. This issue of *America Today* from 1950 included a history of Washington, D.C., as well as an article by Hannah Arendt on concentration camps as a "necessary feature of a totalitarian society." USIA, National Archives.

第一四七期

今日世界

第三屆亞運會來去的龍脈
「阿美娜」，受難人手親像某，其
「民主人士」的悲慘下場
鐘就活堂影登后寶座，漫畫笑話

Figure 5. An issue of *World Today* from 1955, featuring a new Cantonese actress and articles on the PRC's anti-rightist campaign and a new film from "Free China." USIA, National Archives.

In the early 1950s, USIS propaganda itself became a form of relief for refugees. The consulate made copies of popular magazines and publications like *World Today* and *America Today* available to refugees, who could then take them to established neighborhoods in the colony and sell them for profit. *World Today*, a Chinese-language magazine translated and published by USIS, started out as a giveaway and evolved into a paid magazine with a region-wide circulation of one hundred thousand. It eventually (according to its USIS sponsors) took in enough money to pay for its own production costs.[80] During the 1950s, USIS offices distributed the magazine to Chinese-speaking populations across Asia, and starting in 1953 used it to promote support for the government of the Republic of China, alongside its regular content of entertainment news, quizzes, and stories about the United States.[81] Qian Dunxi and his cousin used the money they earned selling U.S. propaganda to raise the capital necessary to sell newspapers (which had a lower profit margin and required more seed money, but which were easier to sell) and finally worked their way up to their own newspaper and magazine stand. That, in turn, provided them enough money to find a house and, eventually, attend school. Wang Guoyi also profited from U.S. publications in the colony, by selling for a small fee, in areas far removed from the American consulate, tracts that the United States otherwise gave away for free.[82] This system had numerous benefits: the United States received free circulation of its publications and market penetration among its target audience of intellectuals in the refugee population, and young refugees found work that enabled them to endure the difficult life of new arrivals in the colonies.

The ROC made its own use out of individual refugees' stories. As an "intellectual," Zhang Shijie registered with ARCI for resettlement in Taiwan. On October 23, 1953, he arrived at Jilong (Keelung) Harbor in Taiwan with two to three hundred other refugees from the Rennie's Mill camp. Because he had been a leader among the refugee group, girls holding bouquets of flowers and reporters and photographers from several newspapers met him at the docks.[83] With his anticommunist rhetoric and absolute conviction that there was no government for China other than the ROC, along with his willingness to retell his story, Zhang Shijie and others like him were a gift to the officials in the U.S. and ROC governments charged with spreading the ideals of the free world across Asia.

American eagerness to exploit Chinese refugees for Cold War gains often placed U.S. officials in direct conflict with the government of Hong Kong, and ultimately with their British ally. Hong Kong was in a precarious position. Not only did it depend on the mainland for access to necessities like drinking water, but it was also vulnerable to security threats, both from the new Communist regime striking out against imperialism, and from subversion from within. But to all this, Chi-kwan Mark has noted, Hong Kong also added the "American threat." When its consulates closed on the mainland, the United States converted the Hong Kong consulate into a listening post, or as Mark has it, the American "informal empire" in Hong Kong.[84] Both covert actions and routine visa processing had caused the consulate to swell to untenable numbers early in the decade, and its activities had to be held in check by the local authorities, because of the colony's precarious position.[85] Ultimately, Mark concludes, the presence of American listening-post activities proved both a threat and a source of stability, inviting backlash from Beijing over such activities while aiding in the larger effort to contain Communist expansion.[86] Refugee aid became a part of this paradox, both aiding the indigent and imposing a political agenda onto them.

The government of Hong Kong not only found itself in frequent conflict with Americans, but also faced additional criticisms from all sides. The ROC wanted freer rein to implement its information and relief programs than the Hong Kong government was willing to give, but the complaints from Communist China and its allies were even more profound. Beijing complained repeatedly about border controls that made it more difficult for Chinese to move between Hong Kong and Guangdong Province, largely because the traditionally mobile population of Guangdong complained to the Communist Chinese government. The border controls implemented by the PRC and Hong Kong varied and were usually reactive; when China had tighter controls over exiting, Hong Kong would relax entry requirements, and when Chinese controls were laxer, Hong Kong would step up border inspections. The Soviet Union accused the UK in the United Nations Economic and Social Council of restricting the right of movement for Chinese in South China and of holding Chinese captive in Hong Kong and making it difficult for them to leave, also suggesting that the "refugee" problem was an invention of United States and UK propaganda designed to embarrass the government of the PRC.[87] The Colonial Office later instructed the UK delegate to the UN on how to respond to these accusations: "It should be emphasized that the difficulties of Hong Kong would be much relieved if the refugees went elsewhere, but that they have fled from China and 'have voted with their feet' to stay in Hong Kong despite their hardships there."[88] Despite their frequent differences in approach, the British joined their American allies in finding both gratifying and useful for the West the idea that an impoverished, uncertain life in a refugee camp under a capitalist colonial government was preferable to that on the Chinese mainland.

Efforts to politicize refugee lives placed the Hong Kong government in a delicate position. It felt compelled to maintain a peaceful relationship with both the PRC and the ROC, though it was obvious that the two Chinese governments did not have anything near the same goals for Hong Kong. The colonial government expressed frequent frustration at the ROC's stated inability to accept more of the refugees for resettlement, and noted that "the Chinese Nationalists are interested in the Hong Kong refugee situation only insofar as they can exploit it to get the use of Hong Kong as a center for their activities."[89] The UK suspected that if the ROC made a new offer to accept refugees, it would only be doing so to serve its own political interests, namely membership in the executive committee of the UN High Commissioner for Refugees and state-to-state negotiations with the UK over refugee admissions. Both of these aims fed the same goal: promotion of the legitimacy of and international recognition for the ROC as the government of China. Moreover, ROC attempts to lobby the UN in pursuit of these interests had the potential to embarrass the United States and the UK. Any UN effort on behalf of the refugees by the mid-1950s would require the leading countries to contribute more funds, which translated to new contributions from the United States and Britain, with perhaps "the odd contribution" from other sources. But the United States claimed it had no more money to give, and the UK could use any money it freed up for Hong Kong more efficiently by sending it directly to the colonial government rather than funneling it through the UN, so the UK asked the United States to rein in its Chinese ally and persuade the ROC not to be too vocal. The United States supported the ROC in its bid to receive a spot on the UN executive committee, but the ROC efforts to draw international attention to the refugees did not end there.[90]

A Crisis Renewed

In the late 1950s, fewer new refugees arrived each year. A new immigration act in Hong Kong in 1958 provided a daily quota of fifty, and officials turned back anyone who tried to enter beyond that. Because of the international situation, however, the Hong Kong government had developed a "touch base" policy—if illegal entrants managed to set foot on colony territory, the authorities allowed them to stay. If it caught them trying to cross the land border on foot or the sea border by swimming or sailing, it turned them back. The first wave of refugees in the wake of 1949 came predominantly for political reasons, but by the mid-1950s, the Hong Kong government believed most Chinese attempting to enter the colony did so for economic reasons. As a result, its terminology underwent a shift from that of "refugees" to "illegal immigrants," and non-forcible repatriation gave way to a policy of deportation.[91]

With the options for resettlement abroad dwindling, the Hong Kong government focused on its effort to integrate the migrants—often indistinguishable from the poor among the total population—into the fabric of colonial life. The colonial government had to balance relief efforts against what was best for the colony as a whole, taking into account the persistent fear that ongoing relief efforts in the colony might encourage still more refugees to enter, a situation the Hong Kong government doubted it could handle. As early as 1952, a British official expressed concern that the combination of easy immigration and aid programs would turn the colony "into a glorified soup kitchen for refugees from all over China," and that fear never abated.[92] For similar reasons, the same official hoped to prevent U.S. organizations from sending food and money for relief work in the overcrowded colony. The Hong Kong government found that both official and private aid programs that offered goods—clothing or food, especially—on an ad hoc basis were of limited utility in the larger process of integrating the refugees into the local society, and occasionally unmindful of the recipients' actual needs.[93] Moreover, with the continuing lack of opportunities for resettling the migrants outside of Hong Kong, what was most needed was more housing, schools, hospitals, and a robust economy to accommodate all who remained.[94]

In 1958, the PRC embarked on its second five-year plan for economic development, also known as the Great Leap Forward, sparking a new wave of refugees. The plan for rapid industrialization and rural collectivization, coupled with natural disasters, created a massive famine that killed millions and created new motivations to cross borders. The question of who was a refugee grew more complex, for unlike the situation in 1950, this time it was not merely an issue of whether or not the UN had a mandate to help a population of people who all parties agreed had fled political persecution. Instead, the question was more fundamental: could individuals who fled economic hardship be called refugees, or were they merely immigrants seeking a better life? What if that economic hardship was the direct result of a Communist campaign? Unlike other parts of the world facing refugee problems, in Hong Kong individuals were fleeing one Chinese society to enter another; ethnically and linguistically, most of the new arrivals could integrate so well into local society that within hours they became impossible to distinguish from long-term residents. The UN declared summer 1959 to summer 1960 "World Refugee Year," and for the first time noted that its "good offices" would be expanded to include even non-mandate refugees. As scholar Peter Gatrell has argued, in Hong Kong "WRY offered the opportunity to be seen to do something, by making a one-off gesture that set no precedent for other requests for assistance in the future."[95] An international fund-raising campaign led to contributions amounting to around US$4 million, which the Hong Kong government funneled directly into existing relief projects.[96]

In the spring of 1962 there was a sudden surge of new migration into Hong Kong. Local officials determined that either there had been a sudden change of policy in Beijing or the upheaval of the Great Leap Forward had caused a breakdown in discipline in the bordering province. Either way, "evidently Communist guards [were] making no effort to prevent these illegal border crossings."[97] British frustration with the new migration came out at a UNHCR meeting, in which D. N. Edwards claimed "that this immigration—illegal immigration—has at times been described as a 'racket.' There is, we know, an organized agency operated for profit, which has been set-up elsewhere to facilitate this pathetic traffic in human beings."[98] New arrivals fleeing the Chinese famine were perhaps distinct from the ongoing "racket" smuggling migrants in and out of Hong Kong, but his speech still managed to imply there was a link between the two. Later talks between the British and Communist Chinese suggested that Beijing had intended to relax the borders in response to criticism from overseas Chinese and internal sources, but that the message filtered down inaccurately, resulting in a large exodus.[99] Given the extent of the humanitarian crisis already existing in the colony, Hong Kong officials felt they had no choice but to repatriate illegal border crossers, though American officials suggested "that positive propaganda and psychological benefits might accrue in giving each refugee 50 pounds of food to take back with him to China."[100] Such a policy did not come without risks, however, as it could induce more refugees to come, if only for the promise of the aid package.

The renewed sense of crisis had the United States in the uncomfortable role of intermediary between its two allies, Nationalist China and

Britain. The Nationalist Chinese government claimed the colonial government sent some thirty thousand refugees back to China against their will, and it offered to reopen resettlement from Hong Kong to Taiwan, give one thousand tons of rice to Hong Kong relief, and work with other countries to solve the human crisis.[101] Hong Kong proved uninterested in these concessions, in part because Taiwan had taken so few refugees the last time around, and in part because regaining control over the border required careful negotiations with Beijing, and cooperation with or publicity for Taipei could interfere with that.[102] In June, Taipei renewed its offer to accept into Taiwan any refugees turned back from entering Hong Kong.[103] Several factors contributed to the openness of this policy, compared with the situation in the mid-1950s. The economy and society in Taiwan were more stable and secure, but the Nationalist position internationally was less secure. Speaking out on behalf of refugees reinforced the Nationalist position as the legitimate government of China, but Nationalist insecurity was reinforced by the fact that this 1962 crisis brought renewed calls from Taipei to take advantage of the chaos to reconquer the mainland.[104] The Nationalists were also offended by deportations back to the PRC. Six Chinese students attempted to enter the colony on April 4, 1962, and were caught by Hong Kong police, who forced them back to the mainland. The ROC condemned that action, along with the thousands of deportations that occurred in April and May of that year, calling them "contrary to all the standards which we all now recognize in dealing with refugees."[105]

The Nationalists were not alone in seeing in the new wave of refugees an opportunity to score some political points. Walter Judd, writing on behalf of a newly formed Emergency Committee for Chinese Refugees, asked American intellectuals and leaders to join forces and find solutions to the problem in Hong Kong. Judd's letter was accompanied by a press release that questioned the PRC's motives for allowing so many to leave China, noting that "either the [Beijing] regime wishes to embarrass Hong Kong governmental authorities; or the Chinese Communists are utilizing the refugee situation to draw attention away from other plans they may have in Southeast Asia; or they are simply trying to relieve the pressures on their limited food supply."[106] Whatever the PRC rationale, Judd's positioning suggests he thought assisting the refugees both a humanitarian necessity and a propaganda coup. Anna Chennault, a prominent Republican and the widow of General Claire Chennault, led a new private organization, Chinese Refugee Relief, in its efforts to assist the Chinese in Hong Kong as well as any who arrived in the United States.[107] Meanwhile, the United

States would also work with British authorities on a relief program and petition other members of the Organization of American States—many of which had a history of accepting Chinese immigrants, albeit in small numbers—to open their doors to refugees as well. In addition to these proposals, the U.S. Senate had some other, more unorthodox ideas; one was to resettle the Chinese on unpopulated Pacific islands, to be governed from afar by the ROC.[108]

All these informal actions received official support when in late May, President Kennedy announced that the United States would authorize admission of several thousand of the refugees now in Hong Kong. He had the authority to do so under a provision in the McCarran-Walter Act that allowed the attorney general to parole migrants into the country without a visa. In this case, the U.S. consulate in Hong Kong would go through existing applications to migrate to the United States and admit anyone in the first or fourth quota preference groups—in other words, those who had skills or education valuable to the United States or immediate family members who were U.S. citizens.[109] Of course, this meant that the United States was not offering to take any of the new refugees at all—they were offering to clear their backlog of visa applications in the name of refugee assistance and the fight against communism. The consulate quickly determined that the numbers of Chinese in Hong Kong registered with the consulate under these preferences were not enough to provide for the "thousands" of refugees Kennedy offered to admit, requiring them to open the process to second and third preferences (parents of citizens and relatives of permanent residents), as well as possibly reopening some of the old RRA applications that had long since expired. Something had to be done, however, as having made the announcement, there would be "damaging results to U.S. prestige foreseen if fewer than several thousand are admitted."[110]

During the 1960s, the United States eventually accepted more than fifteen thousand Chinese refugees from Hong Kong.[111] Given the sheer scale of the overpopulation problem in Hong Kong, this was not an impressive figure, but the United States was limited by immigration restrictionists who preferred solutions that did not undermine the racialized provisions of the McCarran-Walter Act. As in 1953, the measure used immigration policy as an instrument to further U.S. Cold War foreign policy. The United States defined a refugee as someone fleeing from communism, and these new admissions served the purpose of highlighting, once again, how much victims of Communist governments were willing to risk fleeing to the free world. Even while expressing appreciation for the U.S. refugee policy, Nationalist

Chinese officials noted that the regular quota for Chinese immigration remained at 105, making long-term prospects for immigration without occasional special measures like the refugee acts or parole unlikely. The entire situation appeared to be just more evidence that the United States continued in its tradition of placing higher value on European lives than it did on Asian.[112] The British Colonial Office remained unimpressed with the U.S. refugee scheme, which it called "so small and so hedged around with reservations" that it was hard to see it as a genuine solution.[113]

The British were even more concerned about countering the persistent efforts of Nationalist China to use the most recent refugee problem as fodder for anti-PRC propaganda. For the sake of preserving the working relationship between Hong Kong and mainland China, it was necessary to avoid relief efforts or relocation schemes becoming "the source of damaging publicity for them, still less of favorable publicity and increased prestige for the Nationalists or (although this is doubtless less important) for the United States. . . . Since the Chinese regard their food situation as their own affair, they will inevitably regard any talk of an emergency in [any] context as a deliberate political maneuver against them."[114] Although allied with the United States in the Cold War, Britain recognized the PRC, and given the importance of cooperation between the mainland and Hong Kong, it had a very different set of priorities during the entire effort to assist the refugees. While the United States and the ROC worked the crisis to diplomatic advantage, the government of Hong Kong had to find a way to solve the problem without offending either side in the Cold War, but also without causing any more suffering for new arrivals than necessary. The calculated decision to consider new arrivals illegal immigrants rather than a new wave of refugees makes sense in this context.

From its perspective, Hong Kong had spent a decade dealing alone with a humanitarian crisis that the rest of the world found only marginally interesting, and many of its appeals for emigration or monetary assistance largely fell on deaf ears. After the ROC, the country that had accepted the largest number of Chinese refugees was the United States, and its resettlement assistance was decidedly limited. As one undated British report noted, "No other country will accept more than a tiny proportion [of refugees], since Chinese immigrants are nowadays generally suspect."[115] By 1957, it had ceased to consider resettlement abroad any kind of solution, shifting gears instead to focus on integration.[116]

For the Chinese arriving in Hong Kong between 1949 and 1962, the grand, international gesture of assistance never came. The UN and the moneyed first world generally placed a far greater emphasis on refugees and escapees in Eastern Europe. At the same time, there were material differences between the Hong Kong situation and what existed elsewhere, such as the integration of new arrivals into the local community and the dueling Chinese governments. By the end of the 1950s, none of the parties involved particularly wanted the lingering problem of the UN mandate settled. It suited Hong Kong, Great Britain, the PRC, the ROC, and the United States to leave the question open, so as not to force UN involvement in the colony in a way that would complicate each party's interests. But whether or not the UN could assist the immigrants, the related question remained of who, exactly, qualified as a refugee. Without the Cold War, there may not have been an issue, but the political context ensured that refugees from a Communist system became politicized just as soon as they crossed the border.

The refugee response also marks the high point of U.S.-Nationalist Cold War cooperation on migration diplomacy. The United States used both of its refugee acts and the Escapee Program to bolster the American image in Asia and promote the containment of communism by playing up the problems in mainland China. Refugee policy, meanwhile, also selected the best of the migrants for integration into American life. Nationalist China reinforced that process with its own screening measures, ensuring that Chinese American society would be bolstered with educated new immigrants. Meanwhile, the Nationalists also seized on the refugee crisis to promote their own legitimacy and attack that of the government of the PRC, fighting both for continued UN recognition and to maintain support in the diaspora. For much of the 1950s, these goals were quite complementary, but by the late 1950s and early 1960s the Nationalist sense of insecurity was increasing. Moreover, the Nationalists' goals for Hong Kong frequently placed them at odds with the Hong Kong government and, by extension, the British, with the United States riding a fine line in between. Though all these parties were nominally allies on the side of the "free world" against communism, the response to the Hong Kong refugee crisis demonstrates that the Cold War battle lines were never so neatly drawn in Asia as they were in Europe.

Part III

Shifting Exclusions

Chapter 7

Cold War Hostages

Repatriation Policy and the Sino-American Ambassadorial Talks

Though the United States and Nationalist China cooperated successfully in the early Cold War, by the mid-1950s it had grown clear that the United States could not afford to cut out Communist China completely. Certainly the United States and the PRC had both been involved alongside the Korean governments in the painful negotiations that finally declared a truce in the Korean War in 1953. When Secretary of State John Foster Dulles first met Zhou Enlai at international talks on Korea and Indochina in Geneva in 1954, he famously refused to shake the Chinese minister's hand, but their representatives could not help but discuss issues that affected both nations. When Communist China began shelling the offshore islands between Taiwan and the mainland in 1954, it reinforced to American officials how dangerous and unpredictable the Mao Zedong government could be and eventually led the United States to sign a mutual defense pact with Chiang Kai-shek. American Cold War policies in Asia were aligned with the Nationalist government both ideologically and practically, and they demanded that Chiang continue to enjoy international recognition, legitimacy, and China's seat in the United Nations. But increasingly, the Communist government could not be ignored.

Beyond their defensive and economic arrangements, in the early 1950s the United States and Nationalist China cooperated, not always easily, over new immigration, preventing deportations to the mainland, trying to keep remittances from falling into the hands of the Communists, and supporting refugees as propaganda-friendly representatives of people who chose the free world. But not all migration issues could completely cut out the Communist government from consideration, especially when so many migrants had transnational families still living behind the bamboo curtain. When the United States and Communist China were still at war in Korea, Chinese students in the United States and American nationals still in China became Cold War hostages. Both governments had security interests in controlling the movements of the other's citizens. Ultimately, the need of each state to protect its own nationals would be the wild card that forced these governments into direct negotiations. In the contest of the Cold War, the United States consistently tried to avoid direct negotiations on high-level issues for fear that they would undermine the status of Nationalist China, preferring to keep Beijing in a state of international isolation. Instead it was a relatively low-stakes issue, citizen repatriation, that became the forum that required the United States and Communist China to open a direct line of communication.

The Sino-American ambassadorial talks began in September 1955 at Geneva and continued off and on until President Nixon's trip to China in 1972. During the more than 130 sessions, the two sides reached only one negotiated understanding, an "Agreed Announcement" that concerned the repatriation of nationals. So much controversy emerged over the execution of the agreement, however, that the individuals to which it applied became victims of delays caused by the mutual distrust of the two parties. Despite the fact that the talks were between representatives of the United States and Communist China, the Nationalists played an important role in their outcome. The Nationalists' claim to the role of protector of all Chinese abroad held an importance to their claim to legitimacy that was disproportionate to the stakes involved in most migration disputes. It caused them to fight hard to ensure that their voice was included. The repatriation efforts also served as a potent reminder not only that U.S. relations with China were supported by contacts between high-level officials, but that the relationship between the U.S. government and the Chinese people, often in the form of interactions with the INS, the FBI, or other U.S. agencies, could also affect bilateral ties. The exclusion era and its complementary policy of extraterritoriality for Americans in China, though it came to an end in World War II, cast a long shadow over repatriation negotiations. That shadow fed suspicions on both sides that citizens were being used to strike at the other. Interestingly, the repatriates themselves might have been pawns in the geopolitical game, but they were not victims. Migrant choices frequently acted as the most unpredictable element in the process of negotiating their futures.

Prisoners of War

The long history of travel between the United States and China by students, merchants or other businessmen, and missionaries meant that after 1949, a number of temporary migrants found themselves caught on the wrong side of a closed border. In some cases, temporary migrations became permanent. For others, a long-term international struggle began for the right to return home.

Chinese students staying in the United States through the civil war posed both problems and possibilities for both governments. After a hiatus caused by limited transport during World War II, thousands of Chinese students used both private funds and government assistance to study in the United States in the late 1940s. Many had entered with fellowship funding from the Nationalist government, but eventually their stipends stopped coming, and student visas did not permit them to undertake any form of work, even part-time.[1] Some schools responded with independent programs to aid their students, but these limited efforts proved woefully inadequate, given the "desperate situation faced by worthy and needy Chinese students in the United States."[2] The first federal aid program came from the Economic Cooperation Administration (ECA), which allocated $4 million of the funds designated for assisting Nationalist China for the support and maintenance of Chinese students in the United States.[3] These funds came with a caveat, however: students accepting them had to promise to return to China. Roughly one thousand departed between 1949 and 1950.[4] The second measure was Public Law 535, passed in June 1950, which revived a wartime solution to a similar problem by allowing select Chinese students to leave school and work full-time without being held in violation of the terms of their visas.[5]

In seeking a rationale for these expenditures, lawmakers drew upon U.S. foreign policy goals as much as humanitarian concerns. As the Committee on Educational Interchange Policy, a policy committee of the Institute for International Education, explained, "A humanitarian approach can be

profoundly political."[6] In urging Congress to pass these measures, corre-
spondents argued that aiding the students was "the one constructive thing
we can do now to show our sincere friendship with the people of China."[7]
Similarly, congressional debate highlighted the importance of student aid
in encouraging the "democratic forces in China" because "[the students]
are the only remaining bridge we have with a quarter of the inhabitants
of the globe. Unquestionably they are the best bridge we can have with
China for the future."[8] Support for Chinese students often came from the
same voices advocating aid for Chiang Kai-shek, many of them associated
with the China lobby, which was less a formal lobby and more a coalition
of Chinese and Americans seeking greater U.S. government support for the
Nationalists, either out of personal interests or ideological beliefs.[9]

Though China lobby members advocated for Nationalist China, they
did not automatically approve of Chinese immigration. The coalition as
it emerged in the Cold War overlapped significantly with the prominent
"China hands" who advocated for an end to Chinese exclusion. The compromises they willingly made in that case—agreeing to, or even advocating
for a highly restrictive racial quota for only a symbolic number of new
immigrants—offers a reminder that support for China and support for Chinese immigrants were not interchangeable. A leading China lobby figure,
Congressman Walter Judd, who became very active in promoting aid to
Chinese refugees in Hong Kong, received hundreds of letters from Chinese
students and Americans writing on their behalf asking for options to enable
the students to stay in the country. Judd responded almost uniformly that
the annual quota of 105 Chinese immigrants was filled for years to come
and that the only way for the students to stay would be by extending their
studies and remaining on student visas.[10] For most advocates of Chinese
student exchanges, these students would not fulfill the same policy goals
as immigrants, as they would returning to China as pro-American elites.
Both time and public pressure shifted this, however, and by mid-1951 the
INS announced that students who could meet "internal security" standards
would be allowed to stay.[11]

Communist China had a different perspective on these policies. Letters
from returned students to the Ministry of Foreign Affairs described the ECA
scholarships as attempts to buy the students' sympathies and force them into
supporting the Nationalist government and Chiang Kai-shek. That way,
as another letter pointed out, if they ultimately did return to China after
having been provided tuition, living expenses, and even passage home after
graduation, they would arrive promoting a pro-American foreign policy,

perhaps even acting as spies for the Nationalist government.[12] An open letter to Chairman Mao from the Returned Overseas Students Association,
printed in the *People's Daily*, included longer discussion of the many ills that
the U.S. government had visited upon Chinese living in America, and condemned ECA scholarships as a tool used to manipulate Chinese students
in the United States.[13] Of course, it seems unlikely that the United States
or Nationalist China would really dispute these charges—their shared goal
was to educate a cohort of anticommunist leaders who could take control
of Chinese governance after the Beijing government collapsed.

After the Chinese entry into the Korean War in October 1950, aid to
help students return home ceased, and ad hoc measures to prevent departures
increased. In November 1950, the United States prevented a large group
of Chinese students from returning to the mainland through Hong Kong.
Then U.S. government officials stopped a group of students and scholars
in Japan in December 1950 and held them in Tokyo for two months, con-
fiscating some of their luggage and books and finally sending them back
to the United States. The following autumn, in September 1951, U.S. officials in Hawaii interrupted a group of Chinese scientists and, in spite of
the INS having detained and investigated them before their departure from
the port of San Francisco, forced them to return to the U.S. mainland. By
October 1951, Chinese-language newspapers printed announcements that
the United States would prevent all Chinese who studied science from
returning to China.[14] Though preventing departures of technically trained
Chinese students and scholars became de facto policy, the legal grounds for
doing so were not solidified until the 1952 McCarran-Walter Act, which
included language allowing U.S. officials to detain any alien in the country
if immigration officials found that person's departure to be "prejudicial to
the interests of the United States."[15]

In the short term, the departure controls provided kindling for stoking
the anti-American flames in Communist China's Korean War–era propaganda. Calls to "Resist America, Aid Korea" (Kang Mei yuan Chao) got a
boost from the claims that the United States held Chinese students hostage,
inflicting upon them a barrage of misinformation about life in the People's
Republic to reduce their feelings of loyalty. Letters to the *People's Daily* and
the Beijing Ministry of Foreign Affairs claimed the United States employed
a variety of tactics to block Chinese departures, including warnings that
should students return to China, they could be imprisoned, tortured, or
even executed for their ties to the United States. Returned students said
that Chinese who applied to return home—in spite of the great risk of

being rejected—could be fired from their jobs, leaving them still stranded but now unemployed as well. They accused the U.S. government of using the promise of citizenship, work laws, and ECA scholarships as additional inducements to stay and the threat of INS harassment as incentives not to leave. There were rumors as well that some employers in fields with military applications actually forced Chinese employees to sign agreements stating they would never leave. Together, all these accusations and observations from returning students reinforced perceptions in China of underhanded American tactics to prevent all students from returning, which in turn increased Chinese distrust of the U.S. government.[16]

The case of the most famous of the stranded students, Qian Xuesen (in contemporary U.S. documents, Tsien Hsue-shen), provides strong evidence of INS policy undermining U.S.-China relations by destroying the United States' relations with Chinese migrants. Qian arrived in the United States in 1934, studied mechanical engineering at the Massachusetts Institute of Technology, and helped found the Jet Propulsion Laboratory at the California Institute of Technology. When he and his family decided to return to China in the spring of 1950, INS officials warned him that he would not be permitted to go, and sent the FBI to investigate him. In August of that year, after the Qian family had packed up and made airplane reservations, the FBI stopped him from leaving the country with what it claimed were "secret documents." He was accused of past membership in a Communist organization and arrested; he spent three weeks in jail, then posted $15,000 bond. For the next five years, the U.S. government simultaneously ordered the Qian family deported *and* detained, with the result that until they were able to depart, they had no legal status. Chinese accounts of the Qian case suggest that he never intended to remain in America but instead always held on to the dream of returning to China. Biographer Iris Chang, on the other hand, has presented evidence that he was considering settling permanently in the United States until the escalating INS and FBI intimidation destroyed what remained of the good feeling he had developed over the course of his previous sixteen years of American life.[17]

Qian had expertise with applications in space and missile research, making the U.S. government position of denying his talents to China at least understandable, if not quite justifiable. Liu Yongming was a somewhat different story. Liu arrived at the University of Missouri in 1947 to study bridge construction engineering. He never had any intention of staying long term, since he had a wife and child in China. He received his master's of science in 1949, but according to records from the Chinese government, at that point U.S. authorities denied his application for an "exit permit." Around the same time as he learned of this decision, doctors in Missouri diagnosed him with paranoid schizophrenia and installed him in the Missouri State Hospital in Farmington. According to his wife's testimony to the Beijing government, Liu wrote very lucid letters to her from the hospital in 1950. In them, he lamented, "I have no freedom, no freedom to write letters, cut off from the outside world, no one comes to see me, I want to leave this bitter sea as soon as possible, and return to the embrace of my motherland."[18] She said she received no further letters from Liu after mid-1950, and the hospital also stopped sending updates after 1951. From her statements, Communist Chinese officials assumed that Liu was a well man when he first tried to depart, but that subsequent stalling and abuse from U.S. authorities destroyed his sanity, and that they were now holding him hostage. In response to this accusation, the State Department issued a press release to explain that the INS had ordered Liu deported from the United States on January 29, 1951, but that the order was not carried out because it was not possible to obtain the necessary travel documents at that time. Moreover, it claimed that the state hospital had corresponded with Liu's father, but recalled no exchange whatsoever with his wife.[19]

Despite frequent accusations from Beijing, U.S. officials maintained their position that they detained only a handful of Chinese students and scholars, and then only for reasons of national security. Those who had been temporarily prevented from leaving continued to enjoy total freedom of movement within the country, including the right to work. The State Department asserted that neither it nor the Department of Justice had maltreated any of the students.[20] The problem from Beijing's perspective, though, was that of the thousands of students who entered the United States in the late 1940s, few left. Historian Madeline Hsu has argued that these well-educated migrants, by remaining permanently in the United States, helped build a foundation for the liberalization of later immigration laws as well as sow the seeds of the "model minority" idea.[21] They were offered opportunities to stay, then, because they were the right kind of Chinese immigrant, the kind that Americans found increasingly desirable (in limited numbers, of course). The Chinese government interpreted this as proof that the vast majority were not actually free to go as U.S. government officials repeatedly claimed.[22]

Beijing felt it had few reasons to trust the word of the U.S. government, and accusations of FBI and INS harassment of Chinese nationals had a basis in reality. As already demonstrated, in the early 1950s the Justice Department did not simply target a few hundred students and deny them repatriation—it targeted the entire community. In this light, the travails of these stranded students appear as a part of a larger culture of intimidation that specifically targeted Chinese in the United States. That the PRC did not credit the benign reports of the U.S. State Department claiming that the U.S. government had never subjected any of the students or scholars to ill-treatment was neither particularly surprising nor unreasonable.

This profound mistrust went both ways. There were always far fewer Americans in China than Chinese in the United States, and fewer still after 1949. The Hong Kong consulate identified five categories of Americans in China after 1949: long-term expatriates, Chinese Americans, American citizens with Chinese spouses, American POWs from the Korean War who chose to move to China rather than return to the United States, and Americans in jail.[23] The ambassadorial talks and U.S. consular efforts in general dealt only with the last of these categories. Over the years between 1950 and 1953, the Chinese authorities arrested thirty-one missionaries, businessmen, and scholars who had stayed in China, including three students from the first class of Fulbright scholars. Most of these were arrested on charges of espionage, though both contemporary accounts and later memoirs suggest these accusations were tenuous at best. In 1952, the Chinese also captured two American CIA agents. In January 1953, the Chinese attacked an American B-39 conducting leafleting operations in North Korea near the Yalu River and captured eleven U.S. airmen who survived the incident. In March 1953, PRC authorities also seized a yacht sailing in international waters between the ports of Hong Kong and Macao and imprisoned the three Americans onboard.[24] Before any of these jailed Americans could be released, Beijing insisted they be subject to the PRC judicial system, tried and sentenced in accordance with their transgressions.

The lack of diplomatic ties hampered ongoing efforts to exchange nationals before 1954. Each side accused the other—and with good reason—of using the other's citizens as Cold War hostages. The impasse was blowback from years of U.S. extraterritoriality in China and Chinese exclusion from the United States. Americans could no longer appeal to the U.S. government when arrested in China, as the sovereign right of the Chinese government to punish lawbreakers had been recognized, even though the current government had not. Meanwhile, sixty years of exclusion had created an immigration regime in the United States that distrusted and abused Chinese nationals, and the repeal of exclusion did far too little to change that. The failure, post-exclusion, to make significant improvements in the treatment of Chinese in the United States made the prosecution of potentially lawbreaking Americans in China symbolically important to the new Communist government.

Making Repatriation a Diplomatic Issue

Negotiating repatriation across closed borders and without diplomatic relations proved harder than simply sending citizens home. Three things complicated this process. First, the United States began to champion "voluntary repatriation" during the Cold War under the assumption that given the choice, most individuals would not choose to live under communism. The concept took root in Korea, where armistice talks dragged on in part because of the United States' insistence that United Nations commanders offer Chinese POWs the choice of repatriation to Communist China or Nationalist Taiwan (with a similar choice for captured Korean soldiers). Two-thirds of the Chinese POWs chose Taiwan, much to the delight of American and Nationalist propagandists. However, rumors of forced repatriations to the "free" world deepened Communist Chinese suspicion of the United States, though ironically it helped establish the idea of "voluntary repatriation" on a broader scale.[25]

A second problem was determining who wanted to leave. In the case of Americans in Chinese prisons, there was little doubt that all would prefer release and repatriation. For Chinese students and scholars in the United States, the issue proved muddier. Many of the students had built lives in the United States, married, had children, or feared communism. Whatever the reason, some were legitimately not looking for repatriation. In other cases, the fact of INS and FBI harassment of the Chinese community in the United States may very well have made some students eager to return to China, but genuinely afraid to try to go. As one British observer noted, "The [U.S.] Immigration Authorities have evidently acted with some lack of imagination, so there may be something in the assertion that the difficulties they have created have persuaded some students to leave the States. . . . The U.S. Immigration Service is not known for tact or finesse."[26] Every time the United States announced that another group of students previously denied departure would be allowed to go, others stepped forward to apply. Applications to leave started arriving in groups rather than individually, suggesting that some may have felt there to be safety in numbers.

A third complicating factor was the idea of national sovereignty and its link to the right of a nation to protect its citizens abroad and enforce its laws at home. The United States recognized the Nationalists, not the Communists, as the sovereign government with the right to speak on behalf of Chinese students. Allowing Chinese students to return to China voluntarily was one thing, but permitting the Communist government to make specific representations on their behalf, to contact Chinese students to ascertain whether they were being prevented from departing, or allowing a designated third party do so on Beijing's behalf all proved threatening to Taipei's position both internationally and with the United States.

Given this range of issues, it is not surprising that it took a few false starts before bilateral talks got under way and started to accomplish anything. In four meetings during the 1954 Geneva Conferences on Korea and Indochina, PRC ambassador Wang Bingnan and U.S. ambassador U. Alexis Johnson exchanged information and perspectives on the problem of civilian exchanges. Both ambassadors were high-ranking members of their respective foreign services, aiding Chinese premier and foreign minister Zhou Enlai and John Foster Dulles respectively at the conference. During the meetings, both sides made gestures of good faith. The Chinese announced that they would allow families to send letters and packages to Americans in prison in China, and the U.S. government provided a list of fifteen Chinese formerly detained in the United States whom it would now allow to depart.[27] Wang proposed a joint communiqué and third-party representation to protect the interests of Chinese in America and Americans in China, but U.S. officials were not yet ready to accept that suggestion. Two months later, the Taiwan Strait Crisis of 1954–55 began and divided U.S. opinion about the necessity for American authorities to open negotiations with Communist China. On one hand, the PRC's decision to start shelling the offshore islands could be interpreted as an attempt to pressure the United States into talks, but on the other hand, the continued lack of dialogue between the two powers made it likely that the next crisis would escalate into a full-blown conflict.[28]

In early 1955, UN Secretary-General Dag Hammarskjold visited China in an effort to begin negotiations for the release of the airmen captured while under UN command.[29] In Hammarskjold's opinion, the PRC was looking for a way to release the American UN airmen—it had realized that continued incarceration of the men in China would lead to backlash in international public opinion, but the conclusion of a mutual defense treaty between Nationalist China and the United States in December 1954 made it impossible for them to do so.[30] Though not willing to release the airmen immediately and unilaterally, the Chinese government did promise to grant visas to family members of the jailed Americans.[31] This move was designed to challenge the United States, as Zhou Enlai knew that U.S. travel policy would not permit American citizens to visit China under any circumstances. That did not stop him from observing to Hammarskjold that the U.S. refusal to allow family members to visit China demonstrated that the United States did not really care about the men.[32] At the Asian-African conference in Bandung in April 1955, Zhou Enlai made a public statement expressing China's willingness to engage in negotiations with the United States, a move that was well-received at the conference by the governments in attendance, because a potential Sino-American confrontation remained an important threat to the security and stability of the region. Soon after, the shelling of Jinmen and Mazu stopped.

In the summer of 1955, both countries moved to permit more departures. Beijing released seven more individuals from jail and gave twelve others their long-denied exit permits. The United States continued to detain just two students.[33] In July, the Chinese Communist government released four fliers (leaving eleven airmen in detention).[34] As if to emphasize that it was the prospect of talks, and not UN intervention, that led to its decision to release prisoners, the PRC released the other eleven airmen the day before U.S.-Chinese talks formally convened in Geneva. The Nationalist reaction to the release was predictably cynical. A press release from the embassy in Washington downplayed the importance of freeing the airmen, saying that since they were never supposed to be imprisoned in the first place, "it was like a highway robber giving up some of his loot."[35]

On August 1, 1955, Wang and Johnson met in Geneva to discuss the terms for repatriating Americans and Chinese still prevented from returning home, launching the Sino-American ambassadorial talks. Dulles proposed that the agenda include repatriation and "other practical matters now at issue."[36] Scholar Steven Goldstein has noted that Dulles's agenda likely centered on obtaining an agreement renouncing the use of force in the Taiwan Strait and keeping open lines of communication, though certainly the United States as a rule took the protection of its citizens abroad quite seriously and therefore placed the return of its nationals held in the PRC high on the agenda.[37] China had established its policy of peaceful coexistence, and it was looking for a more stable environment within which it could focus on economic development. A desire to end the U.S.-led blockade against the PRC and diminishing the tensions in the region were both instrumental in Beijing's decision to propose negotiations. The PRC also tried to use the discussions to establish "sovereignty and mutual equality."[38] As historian Gordon H. Chang has noted, the United States hoped to lessen the likelihood of a war over Taiwan in addition to achieving the return of its nationals, but Dulles likely did not place particular importance or pin high hopes on what the talks could achieve.[39] Leadership of both countries had much at stake in terms of protecting their international reputations, though neither had full appreciation of the difficulties that the other Chinese government, the Republic of China, could pose for the negotiations.

The Nationalists strongly opposed the talks, believing them to be a dangerous step toward full recognition of Beijing. A pro-Nationalist news story referred to the talks as Beijing's "boldest bid yet to be the voice for all China" and claimed that "in one fell swoop, [Beijing] hopes to cop the prize as the spokesman for Chinese in every corner of the globe." The author called the negotiations a "trap set for Washington by [Beijing]."[40] Taipei emphatically reminded Washington that "all Chinese nationals in the United States are legally under the protection of [the Nationalist] Government. The United States Government has no right to surrender any of them to Chinese Communists."[41] Within the U.S. government, the Committee on Educational Interchange Policy also expressed concern about measures that would substitute Communist officials for the Nationalist embassy in claiming the loyalties of Chinese in the United States.[42] Though Nationalist leaders recognized the plight of the U.S. government in its efforts to obtain the release of its citizens in China, they feared that the mere fact of the talks—whatever they actually accomplished—would be construed by the international community as de facto recognition of the mainland Chinese regime and lead to Beijing replacing Taipei in the UN. In Taiwan, officials followed the developments with apprehension and a general feeling that without a representative of the Nationalist government at the table, Johnson and Wang ought not address general topics related to U.S.-Chinese relations or cross-strait relations.[43]

Nationalist officials couched some of their concerns in the language of Cold War migrations. In an August press conference in Taipei, Nationalist foreign minister George K. C. Yeh linked the issue of Chinese students to that of the Korean War POWs, explaining, "The Government has no objection to any Chinese student in the United States who wishes to go to the mainland, that is, voluntarily. But the United States has no right to deliver such Chinese students physically to the Chinese Communists at the Sino-British border at Hong Kong. . . . This is the principle of voluntary repatriation."[44] Because the United States had in fact been delivering Chinese deportees (though not students) to that border, it was perhaps a fair criticism. Ultimately, however, the Nationalists had no way to prevent the talks from taking place. They only insisted on being kept informed about progress and periodically renewing their protests, especially when the agenda drifted to topics beyond releasing American prisoners.

Once talks began, the differences in how the United States and the People's Republic of China viewed the issue of repatriation and the purpose of the talks quickly emerged. At the first meeting, Ambassador Wang Bingnan suggested a two-point agenda for the talks. The first item was negotiating the "return of civilians of both sides to their respective countries," and the second item borrowed Dulles's formulation of "other practical matters at issue between [the] two sides."[45] Johnson was careful not to allow the "other practical matters" to take precedence over repatriation, explaining that "the United States places unusual stress on protecting the security of its citizens abroad and considered the release of our remaining forty-one nationals a fundamental objective of the talks and a prerequisite to progress on any other subjects China wished to raise."[46] Almost immediately, though, Wang and Johnson ran into trouble on a very basic issue: determining whose repatriation was under negotiation. Wang provided Johnson with name lists of all the Americans known to be in China, both in and out of prison. He requested that Johnson also provide name lists of all Chinese nationals living in the United States, including the seventy-six Chinese students and scholars permitted to depart according to a U.S. announcement made in April.[47] Johnson was neither willing nor able to satisfy the request.

The request for a name list revealed deep-seated differences in ideas of both governance and migration. The PRC wanted a complete list that included all Chinese in the United States, students and long-term residents, but the request seemed to disregard citizenship. One observer from the British Foreign Office commented in March of 1956 that "the Chinese themselves do not appear to know how many Chinese there are in the United States. They keep referring to 'tens of thousands': the recent NATO paper gave the figure as 117,000."[48] Johnson also referred to there being 117,000 Chinese aliens in the United States.[49] U.S. Census data for 1950 counted 117,629 individuals of Chinese ethnicity in the United States—including U.S. citizens of Chinese ancestry.[50] If that was the list the PRC was after, U.S. officials could not agree, as the United States obviously could not allow its own citizens to be contacted for help with "repatriation" to China. Even a list of noncitizens was problematic, though. U.S. officials were not willing to provide the Communist government with full contact information of all Chinese citizens, fearing Beijing could use blackmail to coerce them to repatriate, a concern patterned off the remittances "racket" in previous years. Then, of course, there remained another problem—the United States did not actually have a name list of all the Chinese living within its borders. There was also no obvious means of quickly creating one. Johnson provided a name list of the seventy-six students whose detentions the government had lifted, and reiterated that the Chinese were all free to depart, but that was the extent of what he would or could do.

In addition to the name list, Wang also recommended that each side appoint a third party to represent its affairs in the other's country. The British had been looking after Americans in China since 1950, and the PRC wanted India to do likewise for Chinese in the United States.[51] Chinese students who sought repatriation from the United States to the PRC could not appeal for help, financial or otherwise, to their U.S.-recognized government representative, the Nationalist Chinese Embassy. If the Indian government acted as a third-party representative, students could apply for help from the Indian Embassy, which would then bill the PRC for its expenses. In the interests of reciprocity, it was a fair request, but an intractable problem remained. Under U.S. policy, there already was a Chinese government looking after the interests of Chinese in the United States.

Although the Nationalists did not like the talks in any respect, they expressed particular concern over the prospect of the Indian government taking any kind of responsibility for Chinese students, linking it to a larger threat to Nationalist sovereignty and extraterritorial control of Chinese abroad. The Nationalist embassy in Washington took every opportunity to oppose the plan and restate its insistence that Chinese in the United States remained almost uniformly supportive of the Nationalist government and opposed to communism.[52] The Ministry of Foreign Affairs in Taipei warned its embassy in Washington that "the Chinese Communist Bandits are taking advantage of the so-called 'repatriation of civilians' issue to try to control our 100,000-plus overseas Chinese in America, maliciously tracking their lives, deaths, comings and goings," and then asked that the embassy secretly initiate a letter-writing campaign by Chinese groups in the United States opposing any U.S. agreement with the PRC, targeting Congress and local newspapers.[53] The Nationalist consulate in Los Angeles reported it had "instigated [the Chinese Consolidated Benevolent Association] and the overseas Chinese anti-Communist association to telegram separately President Eisenhower and Secretary Dulles expressing their absolute opposition to any support or compromise with the Communist bandits."[54] The consulate in New York similarly reported contacting overseas Chinese, student groups, and Chinese-language newspapers.[55] Chinese organizations from around the country did write to Eisenhower and to the State Department to protest giving the Chinese Communist government or the Indian Embassy any sort of authority over the Chinese in America, though not necessarily only at the Nationalist government's urging.

The ROC embassy in Washington proved much more sympathetic to the talks than did the ministry officials back in Taipei. Consular officers understood the logic of some students requiring financial assistance to return to mainland China, even if their government publicly doubted such willing returnees existed. Still, the embassy was willing to accept the Indian government in this role only if it did not step beyond providing assistance to students who initiated the contact. It was of paramount importance to the Nationalists not to allow Chinese students and overseas Chinese resident in America to be contacted, harassed, or persuaded to return to China.[56] The Nationalist ambassador remained very wary of the prospect of a signed agreement between the People's Republic and the United States.[57]

Trying to avoid diplomatic complications, when talks of a signed agreement emerged, U.S. officials proposed instead that Beijing and Washington each make a unilateral statement, the terms of which had been agreed upon by both parties. The United States wanted a provision stating that all Americans detained in China would be released immediately—preferably by an agreed deadline. The PRC was not inclined to be that specific; instead, it would perform investigations into the prisoners' individual cases. As if to demonstrate this procedure, during the talks it announced that twelve Americans had been reinvestigated and granted exit permits.[58] The PRC representatives also insisted that any request that lawbreakers be released from prison and allowed to repatriate before their sentences ended was a violation of Chinese sovereignty that would not be tolerated.[59]

On September 10, 1955, the two sides made their "Agreed Announcement" about the repatriation of nationals. After extensive debate, the final text employed carefully chosen language to refer to the timing of the repatriations. The English version used the word "expeditiously," which was slightly more flexible than "promptly" or "immediately," allowing as it did for local laws and processes to be completed. The Chinese chose to translate this word as "*jinsu*," or "as fast as possible."[60] The announcement included provisions allowing the Indian Embassy in the United States and the British Embassy in China to make representations on behalf of anyone who believed his or her departure was being obstructed, to conduct investigations, and to provide financial assistance. All four governments agreed that they would "give wide publicity" to the content of this agreement.[61]

The Agreed Announcement in Action

At first both sides heralded the agreement as a positive step in the advancement of Sino–American understanding, but the months that followed demonstrated strong discrepancies between how the two sides interpreted their responsibilities and the rights of their citizens. As Kenneth Young explained, "Washington and [Beijing] took only six weeks of hard but relatively normal negotiations to conclude this single agreement, but spent eleven years denouncing each other over it."[62] At the first post-announcement meeting between Ambassadors Wang and Johnson at Geneva, Wang was ready to move on to ending the economic blockade against China and easing tensions in the Taiwan Strait, but Johnson replied that he would discuss these matters only once the repatriation of all Americans seeking to return from China was complete. Johnson reported that this statement seemed to have caught Wang off-guard, and he was right.[63] Wang later recalled in his memoir that he had "never imagined" the United States would insist on repatriation being complete before going on to discuss the second agenda item.[64] In reply to Johnson, Wang observed that the number of Chinese in the United States was quite large, so if the talks were to be stalled until all of them had returned to China, then it would be a very long time before the talks could progress.[65]

American and British officials wondered if U.S. citizens were being held hostage to China's larger Cold War agenda. British observers speculated that the rest of the Americans detained in China would be released only if the United States agreed to enter into negotiations on the rest of Wang's agenda, acknowledging that "for the Americans to act thus would admittedly be yielding to blackmail; but at least it might mean liberty for several men now imprisoned."[66] There was some reason to think the British assessment of the situation was accurate. Instructions from the Beijing Ministry of Foreign Affairs to Wang Bingnan explained, "If at the next meeting the American side expresses willingness to enter into talks on the second agenda item, then before the meeting concludes you can give them the dates of departure for ten American criminals." If the United States did not agree to move the talks forward, however, Wang was to say nothing about the prisoners, to show that the American stalling tactics were the cause of bad faith between the two sides.[67] The repatriation talks became a way for Beijing to maintain contact with the United States and seek improvements in relations on other levels, and not merely a means of achieving the return of nationals. Washington, too, came to see the talks as an entry point for discussing tensions in the Taiwan Strait, though this idea met with forceful opposition from Taipei.[68] In late September, Ambassadors Wang and Johnson began discussion on the possibility of an agreement on renouncing the use of force in the area around Taiwan, though Johnson had instructions to continue to raise issues related to repatriation as necessary.[69]

While Wang and Johnson failed to agree on the rest of the agenda, the repatriation project was foundering. The two sides continued to argue over what constituted an obstacle to departure, who was included under the terms of the announcement, and how much power the two "third party" countries had to interpret the agreement and take the initiative in its implementation. At the heart of these issues were mutual claims of bad faith: the United States accused the PRC of stalling when it claimed American prisoners could not be released early, and the Chinese claimed only U.S. coercion would stop the vast majority of Chinese in the United States from returning to China. And in between, the Nationalists' efforts to protect their interests complicated it all.

Many factors kept Chinese from leaving the United States for China. One issue was pure bureaucracy. Students leaving the United States for China did not always have valid passports, but there was no travel route that did not require transit through Hong Kong. Thanks to its swelling ranks of refugees, Hong Kong required proper travel documents and proof that travelers would immediately be accepted into the PRC.[70] Making travel arrangements proved so slow-going that the Communists claimed the United States and Britain used the transit visa system to obstruct the repatriation of Chinese.[71] In response, the British attempted to facilitate repatriation by having guards meet large groups of Chinese in transit and escort them en masse from the ships or planes to the Chinese border.[72] Under this system, repatriation though Hong Kong was possible, but some students waited extended periods from the time they applied to depart until there was a critical mass of students ready to go together.

Beyond passports and transit visas, beginning in late 1955 the United States required Chinese aliens visiting on temporary visas (including student visas) to obtain an entrance permit to Taiwan before it approved visa extensions. This policy stemmed from the difficulty the United States had deporting Chinese to either side of the Taiwan Strait after 1949. If all Chinese aliens in the United States held ROC entry permits, then INS officials could guarantee their acceptance in Taiwan if deporting them became necessary. It applied to mainland students only if they tried to extend their visas, but the Communists viewed it as "a further threat directed against these Chinese students who are unable for the time being to return to China, so that they could not dare to apply for returning to the Chinese mainland in the future."[73] It seemed like an attempt to rally Chinese students in support of the Nationalists. In reality, American immigration officers hoped the policy would serve as an inducement for students loyal to the PRC to abandon plans to extend their studies and simply head home.[74]

The repatriation process offered the United States a unique opportunity to restart the stalled deportation process, but doing so served to complicate the talks. With every group of students returning to China, the INS slipped in a few seamen arrested for overstaying their visas, an individual convicted on drug charges, or other individuals qualifying for deportation on strictly nonpolitical violations of immigration law. These unwilling returnees then told tales that helped increase mistrust of U.S. authorities' treatment of Chinese nationals. Accounts collected in the Ministry of Foreign Affairs archive in Beijing tell of the INS trying to force loyal Chinese to accept deportation to Taiwan or pay unreasonable fees to leave the country.[75] Some complained they were forced to support the KMT or constantly harassed by the FBI, arguing that the INS and the FBI together had created a climate in which most Chinese in the United States wanted to return but could not or dared not.[76] Many of these deportees' accounts explicitly mentioned that their subscriptions to the left-leaning *China Daily News*—the newspaper that faced so much persecution under the Trading with the Enemy Act for facilitating remittances—was the major reason for their persecution as suspected Communists or Communist sympathizers. They also claimed the paper's accurate reporting was how they knew it was safe to return to the mainland. Others told stories of being arrested, imprisoned, or made to do forced labor.[77] Once individuals were deported, no U.S. agency could control how they remembered their American sojourn. In the archives, these deportee stories are mixed in with the student returnees as a category of Chinese migrants unfairly treated by the United States, victimized by the corruption and racism inherent in American immigration laws.

Though these kinds of stories seemed to have the effect of slowing the release of Americans from Chinese prisons, some individuals continued to find their way home. In 1955, the Communists released two American Fulbright scholars imprisoned in Beijing, Allyn and Adele Rickett. With their case, the PRC demonstrated that it would punish "criminals" as was its sovereign right, but the length of the sentence and the availability of early parole could be bent to meet the needs of its negotiators at Geneva. If the British and American reporters who met Allyn upon his arrival in Hong Kong hoped that he would denounce his captors, they were sorely disappointed. He explained, "I was originally given a six-year sentence. But because of the leniency of the Chinese people I was released in advance, and in the course of repatriation, given the utmost consideration. I have great hope that the United States Government will help the Chinese in the United States who are to be repatriated, in the same spirit."[78]

Rickett's statements disappointed the United States, just as the low numbers of Chinese choosing repatriation concerned Communist China. Both governments interpreted the movement of people across the "bamboo curtain" in terms of Communist and capitalist bloc gains and losses, and neither was reaping the public benefits from the repatriations that it had thought it could. As much as possible, the PRC celebrated groups of patriotic Chinese who had thrown off the yoke of Western imperialism and returned to modernize and develop a new, Communist China. Meanwhile, in U.S. accounting, every Chinese who chose to remain in the United States had cast a vote for the free world, just as other Chinese immigrants and refugees had done before.

American officials did not always understand why Chinese might choose to return to the mainland, but they did worry about the political fallout from Communist China's propaganda celebrating their arrivals. In order to limit both, INS developed what it called the "redefector program." The program was not limited to Chinese; INS interviewed anyone who had "escaped" communism only to return apparently voluntarily, in order to ensure that Communist agents were not using threats or blackmail to force former citizens back. Under the program, INS interviewed all Chinese leaving for the PRC to determine why they wanted to return, despite all the bad information coming out of Hong Kong.[79] During the interviews INS would try to persuade the returnee to stay in the United States, though as one astute INS official noted, "there was something of a conflict between our current policy of deporting Chinese on one hand and on the other hand interviewing them to find out if they were coerced to returning and advising them that they need not leave the United States."[80] In theory, at least, deportees had broken U.S. laws, whereas returning students and scholars had not, but the U.S. perception of the destination did not change based on the reasons for departing the United States.

Shortly after the Geneva talks began in August 1955, applications to return to China surged. Some of this might be pent-up demand released by the fact of ongoing negotiations, but the INS also suspected a revival of the early 1950s Chinese letter-writing campaigns, in which the PRC government organized friends and family members to write to contacts in the United States, inform them of the positive developments in the PRC, and encourage them to do their part building a new China. Copies of letters sent to students and collected by INS through the redefector program in 1955 and 1956 revealed several common lines of persuasion to return: appeals to filial piety, praise for the Communist government and its accomplishments, or news that a parent or other relative had fallen ill and required care.

In one case, however, a student brought a letter to INS that she suspected Communist officials had forced her parents to write. She believed that contrary to the text of the letter, their intention was to persuade her not to return. The letter noted her upcoming marriage (she had no plans to marry) and also that "very lately brother D asked about you. . . . Brother D hopes every one will come back here soon for a get-together." Additionally, the letter asked, "Have you seen H lately? She is a good friend of yours. Tell her that I figure she will graduate soon. I also advise her to come back here after her graduation. She is apt to say that I am meddling in her affairs . . . but whether or not she will listen, there is nothing I can do." The letter seemed straightforward enough, until the student explained that actually "Brother D" was a prearranged code between the student and her parents that referred to the Chinese Communist Party and "H" was a code name for the student herself. She interpreted the letter as a warning that the CCP had been asking about her and that her parents did not want her to return; she assumed they wrote it only because someone made them. A note in the INS file explained that her suspicions "were definitely confirmed when later, a relative of the student succeeded in leaving Red China, and a verbal message was brought from the student's parents: no matter what they might write in their letters, they hope the student would not return to Red China."[81]

Though rare, letters like this one convinced INS and FBI officials that there were forces other than patriotism and homesickness pulling students back to China. Chinese-language publications in the United States like the KMT-affiliated *Chinese-American Weekly* advised students to draft their replies to family letters with care. It suggested that students say that they were not inclined to return at the present, but never that they were unable to return. Though the latter might be a way to avoid pressure from family or friends or to protect loved ones from being made to act as bait to lure them back, it would give the U.S. government new waves of trouble at Geneva.[82]

Third–Party Representation

With neither side receiving its citizens back at the rate it would like, each turned to its designated third party to investigate. The PRC requested that India make a public statement about the Agreed Announcement and confirm that the U.S. government had made the text of it available to all Chinese in the United States. Most students who reported seeing the announcement in a newspaper explicitly cited the *China Daily News* as the one to carry it, though it could also have been that readers of that paper were the most likely to express interest in returning anyway. Other students said they had never seen the text of the Agreed Announcement, or that it never appeared in any of the newspapers where they lived. This led Beijing to suspect that the United States was not, as it claimed, doing all it could to ensure that Chinese wishing to leave could depart.[83] The Indian ambassador countered that the announcement had been published in a great many magazines and newspapers but that it did not seem feasible to place it into the hands of every Chinese person in the United States.[84] According to British discussions with the Indian ambassador in Washington, the latter had received only "one or two" inquiries about leaving for China in the first two weeks after the announcement.[85] By the end of November, the Indian Embassy had reported that "they had done a good deal of publicity, particularly in the Chinese language press, but had not had very much response, though there had been some requests for finance." The staff at the embassy was prepared to investigate claims of obstruction, but few students made inquiries.[86]

The PRC remained convinced the United States was manipulating its immigration laws to obstruct Chinese repatriation, so it selected the case of poor, schizophrenic Liu Yongming and asked the Indian embassy to make a formal investigation into his situation. His condition made the mechanics of repatriation difficult, as his transport had to be reconciled with episodes of paranoia. Given his illness, Liu clearly needed a family member to speak on his behalf, but the problem was that there were two candidates for the job. His wife in mainland China had letters that she said expressed Liu's desire to return to the mainland, so Beijing asked the Indian Embassy to investigate the case.[87] However, Liu's father lived in Hong Kong (British reports say he then moved to Taiwan) and wanted Liu to join him, creating a Nationalist interest in his case.[88] Nationalist interest was also piqued by the fact that Liu was the first Chinese national formally named by the Communists as a clear case of U.S. obstruction that required Indian third-party intervention.[89] Liu's future soon became subject to a Communist and Nationalist battle over who had the right to speak for him.

In early January 1956, U.S. officials announced that Liu was doing better and could be repatriated. Hong Kong government authorities met his ship on January 31 and interviewed him to ensure he was returning voluntarily. However well he had been doing when he left, it appeared that somewhere on the Pacific he had taken a turn for the worse. Liu informed the interviewers that actually he had been born in Turkey to Japanese parents, but he was now a Mexican national. He also claimed former residence in Hong Kong and expressed a desire to stay in the colony, rather than go to either China or Taiwan. British observers noted that the one area in which Liu was truly consistent over the course of all their interactions with him was his insistence that he did not want to return to China.[90] While his case was considered, the local Red Cross installed him in a Hong Kong refugee settlement. While he was there, two mainland news reporters approached him, delivering messages from his wife requesting that he return to China. Representatives of the Nationalist government also approached him, bearing greetings from his father and suggesting that he go to Taiwan. The PRC press claimed U.S. agents had stopped Liu at each port of call on his journey and tried to persuade him to return to the United States.[91] On February 5, Liu Yongming's brother, wife, and daughter all arrived from the mainland, and three days later Liu simply crossed quietly into China with them.[92]

Because Liu's illness made ascertaining his personal wishes nearly impossible, the repatriation effort incited accusations of bad faith from all sides. The PRC repeatedly accused the United States and Britain of causing Liu's illness and detaining him against his will. The United States (and the Hong Kong government, to a lesser extent) accused Communist China of ignoring Liu's desires, treating him as a political pawn, and ultimately stealing him back without his consent. The Nationalist Chinese government was unhappy with both sides' handling of the case—with the PRC for claiming the right to protect Liu and then stealing him away, and with the United States for failing to acknowledge that it was the Nationalists, as the recognized government, whose duty it was to look after this most pitiable of Chinese nationals. The issue of where he ultimately lived was not particularly important to any of the governments involved—unlike more famous repatriates like Qian Xuesen, who also returned after the talks started, he would not go on to work in rocket science—and it was far outshone by what he represented in terms of the sovereign rights of governments to protect their nationals.

Just as the Indian government experienced difficulties trying to define its role investigating cases and assisting Chinese in the United States, the British Embassy's efforts to fulfill its role as the third-party protector of American civilians in China led to frequent disagreements. For much of 1956, the British consul assigned to the issue, C. D. W. O'Neill, practically made a career out of his battles with PRC authorities over access to American prisoners, the meaning of the term "expeditiously," and what constituted an obstacle to departure. O'Neill was not always in agreement with the U.S. government on how to interpret the Sino-American Agreed Announcement, but he used his position as intermediary to try to press the Chinese government to expedite the parole process for those still incarcerated. Chinese foreign minister Zhou Enlai complained that as the mediator, O'Neill ought to maintain a neutral stance, but added that China would absolutely not yield under British or American demands anyway.[93]

Because the Indian Embassy had no way to contact all the Chinese without a name list, the PRC reciprocated by permitting O'Neill to visit or communicate with only those prisoners who initiated contact with him.[94] They did eventually permit him to send a copy of the agreement to the prisoners, but discussion over the text of the letter and its translation dragged on for months, and O'Neill wondered if the Chinese authorities were trying to stall to see if the United States would liberalize its rules for Indian Embassy contact with the Chinese.[95] By this point, the continuing talks at Geneva had started to deal with an agreement on the renunciation of force in addition to repatriation, though these continuing arguments about the implementation of the first agreement necessarily made the two sides skeptical about the utility of a second.

In November, Zhou Enlai informed O'Neill that the United States had never told the PRC how many Chinese it had imprisoned and what, if anything, it was doing to reduce their sentences and allow them to depart for China.[96] The British interpreted the statement as a quid pro quo—if the Indian government could visit Chinese in American prisons, in return the PRC might give O'Neill more access to American prisoners. O'Neill noted, "If the Americans went even further, and decided to remit the balance of the sentence of any Chinese in prison who desired to return to the mainland of China, and to deport him here, the Chinese case for retaining Americans in prison here would be correspondingly weakened."[97] The State Department was reluctant to equate American prisoners in China—whom it considered to be political prisoners—with Chinese in U.S. jails who had committed criminal offenses.[98] Nonetheless, the United States began an inquiry into whether it had any Chinese in prison. The review of the prison system ultimately uncovered thirty-four Chinese nationals in prison in the United States. Most were not yet eligible for parole, so their early release would require some sort of presidential commutation of their sentences.[99] Thirty of the prisoners were being held on drug charges, one for manslaughter, and three for murder, so the United States saw no real disadvantage to offering to deport them in place of having them serve out their sentences.[100]

The plan to release and deport Chinese prisoners to the PRC hit its first snag when the Nationalist government learned of it. Although the Nationalists fought adamantly against accepting regular Chinese deportees into Taiwan, once they learned the U.S. government was considering deporting the prisoners to the mainland, they demanded that prisoners be sent to Taiwan instead.[101] The Nationalists also claimed that allowing the Indian government to take the initiative in contacting prisoners who were Chinese citizens was a violation of its own sovereign rights as the government of China. The *Chinese News* reported that the Taipei Ministry of Foreign Affairs "expressed profound regret at the U.S. unilateral and arbitrary action toward the ROC with which she is allied. The government, it was pointed out, has reiterated its right to protect all Chinese residents in the United States, including those serving prison terms." It claimed the entire protest was aimed at the safety and welfare of the Chinese in America; that "if the US would yield to the 'repatriation' of first the Chinese students, now the prisoners, then in the future there [would be] endless [Beijing] demands at the expense of the lives and interests of the entire Chinese population in the States."[102] To Taipei, repatriating prisoners to the mainland was entirely different from simply letting students return home. The Nationalists preferred that their own representatives be the ones to conduct the interviews and that prisoners be given a choice between deportation to China or to Taiwan.[103] However, if the United States allowed the Nationalists to interview the prisoners, the Communists could accuse the United States of abandoning the system of third-party representation they had agreed on. Because Nationalist officials had never shown any inclination before this to visit the prisoners, the State Department, while acknowledging it was the

Nationalists' right to do so, asked them to step back temporarily and not make the visits.[104]

As a compromise, in June 1956, U.S. officials gave all Chinese nationals in its prisons copies of the text of the Agreed Announcement, along with a letter informing them that they would be offered a choice between deportation to China, deportation to Taiwan, or continuing to serve their prison terms in the United States.[105] Washington planned to ask the Red Cross to conduct the interviews, with Indian Embassy representatives present as observers. This way, it could avoid violating either the agreement with the Communists or the "recognized and exclusive right of [the Nationalist] Government to represent interests of Chinese nationals in this country."[106] This impressive display of political theater failed to take an important factor into account: the wishes of the prisoners. It turned out that given the choice between China, Taiwan, and an American prison, most Chinese prisoners preferred to stay in jail. Upon learning the outcome, Beijing claimed the United States designed the entire exercise to embarrass the PRC and refused to acknowledge the project. Because U.S. officials had already committed to the offer, they allowed the Red Cross to step in and arrange for the five Chinese who chose deportation to leave the country.[107]

The extended distraction of releasing Chinese prisoners for deportation did not have any obvious or immediate effect on the situation of imprisoned Americans, but by 1956, some of them reached the end of their sentences. Beijing released Father Marcellus White in May 1956, and he believed the Geneva talks were influential in causing that. He reported that in August 1955, just as the talks began, he experienced what he called "the first change of attitude. Suddenly there was real concern about my condition." He recalled that his captors moved him to better facilities, provided reading materials and bread to eat, then eventually informed him that the United States and the PRC had reached an agreement at Geneva, but that it did not apply to him because he was a criminal. At this point, though, the Chinese finally brought White to court, where they found him guilty of passing along information on China's political, military, and economic situation to friends, family, and church officials in the United States. They sentenced him to four years' imprisonment with credit for time served, though he said later of the trial, "It all seemed so silly." On November 10, they informed White that they planned to release him early on account of good behavior.[108]

In other cases the Geneva talks did not necessarily result in substantial changes. Chinese authorities arrested Jesuit priest Father Charles Joseph

McCarthy in the general sweep of Catholic priests in Shanghai in June 1953, on charges of spying. The British Embassy received a letter from him in September 1956, stating that he felt he was being unjustly prevented from returning to his country of origin. The letter requested that O'Neill make representations on his behalf and that someone from the embassy visit him to discuss the matter. For the first time, the British felt they had an unimpeachable claim to the right to investigate. The McCarthy case became the focus of an extended debate between the British and the Chinese about the circumstances under which the British would be allowed to investigate, though the controversy did nothing to help the priest himself.

Near the end of 1956, O'Neill speculated once again on how and why Americans in China came to be prisoners and the best means of obtaining their release. He noted that there were also Germans detained in China for a time, but that they were released sooner than the Americans, and with comparatively little fuss made over them. He tried to explain the difference between the two groups: "The most obvious answer, and perhaps a sufficient one, is that the Chinese are holding on to the Americans as a matter of policy and because they hope to get something out of the Americans in return for their release. In this sense the American prisoners are victims of unfortunate international circumstances and the German prisoners are lucky. But it is odd that those on whom so much effort has been expended stay in prison, and those for whom comparatively little has been done get out."[109]

Though O'Neill felt that pressing the Chinese government for answers on the McCarthy case was the right thing to do, he also suspected that all his efforts on the priest's behalf only served to ensure that McCarthy would not be released even one day ahead of schedule. The lesson he seemed to take from his experience was that "the Chinese Communist regime is still immature and touchy in its relations with foreign countries. 'Face,' which of course plays a large part in all international relations, still plays an unusually large part here."[110] The PRC finally released McCarthy, along with Fathers Houle, McCormick, and Wagner, when their official sentences ended, on July 14, 1957.

Though the bulk of American prisoners in China were released in the 1950s as a result of the talks, a notable few remained. Names like John T. Downey, Richard G. Fecteau, and Hugh Redmond—all of whom were affiliated with the CIA when captured and therefore being held long-term—as well as that of businessman Robert McCann appeared in the press every now and again, usually when relatives made the long trek to China (with special permission, of course) to see their loved ones in prison. Both the public and local politicians expressed concern for the people they viewed as continuing "hostages" of an enemy regime. The mayor of Downey's home-town expressed his dismay that the United States could so quickly get per-sonnel out of the Soviet Union but had done what he viewed as compara-tively little to help the men in China.[111] Ruth Redmond, mother to Hugh, joined with other relatives in regular letter-writing campaigns in the 1950s, meeting with high-level officials and regularly requesting to meet with the president (first Eisenhower, later Kennedy).[112] The CIA speculated in 1961 that Communist China would never have the incentive to release all the Americans they held, because "the high hostage value [Beijing] attached to the American prisoners in China reflected its interest in maintaining official contacts with the United States." According to the report, a high-ranking official in the Chinese Ministry of Foreign Affairs commented in 1957, "Suppose we release your people today. What guarantees are there that you won't immediately break off the talks which the two governments are hav-ing in Geneva?"[113] McCann was released in 1961 when it became clear he was dying of cancer. Redmond died in jail in 1970. Both Downey and Fec-teau were released in the early 1970s, as détente and Nixon's reconsidered China policy opened new doors to potential cooperation.

In 1957 the State Department reassigned Ambassador Johnson to Thai-land, but after a failed attempt to lower the ranks of the representatives involved, the talks restarted nine months later in Warsaw with U.S. Am-bassador Jacob Beam at the helm of the American delegation. Beam was replaced by John Cabot in 1962. More than a decade after the talks began, prisoners and repatriation remained an issue, but the status of Taiwan, and the Vietnam War, the Soviet Union, and the larger context of the Cold War were the issues keeping the two sides apart. As scholar Yafeng Xia has noted, often the only meaningful negotiations were those that dealt with the tim-ing of the next meeting.[114]

Efforts to continue to repatriate willing Chinese from the United States ran into new trouble in 1960, when diplomatic ties between the PRC and India broke down. In the meantime, the Chinese population in the United States had more than doubled in the previous decade, though travel and re-turn to China continued. In 1963, rumors of China being close to develop-ing an atomic bomb led to criticism of the policies that led to the return of scientists like Qian Xuesen. Some of it came from an unusual source—a So-viet diplomat remarked to an American official how concerned his country was about "a recent report that several prominent and brilliant Chinese American atomic scientists had recently defected to Red China, where they were working on an atomic bomb which should be ready in three years."

The Soviet diplomat chastised the United States, noting that the Soviet Union "did not let its top quality atomic scientists leave the USSR, partly due to secrecy tradition and partly for fear they would pass their skills on to another country other than the United States." He recommended that the United States consider adopting the same policy.[115] The People's Republic of China exploded its first atomic weapon the following year.

Despite periodic suspensions and resumptions, the talks continued through the 1960s. By then, they had fallen into a pattern in which the two sides talked at, rather than to, each other. Still, the connection created by the exigencies of protecting citizens and repatriating nationals had been maintained, and even though the two sides did not sign another agreement on any subject during the talks, they kept the lines of communication open and avoided direct military conflict.

The legacy of the U.S. policy of Chinese exclusion colored the progress of the talks by deepening suspicion between the two parties. U.S. officials felt they were doing nothing to prevent the departure of Chinese who wished to leave the United States, but that the PRC badly mistreated U.S. citizens for political purposes in China. At the same time, Beijing suspected that most if not all of the Americans it held were spies, and that the United States had blocked the departure of thousands of China's own citizens through intimidation, force, and harassment and refused to account for lost or missing citizens or even drove some to insanity through ill-treatment. Although the American officials involved in the talks did not appear to make the link between the long-standing contradictory and harsh policies of the U.S. government toward Chinese immigrants, Beijing clearly did.

What was ultimately at stake for both sides were the lives of a very small percentage of their citizens, but also the very crux of the Sino-American relationship. The Nationalists opposed the talks and intervened in the repatriation attempts because they feared American negotiation with the Communists was a prerequisite to recognizing the PRC. These Nationalist fears later proved well-founded. The fact of the ambassadorial talks forced the United States for the first time to deal with the Chinese Communist government as a power with the potential right to protect and act on behalf of Chinese abroad. Throughout the 1950s, the Nationalists and Communists fought over this right because it bore the crown of legitimacy for the winning party. By the 1960s, Nationalist claims to legitimacy had been weakened by this and other factors, and calls increased in the United States to deal with the reality that the Communist government controlled the mainland and was here to stay.

Chapter 8

Visa Diplomacy

The Taiwan Independence Movement
and Changing U.S.-Chinese Relations

In 1961, the Kennedy administration intervened in a State Department decision and refused to give Taiwan independence activist Thomas Liao (Liao Wenyi) a visa. In 1970, the Nixon administration ignored the Liao precedent and allowed Taiwanese dissident Peng Ming-min (Peng Ming-min) to move to the United States. In both cases, the Nationalist government vociferously protested the visas, claiming that granting either would do irreparable harm to the Sino-American relationship. In the early 1960s the Americans listened, but nine years later they did not. The combination of the growing presence of the Taiwan independence movement in the United States, changes to immigration policy, and major alterations in foreign relations over the course of the decade help to explain the shift.

In the 1960s, Nationalist Chinese relations with the United States grew increasingly strained, and the fact that the United States was an unwitting host to a growing number of Taiwan independence advocates both increased tensions and provided an unexpected avenue for the two countries to cooperate.[1] The root of the problem was that by the time President John F. Kennedy took office, the foundational myth of the Nationalist regime in Taiwan—that it would one day retake the mainland and rule all of China, including Taiwan, in place of the Communists—had started to crumble.

The joint U.S.-Nationalist China strategy to keep the Chinese Communists out of the United Nations collapsed under pressure from newly decolonized states emphasizing self-determination. The Kennedy administration encountered a growing number of prominent American voices calling for a total reconsideration of China policy and recognition of the mainland. The ongoing ambassadorial talks moved away from the original focus on repatriation and instead became a hotline for sharing ideas and discussing differences. The new and sudden influx of refugees to Hong Kong from mainland China's Great Leap Forward–induced famine reported a population defeated and broken, but in no position to rebel against their government. Meanwhile, economic aid to the ROC from the United States dwindled after 1966. The U.S. preoccupation with a widening conflict in Vietnam prevented Chiang Kai-shek from taking advantage of the chaos of China's Cultural Revolution to mount his return.[2] And even without Vietnam, no realistic assessment of Nationalist China's military capabilities believed those forces capable of the vaunted counterattack.

All these changes together made the constant mantra in Taipei that all this was temporary until the day the Nationalists would recover the mainland seem more and more like a desperate ploy to maintain legitimacy, and not a realistic assessment of international affairs. As a result, the Nationalist leaders felt more vulnerable than they had at any point since 1949, and both internal subversion and anything else that could challenge the support of the United States rose to the level of an existential threat. In this context of constant change, growing numbers of Taiwan independence advocates in Taiwan, Japan, and the United States, as well as large numbers of Taiwanese students studying abroad, generated a resurgence of the postwar nationalistic movement that pushed back against both Nationalist and Communist rule and demanded self-determination for Taiwan. As Mei-ling T. Wang has argued, "The roller coaster ride of Taiwan's international standing, to which the Taiwanese felt they were mere innocent by-standers, made the appeal of independence an attractive alternative to the natives."[3]

Preventing the spread of the independence movement and preserving the Nationalist relationship with the United States went hand in hand in the 1960s. By the early 1960s, concerns about the expansion of pro-independence activities into the United States led to a series of testy disputes between Nationalist and U.S. officials, often over the issue of who should be permitted a visa and under what circumstances.[4] Beyond creating a more Taiwanese—and therefore, more sympathetic—base for Taiwan independence activities in the United States, U.S. immigration law also determined the extent to which U.S. officials had the leeway to allow dissidents to enter. Ultimately, both governments turned to the relatively low-stakes grounds of migration policy to achieve their goals, though like so many times before, enough problems accumulated to bring passport and visa issues up to the highest levels. In line with its policies of the last twenty years for new migration from Taiwan, the Nationalist government tried to exercise control over who traveled to the United States and monitor what they did there. The United States, meanwhile, could not afford to assent to every military or defensive demand from Taipei but did make visa decisions in such a way as to signal its support for the struggling government. The decade-long efforts at "visa diplomacy" failed to prevent the impending disaster of de-recognition for the Nationalists, though it might have helped to forestall it until the 1970s. That said, it solidified, rather than weakened, the overseas voices calling for independence.

Two Chinas, One Taiwan, and Thomas Liao

The Taiwan independence movement evolved out of a history of colonialism in Taiwan. From 1895 to 1945 the island was controlled by Japan, and subsequently the Nationalist Chinese government moved in and attempted to establish a new regime. Despite being of the same ethnicity, the Nationalists and native-born Taiwanese did not have a shared agenda for the future of the island. Clashes between the two erupted as early as 1947 in the infamous "228 Incident"—so named because it began on February 28—when Nationalist troops fired on a crowd of Taiwanese antigovernment protesters, inaugurating a wave of violence that left thousands of Taiwanese dead. In the aftermath of 228, many independence advocates fled the island. Thomas Liao (Liao Wenyi) and his brother Joshua were in Shanghai when the massacre occurred, but they had been active in advocating democracy and self-determination for Taiwan. In late 1947 they created one of several competing independence organizations in Hong Kong, but officials there had enough troubles with Chinese Nationalist and Chinese Communist disputes and no desire to extend toleration to a third movement. Eventually the brothers moved to Japan, which had become the home of other pro-independence exiles. There, despite troubles over illegal entry, they eventually settled into political advocacy, eventually trying to unite competing factions in a single provisional government for the Republic of Taiwan in 1956, with Thomas as its head. Using the United Nations' own rhetoric, Thomas Liao submitted dozens of petitions to American diplomats and UN representatives seeking support for self-determination for Taiwan.[5] According to historian Steven Phillips, "By the 1960s, Liao's movement seemed 'tired' as new leaders with ties to students in Japan became more prominent."[6] Instead, the independence movement found new life among Taiwanese students increasingly choosing to study in the United States.

The Taiwan independence movement in the United States developed over the course of the 1950s and 1960s from segmented, regionalized groups of activists to a centralized movement. According to activist Lu Zhuyi, the first and perhaps hardest step was simply getting to the United States. The process involved investigations, exit permits, a passport application, and a difficult approval process by the Ministry of Foreign Affairs, and that was all before the United States issued a visa.[7] Once successful, students tended to follow others from the same schools and hometowns, resulting in Taiwanese students becoming clustered around four areas in the United States: Philadelphia and New York; Chicago and the University of Wisconsin at Madison; Kansas State University in Manhattan, Kansas, and the University of Kansas at Lawrence; and the city of Los Angeles and surrounding areas. These areas were, unsurprisingly, sites hosting major universities. "Academia became a battleground for Taidu [Taiwan independence] advocates. Universities were vital for the recruitment of supporters, offered a forum for meetings and employment of activists, and presented an opportunity to promote study of the island by American scholars."[8] As long as these remained regional centers—they did not have regular contact—there was no real threat of a broad-based movement. But by the late 1950s and early 1960s, that began to change. In the 1950s, Philadelphia-based Chen Yide (Ch'en I-te), Lu Zhuyi (Loo Tsu-yi), and Lin Rongxun founded the "Free Formosans' Formosa" (3F). It was a short-lived, underground organization, but its existence did not manage to remain a secret from the KMT or the U.S. Federal Bureau of Investigation.[9] Lu Zhuyi recalled attracting the interest both of KMT agents, who tried to get his family in Taiwan to write letters compelling him to quit the movement, and the FBI, which called him in for questioning. Lu believes in the latter case that the Nationalists regularly reported that Taiwan independence activists were Communists or Communist sympathizers, then counted on American anticommunism to do the rest.[10] The network of activists dissolved 3F and in 1958 created United Formosans for Independence (UFI) in its place.

Long operated in secrecy, in 1961 UFI made its first public appeals for U.S. support. UFI members still considered Thomas Liao a spiritual leader of the movement, but that put the organization in a difficult position. As detailed in the *New York Times* in 1961, "The Chinese Nationalist Government denounced [Liao] as an impostor and a Communist stooge. The Chinese Communist Government denounces him as an impostor and an imperialist stooge."[11] UFI members counted on Americans seeing the Taiwanese as a third and totally separate group and, ideally, the rightful claimant to the island of Taiwan. That proved a difficult task in a Cold War climate that still demanded loyalty to Chiang Kai-shek in the name of anticommunism, but it sparked real fear in Taipei. Yang Dongjie, a 3F member, boasted that friends had some success getting girlfriends and family members out of Taiwan by writing letters to Soong May-ling (Madame Chiang Kai-shek) threatening to inform prominent Americans about the "real" situation in Taiwan.[12] Though a bit far-fetched, the story illustrates the perception of activists that the KMT feared its antidemocratic rule would become common knowledge and damage support in the United States for its government. Independence advocates gave up that leverage by going public, also staging a series of small public protests concurrent with Republic of China vice president Chen Cheng's visit to the United States.[13]

In Japan, Thomas Liao had some contact first with 3F and then UFI via traveling members, like Yang Dongjie, who stopped off en route to Taiwan. According to Yang, Liao had received an invitation to visit the United Nations (Yang does not mention from whom) but was prevented from going by the KMT.[14] In fact, his visa was stopped by none other than John F. Kennedy himself, in one of the rare cases where visa diplomacy reached the highest levels of government. Liao's 1961 application for a U.S. visa was simply the latest of many. He had been applying for a visa to visit the United States since the mid-1950s, and U.S. officials had been rejecting his applications since then. Along the way, he picked up some valuable supporters, including former foreign service officer (turned Taiwan advocate) George Kerr and Senator William J. Fulbright. Liao had been kept out of the United States for years on the grounds that "his presumed activities here would seriously disturb our relations with the GRC [government of the Republic of China] and hence would be 'prejudicial to the public interest.'" Led by Fulbright, the Senate Committee on Foreign Affairs had been critical of the decision, forcing a comprehensive review of the case, in which the State Department determined that Liao "presents no material threat to the security of the GRC."[15] Having no legal justification for denying the visa, in 1961 the State Department informed Nationalist China that the United States would be lifting the ban. In conversations with National Security Adviser

McGeorge Bundy, Secretary of State Dean Rusk defended the decision, explaining that refusing a visa to a "political refugee" violated American values and traditions, and that it was even worse to do so at the request of an ally. Rusk also asserted that Liao would not "make anything like the amount of noise in the United States that the Chinese claim" and that after the initial fuss, the Nationalist complaints would simply die down.[16]

Despite these reassurances, the issue was a subject of major debate within the White House and extensive negotiations between Washington and Taipei. Robert Komer of the National Security Council once wrote, "The proposed visit of Thomas Liao is a killer." Though sympathetic to State's position, Komer noted that the Nationalists found the idea of giving Liao a visa "an affront."[17] The Liao visa became tied up in the other headline issue of the day, which was the admission of Mongolia to the United Nations. The Nationalists, joined by the United States, had spent the 1950s blocking Mongolia's entry. When word leaked that the United States was considering establishing formal diplomatic ties with the Soviet client state, Nationalists led by Chiang Kai-shek worried that not only had this particular policy changed, but that it might be a signal of a larger shift in Washington toward accommodation. In the summer of 1961, the issue grew more complicated when the Soviet Union began to link admission of Mongolia with the admission of Mauritania, so now voting to keep Mongolia out carried the risk of offending dozens of new African states whose votes were necessary to the even larger U.S. policy goal for the UN: keeping the Nationalists in and the Chinese Communists out. The fact that both the announcement of the Liao visa and possible recognition of Mongolia had been made as a fait accompli, without prior consultation with Taipei, only increased the Nationalists' sense of insecurity.[18] All three issues—Chinese representation in the UN, admission of Mongolia, and a visa for Thomas Liao—were now linked, and the Nationalists proved so irate at how they had been handled that they canceled a scheduled visit from Chiang's son, Chiang Ching-kuo.

The U.S. ambassador in Taipei, Everett Drumright, along with CIA operative Ray Cline, raced to do damage control. State sent instructions to Drumright that explained U.S. policy and emphasized that nothing had changed. But something had: built into the instructions was an assumption that if something like a "two Chinas" formula was necessary to keep the Chinese Communists out of the UN, the Nationalists should consider it. Liao, meanwhile, had to be given a visa, because to refuse "would raise [a] sharp issue here involving individual rights and denial [of] such rights on wholly political grounds."[19] In reply, Chiang Kai-shek made very clear to

Drumright that Mongolia, Liao, and, most important, any talk of "two Chinas" were nonnegotiable, and wavering on these issues was "incompatible with consideration due a close ally." Chiang agreed that Liao was unimportant individually but feared his admission to the United States would rapidly raise his status both abroad and among dissidents in Taiwan.[20] At the same time, Cline's discussion with Chiang Ching-kuo reinforced the weight Taipei placed on these issues. Cline observed that "they live in a queer world in which only the U.S. stands between them and disaster, and in which therefore the faintest indication of a change in U.S. attitudes can seem like a matter of life and death." Uneasiness could lead to "dangerous adventures," like spurring forward plans for an attack to retake the mainland.[21] In an attempt to offer reassurance, Kennedy sent a letter directly to Chiang Kai-shek, asking for direct talks with a trusted emissary to clear up any confusion about the direction of U.S. policy. In that letter, Kennedy promised to have the U.S. Embassy in Tokyo withhold Liao's visa until further talks to clarify matters. He also assured Chiang that he was not committed to establishing diplomatic relations with Outer Mongolia, and promised to work with the Chinese for a better strategy on UN admission.[22] Vice President Chen Cheng agreed to make the trip.

The Chen visit required careful handling. In his briefing on the Liao case, Kennedy was reminded that it had the potential to be explosive either way. Granting the visa would anger Taipei, but "we have been subjected to increasingly strong criticism over our previous stand on denying Liao a visa. We believe that if this criticism is not eased, the Liao case may become a serious political issue in the United States which will give Liao undeserved publicity—a state of affairs which both we and the GRC surely wish to avoid." The legal grounds for the refusal had been undermined by Liao's lack of stature, and the fact that no clear danger could come of allowing him to visit. Since the United States had permitted dozens of other dissidents into the country—some a sore point for even America's closest allies—refusing Liao's visa threatened to turn him into an international cause célèbre.[23] Komer disagreed with this State Department analysis, however, and highlighted the issue as symbolic to Taipei of a changing U.S. China policy. He asked, "Isn't this one place, however, where we can appease the [ROC] (and make our peace with Senator Fulbright)? Even an extended delay till after the [General Assembly] session would help."[24] When Kennedy sat down with Chen, the two men agreed amiably that Liao himself was a "nonentity" to which neither country attached much importance.[25] And yet, they not only discussed at length the basis of his support in the United

States, Japan, and Taiwan, but agreed to defer the issue, which translated on the policy level to deferring Liao's visa. At the same time, the United States forced Chiang to swallow the bitter tea of Mongolian admission to the UN—by abstaining, at least, instead of vetoing the entry. The *New York Times* would report that the United States traded a promise to continue refusing Liao a visa for Chiang Kai-shek's promise not to prevent Mongolia from entering the United Nations.[26]

Mongolia notwithstanding, the strategy for keeping Nationalist China in the UN had to be revised, and U.S. proposals for how to do so deeply concerned Chinese officials. During the Kennedy administration, the old system of declaring a "moratorium" on the question broke down and was eventually replaced with the "important question" sleight of hand, though not before heated discussions between the two sides. The Liao visa was wedged firmly in the middle of this issue: not only was a change on one policy potential evidence of change on them all, but independence advocates supported a variation of the "two Chinas" formula that appalled both Taipei and Beijing. This episode served as a reminder to the Kennedy administration that there was one important principle that bound Nationalist and Communist China together: clear and total rejection of any idea of "two Chinas." As one analyst noted, "When it was recently rumored that Taiwan independence advocate Thomas Liao was to be given a visa for a tour of the US, [Beijing's] cries of outrage were second only to Taipei's."[27]

The State Department tried once again to convince Kennedy of the appropriateness of issuing a visa to Liao, noting that the issue had been deferred but not decided. George Ball argued that the inevitable temporary setback in U.S.-Chinese relations would be temporary and best endured in late 1961 and early 1962 when the UN representation issues were not under discussion and relative tranquility had been restored. In March 1962, Kennedy's answer seemed definitive: whatever the advantages on the public-relations front, he thought it "still to be true that [Liao's] anticipated activities in the United States would be prejudicial to the National interest."[28] In 1965, Liao gave up the fight and agreed to return to Taiwan from his long exile in Japan. Influenced by both rumors that his family in Taiwan was in danger and his own declining image as a movement leader in the face of bright new talent, Liao received a hero's welcome in Taipei and a position in the provincial government.[29] His contributions to the development and growth of the independence movement were undeniable, but his exile and migrations were more than the overtaxed Sino-American relationship could bear.

Limits of Extraterritorial Control

The same immigration laws that helped the Kennedy administration keep Thomas Liao out also kept large numbers of Chinese and other Asian migrants out of the United States. In the decade after Truman condemned the McCarran-Walter Act with harsh words and a veto (which was overridden), every new U.S. president took the opportunity to lament the failings of U.S. immigration law. By the 1960s, the impetus for change had a certain momentum that crossed political parties (though opposition to reform had its own bipartisan appeal). One of the issues driving the change was the fact that the refugee problems in both Europe and Asia had never really gone away. When President Eisenhower reminded Congress in 1960 that it was "World Refugee Year" and that the United States had joined together with other UN member states to look for "permanent solutions" to the decidedly impermanent problem, he also urged the removal of ethnic quotas and an end to the sharp limits on arrivals from Asia.[30] Subsequently, President Kennedy would make his own appeal to Congress late in his short presidency, and Lyndon Johnson would take up the mantle in 1964 and 1965. The result was the Hart-Celler Act of 1965, which Johnson himself lauded as an important, but not at all revolutionary, measure.

For as much as the McCarran-Walter Act represented a Cold War triumph of national security over foreign relations, the Hart-Celler Act of 1965 would represent the opposite. This act would finally be the measure that would end de facto Asian exclusion by doing away with the national origins quotas and creating a general pool of quota slots from which all applicants drew (up to twenty thousand from any given nation). This represented "the nation's shift toward an internationalist approach to containing communism" and a major breakthrough for Chinese immigration.[31] The lifting of the tight numerical limitations eliminated much of the need for fierce competition over those precious few visas or elaborate document fraud measures to enter as derivative citizens (INS continued to field confessions in the 1960s, but few came after the act). The drive and means of passing it came from the domestic reforms shaped by an overwhelmingly Democratic Congress, the civil rights movement, and President Johnson's Great Society program. Even so, the racial assumptions built into the earlier acts were not wholly absent here: despite Hart-Celler's divorcing of the visa priorities from national and ethnic groups, logic suggested that most of the skilled workers or close family of the overwhelmingly European immigrant base in the United States would also be white Europeans. The refugee preference written into the act also had Europe in mind. Reality neverthe-less proved otherwise: the majority of the backlog of people desperate to immigrate but hitherto unable to came from areas that had not been the largest sending areas in the past: Eastern and Southern Europe to a certain extent, but especially Asia.

It turned out that "Hart–Celler didn't come close to working as ex-pected," and the new 1965 immigration laws had a profound long-term ef-fect on Chinese immigration to the United States.[32] The United States had fielded plenty of applications from Chinese prior to the new law, a flow of people that originated from three sources: Chinese living in Taiwan under the Republic of China; Chinese overseas in Southeast Asia, Latin America, or elsewhere who were equally subject to the small quotas; and refugees in Hong Kong after 1949. A smaller, but not insignificant, number were Chinese already in the United States—stranded students and other visi-tors who adjusted to permanent resident status.[33] Not until the late 1970s, when full diplomatic relations were restored between the mainland Chinese government and the United States, would there be significant migration directly from the PRC. In the meantime, the Chinese population in the United States had almost three decades to become increasingly Taiwanese and increasingly educated, leading to two distinct problems. The first was the fact that as Asian nations developed, they lost scholars and scientists to American institutions in a process known as "brain drain." Many students and scholars left Taiwan for temporary tenure in the United States but never returned to contribute their skills and knowledge to the Republic of China. The second was the solidification of the United States as a center for the growing Taiwan independence movement.

First, the easing of visa restrictions led greater numbers of students and scholars to take advantage of the opportunity to study or conduct research in the United States, and perhaps most importantly, made it easier for them to adjust their status to remain on a permanent basis. The "brain drain" out of Taiwan, which sorely needed the scientists and engineers it sent to the United States, created a real dilemma for American consular workers, the gatekeepers who controlled the visas. Walter McConaughy, who spent much of the 1950s guarding against falsified applications from Chinese ap-plicants, was head of the U.S. Embassy in Taiwan by 1967. He lamented that when making their application for a student visa, Chinese graduate students "actually have at that time every intention to remain permanently in the U.S. But they conceal this fact from our Consular officers, in order to qual-ify for a student visa." The 1965 act ensured that later, when they made the formal application to stay, they would qualify for a preference visa based on their professional skills, something that would then allow them to remain without ever having endured the more rigorous screening that immigrant visa applicants encountered in American embassies and consulates in Asia.[34] Although one sardonic suggestion simply "to inculcate ROC youth with the Abraham Lincoln ideal of self-study before a fireplace" came to nothing, officials instead wondered if there would be ways to adjust immigration laws to create greater incentives to leave the United States at the end of a course of study, or to promote the Taiwan economy such that wages aligned more closely with U.S. levels.[35] Although INS yearbooks did not separate migrants from Taiwan from other Chinese immigrant and nonimmigrant arrivals, in the 1960s there is a clear trend for growing numbers of Chinese student visa applications. In reality, the problem of brain drain proved intractable, and the prospect of a permanent Taiwanese diaspora no longer under Nationalist control was a chilling one for some in the KMT.

Beyond the economic and expertise loss, the Nationalists worried over brain drain because of an observed tendency of Taiwanese students to become radicalized abroad. The concern that dissidents could come to the United States and influence the Chinese population already there was not a new one. Now, though, officials' worries increasingly split in two directions: the first was an ongoing fear dating back to the Communist revolution that Chinese emigrants could become Communist spies; and the second was the growing concern that Taiwanese emigrants would link up with dissidents and independence advocates. In both cases, emigrants could use their political lives to undermine both official and popular support for the Republic of China. Cold War–era Taiwanese migration to the United States created a community that opposed both Communist China and Nationalist China, and sought out American attention for the sake of an independent Taiwan. In an atmosphere in which increasing numbers of American scholars and policy watchers began to call for a new approach to China policy, including possible rapprochement with the mainland or a "two Chinas" formula for the United Nations, control over the activism and public statements of Taiwanese students became especially important. Nationalist emigration controls continued to screen emigrants, keeping in check the growth of the permanent Taiwanese American population until the 1980s—but enough students slipped through the cracks to reinforce the growing movement.[36]

Starting in the mid-1960s, the Nationalist government developed a new experiment in extraterritorial control: directing consulates in the United States to refuse requests for passport renewals from individuals involved in Taiwan independence–related activities. Initial memos on the decisions expressed some ambivalence on how effective the policy was in silencing activists, though the refusals did sometimes prevent individuals from changing jobs or processing U.S. residence permits.[37] For example, Taiwan independence advocates Lu Jianhe, Zhou Shiming, and Chen Boshan had their passport extensions denied by the Chicago or New York consulates; Lu subsequently ran into trouble with his residency permits, Zhen could not move to a new state for a job, and Chen found himself facing orders of deportation. Political science student (and future ROC foreign minister) Tian Hongmao agreed to write a statement of regret for his past involvement in the movement in order to get his passport extended and his residency issues resolved.[38] Richard Wang, a graduate of independence hotbed Kansas State, recalled his experience trying to renew his passport in New York in 1963. "The consul threatened that my passport would not be renewed unless I stop telling Americans what was happening in Formosa. He then suggested that I sign a 'letter of explanation' in exchange for the renewal of my passport. I refused." Wang tried, and failed, to get his passport renewed again in 1966. His attempts to get "exit visas" for his parents to leave Taiwan and visit him in the United States also failed.[39] Memos and cables between Taipei and various U.S. consulates clearly identified the passport extension refusals as of uncertain use. Consuls reported back with some regularity cases where it appeared to "work" (that is, when it got the individual in question in trouble with the INS, and in one case even leading to the individual's deportation from the United States), as well as times when it did not (because one way or another, the migrants managed to come up with a green card). Either way, dissidents would either have to leave their organizing activities or, at worst, remain at the status quo, so there was no disadvantage to conducting the experiment.

Though the passport experiments were ongoing, they were not the only means used by the Nationalists to try to regain extraterritorial control over their errant population in the United States. A memorandum for V. K. Wellington Koo, foreign minister of Nationalist China, suggested that China's U.S.-based consulates go even further and advocated numerous courses of action they could take: contact Taiwanese students, warning them not to take part in independence activities; limit exit permits for relatives; request that American universities shut down Taiwanese student associations; send consular representatives to investigate at schools harboring independence activities; investigate applications of Taiwanese students hoping to travel abroad to ensure they were neither independence activists nor planning to attend schools with many activists; share information about Taiwan with schools in the United States; and provide films and other informational materials to schools to counter anti-Taiwan statements from dissidents.[40] A more thorough proposal called for the use of intelligence agents to infiltrate groups; for increased predeparture training and education for students leaving to study abroad; greater cooperation from allied governments; and efforts to ensure that overseas Chinese community organizations remain loyal to the KMT.[41] None of these efforts were particularly new; as Hongshan Li has demonstrated for the period through World War II, "The Nationalist Party had been trying to exert thought control on students since the very beginning."[42] Vigorous predeparture screenings and party-line indoctrination classes, along with supervision while abroad, were meant to keep overseas activities in check and productive for the Nationalists. In the 1950s, the KMT extended the idea more broadly to Chinese immigrants and their American communities. That such efforts did not always succeed did not provide incentive for scaling them back.

The U.S. record on cooperation with these efforts was decidedly a mixed bag. In some cases, Taiwan independence advocates who had been denied passport extensions by the Nationalist Chinese consulates found sympathy in the Immigration and Naturalization Service. Chen Wuxiong, for example, applied to the INS with an expired passport and, at least according to KMT reports, was granted a residence permit (green card) anyway. Similar experiences with other applicants led the ROC's Public Safety Bureau to suggest that the Ministry of Foreign Affairs do more to reverse the "liberal" attitude of the INS.[43] In response to protests from the Nationalists, one INS officer explained that some visitors on educational exchange visas who had been long resident in the United States found success in applying for a waiver of the two-year foreign residency requirement, which once granted would allow them to apply directly for refugee status. This program was not unique to Taiwanese dissidents, but a standing policy that applied to everyone in similar circumstances.[44] The Nationalists appeared to have more success getting assistance from another branch of the U.S. Department of Justice, the FBI. According to independence advocates recounting their experiences years later, "Between 1960 and 1970 the U.S. government and the Chinese Nationalist Party had a deal that the FBI would give the KMT names of Taiwanese independence activists in the U.S. in exchange for the names of Chinese communists."[45] Whoever was collecting the information, MOFA files now contain comprehensive lists of the English and Chinese names, home addresses, and in some cases school activities of individuals perceived to be dissidents.

No amount of increased supervision could make up for relaxed U.S. immigration laws, however, and despite all efforts to stop it, the independence movement in the United States grew during the 1960s. In 1966, activists united the regional study groups to create United Formosans in America for Independence, or UFAI, the first real nationwide organization.[46] By 1970, the organization joined UFI groups in Japan, Canada, and elsewhere to create the World United Formosans for Independence, or WUFI. All the while, other efforts to unify through Taiwanese student groups and the pro-Taiwan press were in process.[47] Just as the Nationalists had feared, active Taiwan independence advocates worked to influence U.S. policy away from its singular support of the Republic of China and used their proximity to New York to try to influence the United Nations to recognize the People's Republic of China and a separate Republic of Formosa. UFIA members made frequent appeals to the public via the press and directly to U.S. officials. One appeal, published in the *New York Times* but reprinted in university newspapers like the University of Oklahoma's *Oklahoma Daily*, called on Americans to recognize that "the U.S., so we are told, is fighting in Vietnam to uphold the principle of self-determination. Your government has repeatedly demanded that the peoples in Cuba and East Europe be permitted to exercise the right of self-determination. Why, then, must Formosans alone be denied the same right?"[48] In 1968, news about a series of arrests of more than two hundred individuals in Taiwan involved in anti-KMT or pro-independence activities reached students in the United States, leading to letters like the one Francis W. Chang of Columbia University sent to Dean Rusk arguing that the "inhumanity and injustice of the Chiang Kaishek regime should not be ignored."[49] As the UN fight heated up in the late 1960s and early 1970s, the World United Formosans for Independence drafted a number of letters in pursuit of their goal of recognition, not only to UN officials but also to representatives of newly established postcolonial states, to seek their support. In a letter to Nyemba Wales Mbekeani, representative from Malawi, WUFI secretary for external affairs Lung-chu Chen appealed on the grounds of shared colonial history for help getting a plebiscite for Formosa on the agenda.[50] This sampling of independence activities demonstrates the larger problem for the Nationalists, that their own citizens were actively campaigning against them in the United States.

The Cold War had made the anticommunist government of Nationalist China important to the United States' policies in Asia despite Taipei's antidemocratic tendencies, but that situation could not last. Taiwanese activists' efforts to reveal the most illiberal aspects of the regime blossomed just as the United States was rethinking its approach to Communist China. As a result, the heavy-handed efforts to exert extraterritorial control on Chinese in America and to influence U.S. visa policy faced new limits.

Changing Tides in U.S.-Chinese Relations

The limits of visa diplomacy became very clear in the case of Peng Ming-min. A scholar of international law with a global education obtained in Japan, Canada, and Paris, Peng had both a reputation for good scholarship and well-respected friends all over the world. No stranger to violence, he had lost an arm in an American bombing raid in Japan just before the end of World War II and returned to Taiwan in time to witness the upheaval of the 228 Incident. He became the youngest full professor at National Taiwan University in 1957. He met with the approval of the Nationalist Party, which sent him to New York to aid the Chinese delegation at the United Nations. Peng had always been engaged politically, but increasingly his ideas about Taiwan and governance moved in a direction far less likely to receive official sanction. In 1964, Peng and two of his graduate students were arrested for attempting to print and distribute a pamphlet described as a Taiwanese declaration of independence. All three men were arrested and accused of advocating for "overthrowing the government by violent means."[51]

The case instantly attracted international attention. Taiwanese in the United States voiced their support, but so did American and Canadian professors and scholars who had worked with Peng or who appreciated his ideas, as well as Amnesty International. In the White House, James Thomson was kept busy replying to their inquiries, explaining that the U.S. government was "severely limited in its ability to interfere in internal matters of this nature" but had communicated to Taipei the extent of public and scholarly concern.[52] Editorials in major newspapers, including the *New York Times* and the *Washington Post*, reinforced the U.S. interest in Peng's future. As a result, the Nationalist embassy in Washington sent back to the Ministry of Foreign Affairs the suggestion that the sentences handed down on the three men be lightened as much as possible to avoid further exasperating the adverse public reaction.[53] That this was done attracted positive notice in a letter from Professor Douglas H. Mendel of the University of Wisconsin–Milwaukee. Mendel not only supported the movement, but in 1970 he also wrote one of the earliest, sympathetic books on it.[54] Mendel commented,

"The sentences were indeed lighter than many Taiwanese in this country expected, and we must all be grateful for that. The press release attributed the reduced terms to the defendants' cooperation; I attribute it to widespread American criticism of the whole episode."[55] With the international interest in Peng this high, official dealings with him became a matter of walking a careful tightrope: neither treating him so harshly that he became a martyr for the cause of independence, nor so leniently that others would be inspired to imitate him. Thomas Liao's return to Taiwan in May 1965 could not have come at a better time for the Nationalist government: combined with the light sentence for Peng, Liao's willingness to return home could be played up in the international press as an indication of the tolerance and openness of life in Taiwan.

The court sentenced Peng to eight years, but he was released after a year and a half for showing "sincere repentance." Even before he was released, offers started rolling in for visiting positions at American and Canadian universities. The most promising of these came from the University of Michigan, which by 1968 had come up with a funding package and made a formal invitation. Peng only needed to obtain two things: permission to leave Taiwan and a visa to enter the United States. Neither proved easy. Worried about Peng's influence both on Taiwanese in the United States and the underground movement in Taiwan, the central government tried to get Peng set up to do research at the prestigious Academia Sinica facility outside Taipei.[56] Following years in which he was not permitted to depart, but during which he said, KMT officials accused him of organizing contacts abroad for Taiwanese independence while he claimed to be subject to around-the-clock surveillance and threats on his life, Peng escaped Taiwan and ended up in Sweden.[57] In his memoir, Peng was purposefully vague about how he actually managed to escape, to avoid implicating those who helped him. Years later, it emerged that American missionary Milo Thornberry and several of his colleagues—inspired by a newspaper report on how one man escaped from East to West Berlin—helped alter a Japanese passport and funded a plane ticket out of Taipei.[58] Amnesty International in Sweden arranged for political asylum if Peng could get to Stockholm. Rumors flew that the CIA had helped extract him, but it was not the clandestine service: it was a handful of Methodists and Presbyterians.[59]

With asylum established in Sweden, Peng began the process of seeking permission to travel to the United States. As he explained to reporter Robert J. Korengold of *Newsweek*, "If I hope to influence Formosa's future, a major factor is U.S. policy. . . . And I can't influence U.S. policy from

Sweden."[60] The Nationalist government wasted no time in making its per-spective clear. Peng left Taiwan on the evening of January 3. On January 29, the Chinese Embassy in Washington sent a memorandum to the U.S. sec-retary of state explaining that Peng's escape was no doubt "motivated by his intention to resume seditious activities abroad." It went on: "In view of the friendly relations existing between the Republic of China and the United States of America, and to anticipate any attempt on Peng's part to carry on his treacherous activities in the United States, it is earnestly requested that instructions be issued by the Department of State to the United States diplomatic and consular establishments abroad to reject any application by Peng to seek entry into the United States or asylum therein should he contact any United States authorities for such purposes."[61] Though they obviously viewed it through a different lens, Peng and ROC officials clearly had a similar sense of his motivation for moving to the United States. The question for the ROC was how to stop him.

Embassy officials in Washington worried that once he applied for a visa, it would be too late for any positive outcomes for the Republic of China. The damage would already be done even if the State Department refused the visa, because that would create a swell of media interest in his case. The Nationalist relationship with the United States was already strained, Chi-nese in the United States looked less frequently to Taipei as their political bedrock, and talk was already running rampant of a "two Chinas" solution to the problem of the United Nations.[62] Reporter Keyes Beech of the *Chicago Daily News* helped present the core problem: "If Peng remains in Sweden he soon will be forgotten as any other Formosan who chose exile rather than live under Chinese Nationalist rule. But in the United States, Peng would be something else. There he could be at least a major embar-rassment, if not an indirect threat to the Nationalist Government."[63] As with the Liao case, there was a fine line to walk to prevent Peng from becoming not just one man, but an international cause. As a result, there was nothing less at stake than relations between Nationalist China and the United States, the strength of the independence movement abroad, the future of National-ist legitimacy and recognition, and the future of Communist China.

President Nixon had started signaling interest in changing the relation-ship with Communist China when he took office, and that made Taipei especially sensitive to the symbolic meaning of a visa. The combination of shifting public opinion (both internationally and domestically) and the Vietnam War gave the once ardent anticommunist incentive to reach out to Beijing and try to seek accommodation. The administration picked up some of the efforts of the Johnson administration, like relaxing travel policy for Americans interested in visiting China, and expanded them. The ambassadorial talks had moved from Geneva to Warsaw, but they continued. Moreover, the issues had changed somewhat since 1961, but the problem of Nationalist Chinese insecurity still threatened the ROC's cooperation with the United States. As one memorandum addressed to National Security Adviser Henry Kissinger explained, "President Chiang will take it as a personal affront if we decide to issue a visa. He will see it in the context of the removal of the permanent Strait patrol, the Warsaw meetings, and our statements and actions concerning relations with Communist China."[64] Once again, the State Department argued that Chiang was too dependent on the United States to make too much of a fuss over a visa, and again, the National Security team countered that in the larger context of the changing relationship in the 1960s, Chiang losing faith in American support could be dangerous. And there was even more to it than that. Allowing Peng into the country would invigorate the independence movement, but that had to be weighed against what it would look like to refuse him. Blowback would be guaranteed by either the appearance that the United States was too deferential to Nationalist China or a clear sign of the United States failing to uphold its own principles of free speech and human rights. This in turn could potentially "cause more publicity unfavorable to the GRC than any harm [Peng] might do by critical statements in the U.S."[65] Complicating everything was the fact that Henry Kissinger knew Peng from their shared time at Harvard University.[66] Peng wrote a personal letter to Kissinger—not his first—on January 23, expressing his concern for his wife and two children left behind in Taipei and asking Kissinger's advice on whether "Formosan authorities can be persuaded by the pressure of international opinion to let them leave."[67] Kissinger did not reply. John Holdridge, a National Security Council staff member, advised him that any reply would convince the Nationalists that President Nixon's closest advisers were "antipathetic" to their interests.[68]

No matter what the foreign policy preferences, simply refusing to grant Peng a visa was harder now than it had been earlier in the decade. The passage of the Hart-Celler Act created more avenues for legal entry and fewer grounds for exclusion than were available earlier in the decade. Nothing in Peng's personal history disqualified him. The arrest and conviction in Taiwan were not enough to make him ineligible for a visa—most crimes would, but this particular conviction was unquestionably political in nature, and there was nothing in his personal history to suggest he would take part in violent revolutionary activities. His public statements proved embarrassing to Nationalist China, but they were not dangerous to that government. So the only grounds on which he might be refused, a subsection of the law that permitted the denial of visas to anyone whose entry "would be prejudicial to the public interest, or endanger the welfare, safety, or security of the United States," did not seem to apply. That particular section of the law—which originated in the 1952 act—had been used to deny visas to people like Fidel Castro, Moise Tshombe, and, of course, Thomas Liao. But the last time this provision had been employed was 1962. The attorney general had broad discretion over such decisions, but that discretion did not include avoiding public criticism, which in this case was likely to be intense.[69] Faced with two unwelcome choices, the State Department country director for the Republic of China, Thomas Shoesmith, argued that if Peng Ming-min could not ultimately be denied entry to the United States, his arrival might at least be delayed until the tension caused by his unexpected escape to Sweden abated. The wisdom of this position seemed to be confirmed in April 1970, when a Taiwanese independence advocate connected to WUFI attempted to assassinate Chiang Ching-guo in New York. WUFI had publicly claimed Peng as their spiritual leader and announced he would be coming to the United States when he escaped Taiwan months earlier.[70] Even if Peng himself had no real connections to what was now considered a "terrorist" organization, his arrival would no doubt invigorate their work.

Peng could not be stalled indefinitely, as he applied for a nonimmigrant visa in March. The University of Michigan reinforced his application by filing a supporting petition asking that he be admitted for temporary employment. One option was to admit him for a year on a nonimmigrant visa on the condition that he not pursue Taiwan independence activities (terms more easily dictated on a nonimmigrant visa, because failure to comply would simply mean nonrenewal—though that was impossible to enforce, as the State Department discovered when visiting Burmese nationalist U Nu ignored similar restrictions).[71] Another option was to refuse the nonimmigrant permit on the grounds that Peng did not have another permanent home to return to, but offer to admit him as an immigrant. This method had the advantage of extended investigations and quota delays that meant postponing the final decision for anywhere from seven to twenty-two months. On the downside, it would also leave U.S. officials much less influence over his political activities. To refuse his entry on the grounds that it would be prejudicial to U.S. interests was rejected by the State Department, though kept alive longer in the National Security Council.[72] As

Peng himself remembers it, "The consul was polite but blunt in letting me know that he would have preferred that I did not request entry." He then recounts being asked about whether he would engage in political activity, which he countered was hard to define. "Our prolonged conversation took a rather surprising turn when the consul asked if I would allow my name to be used on any letterhead. I replied that was unlikely; I had never done that sort of thing."[73] That clumsy attempt to determine the depth of Peng's formal connection to WUFI aside, Peng had few complaints about how his visa case was handled.

During the summer of indecision that followed the application, Kissinger in particular received repeated appeals from other scholars on Peng's behalf. Harvard professor and former ambassador to Japan Edwin O. Reischauer wrote, "If Peng were to be refused entry, I am sure there would be a very strong outcry in this country from a lot of people. In fact, I would join in myself."[74] A. Doak Barnett also wrote from the Brookings Institution, citing "important issues of fundamental and academic freedom involved" that ought to trump any political concerns.[75] Meanwhile, Chinese consulates worked to gather evidence that Peng was pursuing political goals (not academic work) through his speeches and publications, in the hope that it would help give the United States grounds to deny the visa.[76] Despite repeated Nationalist protests over the case, State believed that "since it is hard to see how Peng's admission to the US really could injure any vital GRC interest, even if he were to become actively engaged in the Taiwan Independence movement here, the GRC effort to prevent his admission appears to be little more than a matter of political vengeance or face-saving."[77] By September, as the University of Michigan term opened, it became clear that the United States would not likely refuse to issue the visa. Consular reports back to Taipei offered assurances that it would be a one-year visitor visa with restrictions on political activities; Sweden had helped along the case for a nonimmigrant visa by issuing a reentry permit to Peng, along with a work permit and other materials that made clear Peng had a potential home there.[78] Chiang Kai-shek made one last-ditch effort at heading off the visit with a cable to Nixon arguing, "In view of the friendly relations between our two countries and considering the certainty of exceedingly serious impact on the maintenance of stability in Taiwan and the continued viability of our strength against communism, I strongly urge your excellency to consent [to] issuing instructions to your government organs concerned immediately to bar Peng's admission into your country."[79] Peng arrived in the United States on September 29. As he settled into his life in

Michigan, Nationalist informants keep close watch on him. In his memoir, Peng recalled being followed by KMT agents and slandered "as a 'Communist,' 'adventurer,' 'rapist,' 'CIA agent,' and 'stooge of the United States and Japan.'"[80] Through the end of 1970 and into 1971, ROC officials made repeated complaints about the political activities in which Peng engaged in the United States, hoping his temporary visa could be revoked if enough evidence was acquired. Instead, he stayed for twenty-two years.

That the U.S. government was no longer willing to defer to Taipei on difficult visa cases proved to worried Nationalists that American China policy was changing; but the Peng decision annoyed the Communists as well. As Harvard Law professor Jerome Cohen explained in an op-ed, "A State Department that has been flexibly hinting at its willingness to modify our hostile policy toward Communist China was aware that Peng's admission would be viewed as dimly in [Beijing] as in Taipei." Even perceived support for a Taiwan independence advocate could be viewed in either Chinese government as a shift toward a "two Chinas" (or "one China, one Taiwan") policy. Neither Taipei nor Beijing endorsed such a move. Nevertheless, like every other prominent scholar who voiced an opinion, Cohen supported the visa despite the international consequences.[81]

In Nixon's and Kissinger's attempts to achieve a rapprochement with Communist China, the status of Taiwan proved the major stumbling block. Both in Kissinger's 1971 secret meeting with Zhou Enlai and Nixon's meetings in China the following year, Zhou raised the issue of potential U.S. support for the Taiwan independence movement. In 1971, Zhou asked about the U.S. attitude on the Taiwan independence movement, seeking assurance that it would not be tolerated in the United States or in Taiwan. "Don't you know," he asked Kissinger, "that Chiang Kai-shek is complaining greatly that it was CIA which allowed Peng Meng-min [*sic*] to escape from Taiwan?" Kissinger replied that Peng was a former student of his, but then went on, "First, to the best of my knowledge, CIA had nothing to do with Professor Peng Meng-min's [*sic*] coming to the USA. Second, if the President and Chairman Mao come to an understanding, then it's my job to enforce it in the bureaucracy, and I assure you that it will be enforced."[82] Kissinger was offering assurances that, if need be, the NSA could override State or the consulates on visas, or do whatever else was necessary to keep the movement in check. Nine months later, Nixon had the chance to reinforce Kissinger's commitments. On Peng's escape to the United States, he lamented to Zhou, "Mr. Prime Minister, Chiang Kai-shek did not like it. You did not like it either. Neither did we like it. We had nothing to do with it." Kissinger reminded Zhou of his promise "that we would not support directly or indirectly as a government, or any other form, the Taiwan Independence Movement within the United States," to which Nixon immediately agreed.[83]

Nixon and Kissinger promised not to encourage the movement, but they did not place any real weight on its importance. When an editorial in a Washington newspaper a month later criticized the Shanghai Communiqué for failing to mention the Taiwanese, Nixon turned to Kissinger and asked, "What in the hell is the Taiwanese Independence Movement all about?"[84]

The Taiwan independence movement was not a major political force in the 1960s, but it was a thorn in the sides of Washington, Taipei, and Beijing as all three governments tried to negotiate a new relationship. The use of immigration policy by the United States to grant or deny visas, and by the Nationalist Chinese to control and restrict a political movement they deemed threatening to their political future, proved more ad hoc than consistent. In the context of war, military threats, and loss of recognition, there was no reason for the Nationalist government not to try everything possible to prevent the worst from happening, and unlike most other forums for a changing foreign policy, migration issues proved a low-stakes arena in which to experiment from a government perspective, even if the stakes were high for individual migrants. As a result, the growth of the independence movement was limited to an increasing number of Taiwanese students and scholars in the United States until the combination of American de-recognition and the early 1970s Diaoyutai movement galvanized broader support for independence. But the response of the United States, both in moving from cooperating over the Liao visa to determining it could not refuse the Peng visa, and in using new immigration laws to permit permanent residence for Taiwanese activists, offered a clear signal that Washington was rethinking China policy.

From Kennedy to Nixon, each subsequent administration moved a little closer to the idea of ending Communist China's exclusion, and migration policy became an arena for considering and signaling that. Alongside the intermittent repatriation talks and new ideas about travel policy, declining cooperation with Nationalist efforts to exert extraterritorial control over the Chinese in the United States proved a clear signal of the changes coming. By the end of the decade, the Chinese American community was as politically diverse as any other in the United States. The long-standing Cantonese Chinatowns were filling up with Cold War migrants, who were new Taiwanese students and independence advocates, refugees (who, thanks to ARCI, often had some claim to the status of "intellectuals"), stranded Chinese students who never chose repatriation, and occasionally reunifying family members. U.S. immigration policy, combined with closed Cold War borders, helped create a new Chinese community that would become known as a "model minority." And inasmuch as members of that community looked to Asia for their motherland, it was divided between old-time Nationalists, hopeful supporters of a stronger People's Republic whether Communist or not, leftists and progressives choosing Communist China, and Taiwan independence advocates hoping for a third way. Their transnational ties complicated the ways the governments involved cooperated and competed. As becomes clear in the case of the Taiwan independence movement, visa and passport policy became both assertive and reactive attempts to control the role migrants played in foreign policy.

Conclusion

Coming in from the Cold

Nationalist China's increasing insecurity about American policy and support in the 1960s stemmed not only from concerns over the rise of the Taiwan independence movement but also from constantly changing conditions in Asia. Increasing U.S. commitments to South Vietnam, especially after the hot war began in earnest in 1964, offered the Nationalists opportunities to stand with the United States against communism. Nationalist soldiers and spies committed to intelligence work, training programs, and transport missions; Taiwan also proved valuable as a staging area for American troops and planes.[1] Eventually, as the Vietnam War dragged on, it created a much more urgent need for U.S. communication with Beijing.

It was the long-standing policy of the United States to contain the People's Republic of China and isolate it from global affairs. That policy had included nonrecognition, of course, as well as opposition to seating the PRC in the United Nations in place of (or even alongside) the ROC, the trade embargo that criminalized remittances, the massive propaganda effort to isolate China from both the American public and its diaspora in Asia, and prevention of travel of Americans to the mainland for any reason. Through the 1950s, one expression of this policy was American commitment to the idea that the Republic of China alone had the right to speak for the Chinese people living outside the bamboo curtain, a notion that reached forward to include who governs repatriations, where could deportees be sent, how immigrants were screened, and in what ways refugees were aided. The flaws in this notion crystallized as it became painfully clear that the one group of Chinese people for whom the ROC could not possibly claim to speak were the approximately 700 million Chinese on the mainland.[2] The UN seat remained important to the ROC for the same reason as had speaking up on behalf of Chinese migrants: it "represents an affirmation of [the ROC's] claim to be the only legitimate Government of China."[3] Nevertheless, despite murmurs of support for a changed policy—not to mention the French government's decision to recognize Communist China in 1964—the newly reelected Johnson administration had to contend with its position on Vietnam first and foremost, and the idea of reaching out to China while holding the line in Saigon seemed both weak and unlikely to be effective.[4]

In 1966, the start of the "Great Proletariat Cultural Revolution" on the mainland confused onlookers. All but one of the PRC's ambassadors abroad were recalled for consultations in Beijing, and the fighting between more leftist Red Guards and less political Chinese citizens that seemed to consume the streets also reached the halls of the Ministry of Foreign Affairs.[5] The turmoil of the Cultural Revolution served to isolate the Chinese migrants from the motherland, leading to another drop in remittances and a rise in overall efforts to assimilate into local societies.[6] More directly for U.S. policy, it also served to delay interest in changing the nature of Sino-American relations, as an inward-facing, revolutionary China might be less of a threat to American efforts in Vietnam. By 1968, however, there were indications that some measure of stability had returned when China accepted the date proposed by the Johnson administration to continue the ambassadorial talks.[7] For the Nationalists, the turmoil on the mainland seemed to present a last, best opportunity for staging a counterattack. The missed opportunities in 1962 created a renewed sense of urgency in Taipei. Chiang Kai-shek made repeated appeals to the United States for support, but the Kennedy and Johnson administrations both agreed on the unlikelihood of success and the lack of real support for the KMT on the mainland.[8]

At the end of the 1960s, China began easing its way from the height of Cultural Revolution violence, and the United States was starting the long process of battling its way out from the Vietnam War. Neither conflict would come to a complete close until the mid-1970s, but the potential for a change in the relationship between the United States and Communist China was already in the wind when President Richard Nixon took office in 1969. In the lead-up to rapprochement, both countries turned increasingly to the idea that personal contact—ending the isolation and division that had marked the relationship—was the most likely means of providing a breakthrough. Certainly, the ambassadorial talks had proved antagonistic and frequently fruitless, but in later years their protagonists Johnson and Wang proved to be "the friendliest of enemies," exchanging greetings when the opportunity arose.[9] The early hopes of "détente" offered by the Agreed Announcement, before it became clear just how difficult the project would be to implement, did not find another clear opening until the 1970s, but when it did, migration became a path forward. Migration policy and increased personal contact as Chinese and American nationals crossed back and forth between countries became an important part of the means by which it could happen.

The policy of isolating the PRC using heavy restrictions on trade and travel began to break in the 1960s. When the travel ban went into effect in 1952, the lack of diplomatic ties meant there was no way to protect citizens except through third-party representation, and should more travelers be detained on political grounds, that could create a new source of tension in a region that was not particularly short on it. The protection of nationals was only half the problem: the other half was that allowing travel might allow the Communist government "to use the establishment of trade and cultural relations with the United States as a means of gaining respectability and acceptance into the family of nations."[10] By the end of the 1950s, there had been only a few exceptions to the travel rule: in 1957, the Eisenhower administration authorized some journalists to receive passports for travel to China, though none received visas; family members of Americans serving long sentences in Chinese prisons were permitted to go under the supervision of the International Red Cross; on occasion someone well-known to Mao Zedong or Zhou Enlai, like the journalist and author Edgar Snow, and a couple of odd individuals—one a lawyer investigating a case and the other the personal valet of Dag Hammarskjold of the UN—received valid passports, given the extenuating circumstances involved.[11] Occasionally left-leaning American students or intellectuals visited at the invitation of Beijing, but these unsanctioned trips carried the risk of being stripped of a passport upon return to the United States.[12]

The path toward greater interaction proved difficult to forge, however, because all too frequently American overtures and Chinese interest failed to coincide. Nonetheless, over the course of the 1960s the United States "embarked on a policy of ending the ostracism of Communist China by easing its passport restrictions and permitting American citizens traveling abroad to bring back limited amounts of purchases originating in Communist China."[13] Proponents of a changed China policy suggested small steps forward, like ending bans on trade.[14] Lifting travel controls similarly became a small and safe step that could signal interest without causing undue alarm in Taipei or in the capitals of other American allies, but which would still encourage increasing contact that would include scholarly research, the exchange of journalists, and eventually tourist travel, all of which might help to put the Sino-American relationship on a standing more akin to the tentative contact the United States sustained with Eastern Europe. Moreover, "by permitting desirable projects the United States [could] encourage private American efforts at breaking down Communist China's self-imposed isolation."[15] This kind of personal, private diplomacy would not make the countries instant allies, but it could help push American ideas into a country that had largely resisted them.

Beyond these benefits, one reason to lift U.S.-based restrictions on travel to China was that there was no sense at all that the PRC would let any Americans enter. That being the case, magnanimously offering travel opportunities to at least a few select classes of people would simply demonstrate "that the Chinese Communists have imposed isolation upon themselves and underline the fact that it is [Beijing] not the US which fears and avoids all contacts."[16] In other words, it would signal a new American policy of "containment without isolation" and inform an international audience that it was now the PRC, not the United States, that was perpetuating Chinese exclusion from world affairs.[17] An early test case came in 1964, when Dr. Samuel Rosen, an ear surgeon specializing in relieving deafness, and his wife (and surgical nurse) received an invitation to travel to the mainland. In authorizing the passports, the State Department suggested the Rosens' trip "might help to remind the Chinese people that we are their friends, whatever problems we have with the Communist regime which controls them. It may also give the lie to Communist propaganda that we have no interest in the welfare of the Chinese people themselves."[18] Once the Rosens received official, validated passports from the U.S. government, Chinese officials revoked their invitation. There was so little trust between Beijing and Washington that the idea that the United States might sanction the trip was enough to make the Rosens suspect.[19]

Despite the Rosen setback, the following year the Johnson administration opted to make authorization of travel for medical personnel a general policy. The decision came after a long process of analyzing every possible advantage or disadvantage to the move. When the policy was finally announced in December 1965, James C. Thomson Jr. observed of the press reaction: "Most significant is the 'ho-hum, so what else is new?' attitude of local reporters. It makes our internal huffing and puffing and our sense of boldness all seem a bit pathetic."[20] Beijing officials expressed concerns in 1966 that "by discriminatingly validating passports for travel to mainland China the United States is attempting to dictate to the Chinese who [sic] they may invite to their country." Oddly, this statement is reminiscent of the argument the United States made against ROC attempts to control who could be issued "immigrant" passports after repeal of exclusion. When it was the PRC saying it, however, State Department officials found it "an extremely limp subterfuge."[21]

The authority of the U.S. government to issue passports had been well established in early twentieth-century immigration laws, but the question of the government's ability to restrict their use came under contention in the 1960s. A series of court cases stripped the State and Justice Departments of their ability to respond to violations of travel restrictions, culminating in two decisions in 1967 establishing that there could be no criminal charges against someone who engaged in unauthorized travel, and that there was no right to strip away a citizen's passport for using it in travel to restricted areas.[22] The decisions came in a period when few if any Americans thought of going to the People's Republic, as the early months of the Cultural Revolution did not appear even by secondhand report to be a terribly appealing time for travel. But by 1968 there seemed to be a shift in attitudes, and State Department officials once again discussed the possibility of ending the travel ban. Big changes to U.S. relations with Communist China faced intractable issues, specifically Taiwan, UN representation, and the ongoing Vietnam War, not to mention the secondary impact any major move might have on other U.S. allies in Asia. Instead, there were "advantages to movement on lesser issues—trade and travel restrictions." The advantage to moving first on these low-stakes areas was that "over the long run, any expanded communication with Communist China which might result could contribute to constructive change within China."[23] In other words, ending China's isolation through more people-to-people contact might eventually lead to more liberal ideas in the Chinese leadership. In the meantime, most applications for travel to China for any purpose other than pure tourism were approved, but the general ban on travel to China remained, in part to justify other travel restrictions, such as those in place against travel to North Korea, North Vietnam, and Cuba.[24]

The relaxation of travel restrictions (though not yet an outright end to them) was important to promoting increased contact. At the same time, U.S. presidents still tried to maintain the precarious balance between easing Communist China's exclusion without isolating Nationalist China. To this end President Nixon announced in 1969, "We have relaxed our travel restrictions and purchases with regard to Communist China, but we regard Communist China as an aggressive nation. U.S. policy toward China has not changed, and we will not admit the country to the UN."[25] That effort to placate the Nationalists had limited effect, because the reality was that the two allies had reached different conclusions about what constituted a stable and secure East Asia. The United States preferred some sort of de facto "two Chinas" policy that would allow it to support the nominally democratic KMT regime on Taiwan while opening contact with Communist China on the mainland. The Nationalists preferred an isolated Beijing and sole recognition.

Opening some doors for travel meant not only the opportunity for Americans to visit China, but also for Chinese to come to the United States directly from the mainland. Lingering questions from the 1950s about Chinese Communist infiltration took a new turn in 1971, when the admission of the PRC to the United Nations meant that for the first time since the founding of the People's Republic, there would be a Communist Chinese delegation in New York. Although U.S. officials acknowledged that "Chinese communities in the US are traditionally conservative, ruled by pro-Nationalist leaders through interlocking familial, regional or benevolent organizations," they also expressed some concern that "in the last several years there has been a slow but steady polarization in the communities, with older conservative leaders still holding the upper hand. But the solid front is being eroded by changing times."[26] The audiences that were considered most vulnerable to Communist persuasion were students: Chinese students from Hong Kong and Taiwan who were ambivalent toward Nationalist China, and American intellectuals and students eager to learn and know more about mainland China. Even so, the *New York Times* reported increasing interest in Communist China even among regular residents of Chinatown. Though acknowledging that the Nationalists remained very engaged in overseas Chinese issues, by 1971 there was increasing sympathy for the mainland government. This was not due to any great love of communism, but to the sense that "the Government in Peking is doing much to restore pride to a people too long humiliated and victimized by foreign powers."[27]

The ban on travel to China was officially dropped for all purposes in 1971, just shy of its twenty-year anniversary. The Nixon administration observed, "The reaction has been overwhelmingly favorable with the notable exceptions of nervousness in Moscow and Taipei and silence in [Beijing]. The move has been welcomed as a step toward improved US-PRC relations."[28] Beijing's silence did not last long. In April 1971, China invited the United States table tennis team visiting Japan to visit for a match. Americans took this as a sign that "the People's Republic, like the United States, is serious in its approach to the search for a new relationship."[29] Though the opening suggested new opportunities for exchanges, it also evoked bitterness from two groups. American China scholars long interested in visiting the mainland had spent years trying to get permission from either government to study the country firsthand. "I can lose 21-to-nothing as well as any one of those guys," one graduate student complained to the *New York Times*.[30] Taipei officials, meanwhile, searched for reciprocity and a clear sign of continued status. When the United States reciprocated and invited the PRC national ping-pong team to tour the United States, a private anticommunist organization helped the Nationalists send their own ping-pong team along to shadow them.[31]

With the opening established, journalists, scholars, and members of Congress all lined up for the opportunity to go, and State Department experts on China acknowledged that "over the years, word-of-mouth communication in mainland China, perhaps still the most important form of communication there, has helped keep alive friendly feelings among the Chinese toward Americans."[32] The push for increased contact was not coming only from the United States. Instead, the break in the impasse came also from the Chinese decision to pursue its "people's diplomacy" with the United States: professional foreign relations experts having failed all these years, it was time to leave the question up to the amateurs. The concept meant looking for points of agreement or cooperation with nongovernmental entities abroad in the hope that they would influence their governments' policies in ways beneficial to the PRC.[33] Like "barefoot doctors"—people with no formal training sent to the countryside to practice country medicine—perhaps barefoot diplomats could be anyone coming into contact with the United States.

Numerous choices over the previous twenty years had reinforced the truth of the idea that, good or bad, private diplomacy mattered: the use of personal contacts and letters to influence family members on either side of the Pacific; the prominent support of American voluntary organizations for the refugees in Hong Kong; the impact of the missteps of immigration officers in turning individual and official attitudes in China away from the United States; the experience of being accused and betrayed by neighbors into a Chinese prison; the potential for a defector to influence opinions of an entire community. Migrants kept the connection between the United States and the People's Republic of China alive throughout the isolation of Asia's Cold War. They also influenced the cooperation between Americans and the Republic of China, and the policies governing their movement affected how all three related to one another.

In 1972, the most vital "migration" of all changed the face of the Cold War in Asia: President Richard Nixon visited China. He was only a temporary visitor—and unlike many of the other "temporary" stays in this history, there was no question of him overstaying his visa—but his trip was the culmination of a larger realization in both Beijing and Washington that personal contacts could help forge a new relationship. This one voyage opened the doors for countless others in both directions, as mainland China and the United States returned to the pre-1949 status quo of exchanging students, scholars, diplomats, traders, and immigrants. Opening these contacts had profound impacts on the Republic of China, of course, and true to form that government turned to diasporic supporters to shore up support and ride out the tempest that followed. The end of the twenty-plus-year policy of isolation of mainland China meant new generations of temporary and permanent migrations would now have the task of shaping the way forward.

Migration Diplomacy and U.S.-China-Taiwan Relations

Over the course of three decades, the alliance between the United States and Nationalist China formed, flourished, and flailed. That alliance was held together at its heart by defensive agreements, economic aid and cooperation, shared responsibilities, and international cooperation. It was also forged through transnational migration, traditionally an issue with lower stakes involved, though not, of course, to the migrants themselves. Though the migration diplomacy that was constantly ongoing behind the high-level interactions makes only sporadic appearances in most histories of the bilateral relationship, it played an important role in how the alliance operated between 1943 and 1972.

This book has shown that migration diplomacy was built into the foundation of the alliance between Nationalist China and the United States. First, migration issues were central to the day-to-day management of the relationship. High-level visits, military threats, or sudden crises were exceptional events, while issuing visas and protecting citizens were continuous actions. During the Cold War, the United States used migration issues to show support for Nationalist China in a way that cost it very little, and sometimes fell back on migration issues when other forms of support proved impossible. The Nationalists used it to shape the Chinese voices in the United States in favor of supporting their government, and to maintain recognition and legitimacy. When those rights were contested by Communist China, their importance to the Nationalist regime only increased. Second, migration diplomacy served as a litmus test for the health of the relationship. The United States used migration policy to signal support of the Nationalists in their fights against Japan and then against the Communists, but it also used related issues to open contact with the People's Republic of China. The rapprochement with the PRC had its earliest indications in the ambassadorial talks, and it is possible retroactively to trace the shifting American attitudes toward the two Chinese governments through the migration policies in the years that followed. There is ample evidence that Nationalist officials interpreted U.S. actions this way, as they worried about a larger change in recognition from the very first American acknowledgment of the PRC right to protect and aid Chinese abroad.

In the 1940s, American and Chinese officials developed a working, but fundamentally unequal, alliance to fight against the threat of Japanese militarism. As a result, even the advances for Chinese migrants stemming from the end of exclusion took place on unequal terms. Other measures, such as the end of extraterritoriality, the allowance of shore leave for Chinese sailors, the agreements over Chinese aliens conscripted to U.S. military service, and the Chinese American community's support for Nationalist China's war also reflected the imbalance of power in the relationship. Still, it would be wrong to assume that the Chinese had no clout over American decisions just because they held less power. By expressing their own style of extraterritorial control over Chinese migrants abroad, the Nationalists tried and sometimes succeeded at shaping Chinese American communities in their favor. Attempts to control passports and emigration demonstrated a strong interest in rebuilding those communities in a more elite, educated, middle-class American image, and efforts to represent migrants' interests to the U.S. government attempted to ensure that the diaspora would stay loyal even in the face of Communist competition.

None of these actions ceased during the early Cold War, though the alliance became even more important, and even more unequal, after the Nationalists lost their civil war and settled in Taiwan. In the early 1950s, the United States and Nationalist China reached the heights of their cooperation over policy in Asia, something reflected in their joint mobilization of migration policy to serve Cold War interests. The two governments often disagreed on particulars, but they shared an interest in denying the support of Chinese abroad to the People's Republic of China. New measures from both governments concerning immigration, deportation, family remittances, and refugees sought to accomplish two things: to signal to the world the legitimacy and prestige of both allies, and to ensure that the Chinese American society remained anticommunist and vocal supporters of ongoing cooperation between the United States and Nationalist China. Historian Nancy Tucker has argued that despite the fundamental inequalities in the size, strength, and international influence of these two powers, the assumption that the United States could simply dominate Nationalist China in the Cold War years proved incorrect. Instead, "the Nationalist Chinese have been exceedingly adept at maneuvering within these constraints to shape relations that meet their needs for security, trade, and psychological support."[34] Overseas Chinese and migration policy grew to outsize importance for the Nationalists when they lost direct control over their mainland population, and wielding control over both these factors became a vital tool to help maintain international recognition for twenty years despite the reality of a fully functioning replacement government in China.

Starting as early as 1955 and continuing through the 1960s, however, migration diplomacy signaled a shift in the alliance. Migrants could appeal to either Chinese government—or, in the case of Taiwan independence advocates, to neither—making it impossible for the United States to avoid some variation of a "two Chinas" formulation. U.S. officials were increasingly inclined toward such a formulation anyway by the mid-1950s. They saw the futility of Nationalist talk of recovering the mainland and knew that the Communist government had no real concern of collapse. Students and scholars seeking repatriation forced U.S. officials to deal with the party governing these travelers' homeland; dissidents dissatisfied with the undemocratic rule of the KMT on Taiwan offered a cogent argument for not staying too loyal to that ally; and eventually geopolitical realities like the increasingly desperate American position in the Vietnam War made excluding

Communist China from the international community increasingly untenable. Travel policy and visa diplomacy became a face-saving way to pursue
a new course while propping up the erstwhile ally in the meantime.

Migration diplomacy could be and sometimes was a low-stakes, minor
dispute of not much importance when compared to Mao Zedong shelling the Taiwan Strait or the wars in Korea or Vietnam. But when enough
problems emerged in any aspect of migration policy, it could rise to the
prominence of high-level policy. As a result, managing migration issues well
became vital to managing the overall diplomatic relationship, especially as it
navigated through the tricky course that began by excluding some people,
then some governments, and then others.

This study also demonstrates the importance of not only the state-to-
state relations, but the state-to-people relations as well. The United States
found that the long and tumultuous history of its relationship with the
Chinese people as migrants, and not just with Chinese leaders, affected trust
between countries. Mistreated migrants had the ability to affect the international image of the United States in the Cold War, just as other American
inequalities spilled over onto the global stage. Meanwhile, China's relationship with its own migrants while abroad also carried weighty implications
for its future. For both governments, but especially for Nationalist China as
its status began to slip, the support of the "overseas Chinese" and Chinese
Americans became a way to contest recognition and legitimacy.

This last relationship deserves attention because as much as this is the
story of the ebb and flow of the U.S.-Nationalist China relationship, it is
also the story of the creation of the modern postwar Chinese American
community. The migration policies put to work in service of diplomatic
goals also created and reshaped Chinese communities in the United States.
In recent years, scholars of Asian American history have shown increasing interest in locating the roots of the "model minority" concept that
burst onto the national stage in the pages of the *New York Times Magazine*
in 1966. Scholars have suggested that its origins reach back much further,
to U.S. refugee policy accepting students and well-educated Chinese as
new residents, or back to the fight for the repeal of exclusion, when the
Chinese American community appealed for the right to naturalize as U.S.
citizens by demonstrating assimilability. This book suggests that to find the
origins, scholars will also need to consider Nationalist China's government
policy. Even as the United States expressed a greater preference for educated
elites as immigrants, the Nationalist government developed its own policies
for selecting and sending them as emigrants. Moreover, the KMT tried to

use methods of extraterritorial control to help shape and reshape Chinese American communities to reflect back on the Nationalist government in the best possible light. The Nationalists had a vital interest in having "overseas Chinese Americans" continue to promote the ROC government, and ideally to act as an even stronger advertisement for it than the China lobby could ever be, and in the process ensure that they maintained recognition.

The great irony of these efforts to shape and monitor Chinese communities in the United States is that they sometimes worked a little too well. By outspokenly advocating Nationalist China's democratic values and the embrace of them by Chinese in the United States, the Nationalists inadvertently shone a light on some of the more undemocratic aspects of their control in Taiwan. The heavy-handed attempts to purge American Chinatowns of undesirable (leftist or pro-PRC) elements through the use of American immigration and remittance polices created backlash against the KMT, which in turn was only helped along by the rise of a U.S.-based Taiwan independence movement. In the process, Nationalist efforts helped to build a community that rebelled against attempts at extraterritorial control and dropped the "overseas" from its identity. Not all these changes are rightly attributed to the Nationalist policies, but the international context played an important role.

After 1972, there was no going back. The rapprochement between the PRC and the United States that began in the early 1970s led to new migration after Deng Xiaoping came to power and began his policy of "reform and opening." After 1980, Chinese migrants for the first time came from geographically diverse hometowns, speaking different dialects, and even forcing old Chinatown schools and organizations to adjust to simplified characters. An already diverse Chinese American community became even more varied, and the idea of Chinese Americans speaking with one voice in support of either government grew outdated.

Migration diplomacy remains a vital part of how the United States, China, and Taiwan manage their complicated relationships today. The "visa diplomacy" problems highlighted by Taiwanese independence advocates in the 1960s have emerged as a persistent source of tension. The first democratically elected, Taiwan-born ROC president, Lee Teng-hui, found himself sitting in a plane on a Hawaii tarmac for hours in 1994 while the White House fearfully refused him a visa. Issuing any form of entry permit to the Dalai Lama is also always a matter of some delicacy. Vocal independence movements led by Taiwanese, Tibetans, and Uighurs, often from the safe haven of American shores, have made offering visas to dissidents, escapees, and exiles even more politically charged. After the Tiananmen Square protests in 1989, the U.S. embassy became a refuge for rebel leader Fang Lizhi. Every year, thousands of Chinese request political asylum in the United States in a process that has learned much from the refugee movements of the Cold War. In 2012 two high-profile cases, one right after the other, involved fearful Chinese seeking protection in U.S. consular buildings in China, and now no less than in the Cold War the protection of these people poses serious threats to the working relationship between the countries.

National security also remains instrumental to the management of Sino-American migration. Espionage is a time-honored tradition in international affairs, but the use of immigrant and nonimmigrant visas to inadvertently grant spies permission to enter creates both greater tension and increased scrutiny over applications. The consular officials stationed in Beijing, Shanghai, and about a half dozen other major cities were not trained under the same principles as the old consular officers making their home raids investigating frauds, but they are unquestionably part of the same tradition that has always treated Chinese applicants for travel to the United States with just a touch of suspicion. Ever since the terrorist attacks on New York and Washington in September 2001, in which all of the terrorists entered on legal temporary-visitor visas, the consular service has formed a new sort of front line in security policy and created a terrifying new tension between an open and permissive policy that welcomes the world, against a deeply security-conscious one that limits itself to protecting fortress America.

The connection that all immigrants and their descendants maintain to the homeland remains somewhat mysterious to anxious policy makers as well. Nearly 150 years after the start of Chinese immigration to the United States, the U.S. public panicked during the 1996 presidential election over the appearance of foreign intervention when Chinese Americans became embroiled in a fund-raising scandal. Just a few years later, Taiwanese American scientist Wen Ho Lee was arrested and falsely accused of espionage for China, giving him good reason to suspect there were people in the United States who still viewed Chinese migrants as "perpetual foreigners" and not likely to be loyal Americans. During the international torch run of the 2008 Summer Olympic Games held in Beijing, the evident organization of Chinese nationals or supporters to line the running routes and shout down any pro-Tibet protests served as an uncomfortable reminder of the long, even international, reach of the Chinese state. And beyond all that, the ease of travel and communication in the twenty-first century means that connections between migrants and their homelands will only increase, as will the complications stemming from an abundance of decidedly transnational families. The dilemma of reconciling security interests and foreign policy goals will only increase as more individuals join the Sino-American relationship as migrants.

Note on Sources

As a diplomatic history of migration policy, this book makes particular use of governmental and especially foreign policy records as primary sources, while attempting to stay grounded in the secondary literature on Chinese America. The primary research involved libraries and archives under four governments: the United States, the United Kingdom, the Republic of China, and the People's Republic of China. Wherever possible, I used records from the primary agencies responsible for making and carrying out foreign relations as well as the agencies engaged in governing migration.

In the United States, this meant the National Archives in College Park, Maryland, for the State Department records (record group 59), post records (84), and USIA files (306). The National Archives in Washington, D.C., holds the Immigration and Naturalization Service records (85), and branch offices in New York and California contained more specific files on individual Chinese migrants. Beyond the National Archives, however, foreign relations historians rely heavily on the presidential libraries for official perspectives from the State Department, the White House, and the National Security Agency. This book is no exception, and it made use of records from the libraries of Presidents Franklin Roosevelt through Nixon, scattered across the country. I also used several collections of U.S. congressmen:

Walter Judd (in Minnesota and the Hoover Institution in California), Francis Walter (in Pennsylvania), and Barry Goldwater and John Rhodes (Arizona). Other, private, collections of the ACLU (Princeton), Aid Refugee Chinese Intellectuals Inc., as well as writers Iris Chang and Pardee Lowe (all at the Hoover Institution), also helped fill in the nonofficial perspective. Congressional databases with transcripts of hearings and debates, as well as the State Department's *Foreign Relations of the United States* series, also helped guide my work. In the United Kingdom, I used the National Archives at Kew, focusing primarily on the Foreign Office and Colonial Office files.

My strategy in the Republic of China was similar. I made extensive use of records from the Ministry of Foreign Affairs, which were divided between Academia Historica (both in downtown Taipei and at its facility in Xindian) and the former MOFA facility in Beitou. The latter records have been digitized and moved to Academia Sinica, making them even more accessible to scholars of ROC foreign relations. I also found the records of the Overseas Chinese Affairs Commission and other government offices at Academia Historica particularly useful. Both Academia Sinica's Institute of Modern History and Academia Historica publish documentary collections and compilations of transcribed oral histories on particular subjects, like the Hong Kong refugees and the Taiwan independence movement, that are especially helpful to the overseas historian with limited time in the archives. Beyond that, I used the newspaper and book collections as well as the archives of *Qiaowu Yuebao* (Overseas Chinese affairs monthly) at the National Central Library, and I found propaganda tracts on migrants at numerous university libraries, including National Chengchi University, National Taiwan University, and National Taiwan Normal University. Finally, the records of the Kuomintang proved helpful, though they have moved from their downtown location since my visit.

On the Chinese mainland, the Ministry of Foreign Affairs archive in Beijing once again proved vital for the post-1949 history of the People's Republic. The Number Two Historical Archive in Nanjing also helped to fill in a number of gaps in MOFA and OCAC records for the 1940s. The Guangdong Provincial Archive in Guangzhou offered a better sense of how central policies were carried out on the ground from 1940 all the way through to the 1960s. In Beijing, the National Library also had an excellent collection of historical newspapers, databases, and books, as well as collections of government-published serials like *Qiao Xun* (Overseas Chinese bulletin) and *Qiaoqing Cankao Ziliao* (Reference information on the situation of overseas Chinese). The Nanjing University library also helped me fill in gaps in the Chinese historiography.

As for the secondary source research, I am particularly indebted to the work of scholars like Gordon H. Chang, Madeline Hsu, Peter Kwong, Him Mark Lai, Karen J. Leong, Li Hongshan, Chi-kwan Mark, Mae M. Ngai, Glen D. Peterson, Ren Guixiang, Nancy Bernkopf Tucker, L. Ling-chi Wang, Ellen D. Wu, Kevin Scott Wong, Yafeng Xia, and Renqiu Yu. These scholars are all paving the way forward for a more international, trans-national, and human-centered approach to both Chinese migration and U.S.-Chinese relations.

Notes

Introduction

1. I have written more extensively about the Chinese seamen issues elsewhere. See Meredith Oyen, "Fighting for Equality: Chinese Seamen in the Battle of the Atlantic, 1939–1945," *Diplomatic History* 38.3 (June 2014): 526–48.

2. Lin Yutang, "Chinese Seamen, as Free Men, Should Ship by Consent, Not Coercion," *P.M.*, May 16, 1943, MT 9/4370, the National Archives of the UK (hereafter TNA).

3. Warren Cohen, *America's Response to China: A History of Sino-American Relations*, 5th ed. (New York: Columbia University Press, 2010), 198.

4. The term "migration diplomacy" has recently gained traction among historians, sociologists, and political scientists. As Hélène Thiollet has argued with regard to labor migration in the Middle East, "Migration policy should be analyzed as an indirect form of foreign policy that uses the selection of migrants and quasi-asylum policies as diplomacy." See Thiollet, "Migration as Diplomacy: Labor Migrants, Refugees, and Arab Regional Politics in the Oil-Rich Countries," *International Labor and Working-Class History* 79 (Spring 2011): 103–21. In the Americas, too, there is growing interest in how migration acts as a diplomatic issue. See Christopher Mitchell, "The Future of Migration as an Issue in Inter-American Relations," in *The Future of Inter-American Relations*, ed. Jorge I. Domínguez (New York: Routledge, 2013), 217–36.

5. Notably scholars such as Ellen Wu, Madeline Hsu, and Mae Ngai have published articles (and books) that have moved forward efforts to connect the dots between, for example, the confession program, refugee policy, and the "stranded students" who became the subject of the ambassadorial talks, though none of them have yet brought all these points together, including the diplomatic context for these migration policy decisions, and migration historians

in general have not delved into the official Chinese archives for foreign relations context. Mae Ngai, "Legacies of Exclusion: Illegal Chinese Immigration during the Cold War Years," *Journal of American Ethnic History* 18.1 (Fall 1998): 3–35; Ellen D. Wu, "'America's Chinese': Anti-Communism, Citizenship, and Cultural Diplomacy during the Cold War," *Pacific Historical Review* 77.3 (August 2008): 391–422; Madeline Y. Hsu, "The Disappearance of America's Cold War Refugees, 1948–66," *Journal of American Ethnic History* 31.4 (Summer 2012): 12–33.

6. This is a subject of increasing attention in the literature, both in terms of focus on the activism and actions of average people and local history. See Judy Tzu-Chun Wu, *Radicals on the Road: Internationalism, Orientalism, and Feminism during the Vietnam Era* (Ithaca, NY: Cornell University Press, 2013); Michael Szonyi, *Cold War Island: Quemoy on the Front Line* (New York: Cambridge University Press, 2008); Kate Brown, *Plutopia: Nuclear Families, Atomic Cities, and the Great Soviet and American Plutonium Disasters* (New York: Oxford University Press, 2013); Jadwiga E. Pieper Mooney and Fabio Lanza, eds., *De-Centering Cold War History: Local and Global Change* (New York: Routledge, 2012).

7. Michael Hunt, *The Making of a Special Relationship: The United States and China to 1914* (New York: Columbia University Press, 1983). Other works focused on this period that combine migration and diplomacy well include Elizabeth Sinn, *Pacific Crossing: California Gold, Chinese Migration, and the Making of Hong Kong* (Hong Kong: Hong Kong University Press, 2013); Adam McKeown, *Melancholy Order: Asian Migration and the Globalization of Borders* (New York: Columbia University Press, 2011).

8. Hongshan Li, *U.S.-China Educational Exchange: State, Society, and Intercultural Relations, 1905–1950* (New Brunswick, NJ: Rutgers University Press, 2007); John R. Haddad, *America's First Adventure in China: Trade, Treaties, Opium, and Salvation* (Philadelphia: Temple University Press, 2013); Peter Rand, *The Adventures and Ordeals of the American Journalists Who Joined Forces with the Great Chinese Revolution* (New York: Simon & Schuster, 1995); Erleen J. Christensen, *In War and Famine: Missionaries in China's Honan Province in the 1940s* (Montreal: McGill–Queen's University Press, 2005).

9. Erika Lee, *At America's Gates: Chinese Immigration during the Exclusion Era, 1882–1943* (Chapel Hill: University of North Carolina Press, 2003); Madeline Hsu, *Dreaming of Gold, Dreaming of Home: Transnationalism and Migration between the United States and South China, 1882–1943* (Stanford, CA: Stanford University Press, 2000); Sucheng Chan, ed., *Chinese American Transnationalism: The Flow of People, Resources, and Ideas between China and America during the Exclusion Era* (Philadelphia: Temple University Press, 2005). Other works that highlight this era include Estelle Lau, *Paper Families: Identity, Immigration Administration, and Chinese Exclusion* (Durham, NC: Duke University Press, 2007); Yucheng Qin, *The Diplomacy of Nationalism: The Six Companies and China's Policy toward Exclusion* (Honolulu: University of Hawai'i Press, 2009); Sucheng Chan and K. Scott Wong, eds., *Claiming America: Constructing Chinese American Identities during the Exclusion Era* (Philadelphia: Temple University Press, 1998).

10. For the 1980s and beyond see Peter H. Koehn and Xiao-Huang Yin, eds., *The Expanding Roles of Chinese Americans in U.S.-Chinese Relations* (Armonk, NY: M. E. Sharpe, 2002); Julia Meredith Hess, *Immigrant Ambassadors: Citizenship and Belonging in the Tibetan Diaspora* (Stanford, CA: Stanford University Press, 2009).

11. Gordon H. Chang, *Friends and Enemies: The United States, China, and the Soviet Union, 1948–1972* (Stanford, CA: Stanford University Press, 1990); Chen Jian, *Mao's China and the Cold War* (Chapel Hill: University of North Carolina Press, 2000); Shu Guang Zhang, *Economic Cold War: America's Embargo against China and the Sino-Soviet Alliance, 1948–1963* (Stanford, CA: Stanford University Press, 2002); Yafeng Xia, *Negotiating with the Enemy: U.S.-China Talks during the Cold War, 1949–1972* (Bloomington: Indiana University Press, 2006); and Simei Qing, *From*

Allies to Enemies: Visions of Modernity, Identity, and U.S.-China Diplomacy, 1945–1960 (Cambridge, MA: Harvard University Press, 2007).

12. Akira Iriye, *Global and Transnational History: The Past, Present, and Future* (New York: Palgrave Pivot, 2012); Luc van Dongen, Stephanie Roulin, and Giles Scott-Smith, *Transnational Anti-communism and the Cold War: Agents, Activities, and Networks* (New York: Palgrave Macmillan, 2014); Linda Basch, Cristina Blac-Szanton, and Nina Glick Schiller, *Towards a Transnational Perspective on Migration: Race, Class, Ethnicity, and Nationalism Reconsidered* (New York: New York Academy of Sciences, 1992); Sarah B. Snyder, *Human Rights Activism and the End of the Cold War: A Transnational Perspective on the Helsinki Network* (New York: Cambridge University Press, 2013); Nicholas J. Cull, *The Cold War and the United States Information Agency: American Propaganda and Public Diplomacy, 1945–1989* (New York: Cambridge University Press, 2009).

13. K. Scott Wong, *Americans First: Chinese Americans and the Second World War* (Cambridge, MA: Harvard University Press, 2002); Xiaojian Zhao, *Remaking Chinese America: Immigration, Family, and Community, 1940–1965* (New Brunswick, NJ: Rutgers University Press, 2002); Mae M. Ngai, *Impossible Subjects: Illegal Aliens and the Making of Modern America* (Princeton, NJ: Princeton University Press, 2005); Cindy I-Fen Cheng, *Citizens of Asian America: Democracy and Race during the Cold War* (New York: NYU Press, 2013); Ellen D. Wu, *The Color of Success: Asian Americans and the Origins of the Model Minority* (Princeton, NJ: Princeton University Press, 2014).

14. Donna Gabaccia, *Foreign Relations: American Immigration in Global Perspective* (Princeton, NJ: Princeton University Press, 2012); Eiichiro Azuma, *Between Two Empires: Race, History, and Transnationalism in Japanese America* (New York: Oxford University Press, 2005); Carl Bon Tempo, *Americans at the Gate: The United States and Refugees during the Cold War* (Princeton, NJ: Princeton University Press, 2008).

1. Unequal Allies

1. Hannah Pakula, *The Last Empress: Madame Chiang Kai-shek and the Birth of Modern China* (New York: Simon & Schuster, 2009), 412, 418.

2. Memorandum to James McConaughy from Frank McNaughton, February 18, 1943, box 4, February 1–19, 1943, Frank McNaughton Papers, Presidential Library of Harry S. Truman, Independence, MO (hereafter HST Library).

3. T. Christopher Jespersen, *American Images of China, 1931–1949* (Stanford, CA: Stanford University Press, 1999), 66.

4. Ibid., 28–30; see also Karen J. Leong, *The China Mystique: Pearl Buck, Anna May Wong, Meiling Soong, and the Transformation of American Orientalism* (Berkeley: University of California Press, 2005).

5. Nancy Bernkopf Tucker, ed., *China Confidential: American Diplomats and Sino-American Relations, 1945–1996* (New York: Columbia University Press, 2001), 20–21.

6. This point is elaborated on in Jonathan Fenby, *Chiang Kai-shek: China's Generalissimo and the Nation He Lost* (New York: Carroll & Graf, 2004), 208–9.

7. On World War II–era U.S.-Chinese relations see Rana Mitter, *Forgotten Ally: China's World War II, 1937–1945* (Boston: Houghton Mifflin Harcourt, 2013); Barbara W. Tuchman, *Stilwell and the American Experience in China, 1911–1945* (New York: Macmillan, 1971); Wesley M. Bagby, *The Eagle-Dragon Alliance: America's Relations with China in World War II* (Newark: University of Delaware Press, 1992).

8. Adam McKeown, *Melancholy Order: Asian Migration and the Globalization of Borders* (New York: Columbia University Press, 2008).

9. Karen J. Leong, "Foreign Policy, National Identity, and Citizenship: The Roosevelt White House and the Expediency of Repeal," *Journal of American Ethnic History* 22.4 (Summer 2003): 3–30; Renqiu Yu, "Little Heard Voices: The Chinese Hand Laundry Alliance and the *China Daily News'* Appeal for Repeal of the Chinese Exclusion Act in 1943," *Chinese America, History and Perspectives*, 1990, 21–35; Xiaohua Ma, "A Democracy at War: The American Campaign to Repeal Chinese Exclusion in 1943," *Japanese Journal of American Studies* 9 (1998): 121–42; Yui Daizaburo, "From Exclusion to Integration: Asian Americans' Experiences in World War II," *Hitotsubashi Journal of Social Studies* 24.2 (1992): 55–67; John Hayakawa Torok, "'Interest-Convergence' and the Liberalization of Discriminatory Immigration and Naturalization Laws Affecting Asians, 1943–65," *Chinese America, History and Perspectives*, 1995, 1–28; L. Ling-chi Wang, "Politics of the Repeal of Chinese Exclusion Laws," in *The Repeal and Its Legacy: Proceedings of the Conference on the 50th Anniversary of the Repeal of the Exclusion Acts, Nov. 12–14* (Brisbane, CA: Chinese Historical Society of America, 1993), 66–80.

10. "Roosevelt recognized China's potential," but also knew the state would be under American tutelage for some time to come. Warren F. Kimball, *The Juggler: Franklin Roosevelt as Wartime Statesman* (Princeton, NJ: Princeton University Press, 1991), 85–86.

11. For a full discussion of the perceived necessity of extraterritoriality given the lack of codified law in China see Elbert D. Thomas, "Extraterritoriality in China," Senate Document No. 102, 78th Cong., 1st Sess. (Washington, DC: Government Printing Office, 1943), 2–8. On the American court in Shanghai see Eileen P. Scully, *Bargaining with the State from Afar: American Citizenship in Treaty Port China, 1844–1942* (New York: Columbia University Press, 2001).

12. They agreed to the principle at that time, but abolition of extraterritoriality was still a matter of intense debate. See H. G. W. Woodhead, *Extraterritoriality in China: The Case against Abolition* (Tientsin: Tientsin Press, 1929).

13. K. C. Chan, "The Abrogation of British Extraterritoriality in China, 1942–43: A Study of Anglo-American-Chinese Relations," *Modern Asian Studies* 11.2 (1977): 258.

14. Wesley R. Fishel, *The End of Extraterritoriality in China* (New York: Octagon Books, 1974).

15. Chan, "Abrogation of British Extraterritoriality," 264.

16. Mainland Chinese battles with the Japanese occupied some two-fifths of the Japanese army in the summer of 1942, and as such it was vital to keep the Chinese fighting. Jonathan Spence, *The Search for Modern China* (New York: W. W. Norton, 1990), 470.

17. Memo by Walter A. Adams, March 19, 1942, in U.S. Department of State, *Foreign Relations of the United States, 1942, China* (Washington, DC: Government Printing Office, 1942) (hereafter *FRUS 1942 China*), 270.

18. "Exclusion and Extraterritoriality," *Contemporary China: A Reference Digest* 1.26 (May 18, 1942): 1.

19. Him Mark Lai (Mai Liqian), *Cong Huaqiao dao Huaren: Ershi Shiji Meiguo Huaren Shehui Fazhan Shi* (Hong Kong: Sanlian Shudian, 1992), 330.

20. The captain was acquitted of all charges, and the company never paid compensation to the family of the fallen sailor; both actions infuriated and energized Chinese protesters. Translation from the *Chinese Nationalist Daily*, December 16, 1942, MT 9/4370, TNA; *People v. Rowe*, 36 N.Y.S.2d 980.

21. Harry Paxton Howard, "Chinese Seamen's Fight Shows Exclusion Act Should Be Repealed!," and Post War World Council News Service, "Shore Leave for Chinese Sailors

Requested," June 6, 1942, vol. 2460, Chinese Shore Leave, Records of the American Civil Liberties Union, Princeton University, Princeton, NJ (hereafter ACLU).

22. Memorandum by Miss Ruth E. Bacon of the Division of Far Eastern Affairs, June 4, 1942, *Foreign Relations of the United States: Diplomatic Papers, 1943, China* (Washington, DC: Government Printing Office, 1957), 788–89 (hereafter *FRUS 1943 China*).

23. The impetus for change at this particular moment in the war was likely driven by developments in fighting. In June 1942 the battle of Midway offered both a much-needed military success for the Allies and a stark reminder of just how important the continued Chinese contribution really was in the fight against Japan. Alan J. Levine, *The Pacific War: Japan versus the Allies* (Westport, CT: Praeger, 1995), 66–67.

24. In some cases, desertions were likely motivated by a desire to immigrate to the United States: many open, well-paying jobs in U.S. Chinatowns and in upstate New York were understandably more desirable than returning to the dangerous battle of the Atlantic. See my previous work on Chinese seamen: Meredith Oyen, "Fighting for Equality: Chinese Seamen in the Battle of the Atlantic, 1939–1945," *Diplomatic History* 38.3 (June 2014).

25. Peter Kwong, *Chinatown, New York: Labor and Politics, 1930–1950* (New York: New Press, 1979), 125.

26. Shaughnessy called the experiment "a bit too theoretical, even a bit fantastic." Memorandum for Major Schofield from Shaughnessy, July 8, 1942, 56084/639, Records of the Immigration and Naturalization Service, Record Group (RG) 85, National Archives and Records Administration, Washington, DC (hereafter NARA).

27. Telegram from Secretary of State to Ambassador in the United Kingdom, September 5, 1942, *FRUS 1942 China*, 287. The initiative for abolition shifted several times between Britain and the United States; Fishel recounts a British proposal from April 1942, and then notes that by autumn the two countries were acting on U.S. initiative. Fishel, *End of Extraterritoriality*, 209–10.

28. Memorandum of Conversation by the Assistant Chief of the Division of Far Eastern Affairs, May 8, 1942, *FRUS 1942 China*, 279; Telegram from Secretary of State to Ambassador in the United Kingdom, September 5 1942, *FRUS 1942 China*, 287.

29. See Martha Byrd, *Chennault: Giving Wings to the Tiger* (Tuscaloosa: University of Alabama Press, 1987), 170; Graham Peck, *Two Kinds of Time* (Boston: Houghton Mifflin Co., 1950), 473–75.

30. Memorandum of Conversation, by the Chief of the Division of Far Eastern Affairs, October 9 1942, *FRUS 1942 China*, 307.

31. The Ambassador in China (Gauss) to the Secretary of State, October 12, 1942, *FRUS 1942 China*, 311.

32. Chan, "Abrogation of British Extraterritoriality," 276.

33. Series 3, minutes, June 8, 1942, box 823, folder 2, "Immigration: Chinese Exclusion Laws," ACLU.

34. Walter Kong, "How We Grill the Chinese," *Asia and the Americas*, September 1942, 520–23; Richard Walsh, "Our Great Wall against the Chinese," *New Republic*, November 23, 1942. The Walsh article was also translated and reprinted in the Chinese newspaper *Da Gong Bao*, highlighting the extent to which the repeal debate was being followed in Asia. "Quxiao Meiguo dui Hua yimin xianzhi," *Da Gong Bao*, May 25, 1943.

35. General Intelligence Survey in the United States, FBI, November 1942, box 3162, 800.20211, Records of the Department of State RG 59, National Archives and Records Administration, College Park, MD (hereafter Archives II).

36. U.S. Congress, House, *An Act to Authorize the Deportation of Aliens to Countries Allied with the U.S., Hearing before the House Committee on Immigration and Naturalization on H.R. 2076*, 77th Cong., 2nd Sess., 1942, 50–51.

37. The Secretary of State to the Ambassador in the United Kingdom (Winant), November 11, 1942, *FRUS 1942 China*, 347–48.

38. Secretary of State to the Ambassador in the United Kingdom (Winant), November 11, 1942, *FRUS 1942 China*, 347.

39. Memorandum by the Assistant Chief of the Division of Far Eastern Affairs of the Conversation with the Minister Counselor of the Chinese Embassy, November 13, 1942, *FRUS 1942 China*, 350.

40. Stephen G. Craft, *V. K. Wellington Koo and the Emergence of Modern China* (Lexington: University Press of Kentucky, 2004), 18.

41. "New Day in China," *New York Times*, January 13, 1943; "Sovereign China," *Washington Post*, January 13, 1943. Clippings from Zhu Mei dashiguan wei jiansong ge bao guanyu Zhong Mei xinyue pinlun dengshi de laihan, 18/1642, Records of the Ministry of Foreign Affairs (hereafter MOFA), Number Two Historical Archive, Nanjing, PRC (hereafter Nanjing). Before the founding of the United Nations as an international organization in 1945, the term "United Nations" was used to refer to the Allied powers in World War II.

42. Statement by Dr. Wang Chung-hui, Secretary General of the Defense Council, January 13, 1943, 18/1721, MOFA, Nanjing.

43. Chiang Kai-shek to the Chinese Armed Forces and people on the conclusion of the new Sino-American and Sino-British treaties, January 12, 1943, 18/1721, MOFA, Nanjing.

44. Chan, "Abrogation of British Extraterritoriality," 290.

45. Fishel, *End of Extraterritoriality*, 214.

46. Wang, "Politics of the Repeal," 79–80.

47. K. Scott Wong, *Americans First: Chinese Americans and the Second World War* (Cambridge, MA: Harvard University Press, 2002), 123. He also highlights the letter-writing campaigns discussed later in this chapter, 119–20.

48. Yu, "Little Heard Voices," 21.

49. Ibid., 30.

50. Fred W. Riggs, *Pressures on Congress: A Study of the Repeal of Chinese Exclusion* (New York: King's Crown Press, Columbia University, 1950).

51. Guoli zhengzhi daxue shixi xuesheng Cheng Hougu, Meizhou Si, Shixi baogao, n.d., 18/3086, MOFA, Nanjing; U.S. Congress, House, *A Bill to Grant to the Chinese Rights of Entry to the United States and Rights to Citizenship*, HR 1882, 78th Cong., 1st Sess., 1943, 1–2.

52. U.S. Congress, House, Congressman Ramspeck on the repeal of Chinese exclusion, 78th Cong., 1st Sess., October 21, 1943, 89:8631; Him Mark Lai, *Cong Huaqiao*, 330.

53. U.S. Congress, House, Congressman Dewey on the repeal of Chinese exclusion, 78th Cong., 1st Sess., October 21, 1943, 89:8627.

54. U.S. Congress, House, *A Bill to Provide for the Admission to the United States of Alien Chinese Wives of American Citizens*, HR 1607, 78th Cong., 1st Sess., 1943, 1.

55. U.S. Congress, House, Committee on Immigration and Naturalization, *To Provide for the Admission to the U.S. of Alien Chinese Wives of American Citizens, Hearings before the Committee on Immigration and Naturalization on H.R. 1607*, 78th Cong., 1st Sess., 1943, 10b.

56. Memorandum of Conversation, by the Advisor on Political Relations (Hornbeck), March 10, 1943, *FRUS 1943 China*, 769–70.

57. Riggs, *Pressures on Congress*, 117.

58. Meiguo xiugai yimin lu, undated memorandum, 172–1/1940–1, MOFA, Academia Historica, Taipei, Taiwan, ROC (hereafter Academia Historica).

59. "Wo qixie qing xiuzheng Meiguo yimin fa," *Xin Hua Ribao*, March 4, 1943.

60. Him Mark Lai, *Cong Huaqiao*, 330.

61. U.S. Congress, House, Committee on Foreign Affairs, *Testimony of Bishop Paul Yu Pin, Vicar Apostolic of Nanking, and Statement of Rev. Ronald Norris, C.P. before the Committee on Foreign Affairs*, 78th Cong., 1st Sess., 1943, 2–14.

62. "Mei ying feichu huaren rujing xiuli," *Da Gong Bao*, March 4, 1943.

63. "Chufei Huaren yi Mei Zhang'ai, Mei zhongyuan yi kaishi shenyi," *Da Gong Bao*, March 5, 1943; "Quxiao xianzhi Huaren ru Mei, Mei zhongyuan yimin weihui kaolu zhong," *Da Gong Bao*, March 19, 1943; "Mei zhunxu huaqiao rujing an: Zhongyuan yimin weihui jiang taolun ge ti an zhuzhang xianding shu'e," *Da Gong Bao*, April 19, 1943.

64. Telegram from American Embassy Chongqing to Secretary of State, May 24, 1943, box 1, folder 855, Chungking Embassy General Records 1943–54, Records of the Foreign Service Posts RG 84, Archives II.

65. Samples of Japanese Radio Comments on America's Exclusion Act, Confidential Print, *Committee on Immigration and Naturalization, House of Representatives*, 78th Cong., 1st Sess., 4, in "Chinese Exclusion Acts," box 7, Samuel Rosenman Papers, Presidential Library of Franklin Delano Roosevelt (hereafter FDR Library).

66. Memorandum of Conversation, by the Assistant Secretary of State, May 13, 1953, *FRUS 1943 China*, 770.

67. He observed that they were generally not organized on a "national scale." It can be hard to generalize about these advocates, because (for example) individual Catholics or Presbyterians, and sometimes whole congregations, supported repeal, but the national church did not necessarily want to weigh in. Riggs, *Pressures on Congress*, 92, 101.

68. Witnesses promoting repeal included Arthur Hummel of the Asiatic Division of the Library of Congress, novelist Pearl Buck, Richard J. Walsh of the magazine *Asia and the Americas*, Walter Judd, and a number of private citizens or missionaries who had lived in China.

69. Samples of Japanese Radio Comments on America's Exclusion Act, 5.

70. Scholars have supported some of these assertions. See Akira Iriye, *Across the Pacific: An Inner History of American–East Asian Relations* (New York: Harcourt, Brace & World, 1967), 28–32, 111–37; Izumi Hirobe, *Japanese Pride, American Prejudice: Modifying the Exclusion Clause of the 1924 Immigration Act* (Stanford, CA: Stanford University Press, 2001). Izumi notes that many Japanese officials viewed the increasing confrontation between the United States and Japan as a racial issue and says, "The exclusion clause in the immigration act of 1924 was one of the few factors to significantly disturb U.S.-Japanese relations during the two decades before the Pacific War" (224). Japanese immigration was limited through the Gentlemen's Agreement in 1907–8 until it was also formally included in the 1924 act. Because the Japanese agreement was nullified by the later Asian exclusion acts, some historians have argued that U.S. immigration laws were a factor leading to the eventual hostilities between the United States and Japan in the Pacific, demonstrating the sometimes high cost of bad—which is to say, blatantly discriminatory—immigration law.

71. U.S. Congress, House, Committee on Immigration and Naturalization, *To Repeal the Chinese Exclusion Acts, to Put the Chinese on a Quota Basis, and to Permit Naturalization, Hearings before the House Committee on Immigration and Naturalization on H.R. 1882 and H.R. 2309*, 78th Cong., 1st Sess., 1943.

72. Riggs, *Pressures on Congress*, 65.

73. Ibid.

74. Yu, "Little Heard Voices," 29.

75. Ibid.

76. According to the Overseas Chinese Affairs Commission, in 1943 there were 8,715,733 Chinese living abroad (including 59,692 Chinese in Taiwan), and 102,554 living in the United

States of America, including Hawaii. A total of 3,635,062 Chinese lived in British territories or colonial possessions in 1943, not counting the commonwealth nations of Canada, Australia, and New Zealand, which accounted for an additional 66,400 Chinese. Haiwai huaqiao renkou febu tongji, sa er nianji qiaowu tongji, 18/1677, MOFA, Nanjing.

77. Neil Gotanda, "Exclusion and Inclusion: Immigration and American Orientalism," in *Across the Pacific: Asian Americans and Globalization*, ed. Evelyn Hu-Dehart (Philadelphia: Temple University Press, 1999), 145.

78. Riggs, *Pressures on Congress*, 179–80.

79. Ibid., 47; Citizens' Committee for Repeal of Chinese Exclusion Final Report to Members, November 30, 1943, MC#001, box 823, folder 2, ACLU.

80. Wang, "Politics of the Repeal," 73.

81. Riggs, *Pressures on Congress*, 56–59.

82. "Our Chinese Wall" (New York: Citizens' Committee to Repeal Chinese Exclusion, 1943), 3, in File 832/25, ACLU.

83. Ibid., 6.

84. Yui Daizaburo, "From Exclusion to Integration: Asian Americans' Experiences in World War II," *Hitotsubashi Journal of Social Studies* 24.2 (1992): 55–67.

85. For a discussion of how U.S. labor organizations reacted to the repeal campaign see Riggs, *Pressures on Congress*, 65–74. The Roosevelt administration was not content to let the AFL opposition go unaddressed, though: there were several efforts to bend William Green's ear on the matter. "Memorandum for Judge Samuel I. Rosenman, August 24, 1943, Chinese Exclusion Acts, box 7, Rosenman Papers, FDR Library.

86. Meeting on Oriental Exclusion Act, Boston, November 12, 1942, File: Oriental Exclusion, box 823, folder 2, ACLU.

87. Express Telegram #533 to Ministry of Foreign Affairs, Chongqing, from Chinese Consulate in Los Angeles, May 4, 1943, 172–1/1941, MOFA, Academia Historica.

88. Letter to Board of Trustees, Seattle Chamber of Commerce, from Kiang Yi-seng, Chinese Consul at Seattle, May 28, 1943, 172–1/1941, MOFA, Academia Historica.

89. Report of the Consulate in Seattle to the Ministry of Foreign Affairs, Chongqing, July 20, 1943, 172–1/1941, MOFA, Academia Historica.

90. "Readers Have Their Say / A Word for the Chinese. Letter to the Editor from Dr. Kiang Yi Seng, Chinese Consul at Seattle," June 7, 1943, 172–1/1941, MOFA, Academia Historica.

91. U.S. Congress, House, *To Grant to the Chinese Rights of Entry to the U.S. and Rights to Citizenship, a Hearing before the Committee on Immigration and Naturalization on H.R. 1882*, 78th Cong., 1st Sess., 1943.

92. Memorandum of Conversation, by the Advisor on Political Relations (Hornbeck), May 29, 1943, *FRUS 1943 China*, 771–73.

93. Memorandum of Conversation, by the Secretary of State, June 11, 1943, *FRUS 1943 China*, 781.

94. Further evidence that in spite of her lack of formal public statements related to repeal, Madame Chiang Kai-shek was also working behind the scenes in support of the measure. Cable no. 228, from Washington Embassy to MOFA Chongqing, June 19, 1943, 172–1/1941, MOFA, Academia Historica.

95. Renqiu Yu, "Little Heard Voices," 26–28; Wong, *Americans First*, 119–20. Wong recognizes the contributions of interested Chinese Americans to the debate and the ways in which they discussed the issue internally, noting that they were not an obvious part of the public campaign.

96. U.S. Congress, Senate, *Repealing Chinese Exclusion Acts, Establishing Quotas, etc.*, Senate Rept. 535, 78th Cong., 1st Sess., *Serial Set Collection*, 1943.

97. Letter from C. E. Gauss, U.S. Embassy in Chongqing, to Secretary of State, Enclosing Editorial Translation, "Magnuson's Bill," from *Central Daily News*, Chongqing, October 26, 1943, box 1, folder 855, Chungking Embassy General Records 1943–54, RG 84, Archives II.

98. Note from Chongqing to Washington, October 25, 1943, box 1, folder 855, Chungking Embassy General Records 1943–54, RG 84, Archives II.

99. Memorandum of Conversation, October 24, 1943, box 1, folder 855, Chungking Embassy General Records 1943–54, RG 84, Archives II.

100. Removal of Legislative Discrimination against the Chinese, from the Standpoint of American National Interests, Microfilm C0012, reel 1, RG 59, Archives II.

101. The repeal of Chinese exclusion passed in both houses by voice vote, so there is no record of the final count. Some objections were registered for both votes, but not enough to prevent passage. See "H.R. 3070 A Bill to Repeal Chinese Exclusion," *Congressional Record* 78:1 (October 21, 1943), 8635 (November 26, 1943), 10019.

102. Telegram to Washington, November 30, 1943, box 1, folder 855, Chungking Embassy General Records 1943–54, RG 84, Archives II.

103. MOFA Central Press Release, undated, 172–1/1940–1, MOFA, Academia Historica.

104. Report from the Seattle Consulate, January 14, 1944, 172–1/1941, MOFA, Academia Historica.

105. Report from the Honolulu Consulate, December 21, 1943, 172–1/1941, MOFA, Academia Historica.

106. American Consul Bombay to State, November 3, 1943, box 1, folder 855, Chungking Embassy General Records 1943–54, Records of the Foreign Service Posts RG 84, Archives II.

107. Memorandum of Conversation, November 30, 1942, November–December 1942, box 214, Adolf A. Berle Papers, FDR Library; Memorandum of Conversation, July 27, 1943, April–July 1943, 2 of 2, box 215, Adolf A. Berle Papers, FDR Library.

108. Request for Removal of Statutory Discrimination Now Existing against Immigration of East Indians, December 15, 1943, October–December 1943, box 215, Adolf A. Berle Papers, FDR Library.

109. Letter to Samuel Dickstein from FDR, March 5, 1945, OF 133 Immigration, box 1, Roosevelt Official File, FDR Library.

110. Ellen D. Wu has traced the "model minority" myth that emerged surrounding the Asian American community in the 1960s to the wartime battle for more-inclusive immigration policies. Wu, *The Color of Success: Asian Americans and the Origins of the Model Minority* (Princeton, NJ: Princeton University Press, 2014).

2. The Diaspora Goes to War

1. "Readers Have Their Say / A Word for the Chinese. Letter to the Editor from Dr. Kiang Yi-Seng, Chinese Consul at Seattle," June 7, 1943, 172–1/1941, MOFA, Academia Historica.

2. Wang Gungwu, "Upgrading the Chinese Migrant: Neither *Huaqiao* nor *Huaren*," in *The Last Half Century of Chinese Overseas*, ed. Elizabeth Sinn (Hong Kong: Hong Kong University Press, 1998), 15–34; Soon Keong Ong, "'Chinese, but Not Quite': *Huaqiao* and the Marginalization of the Overseas Chinese," *Journal of Chinese Overseas* 9 (2013): 1–32.

3. Ong, "'Chinese, but Not Quite,'" 4.

4. Chinese abroad provided the funding for the Nationalist revolution that took down the Qing dynasty, though as Soon notes, Sun Yat-sen's famous quote that "overseas Chinese are

the mother of the revolution" (huaqiao wei geiming zhi mu) is probably apocryphal. Ong, "'Chinese, but Not Quite,'" 13–14.

5. Philip Kuhn, *Chinese among Others: Emigration in Modern Times* (Lanham, MD: Rowman & Littlefield, 2008), 267. The OCAC was a cabinet-level post in the Executive Yuan; when the People's Republic of China established its own OCAC, it would become a department within the Ministry of Foreign Affairs.

6. L. Ling-chi Wang, "Politics of the Repeal of Chinese Exclusion Laws," in *The Repeal and Its Legacy: Proceedings of the Conference on the 50th Anniversary of the Repeal of the Exclusion Acts, Nov. 12–14* (Brisbane, CA: Chinese Historical Society of America, 1993), 66–80.

7. Kuhn, *Chinese among Others*, 267–68. Kuhn focuses his examples on Southeast Asia, but this system was also in place in North America.

8. Him Mark Lai, *Chinese American Transnational Politics*, ed. Madeline Hsu (Urbana: University of Illinois Press, 2010), 23.

9. Zhang Xizhe, "Kang Ri zhanzheng shiqi Guomin Zhengfu de qiaowu gongzuo," *Huaqiao yu kang Ri zhanzheng lunwen ji*, vol. 1 (Taipei: Huaqiao Xiehui Zonghui, 1999), 1–20.

10. The countries/territories were Vietnam, Burma, Thailand, Malaya, British North Borneo, Sarawak, the Dutch East Indies, the Philippines, Hong Kong, the United States, Canada, Mexico, Guatemala, Nicaragua, Panama, Cuba, Peru, Chile, Australia, New Zealand, the U.S. Territory of Hawaii, and South Africa. Sayi nianji qiaowu tongji, 43–45, 28/1/2, Guangdong Provincial Archive, Guangzhou, PRC (hereafter Guangzhou).

11. Huaqiao daiyu zhi gaishan, huaqiao dengji banfa he gaishan huaqiao zhuangkuang de yijian shu, 1940–45, 18/3058, MOFA, Nanjing.

12. Ibid.

13. Ibid.

14. Zhanhou nanyang huaqiao wenti zuotanhui taolun jingguo ji jielun, March 15, 1943, 370/210, Records of the Overseas Chinese Affairs Commission (OCAC), Nanjing.

15. The potential seriousness of the conflict of interest experienced by dual nationals in times of war was something the United States had recent experience with, in the Japanese American population during World War II; for example, see *Kawakita v. United States* (Sup. Ct. 1952).

16. Letter to Hollington Tong from Willys R. Peck, January 3, 1944, 811.2222 (1940), box 3744, RG 59, Archives II.

17. Chinese men who were otherwise barred from naturalization could become U.S. citizens after service in World War I. K. Scott Wong, *Americans First: Chinese Americans and the Second World War* (Cambridge, MA: Harvard University Press, 2002), 163.

18. Candice Bredbenner, "A Duty to Defend? The Evolution of Aliens' Military Obligations to the United States, 1792 to 1946," *Journal of Policy History* 24.2 (2012): 231–32, 236–37; William W. Fitzhugh Jr. and Charles Cheney Hyde, "The Drafting of Neutral Aliens by the United States," *American Journal of International Law* 36.3 (July 1942): 382.

19. See Deportation Investigation Case Files, 12020/34419 to 12020/35405, boxes 57 and 58, RG 85, San Bruno National Archives and Records Administration, San Bruno, CA.

20. Telegram 27776, from Chinese Embassy in Washington, DC, to Ministry of Foreign Affairs, Chongqing, April 18, 1942, 18/1544, MOFA, Nanjing.

21. Memorandum of Conversation, February 25, 1943, Status under Selective Service of Chinese Students in the United States, 811.2222 (1940), box 3742, RG 59, Archives II. The United States resisted Chinese attempts to get a reciprocal draft agreement along the lines offered to Mexico, arguing that the latter was a unique case and the procedures set in place would already be enough to protect Chinese students.

22. Letter, Breckinridge Long, Assistant Secretary for the Secretary of State, to the Honorable Francis Biddle, Attorney General of the United States, February 18, 1942, Chinese Students, 56066/683, box 2003, RG 85, NARA.

23. Memorandum of Conversation, February 22, 1943, Status under Selective Service of Chinese Students in the United States, 811.2222 (1940), box 3742; Status Memorandum to Hershey, August 12, 1943, 811.2222 (1940), box 3743, RG 59, Archives II.

24. Meeting held on March 31, 1943, in the Department of State between Officers of the Chinese Embassy, the Selective Service System, the War Department, and the Department of State on the Subject of Military Service of Chinese Nationals in the United States, 811.2222 (1940), box 3742, RG 59, Archives II.

25. Wong notes that not everyone chose to do so, citing the example of Tung Pok Chin, whose well-known memoir *Paper Son* details his decision not to "confess" either while in the navy or when the confession program offered a second opportunity in the 1950s (see chapter 3 of this work for more on the paper son issue). Wong, *Americans First*, 174–75.

26. In this document, the term *huaqiao* is translated as "overseas Chinese," and the term *Mei ji huaren* is translated as "Chinese Americans." According to ROC nationality law, both groups were considered Chinese nationals, and therefore the ROC made representations on behalf of not only Chinese residents in the United States, but also American Chinese, the latter of which U.S. authorities did not consider to be within Chinese jurisdiction. Telegram 32315, from Liu Enchu, Chairman, Chinese Consolidated Benevolent Association of New York, to Ministry of Foreign Affairs, Chongqing, December 5, 1942, 18/1544, MOFA, Nanjing.

27. Letter to Secretary of State from Arthur R. Ringwalt, September 4, 1944, 811.2222 (1940), box 3744, RG 59, Archives II.

28. Wong, *Americans First*, 60.

29. Meeting on March 31, 1943, 811.2222 (1940), box 3742, RG 59, Archives II. The week of the meeting, 59 of 125 Chinese ordered to report to local draft boards failed to appear.

30. As Parker noted, "There is no use to say to the Chinese that you may elect to go to your country if there are no boats." Meeting on March 31, 1943, 811.2222 (1940), box 3742, RG 59, Archives II. There was no objection to signing such an agreement in principle, and in fact, the two finally did sign a mutual induction agreement in early 1944.

31. Xie Keliang, "Liuxuesheng weisheme yao fu bingyi?" *Minqi Ribao*, March 8, 1943.

32. Hershey did not reject all such claims. Nicholas A. Krehbiel, *General Lewis B. Hershey and Conscientious Objection in World War II* (Columbia: University of Missouri Press, 2011), 16–17.

33. Letter to Lewis B. Hershey from Cordell Hull, June 5, 1943, 811.2222 (1940), box 3742, RG 59, Archives II.

34. Memorandum, May 3, 1943, 811.2222 (1940), box 3742, RG 59, Archives II.

35. Memorandum of Conversation, December 9, 1943, Exemption of Chinese from Military Service in the United States, 811.2222 (1940), box 3743, RG 59, Archives II.

36. Letter to Hershey from Edward Stettinius, August 7, 1944, 811.2222 (1940), box 3744, RG 59, Archives II.

37. Letter to Hollington K. Tong from Willys R. Peck, January 3, 1944, 811.2222 (1940), box 3744, RG 59, Archives II.

38. Letter to Willys R. Peck from Yang-lung Tong, February 21, 1944, 811.2222 (1940), box 3744, RG 59, Archives II.

39. Memo for the file, July 11, 1944, 811.2222 (1940), box 3744, RG 59, Archives II.

40. Memo for the file, February 26, 1944, 811.2222 (1940), box 3744, RG 59, Archives II.

41. Him Mark Lai, "Roles Played by Chinese in America during China's Resistance to Japanese Aggression and during World War II," *Chinese America* (1997): 99; Wong, *Americans First,* 58; Ronald Takaki, *Strangers from a Different Shore* (New York: Little, Brown and Co., 1998), 399–400. Wong also details the history of some units composed primarily of Chinese Americans, used as liaisons in China. See Wong, *Americans First,* chap. 5.

42. Eric Muller, *Free to Die for Their Country: The Japanese American Draft Resisters of World War II* (Chicago: University of Chicago Press, 2001).

43. Yui Daizaburo, "From Exclusion to Integration: Asian Americans' Experiences in World War II," *Hitotsubashi Journal of Social Studies* 24.2 (1992): 55–67.

44. Stephen Fitzgerald, *China and the Overseas Chinese: A Study of Peking's Changing Policy, 1949–1970* (Cambridge: Cambridge University Press, 1972), 8.

45. Zhanhou nanyang huaqiao wenti zuotanhui taolun jingguo ji jielun, March 15, 1943, 370/210, OCAC, Nanjing; Youguan zhanhou qiaomin qiao guanli yu jiaoyu wenti de ziliao, 1944, 18/1711, MOFA, Nanjing.

46. Di liu ci gongzuo baogaoshu, zhu Meiguo zongzhibu zhiji zhang Huang Boyao jincheng, December 10, 1943, Te 8/3.1/14, Archives of the Kuomintang, Taipei, Taiwan, ROC (hereafter KMT). Of the 104 Chinese schools in the Americas, 58 were in the United States, 27 in Canada, 9 each in Mexico and Cuba, and 1 in Guatemala. Independently owned and operated Chinese schools unknown by the Chinese government may have existed in addition to these. Qiaowu weiyuanhui songlai "sa er nianji qiaowu tongji," 84–85, 1943, MOFA, Nanjing.

47. Wong, *Americans First,* 15.

48. Some scholars see this as a marked contrast to Kuomintang overseas Chinese policy, which tried simultaneously to gain support for the fight against Japan and support for the party in its battle against internal elements. Ren Guixiang, "Kang Ri zhangzhen shiqi Guo Gong liang dang qiaowu zhengce bijiao yanjiu," *Kaifang Shidai,* 1995, 74.

49. Ibid.

50. Ren Guixiang and Chao Hongying, *Huaqiao Huaren yu Guo Gong Guanxi* (Wuhan: Wuhan Publishing House, 1999), 155–56.

51. Ibid., 158–59. One Chinese American apparently gave up on his long-standing support of the Kuomintang after seeing for himself how much the Communists worked to fight the Japanese and how little the Nationalists did (162).

52. Ren Guixiang, "Kang Ri zhangzhen shiqi," 75.

53. Ibid., 67. In addition to KMT-CCP contests for overseas Chinese support, the Japanese puppet government in Nanjing, led by Wang Jingwei, also made efforts to court the overseas Chinese.

54. General Intelligence Survey in the United States, FBI, September 1942, 800.20211, box 3162, RG 59, Archives II.

55. General Intelligence Survey in the United States, FBI, November 1942, 800.20211, box 3162, RG 59, Archives II.

56. Zhong gong zhi guojixing yu yinmou, undated (1940s series), Te 5/30.2, KMT.

57. Zhongguo Guomindang zhu Meiguo zhibu, Huang Boyao zhi Wu Tiecheng han, December 28, 1943, Te 8/3.1/22, KMT.

58. Qiaowu weiyuanhui sanshi niandu shizheng jihua, December 1942, 370/19, OCAC, Nanjing.

59. Chun-hsi Wu, *Dollars, Dependents and Dogma: Overseas Chinese Remittances to Communist China* (Stanford, CA: Hoover Institution, 1967), 28–39.

60. Telegram 07433 from Consulate in San Francisco to Ministry of Foreign Affairs, Chongqing, March 30, 1942, 18/1544, MOFA, Nanjing. Not all the overseas Chinese villages

fell under Japanese occupation, but many of the banks used to transfer funds were located in Hong Kong or Guangzhou. So the Chinese government was left trying to find an alternate route for funds to get from New York to rural Guangdong, sidestepping the Japanese-occupied coast. It was a problem they would try to solve the entire war without success.

61. Telegram 31360 from Chinese Consulate in San Francisco to MOFA Chongqing, October 23, 1942, 18/1544, MOFA, Nanjing; see also, in the same file, Telegram 28031 from the Chinese Consulate in Honolulu, April 27, 1942; Telegram 30102 from the Chinese Consulate in Seattle, August 14, 1942; and Telegram 30122 from the Zhongguo Huaqiao Kang Ri Hui, August 15, 1942, MOFA, Nanjing.

62. Zhu Mei zongzhibu zhi weiyuan Kuang Bingshun shang Wu Tiecheng cheng, December 13, 1943, Te [Special] 8/3.2/33, KMT.

63. The famine was centered in the four districts and near the East River (Dong Jiang si yi), from which the vast majority of Chinese Americans came. The "Four Districts" refers to Xinhui, Enping, Kaiping, and Taishan. Qiaowu weiyuanhui Guangdong qiaowuchu gongzuo gaikuang, chuzhang Zhang Tianjue baogao, 1946–48, 28/1/3, Guangzhou.

64. Letter from General Relief Fund Committee of CCBA New York, January 15, 1943, and Letter from Chinese Emergency Relief Society, July 31, 1943, 28/2/30, Overseas Chinese Office, Guangzhou. A contemporary exchange rate of 10 Chinese yuan to 3 U.S. dollars is given in Liu Weilin, "Meiguo gebu kang ri jiu guo zuzhi ji mukuan fenxi," *Huaqiao yu kang Ri zhanzheng lunwen ji*, vol. 2 (Taipei: Huaqiao Xiehui Zonghui, 1999), 480.

65. Zhang Xizhe, "Kang Ri zhanzheng shiqi Guomin Zhengfu," 7. In the first few months of the war in 1937, U.S. overseas Chinese contributed 1 million Chinese yuan through relief associations. Liu Weilin, "Meiguo gebu kang ri jiu guo zuzhi," 480.

66. Not to be confused with United China Relief, an American fund-raising organization that was led by old China hands and China watchers, composed of a coalition of organizations that had been working in China before the war. United China Relief became the means through which most non-Chinese Americans showed their support to China. The fact that there was not closer cooperation between this group and the Chinese-created China War Relief Association of America acts as a reminder of how segregated the two populations remained during the war.

67. Liu Weilin, "Meiguo gebu kang ri jiu guo zuzhi," 485–86. The US$56 million figure includes not only the $25 million contributed through the Chinese Relief Associations, but also separate contributions in the forms of the US$918,128 raised for the Chinese Air Force, contributions to Chinese war bonds, contributions for Cantonese refugees in South China, and remittances. According to Ren Guixiang, some sources even put the figure as high as US$132.3 million, but because the US$56 million figure comes from the ROC Treasury Department's records, it seems more believable. Ren Guixiang, "Kang Ri zhangzhen shiqi," 83–84. Most Chinese sources accept the $56 million figure, which originates with Taiwan Huaqiao Geming Shi Bianmu Weiyuanhui, *Huaqiao Geming Shi*, vol. 2 (Taipei: Taiwan Zhengzhong Shuju, 1981), 705–6, though *Huaqiao Huaren Baike Quanshu, Lishi juan* (Beijing: Huaqiao chubanshe, 2002), revives the US$132.3 million figure. Him Mark Lai discounts the $56 million estimate and thinks it unlikely that Chinese American contributions exceeded the $25 million mark: Him Mark Lai (Mai Liqian), *Cong Huaqiao dao Huaren: Ershi Shiji Meiguo Huaren Shehui Fazhan Shi* (Hong Kong: Sanlian Shudian, 1992), 118, n50. Him Mark Lai does not seem to take remittances and other contributions for relief efforts in Guangdong Province into account, but $31 million is a large discrepancy. None of these figures include small contributions (largely undocumented) made directly to the Communist forces on the mainland and in Hong Kong, like the Eighth Route Army and New Fourth Army.

68. Maochun Yu, *The Dragon's War: Allied Operations and the Fate of China, 1937–1947* (Annapolis, MD: Naval Institute Press, 2013).

69. Liu Weilin, "Meiguo gebu kang ri jiu guo zuzhi," 489–90.

70. The exception was the American colony of the Philippines, which placed fewer restrictions on remittances and sending funds to China than did the other colonial governments in Southeast Asia, and as a result, contributions from the islands were three times that of Chinese in Malaya. Huang Xiaojian, "Guanyu huaqiao kang Ri zhanzheng yanjiu de ruogan wenti," *Huaqiao yu kang Ri zhanzheng lunwen ji*, 1:28–29.

71. Him Mark Lai, *Cong Huaqiao dao Huaren*, 91.

72. Wong, *Americans First*, 38.

73. In 1938, San Francisco won, 7–0. "S.F. Rice Bowl Victor," *Chinese Digest*, March 1938, Chinatown—Overseas Chinese, box 200, Papers of Pardee Lowe, Hoover Institution.

74. Li Yinghui, "Kangzhan shiqi huaqiao kang Ri juanxian yu xiangguan fenzheng," *Huaqiao yu kang Ri zhanzheng lunwen ji*, vol. 1 (Taipei: Huaqiao Xiehui Zonghui, 1999), 64.

75. General Intelligence Survey in the United States, FBI, November 1942, 800.20211, box 3162, RG 59, Archives II.

76. "Torture Slaying Laid to War Drive," August 8, 1939, box 201, Papers of Pardee Lowe, Hoover Institution.

77. Him Mark Lai, *Cong Huaqiao dao Huaren*, 92–93; Li Yinghui, "Kangzhan shiqi huaqiao," 64–65. There were also documented cases of forced donations among the Chinese of Cuba and the Philippines.

78. Him Mark Lai, *Cong Huaqiao dao Huaren*, 93.

79. Li Yinghui, "Kangzhan shiqi huaqiao," 65–66.

80. General Intelligence Survey in the United States, FBI, August 1943, 800.20211, box 3165, RG 59, Archives II.

3. A Fight on All Fronts

1. Rana Mitter, *Forgotten Ally: China's World War II, 1937–1945* (Boston: Houghton Mifflin Harcourt, 2013), 6–7.

2. Qiaowu weiyuanhui Guangdong qiaowuchu baogao shu, 1946–48, 28/1/3, OCAC, Guangzhou.

3. Ben Shephard, *The Long Road Home: The Aftermath of the Second World War* (New York: Alfred A. Knopf, 2011).

4. Charges of corruption were common during the war and after. See Wesley M. Bagby, *The Eagle-Dragon Alliance: America's Relations with China in World War II* (Newark: University of Delaware Press, 1992), 127–28; Suzanne Pepper, *Civil War in China: The Political Struggle, 1945–1949* (Lanham, MD: Rowman & Littlefield, 1999), 423.

5. The full, international history of UNRRA was published shortly after the work was completed in a three-volume set. George Woodbridge, *UNRRA: The History of the United Nations Relief and Rehabilitation Administration*, 3 vols. (New York: Columbia University Press, 1950).

6. A history of the IRO was also published as its work came to an end. See Louise W. Holborn, *The International Refugee Organization, a Specialized Agency of the United Nations: Its History and Work, 1946–1952* (London: Oxford University Press, 1956).

7. Report on 5th Part of 1st Session, PCIRO, February 18, 1948, Foreign Office (FO) 371/107252, the National Archives of the UK (TNA): Public Record Office (PRO); Telegram

from State to U.S. Embassy Nanjing, March 20, 1947, IRO Constitution, December 19, 1946–May 31, 1947, box 4, Records Relating to the Intergovernmental Committee on Refugees, Country Files, 1938–41, RG 59, Archives II.

8. Memorandum of Conversation, IRO Constitution, April 24, 1947, IRO Constitution, December 19, 1946–May 31, 1947, box 4, Records Relating to the Intergovernmental Committee on Refugees, Country Files, 1938–41, RG 59, Archives II.

9. CNRRA Report on Externally Displaced Persons, June 1, 1946, 370/77, OCAC, Nanjing.

10. Katrine R.C. Greene, "Repatriating China's Expatriates," *Far Eastern Survey* 17.4 (February 25, 1948): 45.

11. Ibid., 46.

12. Qiaowu weiyuanhui xunling di 37588 hao, November 3, 1947, 28/1/49, OCAC, Guangzhou; Huping Ling, *Chinese Chicago: Race, Transnational Migration, and Community since 1870* (Stanford, CA: Stanford University Press, 2012), 206.

13. Marcia Reynders Ristaino, *Port of Last Resort: The Diaspora Communities of Shanghai* (Stanford, CA: Stanford University Press, 2001), 259.

14. United States Displaced Persons Commission, *Memo to America: The DP Story, the Final Report of the U.S. Displaced Persons Commission* (Washington, DC: Government Printing Office, 1952), 37–39.

15. The citizenship papers lost from the APL office were apparently recovered by a ring of criminals in Hong Kong, who tried to sell them back to their owners (or other takers) for HK$300 or more. Memorandum by American Consul General Canton, June 14, 1946, 130.00, box 3, Canton Security General, RG 84, Archives II; Despatch from Consul General Canton to Department of State, November 20, 1947, 811.11, box 79, Nanjing Embassy General, RG 84, Archives II.

16. In Chinese, *Huayi Meiguoren*. Ellen D. Wu has argued that the U.S. government found it more convenient to see Chinese Americans as overseas Chinese in the context of the Cold War in the 1950s. Though this was true for overseas information work, the repatriation negotiations serve as a reminder that this preference was contingent on external events. Wu, *The Color of Success: Asian Americans and the Origins of the Model Minority* (Princeton, NJ: Princeton University Press, 2014), 113.

17. Qiaowu weiyuanhui Guangdong qiaowuchu gongzuo gaikuang, chuzhang Zhang Tianjue baogao, 1946–48, 28/1/3, OCAC, Guangzhou.

18. Holborn, *International Refugee Organization*, 361. UNRRA efforts were first taken over by the Preparatory Commission of the International Refugee Organization (PCIRO), which in September 1948 became the International Refugee Organization (IRO). In addition to the overseas Chinese, the IRO also repatriated 1,809 displaced Europeans stranded, stateless, in China, a project that received a disproportionate share of the attention of both the UNRRA and the IRO in their efforts in Asia.

19. Huadong Xun, Minzhewei guanyu nanmin chuguo chuli banfa, September 20, 1950, 113–00125–01(1), Ministry of Foreign Affairs Archives, Beijing, People's Republic of China (hereafter MOFA Beijing).

20. Letter to Findlay Andrews from IRO Geneva, June 19, 1950, 113–00075–04(1), Guoji nanmin zuzhi yuadongju jieshu gongzuo youguan qingkuang, MOFA Beijing.

21. Telegram UNRRA Nanjing to UNRRA Hong Kong, March 19, 1947, and IRO Far East Office Narrative Report, September 1948, both 370/77, OCAC, Nanjing.

22. Letter from Jennings Wong to Dr. George Yeh, Vice Minister MOFA, April 16, 1948, 642/0056, Guojinanminzuzhi zhian (11-INO-05765), MOFA Taipei; Draft Provisions concerning

Payments of China's Contributions to IRO, 1948, FO 371/72052, TNA; Telegram, Shanghai to Foreign Office, December 2, 1948, FO371/2086C, TNA.

23. Savinggram to Mayor, Municipal Government of Amoy, from Horner H. C. Chen, IRO Amoy Suboffice, March 11, 1949, 642/0063, Guojinanminzuzhi zhian (11-INO-05773), MOFA Taipei; Letter to George Yeh from William N. Collison, July 22, 1949, 642/0065, Guojinanminzuzhi (11-INO-05774), Ministry of Foreign Affairs Archive, Institute of Modern History, Academia Sinica, Republic of China, Taipei, Taiwan, ROC (hereafter MOFA Taipei).

24. IRO Narrative Report, November 1948; Letter to H. W. Tuck, IRO Director-General, from Wu Nan-Ju, January 12, 1949, 642/0063, Guojinanminzuzhi zhian (11-INO-05773), MOFA Taipei.

25. Minutes, Emergency Measures Being Considered for the Evacuation of Jewish and White Russian DPs, FO 371/72086B, TNA.

26. "Meidi zai Ruishi xunlian jiandie," *People's Daily*, January 9, 1950.

27. Huadong Xun, Minzhewei guanyu nanmin chuguo chuli banfa, September 20, 1950, 113–00125–01(1), MOFA Beijing; MOFA to Shanghai, telegram, May 22, 1956,113–00287–01(1), Chuli he jieshu Lianheguo Guojinanminzuzhi Shanghaizhi wenti, MOFA Beijing.

28. Qiaowu weiyuanhui di ererjiu cichang huiyi shi richeng, Qiaomin churujing shishi banfa, September 19, 1945, 370/10, OCAC, Nanjing.

29. Qiu Hanping, *Zhanhou huaqiao wenti* (Fuzhou: Fujian Yinhang jingji yanjiusuo, 1945), 46–47.

30. Much has been written about the exclusion era and immediate post-exclusion-era immigration process for the Chinese. See in particular Erika Lee, *At America's Gates: Chinese Immigration during the Exclusion Era, 1882–1943* (Chapel Hill: University of North Carolina Press, 2007); Estelle T. Lau, *Paper Families: Identity, Immigration Administration, and Chinese Exclusion* (Durham, NC: Duke University Press, 2006).

31. U.S. Congress, Senate, Committee on Immigration and Naturalization, *Study of Problems Relating to Immigration and Deportation and Other Matters, Part 4 Hearings before the Committee on Immigration and Naturalization*, 78th Cong., 1st Sess., 1945.

32. See Xiaojian Zhao, *Remaking Chinese America: Immigration, Family, and Community, 1940–1965* (New Brunswick, NJ: Rutgers University Press, 2002), 24–25.

33. American Consul at Guangzhou to Department of State, 811.11, box 119, General Records of the Hong Kong Consulate 1945–49 (hereafter General HK Consulate), RG 84, Archives II.

34. Zhao, *Remaking Chinese America*, 82.

35. Telegram from Nanjing HQ Command to Hong Kong Consulate, July 19, 1947, 811.11, box 118, General HK Consulate, RG 84, Archives II.

36. Telegram from the U.S. Embassy to American Consulate in Guangzhou, August 14, 1947, 811.11, box 118, General HK Consulate, RG 84, Archives II; see also Letter to Consul General from Lau Lin Yau, November 7, 1947, 811.11, box 119, General HK Consulate, RG 84, Archives II.

37. American Consul General to Secretary of States, June 17, 1947, 811.11, box 119, General HK Consulate, RG 84, Archives II.

38. Historian Elaine Tyler May has argued that Hollywood marriages—both on and off screen—helped to normalize the Victorian ideal of romantic love in American marriages and make it mainstream by the 1920s. May, *Great Expectations: Marriage and Divorce in Post-Victorian America* (Chicago: University of Chicago Press, 1980), 75.

39. Kristin Celello, *Making Marriage Work: A History of Marriage and Divorce in the Twentieth-Century United States* (Chapel Hill: University of North Carolina Press, 2009), 67.

40. Telegram from Hopper to State, March 27, 1947, 811.11, box 119, General HK Consulate, RG 84, Archives II.

41. Telegram State to Hopper, April 10, 1947, and Telegram Secretary of State to Hong Kong Consulate, April 22, 1947, 811.11, box 119, General HK Consulate, RG 84, Archives II.

42. Hopper to Middleton, Thompson, April 23, 1947, 811.11, box 119, General HK Consulate, RG 84, Archives II.

43. "Picture brides" were Japanese and Korean women who arrived in the United States legally before 1924 to marry men with whom their families had exchanged pictures. Middleton to Hopper, undated (1947), 811.11, box 119, General HK Consulate, RG 84, Archives II.

44. Marshall to American Consul Hong Kong, May 28, 1947, 811.11, box 119, General HK Consulate, RG 84, Archives II.

45. American Consul at Guangzhou to Department of State, 811.11, box 119, General HK Consulate, RG 84, Archives II.

46. I. F. Wixon Memorandum to Ugo Carusi, INS, July 1, 1947, 811.11, box 79, General Records of the U.S. Embassy in Nanjing, China, 1946–48 (hereafter General Records Nanjing), RG 84, Archives II. The equation of female arrivals with prostitutes was rooted in the gender imbalance in U.S. Chinatowns and cultural differences with regard to marriage. Chinese women arriving during the exclusion era often provided additional affidavits attesting to their respectable characters and solid reputations to avoid being taken for prostitutes; lower-class women were given additional scrutiny. See Lee, *At America's Gates*, 94–95.

47. Hopper to Dept., November 19, 1947, 811.11, box 79, General Records Nanjing, RG 84, Archives II; Canton to Dept., October 6, 1947, 811.11, box 79, General Records Nanjing, RG 84, Archives II.

48. John Cabot, U.S. Consul Shanghai, to Lewis Clark, American Embassy Nanjing, April 26, 1948, 811.11, box 119, General Records Nanjing, RG 84, Archives II. The navy was in the habit of requiring prior approval for all American sailors seeking to marry foreigners in the Pacific, citing as an example of a security risk a young woman who had relatives recently repatriated to Soviet Russia whom Soviet representatives in the United States could pressure into making decisions adverse to U.S. security interests. Oscar C. Badger, Vice Admiral, U.S. Navy, Commander Naval Forces, Western Pacific, to J. Leighton Stuart, U.S. Ambassador to China, undated (1948), 811.11, box 119, American Embassy Nanjing, RG 84, Archives II.

49. Him Mark Lai, *Becoming Chinese American: A History of Communities and Institutions* (Walnut Creek, CA: Alta Mira Press, 2004), 23.

50. For a full discussion of the "paper sons" system and Chinese use of the U.S. court system to gain entry see Lucy Salyer, *Laws Harsh as Tigers: Chinese Immigrants and the Shaping of Modern Immigration Law* (Chapel Hill: University of North Carolina Press, 1995); and Mae M. Ngai, *Impossible Subjects: Illegal Aliens and the Making of Modern America* (Princeton, NJ: Princeton University Press, 2004), 202–6.

51. Chinese immigrating to or resident in the United States before 1965 were almost exclusively natives of a few particular counties within Guangdong Province; as a result, the Guangzhou consulate was primarily responsible for processing applications. After 1949, when the Guangzhou consulate was closed, Hong Kong became solely responsible for all immigration and citizenship applications from China or Hong Kong.

52. Office Memorandum Canton (Guangzhou), Chinese-American Citizenship and Immigration Work, May 5, 1947, Canton Consulate General Security Segregated General Correspondence (hereafter Canton Security General), 000–720, box 4, RG 84, Archives II; Report, Kenneth Wu to Consul at Guangzhou, October 30, 1947, 811.11, box 5, Canton Security General, RG 84, Archives II.

53. Telegram Burke to Secretary of State, July 20, 1947, 000–720, box 4, Canton Security General, RG 84, Archives II.

54. INS began to use telegraph codes to represent characters, but many of the Chinese applicants had more than one name (a birth name, a school name, a marriage name, etc.), so even that system did not completely eliminate difficulties identifying files.

55. Memo Gordon L. Burke to John J. Muccio, January 5, 1948, 811.11, box 129, General HK Consulate, RG 84, Archives II.

56. Qiaowu weiyuanhui xunling, no. 45259, 1948, 28/1/49, OCAC, Guangzhou.

57. Letter John J. Muccio, American Embassy Manila, to Christian M. Ravental, Director General of the Foreign Service, January 22, 1948, 811.11, box 129, General HK Consulate, RG 84, Archives II.

58. Chuck Fong, Office Memorandum on Citizenship and Visa Problems in the Canton Consular District, June 23, 1947, 000–720, box 4, RG 84, Archives II.

59. Hopper to American Consul in Guangzhou, January 18, 1948, General HK Consulate, 811.11, RG 84, Archives II.

60. Letter to Ambassador Stuart, Nanjing, from Louis H. Chin et al., September 30, 1948, 811.11, box 119, American Embassy Nanjing, RG 84, Archives II.

61. Most did not wait two years, but with INS officials in the United States suspecting consular officials in Guangzhou and Hong Kong of fraud, they were often determined to investigate each case as thoroughly as possible. Chinese stayed in detention while INS sought out and interviewed their family members, examined the records of their entries, and corresponded with U.S. consular officials. The high numbers of Chinese arriving in the postwar era meant that some of the time in detention involved waiting for INS to start to examine the case.

62. Memorandum from the Chinese Consul in San Francisco to the Guangzhou Office of the OCAC, May 20, 1948, 28/1/49, OCAC, Guangzhou. The suicide became ammunition for the CCP's anti-American propaganda—it and other examples of American mistreatment of Chinese immigrants were reported in "Wo guo liu Mei shiwang qiaobao lue shou Meidi qishi pohai," *Renmin Ribao*, November 15, 1948, 3.

63. Glen Peterson, *Overseas Chinese in the People's Republic of China* (New York: Routledge, 2012), 27.

64. Hongshan Li, *U.S. China Educational Exchange: State, Society, and Intercultural Relations, 1905–1950* (New Brunswick, NJ: Rutgers University Press, 2008), 110.

65. Ibid., 119.

66. Ibid., 149.

67. Memorandum from the Ministry of Foreign Affairs, n.d., 172–1/1940–2, MOFA, Academia Historica.

68. See Lee, *At America's Gates*; Ronald Takaki, *Strangers from a Different Shore* (New York: Little, Brown and Co., 1998).

69. Memorandum from MOFA, North America Section, September 9, 1944, 172–1/1940–2, MOFA, Academia Historica.

70. Memorandum to MOFA from Ping, May 9, 1944, 172–1/1940–3, MOFA, Academia Historica.

71. The documents on this policy position it as a direct response to the U.S. repeal of exclusion. Other net immigration countries, like Canada or Australia, had not yet reformed their Chinese immigration laws when it was being drafted, though it is safe to assume that if it worked with the United States it might be fruitfully applied elsewhere. That said, some of the documents do speak in a more general sense of improving the overall "quality" of Chinese migrants abroad for the sake of improving China's status in the world.

72. OCAC to MOFA no. 8173, on regulations for immigration to America, December 27, 1944, 172–1/1940–2, MOFA, Academia Historica.

73. Memorandum from the Ministry of Foreign Affairs (undated), 172–1/1940–2, Academia Historica. This policy was articulated explicitly with regard to new U.S. immigration, though because screening procedures applied to all students moving abroad, whatever their destination, there is no reason to think a variation of it would not have been used anywhere else Chinese under ROC purview might have migrated.

74. Immigration to the U.S. (undated memorandum), 172–1/1940–3, MOFA, Academia Historica.

75. MOFA note to the American Embassy, no. Mei-36/10613, May 22, 1947, 172–1/1940–4, MOFA, Academia Historica.

76. Letter from the Consulate General Shanghai to Secretary of State, April 16, 1947, 855–56, box 95, American Embassy Nanjing, RG 84, Archives II.

77. Letter from Consul at Shanghai to Secretary of State, September 18, 1947, 855–56, box 95, American Embassy Nanjing, RG 84, Archives II.

78. Conversation between J. E. McKenna and S. T. Chen concerning Chinese Quota Immigrants to the United States, May 4, 1948, 172-1–2/1940–4, MOFA, Academia Historica.

79. Huaqiao weiyuanhui di san ci changwu huiyi yishi richeng, July 6, 1948, 370/13, OCAC, Nanjing. After the ROC government moved to Taiwan in 1949, investigations into the background of potential immigrants grew difficult if not impossible, given the lack of access to mainland home villages, but the formality was maintained as part of the procedure for obtaining a passport for immigrating to America.

80. Message from the Guangzhou OCAC Office, January 21, 1948, 28/1/49, OCAC, Guangzhou.

81. Renqiu Yu, *To Save China, to Save Ourselves: The Chinese Hand Laundry Alliance of New York* (Philadelphia: Temple University Press, 2011); Him Mark Lai, *Chinese American Transnational Politics*, ed. Madeline Hsu (Urbana: University of Illinois Press, 2010); Peter Kwong, *Chinatown, New York: Labor and Politics, 1930–1950* (New York: New Press, 1979).

82. Handwritten letter from Chen Zianywen and Yu Uen Lee, November 10, 1946, OF 150 Miscellaneous (1945–46) (1 of 2), White House Central Files, Truman Papers, Harry S. Truman Presidential Library (hereafter HST Library).

83. Collection of letters from Chinese in the United States, January 25, 1946, China: 1946, box 150, Papers of HST, PSF Subject File, 1940–53, China Lobby File, HST Library.

84. Letter to Dean Acheson from Albert Chow, October 18, 1949, China 1950–52, box 151, Papers of HST, PSF Subject File, 1940–53, China Lobby File, HST Library.

85. Him Mark Lai, *Chinese American Transnational Politics*, 123–36.

86. ORE 7, Central Intelligence Group, "Chinese Minorities in Southeast Asia," December 2, 1946, www.foia.cia.gov, accessed June 19, 2006.

87. General Intelligence Survey in the United States, FBI, September 1942, 800.20211, box 3162, RG 59, Archives II.

88. Him Mark Lai, "The Chinese Marxist Left in America to the 1960s," *Chinese America: History and Perspectives* 6 (1992): 3–81.

89. "Laoda haozhao haiwai huaqiao zhiyuan zuguo jiefang yundong," *Renmin Ribao*, September 8, 1948, 2.

90. Zhanhou qiaomin jiaoyu shishi fang'an, June 22, 1944, 18/1711, MOFA, Nanjing.

91. Qiaowu weiyuanhui Liu weyuanzhang Weichi liu yue shi'er ri dui haiwai qiaobao guangbo ci, 28/1/1, OCAC, Guangzhou.

4. Chinese Migrants as Cold Warriors

1. Nancy Bernkopf Tucker, *Taiwan, Hong Kong, and the United States, 1945–1992: Uncertain Friendships* (New York: Twayne Publishers, 1994), 30–32.

2. The other NATO exceptions that recognized Communist China in the early 1950s were all Scandinavian countries.

3. Tucker, *Taiwan, Hong Kong, and the United States*, 35.

4. Ibid., 40–42.

5. Matthew A. Light, "What Does It Mean to Control Migration? Soviet Mobility Policies in Comparative Perspective," *Law and Social Inquiry* 37.2 (Spring 2012): 395. Communist China employed many of these same controls, though with some clear exceptions that largely related to the overseas Chinese: intermittent free migration between Guangdong and Hong Kong and freedom of return for Chinese abroad.

6. Mae M. Ngai, *Impossible Subjects: Illegal Aliens and the Making of Modern America* (Princeton, NJ: Princeton University Press, 2004), 243.

7. Discussion of Points of Objection to Certain Provisions of S. 2550 Raised in the White House Memorandum, OF 133 S. 716, S2550, HR 5678, box 682, Official File, Papers of HST, HST Library.

8. *Congressional Record*, 82nd Cong., 2nd Sess., 1952, 98, pt. 5:5608, 5612, 5616.

9. Letter to Monsignor O'Grady from Truman, May 28, 1952, OF 133 S. 716, S2550, HR 5678, box 682, Official File, Papers of HST, HST Library.

10. Veto Message, June 25, 1952, OF 133 S. 716, S2550, HR 5678, box 682, Official File, Papers of HST, HST Library.

11. Carl Bon Tempo, *Americans at the Gate: The United States and Refugees during the Cold War* (Princeton, NJ: Princeton University Press, 2008), 29.

12. Lee, Lim P.; Hong, Edward; Hong, CY, box 8; and Sing, Jack Wong, box 10, Presidential Committees, Commissions and Boards (RG 220), HST Library.

13. *Whom We Shall Welcome: Report of the President's Commission on Immigration and Naturalization* (Washington, DC: Government Printing Office, 1953), 52.

14. Ngai, *Impossible Subjects*, 246. The debate not only cut across party lines, but it was essentially between two camps of immigration restrictionists, demonstrating just how much agreement there was in Congress on these issues.

15. Guanyu huaqiao qiaojuan chu ru guo shen pi yuanze de zhishi, December 31, 1955, 118–00317–01, MOFA Beijing.

16. "Renmin zhengfu zenme jiedai guiqiao, nanqiao," *Qiao Xun*, no. 108, January 20, 1953, Beijing, 1948.

17. Guanyu huaqiao qiaojuan chu ru guo shen pi yuanze de zhishi, December 31, 1955, 118–00317–01, MOFA Beijing.

18. "Fu Mei ding'e yimin shenhe banfa zhi xiugai," *Qiaowu Yuebao* 12, June 1942, Taipei, 10.

19. Tucker, *Taiwan, Hong Kong, and the United States*, 40–42; Nancy Bernkopf Tucker, *The China Threat: Memories, Myths, and Realities in the 1950s* (New York: Columbia University Press, 2012), 69–71.

20. Athan Theoharis, "The Truman Administration and the Decline of Civil Liberties: The FBI's Success in Securing Authorization for a Preventative Detention Program," *Journal of American History* 64.4 (March 1978): 1011.

21. Memo, Director, FBI, to the Attorney General, March 18, 1955, "Justice Department Plans in Event of Formosan Open Hostilities," DETCOM File 100–356062 / Section 16, FBI FOIA Reading Room, Washington, DC.

22. Memo, [deleted] to the Director, FBI, "Justice Department Plans in Event of Formosan Open Hostilities," April 4, 1955, DETCOM File 100–356062 / Section 16, FBI FOIA Reading Room.

23. "Memorandum for Mr. [deleted]," May 11, 1955, DETCOM File 100–356062 / Section 17, FBI FOIA Reading Room.

24. U.S. Immigration and Naturalization Service (USINS), *Annual Report*, 1955, 1956.

25. Suggested contemporarily by Whittaker Chambers, *Witness* (New York: Random House, 1952), and more recently through such works as John Earl Haynes, *Verona: Decoding Soviet Espionage in America* (New Haven, CT: Yale University Press, 1999).

26. Office Memo, Boyd to Kelly, January 4, 1952, Chinese Inspection–NY, box 3277, RG 85, NARA.

27. Mimie Ouei to O. Edmund Clubb, June 14, 1951, reel 20, frames 925–26, MF C-0012, RG 59, Archives II.

28. "Harm done U.S. interests by delays and obstacles holding up deserving Chinese and others seeking to enter U.S. from Hong Kong," memorandum, June 18, 1951, reel 20, frames 775–78, MF C-0012, RG 59, Archives II.

29. Memorandum to All District Directors from Benjamin G. Habberton, Acting Commissioner, July 23, 1953, 21.1, box 21, Papers of Iris Chang, Hoover Institution.

30. Ibid.

31. As Mae Ngai has noted, estimates were that "at least half of all Chinese immigrants during the exclusion era entered the United States illegally." Ngai, *Impossible Subjects*, 204.

32. FSD 931, December 9, 1955, box 7, folder 1-C/4, Records of the Bureau of Security and Consular Affairs, RG 59, Archives II.

33. FSD 1485, June 5, 1956, box 7, folder 1-C/4, Records of the Bureau of Security and Consular Affairs, RG 59, Archives II.

34. Ibid. These problems were raised at the talks in Geneva; see chapter 7.

35. Interview with Everett Drumright, December 5, 1988, Foreign Affairs Oral History Collection of the Association for Diplomatic Studies and Training, Library of Congress, http://www.loc.gov/item/mfdipbib000311/.

36. Ngai, *Impossible Subjects*, 209–10.

37. Memo to Henderson, Robertson, Morton, and McLeod, from Jack B. Minor, January 4, 1956, report of committee from Far Eastern Affairs, box 7, 1-C/4, Records of the Bureau of Security and Consular Affairs (hereafter SCA), RG 59, Archives II.

38. Memo, to SCA McLeod from SY Flinn, July 17, 1956, box 1, Bureau of Far East Asian Affairs, Office of Asian Communist Affairs (hereafter ACA), 220.1 Passport Fraud 1956, RG 59, Archives II.

39. Ngai, *Impossible Subjects*, 202–24; Him Mark Lai, *Becoming Chinese American: A History of Communities and Institutions* (Walnut Creek, CA: Alta Mira Press, 2004), 26–32; Xiaojian Zhao, *Remaking Chinese America: Immigration, Family, and Community, 1940–1965* (New Brunswick, NJ: Rutgers University Press, 2002), 174.

40. Memo of Conversation, 3/2/56, Grand Jury Summons to SF Chinese Organizations in Regard to Passport Fraud Investigation, 1-C/3.1, box 6, SCA, Archives II.

41. FBI Memo to Mr. Dennis A. Flinn, from John Edgar Hoover, May 22, 1956, Movement of Communist Chinese, 56364/51.6, RG 84, NARA; Memo of Conversation, March 13, 1956, US Grand Jury Investigations of Chinese Passport Fraud Cases, ACA, folder 220.1 Passport Fraud 1956, ACA, RG 59, Archives II.

42. Tung Pok Chin, *Paper Son: One Man's Story* (Philadelphia: Temple University Press, 2000).

43. A point made best by Ngai, *Impossible Subjects*, 223–24.

44. *The Chinatown Files*, DVD, dir. Amy Chen (New York: Filmmakers Library, 2001).

45. Mei diguozhiyi soucha huaqiao huzhao de qingkuang huibao, March 16, 1956, 11–00241–05(1), MOFA-Beijing. Beijing MOFA officials also noted with interest that the ROC has protested the actions.

46. "Meiguo zhengfu konggao Liu Chengji pohuai yiminfa he guihuafa," March 14, 1957, *Qiaoqing Cankao Ziliao* 503, 4445.

47. "Zai Meiguo yimin kelixia Li Shou yu yu zhong zisha," April 11, 1957, *Qiaoqing Cankao Ziliao* 510–11, 4514.

48. "Smuggling Chinese: A Threat to U.S. Security," *New York Daily News*, April 30–May 4, 1956, 172–3/0594, MOFA, Academia Historica, Taipei.

49. Jack Chen, *The Chinese of America* (San Francisco: Harper & Row, 1980), 214; Peter Kwong, *Chinatown, New York: Labor and Politics, 1930–1950* (New York: New Press, 1979), 145–47; Brett de Bary Nee and Victor Nee, "The Kuomintang in Chinatown," in *Counterpoint: Perspectives on Asian America*, ed. Emma Gee (Los Angeles: University of California Press, 1976), 150; and Him Mark Lai, "Chinese Politics and the United States Chinese Communities," ibid., 158.

50. *Annual Report*, 1950–1960 (USINS). Some of the 55 Chinese deported for entering with false documents or a few of the 115 "entering without proper documents" may have been suspected subversives.

51. *Annual Reports*, 1950–1960 (USINS).

52. Letter, Chinese Embassy to US Department of State, November 21, 1951, Formosa, Deportation of 48 Chinese Aliens to, File 56204/20 (Formosa-Deportation), box 2876, RG 85, NARA.

53. Letter, US Department of State to Chinese Embassy, undated, Formosa-Deportation, RG 85, NARA.

54. USINS, *Annual Report*, 1950, 54.

55. USINS, *Annual Report*, 1951, 58–59.

56. USINS, *Annual Report*, 1955, 20.

57. USINS, *Annual Report*, 1953, 43.

58. 56204/81, Walter McConaughy to A. R. Mackey, July 3, 1953, box 2878, RG 85, NARA.

59. 56204/81, Memorandum to Commissioner from Bruce Barber, San Francisco director, July 7, 1953, box 2878, RG 85, NARA.

60. *United States v. Leong Choy Moon*, 218 F. 2d 316 (1954).

61. *Cheng Fu Sheng v. Rogers*, 177 F. Supp. 281 (1959).

62. *Cheng Fu Sheng v. Barber*, 269 F. 2d 497 (1959).

63. *Chao-Ling Wang v. Pilliod*, 285 F. 2d 517 (1960); *Cheng Kai Fu v. Immigration and Naturalization Service*, 386 F. 2d 750 (1967).

64. Memorandum to Commissioner from Philip Forman, February 6, 1940, 56204/81, box 2878, RG 85, NARA.

65. Memorandum for the file, State letter to INS, April 25, 1951, 56204/81, box 2878, RG 85, NARA.

66. C. G. Kemball to Harry Jones, April 1, 1954, FO369/4981, TNA.

67. Saving Telegram no. 477, C. Steel to Foreign Office, June 30, 1954, FO 39/4982, TNA.

68. Depending on the source, Jue's name is also variously given as Jew Ten, Jue Gar King, and Chow Ka King. See *Jew Ten v. Immigration and Naturalization Service*, 307 F. 2d 832 (1962).

69. "Jue Indicted on Immigration Charge," *San Francisco Chronicle*, July 15, 1953, box 201, Papers of Pardee Lowe, Hoover Institution.

70. Application for parole, George K. Jue, May 15, 1954, box 5, folder 14, Papers of John J. Rhodes, Arizona State University Archives and Special Collections, Tempe.

71. *Jew Ten v. Immigration and Naturalization Service*, 307 F. 2d 832 (1962); Memorandum from Director of Office of Security to SAC San Francisco, Re George K. Jue, December 2, 1953, 426.6/0010, Mei yiminju song Zhou Jiajing lai Tai, MOFA Taipei.

72. Memo from Clough to Robertson, Office of Chinese Affairs, September 17, 1957, box 3, folder 210, Jue, George, RG 59, Archives II.

73. Despite a thorough search, nothing in Walter's papers at Lehigh University offers any insight into his particular thinking on Jue, though he was clearly amenable to (and sponsored) other private bills for Chinese nationals. The accusation—backed up by the INS investigative report—that Jue was a habitual offender by repeatedly helping Chinese immigrate with falsified documents is likely the reason for Walter's vendetta. Having helped to write the 1952 immigration law, he proved uniquely committed to upholding it. Papers of Congressman Francis E. Walter, Lehigh University Special Collections, Bethlehem, PA.

74. Letter to George K. Jue from Roy W. Howard, October 15, 1957, 426.6/0010, MOFA Taipei.

75. Edward Ranzal, "Chinese Leader Is Indicted Here: Sing Kee, D.S.C. Winner in World War I, Accused of Bringing in Aliens," *New York Times*, May 4, 1956, 1.

76. "Senate Unit Kills Bill to Bar Alien's Ouster," *Washington Evening Star*, July 7, 1955, box 5, folder 14, Rhodes Papers, ASU Archives.

77. Letter to John J. Rhodes from Emanuel Celler, June 5, 1955, box 5, folder 14, Rhodes Papers, ASU Archives.

78. Classified Memorandum of Information from Immigration and Naturalization Service Files of George K. Jue, Beneficiary of I.N. A505, box 5, folder 14, Rhodes Papers, ASU Archives.

79. Memorandum from ROC Embassy in the United States to MOFA Taipei, June 20, 1956, 426.6/0010, MOFA Taipei.

80. Memo from Clough to Robertson, Office of Chinese Affairs, September 17, 1957; Memo from Clough to Robertson, Office of Chinese Affairs, October 14, 1957, box 3, folder 210, Jue, George, RG 59, Archives II.

81. Memorandum of Conversation with Frank Ford, ed., Scripps-Howard Newspapers, October 14, 1957, box 3, folder 210, Jue, George, RG 59, Archives II; Lynn Pan, *Sons of the Yellow Emperor: A History of the Chinese Diaspora* (New York: Kodansha International, 1994), 175–78.

82. Telegram to Roy W. Howard from George K. C. Yeh, October 8, 1957, 426.6/0010, MOFA Taipei.

83. Telegram to MOFA from Dong Xianguang in Washington, DC, February 12, 1957, 426.6/0010, MOFA Taipei.

84. Letter to Robert Murphy, Deputy Under Secretary for Political Affairs, from INS, undated (1957), box 3, folder 210, Jue, George, RG 59, Archives II.

85. Telegram to MOFA from ROC Consulate in San Francisco, October 1, 1957, 426.6/0010, MOFA Taipei.

86. Telegram to MOFA from Dong Xianguang in Washington, DC, September 18, 1957, 426.6/0010, MOFA Taipei.

87. Memo from Clough to Robertson, Office of Chinese Affairs, September 17, 1957, box 3, folder 210, Jue, George, RG 59, Archives II.

88. Qiao bao lun Mei qiansong Zhou Jiajing lai Tai an, November 27, 1962, 426.6/0010, MOFA-Taiwan; "Jue Asks Court to Reconsider Deportation Order," *China Post*, October 16, 1961, box 276, Papers of Pardee Lowe, Hoover Institution.

89. Letter to George Yeh from Roy Howard, October 9, 1962, 426.6/0010, MOFA Taipei.

90. Qiao bao lun Mei qiansong Zhou Jiajing lai Tai an [An overseas Chinese newspaper discusses the U.S. deportation of George K. Jue to Taiwan], November 27, 1962, 426.6/0010, MOFA Taipei.

91. Letter to Judy Eisenhower from Lawrence N. Dicostanzo, June 26, 1984, box 162, folder 8, Papers of Barry Goldwater, Arizona State University Archives and Special Collections, Tempe; U.S. Naturalization Record Indexes, 1791–1992.

92. Semi-Annual Report on Educational Exchange Program, Hong Kong to State, January 27, 1954, RG 84, Archives II.

93. Fitzgerald, James E., box 7, Presidential Committees, Commissions and Boards (RG 220), HST Library.

5. Remitting to the Enemy

1. The dynamics of this system have been meticulously documented for the county of Taishan (which up to 1960 was the home county of "well over half" of all Chinese in the United States) by Madeline Hsu in *Dreaming of Gold, Dreaming of Home: Transnationalism and Migration between the United States and South China, 1882–1943* (Stanford, CA: Stanford University Press, 2000). In her history, remittances, letters, and magazines helped to create a transnational community that defied U.S. immigration restrictions and racism and allowed families to flourish across national boundaries.

2. This argument is made by Glen Peterson in *Overseas Chinese in the People's Republic of China* (New York: Routledge, 2012), 27–54.

3. In the former case, Stephen Fitzgerald, *China and the Overseas Chinese: A Study of Peking's Changing Policy, 1949–1970* (Cambridge: Cambridge University Press, 1972); Chun-hsi Wu, *Dollars, Dependents and Dogma: Overseas Chinese Remittances to Communist China* (Stanford, CA: Hoover Institution, 1967). In the latter, Cindy I-Fen Cheng, *Citizens of Asian America: Democracy and Race during the Cold War* (New York: NYU Press, 2013); Gloria Heyung Chun, *Of Orphans and Warriors: Inventing Chinese American Culture and Identity* (New Brunswick, NJ: Rutgers University Press, 2000); Renqiu Yu, *To Save China, to Save Ourselves: The Chinese Hand Laundry Alliance of New York* (Philadelphia: Temple University Press, 2011). One notable exception is Peterson, *Overseas Chinese in the People's Republic of China*, which deals briefly with both sides of the issue.

4. This is a subject that I have explored in more depth elsewhere. Meredith Oyen, "Communism, Containment, and the Chinese Overseas," in *The Cold War in Asia: The Battle for Hearts and Minds*, ed. Zheng Yangwen, Hong Liu, and Michael Szonyi (Boston: Brill, 2010), 59–93.

5. "Suggestions for increasing the effectiveness of our propaganda campaign," memorandum to FE/P Connors, from CA Stuart, January 5, 1951, reel 24, frames 574–5, RG 59, Archives II.

6. Free World 1.8; Free World 1.9; Free World 4.2. Publications about the United States, Free World Chinese, box 113, Records of the USIS, RG 306, Archives II.

7. The story of Wong's trip has been told more completely in Ellen D. Wu, *The Color of Success: Asian Americans and the Origins of the Model Minority* (Princeton, NJ: Princeton University Press, 2014), 126–34; Cheng, *Citizens of Asian America*, 95–102.

8. "Leader Specialists Program: Jade Snow Wong," Operations Memo, to State from Hong Kong Consul General, July 17, 1952, folder Visiting Persons, box 3, USIS, Hong Kong, RG 84, Archives II.

9. Semi-Annual Report on Educational Exchange Program, Julian F. Harrington, Hong Kong to State, July 21, 1954, folder Educational Exchange, Reports, box 5, USIS, Hong Kong, RG 84, Archives II.

10. Inspection Report of USIS Hong Kong, June 6–9, 1955, folder Hong Kong, box 4, Inspection Reports, USIA, RG 306, Archives II.

11. Wu, *Color of Success*, 142.

12. For examples see the determination to repatriate U.S. nationals after World War II in chapter 3, the dismissal of Nationalist government intervention in screening migrants in chapter 4, and the representation issues in chapter 7.

13. Mae M. Ngai, *Impossible Subjects: Illegal Aliens and the Making of Modern America* (Princeton, NJ: Princeton University Press, 2004), 208.

14. Him Mark Lai, *Chinese American Transnational Politics*, ed. Madeline Hsu (Urbana: University of Illinois Press, 2010), 30; Gaijin dui mei xuanchuan gongzuo jiantao hui jilu, February 19, 1957, 707.6/0014, MOFA Taipei.

15. Him Mark Lai, *Chinese American Transnational Politics*, 31; Ross Y. Koen, *The China Lobby in American Politics* (New York: Macmillan, 1960), 31–32.

16. Cheng, *Citizens of Asian America*, 151.

17. Telegram, W. F. Long, Chairman, the Chinese Six Companies Anti-Communist League, to Vice President Alben Barkley, March 2, 1952, Petitions and Memorials to the Senate Committee on Foreign Relations, 82nd Congress, 82A-J8 (372), 2 of 2 (Sen. P/M, 82nd), Records of the United States Senate, Record Group 46 (RG 46), NARA.

18. Telegram, Samuel Y. Ong and Frank M. Ong, Directors-General, Hip Sing Association in America, to Sam Rayburn, Speaker of the House of Representatives, September 16, 1955, Petitions and Memorials to the House Committee on Foreign Affairs, HR84A-H5.1, 1 of 2 (HR P/M, 84th), Records of the United States House of Representatives, RG 233, NARA.

19. "17,000,000 Overseas Chinese Opposed Admission of Red China into United Nations," November 21, 1967, *New York Times*, Chinatown, box 200, Pardee Lowe Papers, Hoover Institution.

20. Telegram, Dr. Henry S. Luke, President, Seattle Chinese Benevolent Association, to Senator Warren Magnuson, August 22, 1951, Sen P/M, 82nd, 1 of 2, RG 46, NARA.

21. Cheng, *Citizens of Asian America*, 159–60; Daryl J. Maeda, *Chains of Babylon: The Rise of Asian America* (Minneapolis: University of Minnesota Press, 2009), 88.

22. Him Mark Lai, "The Chinese-Marxist Left, Chinese Students and Scholars in America, and the New China: Mid-1940s to Mid-1950s," *Chinese America: History & Perspectives* 18 (January 2004): 16.

23. Yu, *To Save China*, 165.

24. Cheng, *Citizens of Asian America*, 160–61.

25. Donna Gabaccia, *Foreign Relations: American Immigration in Global Perspective* (Princeton, NJ: Princeton University Press, 2012), 117–20.

26. Memorandum of Conversation, Dr. Cheng Yen-fen, December 2, 1953, folder 350, box 17, Taiwan—Taipei Consulate Confidential Files, RG 84, Archives II.

27. A. H. B. Hermann to E. T. Biggs, April 21, 1954, FO 371/110376, Foreign Office, TNA.

28. Niuyue qiaobao lun zhengfu huaqiao zhengce, November 20, 1958, 462.2/0010, MOFA Taipei.

29. Zhongyang renmin zhengfu huaqiao shiwu weiyuanhui di yi ci qiaowu kuoda huiyi, June 26, 1951, 235/2/3–125, Guangzhou.

30. Wu, *Dollars, Dependents and Dogma*, 83; *Gongfei qiaohui de yanjiu* (Taipei: Qiaowu weiyuanhui diqing yanjiu shi, 1969), 20–21.

31. Yang Shihong, "Xin Zhongguo Qiaohui Gongzuo de Lishi Kaocha (1949–1966)," *Dangdai Zhongguo Shi Yanjiu* 9.2 (March 2002): 89.

32. Guonei qiaowu gongzuo ruogan zhengce wenti, Zhong qiaowu dangzu, July 25, 1955, 235/2/9–67, Guangzhou.

33. Another—somewhat ingenious—scheme reported by *Time* claimed that Chinese Communist agents were in the Philippines spending pesos to buy up money orders sent by migrants in Hawaii to families in Manila, then changing the decimal points before cashing them in Hong Kong, raking in some US$4 million in the process. "Money-Order Racket," September 24, 1951, *Time* magazine, Chinatown, box 200, Pardee Lowe Papers, Hoover Institution.

34. "Chinese Reds Face Crises in Finances," *New York Times*, December 4, 1949, 5; "Communist China Seeks Cash Here in Secret Campaign to Sell Bonds," *New York Times*, February 5, 1950, 1.

35. Peterson, *Overseas Chinese*, 50–51, 73.

36. Zhongyang renmin zhengfu huaqiao shiwu weiyuanhui di yi ci qiaowu kuoda huiyi, June 26, 1951, 235/2/3–125, Guangzhou.

37. South China branch Office Propaganda Department to CCP Central Propaganda Department, Qiaowei, February 11, 1952, 204/3/16–101, Guangzhou.

38. Guonei qiaowu gongzuo ruogan zhengce wenti, Zhong qiaowu dangzu, July 25, 1955, 235/2/9–67, Guangzhou.

39. Peterson, *Overseas Chinese*, 31. There was a long history of using letters for these purposes.

40. Gui guo liuxuesheng guanyu Meiguo kouliu woguo liuxuesheng wenti zuotanhui jilu, November 1953–February 1954, 111–00052–04, MOFA Beijing.

41. Other banks quickly followed suit. Peterson, *Overseas Chinese*, 32.

42. CCP Central Propaganda Department to South China Branch Office Propaganda Department, March 18, 1952, 204/3/16–98, Guangzhou.

43. Guangdong Sheng renmin zhengfu, Notice 54, Guanyu jinyibu jiaqiang chuli huaqiao laixin de yijian, November 15, 1954, 235/1/115–89, Guangzhou.

44. Guanyu zaixuanju zhong gaibian huaqiaohu dizhu shenfen de yijian, July 17, 1956, OCAC, 250/1/44–119, Guangzhou.

45. Glen D. Peterson, "Socialist China and the *Huaqiao*: The Transition to Socialism in the Overseas Chinese Areas of Rural Guangdong, 1949–1956," *Modern China* 14 (July 1988): 326.

46. Peterson, *Overseas Chinese*, 33.

47. Huaqiao konggaoxin yi su, January 10, 1952, 204/3/16–104, Guangzhou.

48. Ibid.

49. Cheng, *Citizens of Asian America*, 161, 168.

50. George de Carvalho, "No Action in Chinatown on Red Racket," November 26, 1951, *San Francisco Chronicle*, Chinatown–Korean War, box 201, Pardee Lowe Papers, Hoover Institution.

51. Press Release, April 18, 1951, reel 24, frames 80–81, C0012, RG 59, Archives II.

52. Letter from Secretary of the Treasury to Senator Knowland, December 3, 1951, reel 24, frames 83–4, C0012, RG 59, Archives II.

53. "Red Ransom Racket Smashed," December 3, 1951, *San Francisco Chronicle*, Chinatown–Korean War, box 201, Pardee Lowe Papers, Hoover Institution.

54. Wu, *Dollars, Dependents and Dogma*, 42. Wu's account is based on Chinese-language newspaper reports coming out of Hong Kong.

55. "Chinese Extortion Brings Death Here," *New York Times*, December 9, 1951, 4.

56. The Canadian and Jamaican governments reported evidence of extortions. Secretariat, Jamaica, to W. I. J. Wallace, Colonial Office, April 17, 1952, CO1033/3, TNA; H. R. Horne,

Office of the High Commissioner for Canada, to J. O. Floyd, Foreign Office, January 14, 1952, CO1033/3, TNA. An American interview with a Chinese man in Singapore revealed the interviewee's opinion that "the families of wealthy Chinese . . . are in effect being held for ransom by the Communists." They noted, however, that the same man "almost unbelievably" could not identify his family's hometown in China, and they therefore questioned his overall credibility. Memo of Conversation, August 16, 1951, reel 24, frames 285–86, MF C0012, RG 59, Archives II.

57. Memo of Conversation, undated 1951, reel 24, frame 287, MF C0012, RG 59, Archives II.

58. Chinese Delegation to the United Nations to the Delegation of the United Kingdom, enclosing "a letter of appeal to the General Assembly from the Chinese Community of Singapore," January 7, 1952, CO 1033/3, TNA; Saving 840, Governor of Singapore to the SSC, May 19, 1952, CO1033/3, TNA.

59. State Department Memorandum, "What is being done about Chinese Communist extortion from relatives in the United States?," reel 24, frames 948–49, C0012, RG 59, Archives II.

60. "Guoqu yinian gongfei ruhe pohai huaqiao," *Qiaowu Yuebao*, issue 6, December 1952, Taipei, 59–62.

61. There were in fact ample examples of both of these situations occurring. Peterson, *Overseas Chinese*, 32–33.

62. Donghuadong Jie Meizhou qiaojuan qiaohui qingkuang chubu diaocha baogao, August 1954, 235/1/115, Guangzhou.

63. "The US-KMT 'Extortion Letter' Fraud," March 18, 1952, TNA; FO 371/99376, "China News Commentary," no. 25, March 10, 1952, CO 1033/33, TNA.

64. Wu, *Dollars, Dependents and Dogma*, 93.

65. Madeline Hsu has shown that magazines printed in Taishan became a vital way to connect migrants abroad to developments at home. Hsu, *Dreaming of Gold*, 124–55; Cheng, *Citizens of Asian America*, 158.

66. For a comprehensive discussion of the Chinese press in the United States in these years see Him Mark Lai, "The Chinese Press in the United States and Canada after World War II: A Diversity of Voices," *Chinese America: History and Perspectives* 4 (1990): 107–55.

67. *China Daily News*, report by Chester A. Reilly, June 9, 1950, 100–63825, New York, Federal Bureau of Investigation (hereafter FBI).

68. Tung Pok Chin and Winifred C. Chin, *Paper Son: One Man's Story* (Philadelphia: Temple University Press, 2000), 84–93.

69. *China Daily News*, report by Roland G. Kearns, June 11, 1953, 100–63825, New York, FBI.

70. "Taishan guiqiao daibiaohui jueding jiaqiang dui guowai huaqiao xuanchuan," *Qiao Xun* 7.21 (September 1950): 6.

71. Huaqiao baozhi he Xianggang baozhi caiyong huaqiao guangbo gao qingkuang de diaocha baogao, November 1954, National Library of China, Beijing, PRC.

72. "The *China Daily News* Case," issued by the Committee to Support the *China Daily News*, box 926, folder 12, MC001, ACLU; Yu, *To Save China*, 186–88.

73. "Jiang te tixu pohuai Huaqiao Ribao, Niuyue qiaobao zu yong bao weiyuanhui, shi zuo houdun," *Qiao Xun* 30.15 (March 1951), Beijing.

74. *China Daily News*, Report by Roland G. Kearns, July 22, 1952, 100–63825, New York, FBI.

75. Ibid.

76. "Three More Men Named in Chinese Racket," *New York Times*, April 30, 1952, 2.

77. Yu, *To Save China*, 188; *United States of America v. China Daily News, Inc. and Eugene Moy*, Appendix to Brief of Defendants-Appellants, *China Daily News* Inc. and Eugene Moy, series 3, box 926, folder 13, C138–159, ACLU.

78. *United States of America v. China Daily News, Inc. and Eugene Moy*, Appendix to Brief of Defendants-Appellants, *China Daily News* Inc. and Eugene Moy, pp. 89a–90a, series 3, box 926, folder 13, C138–159, ACLU.

79. American Civil Liberties Union Memorandum, Re: *China Daily News*—Eugene Moy Case, February 8, 1956, series 3, box 926, folder 12, ACLU.

80. Ibid.

81. Press Release, April 18, 1951, reel 24, frames 80–81, C0012, RG 59, Archives II.

82. Ngai, *Impossible Subjects*, 223.

83. Yu, *To Save China*, 190, 203.

84. Phong claimed that he sent remittances until he learned of the restrictions and then immediately stopped. "China Fund Verdict—Not Guilty," *San Francisco Chronicle*, June 12, 1955. In the aftermath of Phong's acquittal, the case against George Chew for Trading with the Enemy was also dropped. "U.S. to Drop Red China Funds Case," June 13, 1953, *San Francisco Chronicle*, Chinatown, box 201, Pardee Lowe Papers, Hoover Institution.

85. *United States of America v. China Daily News, Inc. and Eugene Moy*, Appendix to Brief of Defendants-Appellants, *China Daily News* Inc. and Eugene Moy, pp. 89a–90a, series 3, box 926, folder 13, C138–159, ACLU.

86. Yu, *To Save China*, 188–89.

87. Letter of Ida Pruitt for the Friends of Eugene Moy, December 9, 1955, series 3, box 926, folder 12, ACLU.

88. American Civil Liberties Union Memorandum, Re: *China Daily News*—Eugene Moy Case, February 8, 1956, series 3, box 926, folder 12, ACLU.

6. Crossing the Bamboo Curtain

1. Interviews with Zhang Shijie, Wang Guoyi, Hao Cihang, and Sai Dunxi, in *Xianggang Diaojingling ying de dansheng yu xiaoshi, 1949–1997*, Oral History Series No. 12, ed. Hu Chunhui (Taipei: Academia Historica, 1997), 53–87, 103–43, 171–89, 191–207.

2. Hu Yueh, "The Problem of Chinese Refugees in Hong Kong," *Asian Survey* 2.1 (March 1962): 30.

3. "Zhongyang renmin zhengfu gong'an bu gongbu luke wanglai Xianggang, Aomen guanli banfa," *Qiao Xun*, vol. 49, August 19, 1951, Beijing.

4. "Hong Kong Is Now No Refugee Heaven," *New York Times*, July 11, 1951, 3. Harsh punishments are hard to document, but unsuccessful escapees did face prison sentences; see Hong Kong, Foreign Service Despatch 291 from Hong Kong, August 24, 1955, box 7, folder 1-C/4, Records of the SCA, RG 59, Archives II.

5. Kathleen Newland, "The Impact of U.S. Refugee Policies on U.S. Foreign Policy: A Case of the Tail Wagging the Dog?," in *Threatened People, Threatened Borders: World Migration and U.S. Policy*, ed. Michael S. Teitelbaum and Myron Weiner (New York: W. W. Norton, 1995), 190–214; Ellen Percy Kraly, "U.S. Refugee Policies and Refugee Migration since World War II," in *Immigration and U.S. Foreign Policy*, ed. Robert W. Tucker, Charles B. Keely, and Linda Wrigley (Boulder, CO: Westview Press, 1990), 73–98.

6. See Kim Salomon, *Refugees in the Cold War* (Lund, Sweden: Studentlitteratur, 1991); Gil Loescher, *The UNHCR and World Politics: A Perilous Path* (New York: Oxford University Press, 2001); Peter Gatrell, *Free World? The Campaign to Save the World's Refugees, 1956–1963* (New York: Cambridge University Press, 2011).

7. Chi-kwan Mark, "The 'Problem of People': British Colonials, Cold War Powers, and the Chinese Refugees in Hong Kong, 1949–62," *Modern Asian Studies* 41.6 (2007): 1145–81.

8. Carl Bon Tempo, *Americans at the Gate: The United States and Refugees during the Cold War* (Princeton, NJ: Princeton University Press, 2008); Michael G. Davis, "Impetus for Immigration Reform: Asian Refugees and the Cold War," *Journal of American-East Asian Relations* 7.3–4 (Fall–Winter 1998): 127–56.

9. Hsu has also argued that Chinese refugees have been largely left out of prominent studies of Asian American and Chinese American history. Madeline Hsu, "The Disappearance of America's Cold War Chinese Refugees, 1948–1966," *Journal of American Ethnic History* 31.4 (Summer 2012): 12–33.

10. Alexander Grantham, *Via Ports: From Hong Kong to Hong Kong* (Hong Kong: Hong Kong University Press, 1965), 155.

11. Rennie's Mill was named for a Canadian (surnamed Rennie) who had once owned a mill on the location. After the business went bankrupt, he hanged himself, and the Chinese renamed the location "diao jing ling," or "hanged neck summit." The name was unlucky, however, so when the camp was settled, it was changed to a homonym with a better meaning, "ideal scenery summit." In Cantonese, "diao jing ling" is pronounced "tiu keng leng," and it became the commonly used name for the area in Hong Kong all the way until the Hong Kong government finally evacuated the last of its residents in 1996. See interview with Wang Guoyi, in Hu Chunhui, *Xianggang Diaojingling*, 109.

12. Interview with Hao Cihang, in Hu Chunhui, *Xianggang Diaojingling*, 182–83. The regulations about cooking and lamps stemmed from a fear of fires breaking out and engulfing the community; one particularly disastrous fire in 1953 destroyed a large section of the camp.

13. Ibid., 120.

14. According to novelist Martin Booth, the Rennie's Mill population continued to be dominated by Nationalist patriots in the 1980s, flying the ROC flag and remaining steadfastly loyal to the old Generalissimo. Martin Booth, *The Dragon and the Pearl: A Hong Kong Notebook* (London: Simon & Schuster, 1994), 252–55.

15. UNHCR Summary Record of 13th Meeting, December 4, 1954, "The Situation of Chinese Refugees in Hong Kong," CO 1030/382, TNA.

16. Memorandum, Bacon to Johnson, ECOSOC and Refugee Reports in Recent Committee Three Meetings, December 31, 1952, reel 25, RG 59, Archives II. The United States also came to the aid of White Russians by providing refugee visas more easily than it ever did for the Chinese.

17. Glen Peterson, "To Be or Not to Be a Refugee: The International Politics of the Hong Kong Refugee Crisis, 1949–55," *Journal of Imperial and Commonwealth History* 36.2 (June 2008): 177.

18. Edvard Hambro, *The Problem of Chinese Refugees in Hong Kong* (Leiden: A. W. Sijthoff, 1955), 4.

19. Letter from Mervyn Brown, UK delegate to the UN, to L. J. Evans, UN Economic and Social Department, Foreign Office, February 27, 1954, CO 1030/381, TNA.

20. Letter to McConaughy from Clough, December 28, 1953, reel 25, C0012, RG 59, Archives II.

21. Hambro, *Problem of Chinese Refugees*, 18, 32. One of the main problems in Hong Kong was that the new arrivals were not the only ones in desperate need of relief; his mission estimated that 885,000 Chinese entered the colony after World War II, and that most of that number required assistance.

22. Ibid., 34–40. There was also the question of some thirty thousand Chinese in similar predicaments in Macao and elsewhere in Asia who would have to be considered as well if the UN mandate applied to Hong Kong. The UK hoped to avoid a formal decision one way or the other, because it did not want the UN coming in and taking over the refugee situation from local authorities. The UK found it "politically embarrassing" to have outside groups administering relief programs in the colony. The UN mandate on refugees was due to expire in 1958, so if the UN could go that long without reaching a definite determination on the situation in Hong Kong, the UK would be spared the intervention. Brief for UK representative to the UN, December 6, 1954, CO 1030/382, TNA.

23. Chi-kwan Mark, *Hong Kong and the Cold War: Anglo-American Relations, 1949–1957* (New York: Oxford University Press, 2004), 209–10. Additionally, the UK had not extended its participation in the UN Convention Relating to the Status of Refugees to its colonial territories. Peterson, "To Be or Not to Be," 174.

24. Peterson, "To Be or Not to Be," 184.

25. The Hong Kong government did deport illegal immigrants later in the decade, though the idea proved unpopular with the press in the United States and Taiwan.

26. Hambro, *Problem of Chinese Refugees*, 185.

27. Ibid., 186. The survey was a sample of all postwar immigrants, including those legitimately classified as political refugees and those classified as economic immigrants. The political refugees were more likely to seek resettlement elsewhere than the economic immigrants, who tended to prefer integration into Hong Kong. Hambro gives the total number of postwar immigrants as 885,000.

28. Moy was well-known but not always well liked, and the fact that he was the one approaching the IRC could have colored the response. Ena Chao, "Lengzhan yu Nanmin yuanzhu: Meiguo 'Yuanzhu Zhongguo Zhishi Renshi Xiehui,' 1952–59," *Ou Mei Yanjiu* 27.2 (June 1997): 69.

29. Ibid., 65–108; Peterson, "To Be or Not to Be," 177–80; Mark, "'Problem of People,'" 11–12; Hsu, "Disappearance," 19. ARCI also left a complete record of its activities in the Hoover Institution archives, which makes it a more accessible target of study.

30. Memorandum from Chinese Embassy to Walter Judd, March 27, 1952, box 166, folder 166.1, Judd Papers, Hoover Institution.

31. *Congressional Record*, 82nd Cong., 2nd Sess., 1952, 98, pt. 10: A275.

32. Memorandum to ARCI Executive Committee from Oram, Re Fall Fundraising Campaign, October 5, 1953, attached to 5th Executive Committee, May 15, 1952, box 2, folder Executive Committee (I), ARCI Records, Hoover Institution.

33. Memorandum to ARCI and AMBAC from Marvin Liebman, September 16, 1954, attached to 21st Executive Committee, September 16, 1954, box 2, ARCI Records, Hoover Institution.

34. "Group Seeks to Aid Chinese Scholars," *New York Times*, April 29, 1952, 2.

35. Escapee Program Submission, FY 1954, reel 25, C0012, RG 59, Archives II.

36. Memorandum, Martin to McConaughy, Developments in Escapee Program, October 27, 1952, reel 25, RG 59, Archives II.

37. C0012, Memorandum, Briefing Material for the Secretary, March 7, 1952, reel 24, frames 948, 955–56, RG 59, Archives II.

38. Hambro, *Problem of Chinese Refugees*, 188.

39. Results to Date and Prospects for the Future—an Appraisal of ARCI's Program by B. A. Garside, October 1953, Purpose and Program of ARCI, box 1, ARCI Records, Hoover Institution.

40. Report to ARCI Executive Committee by the Executive Director, December 10, 1953, attached to 18th Executive Committee, December 10, 1953, box 2, ARCI Records, Hoover Institution.

41. Escapee Program Submission, FY 1954, reel 25, C0012, RG 59, Archives II; Chao, "Lengzhan yu Nanmin yuanzhu," 87.

42. Mark, *Hong Kong*, 206–7.

43. Letter from George A. Fitch to B. A. Garside, November 28, 1952, box 5, folder ARCI Agenda 1952, ARCI Records, Hoover Institution.

44. Savingram 1449 from Hong Kong to SSC, "Activities of the Judd Committee," September 8, 1952, CO 1023/117, TNA.

45. The 1965 Immigration Act added status as a refugee from communism to the list of visa preferences, but the United States did not have a refugee policy based on humanitarian, not political, qualifications until Congress passed the Refugee Act in 1980. Kraly, "U.S. Refugee Policies," 84.

46. Norman L. Zucker, "Refugee Resettlement in the United States: Policy and Problems," *Annals of the American Academy of Political and Social Science*, vol. 467 (May 1983), 172–75.

47. Pub. L. No. 83–203 §§ 2–4, 67 Stat. 400, 405–7 (1953).

48. Bon Tempo, *Americans at the Gate*, 55.

49. Ibid., 50–51.

50. Eventually, Scott McLeod, head of the SCA, was replaced as the administrative head of the program, some changes to the sponsorship process were made, and together this allowed the screenings to go much faster. Ibid., 57.

51. Memo to Gerety from Halleck Rose, RRP, January 31, 1956, box 8, folder Far East, SCA-ORMA, RG 59, Archives II.

52. Report on the Survey of the Investigative Section and RRP in the Consulate General in Hong Kong, July 14, 1955, box 8, folder Far East, SCA-ORMA, RG 59, Archives II; Memo to Gerety from Halleck Rose, RRP, January 31, 1956, box 8, folder Far East, SCA-ORMA, RG 59, Archives II.

53. Memo to Gerety from Halleck Rose, RRP, January 31, 1956, box 8, folder Far East, SCA-ORMA, RG 59, Archives II.

54. Memo to Gerety from Jean J. Chenard, January 31, 1956, box 8, folder Far East, SCA-ORMA, RG 59, Archives II.

55. "Zenyang shenqing tebie yimin fu Mei," *Huaqiao Yue Bao* 25 (July 1944): 7–11; "Fu zhu Niuyue qiaowu weiyuanhui," *Huaqiao Yue Bao* 40 (October 1945): 40–41.

56. New York to Taipei, Fu Mei tebie yimin zajuan, May 10, 1956, 172–3/0792, MOFA, Academia Historica, Taipei.

57. 18th Executive Committee, December 10, 1953, box 2, ARCI Records, Hoover Institution.

58. Paine Knickerbocker, "Five Happy Refugees from China Dock Here," January 9, 1955, *San Francisco Chronicle*, in China File, ARCI General Records 1952–59, box 165, Judd Papers, Hoover Institution.

59. Report on the Refugee Relief Program, attached to the 19th Executive Committee, September 13, 1955, box 2, ARCI Records, Hoover Institution.

60. "Re: U.S. Refugee Relief Act of 1953 as It Concerns Chinese Applicants," October 8, 1953, 172–3/0792, MOFA, Academia Historica, Taipei.

61. Memorandum, Pierce J. Gerety to F. E. Robertson, March 7, 1956, box 10, folder Refugee Relief Act of 1953, RG 59, Archives II.

62. Memorandum to All Regional Commissioners and District Directors from the Commissioner, May 25, 1955, box 43, 56336/243(h) pt. 1, RG 85, NARA.

63. There is more on these students in chapter 7. See also Hsu, "Disappearance," 16.

64. U.S. Congress, Senate, Committee on the Judiciary, *Amendments to the Refugee Relief Act of 1953*, 84th Cong., 2nd Sess., 1956, 6–7.

65. Foreign Service Despatch from AmConsulate, Fukuoka, December 30, 1955, 56351/4.12, RG 85, NARA.

66. Immigration and Naturalization Service, *Annual Report*, 1961 (Washington, DC: Government Printing Office, 1961), 24.

67. Report on ARCI by G. W. Aldington, November 17, 1952, CO 1023/117, TNA. ARCI would later come under suspicion from both the PRC and historians that it had been a CIA front organization. Hugh Wilford claims as much in *The Mighty Wurlitzer: How the CIA Played America* (Cambridge, MA: Harvard University Press, 2009), 31–36. Even though many of the ARCI elite were affiliated with other CIA activities, however, there is no direct evidence that it was ever actually a front for CIA activities in Hong Kong.

68. Sir A. Grantham to SSC, "Chinese Refugees," January 25, 1952, CO 1023/117, TNA.

69. Conflicts between supporters of the KMT and CCP broke out periodically. Frank Welsh, *A Borrowed Place: The History of Hong Kong* (New York: Kodansha International, 1993), 444, 453–56.

70. Aristide Z. Zolberg et al., *Escape from Violence: Conflict and the Refugee Crisis in the Developing World* (Oxford: Oxford University Press, 1989), 156–61.

71. "Mei 'xin nanmin fa'an' zhun er qian 'Zhongguo nanmin' rujing, Jiang bang fenzi tujie 'tongyi' rujing de jihui chengji leisuo," *Qiao Xun*, no. 169 (October 29, 1953), Beijing.

72. State Instruction: U.S. Escapee Program Activities in the Far East, February 10, 1955, 250–461, box 6, USIS, Hong Kong, RG 84, Archives II. The Escapee Program was completely distinct from the Refugee Relief Act; the former assisted a select few Chinese with resettlement, whereas the latter offered visas for immigration to the United States. Some Escapee Program beneficiaries ultimately entered the United States under RRA visas, but these were two separate, complementary programs. All refugee work in East Asia fell under the purview of FERP, the Far East Refugee Program.

73. Ibid.

74. Chinese scholar Li Xiaogang has studied what he calls a major contradiction in U.S. refugee policy and U.S. anticommunism with regard to Europe, noting that although the United States wanted to make good use of the escapees for its information work, it would have suited long-term American goals better if dissidents remained in their countries of origin and struggled for internal change. Moreover, even with American propaganda touting the existence of refugees as proof of the bankruptcy of the regimes they fled, these regimes' leadership often benefited from having troublemakers depart. The United States was also often limited by its efforts not to incite too many defections. For the governments being left behind, U.S. information work was a small price to pay for internal stability. See Li Xiaogang, *Nanmin Zhengce yu Meiguo Waijiao* [Refugee policy and U.S. foreign relations] (Beijing: Shijie Zhishi, 2004), 46–52.

75. Two programs interviewed Chinese refugees and European migrants leaving the mainland, "Uplift" and "Charity." The full reports can be found in Records of the Division of Acquisition and Distribution, Office of Libraries and Intelligence, Special Assistant for Intelligence, 1947–55, Hong Kong Interrogation Reports, 1953–55, RG 59, Archives II.

76. Foreign Service Despatch 291 from Hong Kong, August 24, 1955, box 7, folder 1-C/4, Records of the SCA, RG 59, Archives II.

77. It is not clear if the version in the files contains the altered details or the original story; the value of the narrative as a propaganda effort, however, remains either way.

78. Memorandum from James Campbell, U.S. Escapee Program Activities in the Far East, March 16, 1955, box 6, USIS Hong Kong, RG 84, Archives II.

79. Grantham, *Via Ports*, 155–56. As John M. Carroll has noted, there is a debate in the historiography on the fire as to whether it was the disaster of the fire that spurred the British government to provide funds for the Hong Kong government to build resettlement complexes and its first public housing apartment blocks, or if the process of creating public housing had already begun but became more palatable to the Chinese elite in the economy in the wake of the fire. John M. Carroll, *A Concise History of Hong Kong* (Lanham, MD: Rowman & Littlefield, 2007), 145.

80. ADST Foreign Affairs Oral History Project, interview with Arthur Hummel by Charles Stuart Kennedy, April 13, 1994, transcript in Lauinger Library Special Collections, Georgetown University, Washington, DC.

81. "Recommended Changes in USIS Hong Kong Magazine 'World Today,'" March 2, 1953, *World Today*, box 3, Classified General Records of the USIS Hong Kong, 1951–55, RG 84, Archives II.

82. Interview with Qian Dunxi, in Hu Chunhui, *Xianggang Diaojingling*, 201–2; Interview with Wang Guoyi, ibid., 143. The men give different buying and selling prices for the magazines, but both remember relying heavily on the income they earned from selling them. In the interview with Wang Guoyi, Hu Chunhui recalls that the United States stopped these publications only when it recognized the PRC and shifted the money toward cultural exchanges.

83. Interview with Zhang Shijie in Hu Chunhui, ibid., 53–87.

84. Mark, *Hong Kong*, 177–78.

85. Ibid., 2; Memo, to SCA McLeod from SY Flinn, July 17, 1956, 220.1 Passport Fraud 1956, box 1, ACA, RG 59, Archives II.

86. Mark, *Hong Kong*, 213.

87. UN Economic and Social Council, 24th Session, July 24, 1957, CO 1030/778, TNA.

88. Letter to J. A. Snellgrove from K. G. Ashton, September 6, 1957, CO 1030/778, TNA.

89. Letter to Mr. Wallace, from K. G. Ashton, March 2, 1959, CO 1030/781, TNA.

90. J. B. Johnston to Alexander Grantham, May 17, 1957, CO 1030/777, TNA.

91. For example, as late as 1962, the ROC government and Free China Relief Association (a quasi-nongovernmental organization) publicized the story of a group of students arrested while sailing to Hong Kong and deported by the British authorities, indicting the whole of the free world for its failure to adhere to humanitarian principles. "Deportation of Young People Seeking Freedom in Hong Kong," April 4, 1962, file 642/0047, Xianggang Nanbao wenti ziliao, MOFA Taipei.

92. Letter to C. H. Johnston from J. B. Sidebothem, October 24, 1952, CO 1023/117, TNA.

93. For example, Britain's own War Department tried to donate some ninety-six thousand pairs of women's woolen underpants left over from post–World War II relief efforts in Europe. The Hong Kong government was forced to thank them for the offer but acknowledged that it could make only limited use of such things in the subtropical colony. Letter to A. G. W. Drew from J. A. Snellgrove, November 18, 1957, CO 1030/779, TNA.

94. Suggestions for what needed to be undertaken can be found in Louise W. Holborn, *Refugees, a Problem of Our Time: The Work of the United Nations High Commissioner for Refugees, 1951–1972* (Metuchen, NJ: Scarecrow Press, 1975), 680–86; Hambro, *Problem of Chinese Refugees*, 86–124.

95. Gatrell, *Free World?*, 60.

96. Holborn, *Refugees*, 692–93.

97. Hong Kong to State, May 11, 1962, China Cables 5/61, National Security Files (hereafter NSF), box 25, Presidential Library of John F. Kennedy, Boston (hereafter JFK Library).

98. Statement of D. N. Edwards, UK, Afternoon Session of the UNHCR, May 15, 1962, 172–3/5141, Academia Historica, Taipei.

99. Hong Kong to State, May 22, 1962, China Cables 5/61, NSF, box 25, JFK Library.

100. Geneva to State, May 21, 1962, China Cables 5/61, NSF, box 25, JFK Library.

101. Letter from Dr. Tianfu E. Tsiang, Permanent Representative of China, to Secretary-General of the United Nations, May 25, 1962, 172–3/5141, Academia Historica, Taipei.

102. The British also added that Hong Kong had plenty of rice. State to Taipei, May 24, 1962, China Cables 5/61, NSF, box 25, JFK Library.

103. Message ROC to Hong Kong authorities, June 5, 1962, 172–3/5141, Academia Historica, Taipei. Unlike in 1950, though, there was no reason in 1962 to think the majority of new arrivals preferred to resettle in Taiwan. The first influx of refugees were often affiliated personally or professionally with the Nationalist regime; this second wave consisted of individuals fleeing economic disaster and widespread famine. If the ROC government was aware of just how few of these new migrants would prefer to start a new life in Taiwan, the offer may have been a face-saving measure.

104. These were more than idle calls—Nationalist leaders presented Kennedy with plans and requested his support and assistance in various measures, ranging from small personnel drops to much larger incursions. CIA report, Chiang Kai-shek views on advisability of GRC action against the Chinese mainland, Return to the Mainland 1/1/62–5/2/62, NSF, box 23, JFK Library.

105. Cheng Pao-nan to UNHCR, May 15, 1962, 172–3/5141, Academia Historica, Taipei.

106. Copy of form letter from Walter H. Judd, Ad Hoc Organizing Committee, Emergency Committee for Chinese Refugees, May 22, 1962, 172–3/5141, Academia Historica, Taipei.

107. Catherine Forslund, *Anna Chennault: Informal Diplomacy and Asian Relations* (Lanham, MD: Rowman & Littlefield, 2002), 44–45.

108. S. Res. 346, May 24, 1962, 87th Cong., 2nd Sess.

109. State to Hong Kong, May 24, 1952, China Cables 5/61, NSF files, box 25, JFK Library.

110. Hong Kong to State, May 26, 1962, China Cables 5/61, NSF files, box 25, JFK Library.

111. INS *Annual Reports* (1962–66); Roger Daniels, *Coming to America: A History of Immigration and Ethnicity in American Life* (New York: Perennial, 2002), 337.

112. Report from Chinese Embassy in Washington to MOFA, undated (May 1962), 172–3/5129, Academia Sinica, Taipei.

113. Telegram 575 to Hong Kong from Colonial Office, June 7, 1962, CO 1030/1312, TNA.

114. Telegram 580 to Hong Kong from Colonial Office, June 7, 1962, CO 1030/1312, TNA.

115. Chinese Refugees in Hong Kong, n.d., CO 1030/781, TNA. This may have been a reference to U.S. suspicion of illegal Chinese immigrants, which peaked in the mid-to-late 1950s.

116. Mark, "'Problem of People,'" 37.

7. Cold War Hostages

1. Yelong Han, "An Untold Story: American Policy toward Chinese Students in the United States, 1949–1955," *Journal of American–East Asian Relations* 1 (Spring 1993): 79–81.

2. For example, the University of Minnesota reported in 1949 that it raised $4,000 for forty-eight Chinese students in need. Letter, E. G. Williamson to Walter Judd, July 12, 1949, Judd, box 22, location 143.C.20.3B, Foreign Affairs Committee, 1943–62, Minnesota Historical Society, St. Paul (hereafter MHS).

3. Yelong Han, "Untold Story," 80.

4. Hongshan Li, *U.S. China Educational Exchange: State, Society, and Intercultural Relations, 1905–1950* (New Brunswick, NJ: Rutgers University Press, 2008), 171.

5. *Congressional Record*, 82nd Cong., 1st Sess., 1951, 97, pt. 12:A1469–70.

6. Committee on Educational Interchange Policy, *Chinese Students in the United States, 1948–55: A Study in Government Policy* (New York: Institute of International Education, 1956), 12–13.

7. Letter, Clarence Linton, President of the National Association of Foreign Student Advisors, to Senator Tom Connally, August 1, 1949, Chinese-U.S. Foreign Policy, Sen. 81A-F8 (282–1) (Ch-U.S. For Pol, 81st), RG 46, NARA.

8. *Congressional Record*, 81st Cong., 1st Sess., 1949, 95, pt. 8:10505.

9. Ross Y. Koen, *The China Lobby in American Politics* (New York: Macmillan, 1960), 28–29.

10. Letters from Chinese Refugees Seeking Visas (Visas), Judd, box 32, location 149.F.3.6F, Justice Department, 1945–51 (Justice), MHS.

11. "Sensible Solution," *San Francisco Chronicle*, May 31, 1951, Chinatown, box 201, Pardee Lowe Papers, Hoover Institution.

12. "Ou Mei tongxuehui kangyi Meiguo zhengfu zunao Zhongguo liuxuesheng hui guo," December 5, 1953, 111–00052–04; Zhang Xiongwu tan Meidi zunao liuxuesheng de shouduan, undated, 111–00052–04, MOFA Beijing.

13. Many of these letters used very similar language. "Guiguo huaqiao xuesheng gei Mao Zhuxi xie xin," *Renmin Ribao*, November 16, 1950, 1.

14. Guanyu Mei diguoizhuyi zi 1950 nian qi wuli zunao wo liuxuesheng guiguo de yi xie shishi, May–August 1952, 118–00425–01(1), MOFA Beijing; Yelong Han, "Untold Story," 81.

15. Yelong Han, "Untold Story," 83.

16. Gui guo liuxuesheng guanyu Meiguo kouliu woguo liuxuesheng wenti zuotanhui jilu, November 1953–February 1954, 111–00052–04, MOFA Beijing.

17. Zhou Yihuang, "Zhong Mei huitan yu Qian Xuesen hui guo," *Dangshi Tiandi* (June 1998), 16–19; Iris Chang, *Thread of the Silkworm* (New York: Basic Books, 1995).

18. Letter from Wang Bingnan to U. Alexis Johnson, December 28, 1955, 111–00117–08, MOFA-Beijing.

19. Department of State Press Release no. 714, December 30, 1955, FO 371/12079, TNA.

20. Department of State Bulletin, May 24, 1954, 111–00011–01, MOFA Beijing.

21. Madeline Hsu, "Befriending the 'Yellow Peril': Chinese Students and Intellectuals and the Liberalization of U.S. Immigration Laws, 1950–1965," *Journal of American–East Asian Relations* 16.3 (Fall 2009): 145.

22. Wei ju ming liuxuesheng qi jiao Lundun Zhongguo yinhang zhuan Rineiwah Zhongguo daibiaotuan de xin, June 1, 1954, 111–00054–06, MOFA-Beijing; Yu Jun laixin, er, June 16, 1954, 111–00054–06, MOFA-Beijing.

23. Foreign Service Despatch no. 1493, June 4, 1956, 233 Americans in China 1956–57, General File, box 1, Hong Kong Classified General Records, RG 84, Archives II; "American Citizens in Prison in Communist China," April 24, 1953, FO 371/105312, TNA.

24. U.S. Memorandum to Soviet Ministry of Foreign Affairs, "Treatment of Americans by Chinese Communist Authorities," September 1953, FO 371/105312, TNA.

25. The repatriation process proved controversial, and later allegations of coercion in UN POW camps may have resulted in some decisions being something less than voluntary. See

Rosemary Foot, *A Substitute for Victory: The Politics of Peacemaking at the Korean Armistice Talks* (Ithaca, NY: Cornell University Press, 1990), 108–29.

26. File Minutes, unsigned, August 8, 1955, FO 371/115164, TNA.

27. This was part of a larger policy shift. In 1954 the United States adjusted the grounds for preventing departures to exclude individuals with technical knowledge "generally available in the scientific or technical literature," along with new provisions limiting measures to times of open hostility. Memorandum to SAC Washington Field from FBI Director, January 26, 1955, 11.6, Thread of the Silkworm Research Materials, box 11, Iris Chang Papers, Hoover Institution.

28. Leonard A. Kusnitz, *Public Opinion and Foreign Policy: America's China Policy, 1949–1979* (Westport, CT: Greenwood Press, 1984), 71–73; Alfred D. Wilhelm, *The Chinese at the Negotiating Table: Style and Characteristics* (Washington, DC: National Defense University Press, 1994), 169–72.

29. Hammarskjold's trip was in response to a resolution in the UN to take action to obtain the release of fliers imprisoned in China, and it was undertaken with U.S. cooperation and agreement: Discussions between the Secretary-General of the United Nations and the Chinese Prime Minister in Peking, FO 371/115180, TNA. The British speculated that Hammarskjold might be the only person in the world acceptable to both the Chinese and the Americans as a go-between.

30. Letter from M. G. L. Joy to Far East Department, February 22, 1955, transmitting report of January 14, 1955, on Hammarskjold visit to China, FO 371/115180, TNA.

31. Officials in Beijing also grumbled over the idea of the United Nations placing pressure on China on behalf of the United States while keeping their government out. Guanyu Zhong Mei huitan yu Yindu fangmian lianxi de tanhua gao, n.d., 118–00518–02, MOFA Beijing.

32. Letter to Henry Cabot Lodge of the U.S. delegation to the UN from Hammarskjold, March 22, 1955, FO 371/115180, TNA.

33. American Civilians in Communist China, May 3, 1955, box 16, folder Ralph N. Clough "Prisoner Officer," Bureau of Far Eastern Affairs, Republic of China, RG 59, Archives II.

34. The international reaction to this move was positive, but the PRC bristled at press reports that the UN was principally responsible for the decision. It insisted that it had based its decision solely on an assessment of China's situation and the cases of the men involved. Zhou zongli dao Meinong dian, July 15, 1955, 105–00061–03, MOFA Beijing. Zhou Enlai also complained about U.S. statements thanking Hammarskjold for his assistance in securing the releases. Beijing had welcomed Indian mediation but felt the UN secretary-general had only engaged in diplomatic posturing. Zhou zongli jiejian Lai Jiawen dashi shi tanhua de jiyao, July 7, 1955, 105–00061–02, MOFA Beijing.

35. Press Release from the Chinese Embassy in Washington, DC, September 1, 1955, 405.21/0181–0182, MOFA Taipei.

36. Wilhelm, *Chinese at the Negotiating Table*, 186.

37. Steven M. Goldstein, "Dialogue of the Deaf? The Sino-American Ambassadorial-Level Talks, 1955–1970," in *Re-examining the Cold War: U.S.-China Diplomacy, 1954–1973*, ed. Robert S. Ross and Jiang Changbin (Cambridge, MA: Harvard University Press, 2001), 204–5.

38. Yafeng Xia, *Negotiating with the Enemy: U.S.-China Talks during the Cold War, 1949–1972* (Bloomington: Indiana University Press, 2006), 79.

39. Gordon H. Chang, *Friends and Enemies: The United States, China, and the Soviet Union, 1948–1972* (Stanford, CA: Stanford University Press, 1990), 155–57.

40. T. C. Tang, "Peiping's Chicanery at Geneva," August 26, 1955, 172–3/5239, MOFA Taipei.

41. "U.S.-Peiping Talks to Resume Today," *New York Times*, August 8, 1955, 5; "U.S. Cautioned by Formosa," *New York Times*, August 20, 1955.

42. Committee on Educational Interchange Policy, *Chinese Students in the United States*, 12.

43. MOFA Telegram no. 3293/3294, July 29, 1955, 405.21/0181–0182, MOFA Taipei.

44. Yeh Press Conference in Taipei, August 4, 1955, 405.21/0181–0182, MOFA Taipei.

45. Beyond the stated agenda, the two sides agreed as a matter of procedure not to make public statements about progress without first informing the other and to keep the contents of the meetings private. U.S. Department of State, *Foreign Relations of the United States, 1955–1957*, vol. 3, *China* (hereafter *FRUS 1955–57 China*), Telegram from Ambassador U. Alexis Johnson to the Department of State, August 1, 1955, 1–2.

46. U. Alexis Johnson, *The Right Hand of Power* (Englewood Cliffs, NJ: Prentice-Hall, 1984), 242.

47. Telegram from Ambassador Johnson to the Department of State, August 2, 1955, *FRUS 1955–57 China*, 7–9.

48. W. E. Syman in Minutes, March 13, 1956, FO 371/120979, TNA. By contrast, the ROC was very much aware of the size of the Chinese population—its internal memorandums reference "our 100,000 plus overseas Chinese in America." For the ROC, the term "overseas Chinese" included American citizens. MOFA to Embassy in U.S., no. 492, August 13, 1955, 405.21/0181–0182, MOFA Taipei.

49. Johnson, *Right Hand of Power*, 243.

50. U.S. Census, 1950.

51. Telegram from Ambassador Johnson to the Department of State, August 2, 1955, *FRUS 1955–57 China*, 7–9.

52. Memorandum of Conversations, Walter Robertson, Walter McConaughy, and Ambassador V. K. Wellington Koo, August 9, 1955, *FRUS 1955–57 China*, 22–24.

53. MOFA to Embassy in U.S., no. 492, August 13, 1955, 405.21/0181–0182, MOFA Taipei.

54. Telegram to MOFA, no. 3257, August 13, 1955, 405.21/0181–0182, MOFA Taipei.

55. ROC Consulate in New York to MOFA, August 12, 1955, 405.21/0181–0182, MOFA Taipei

56. MOFA Telegram no. 3746, 3747, August 26, 1955, 405.21/0181–0182, MOFA Taipei.

57. Washington to MOFA, no. 4016, September 11, 1955, 172–3/5239, MOFA Taipei.

58. "Wo xuanbu shi er ming Meiqiao suishi keyi li jing, Meiguo Yingguo fangmian guangfan biaoshi huanyin," *Renmin Ribao*, September 10, 1955, 1.

59. Guanyu di shi san ci Zhong-Mei huitan de qingshi, September 1, 1955, 111–00008–01, MOFA Beijing.

60. Juemi, guanyu Zhong-Mei tanpan de qingshi, September 8, 1955, 111–00008–02(1), MOFA Beijing.

61. Agreed Announcement of the Ambassadors of the United States of America and the People's Republic of China, September 10, 1955, *FRUS 1955–57 China*, 85–86.

62. Kenneth Todd Young, *Negotiating with the Chinese Communists: The United States Experience, 1953–1967* (New York: Published for the Council on Foreign Relations by McGraw-Hill, 1968), 64.

63. Telegram from Ambassador U. Alexis Johnson to the Department of State, September 14, 1955, *FRUS 1955–57 China*, 89–90.

64. Wang Bingnan, *Zhong mei huitan jiu nian huigu* (Beijing: Shijie Zhishi, 1985), 56.

65. Diandang 368 hao yifa Rineiwah—Neirong dui Meifang pianmian fabiao shumian shengming, September 15, 1955, 111–00066–07(1), MOFA Beijing.

66. Telegram 912 from Peking to FO, October 4, 1955, FO 371/115119, TNA.

67. Guanyu Zhong Mei huitan de qingshi [Request for instructions regarding Sino-American talks], September 18, 1955, 111–00008–07, MOFA Beijing.

68. Taipei thought even the discussion was a threat to its position. Aide-Memoire, January 25, 1956, 405.21/0100, MOFA Taipei.

69. Goldstein, "Dialogue of the Deaf?," 210–11.

70. Zhang fubuzhang jiejian Yindu daiban tanhua jiyao, November 3, 1955, 105–00062–01, MOFA Beijing.

71. Letter from Basil Turnell, Colonial Office, to I. J. M. Sutherland, January 20, 1956, FO 371/120979, TNA.

72. Telegram no. 32 from Peking to FO, January 12, 1956, FO 371/120979, TNA.

73. Telegram 1109 from Peking to Foreign Office, transmitting statement from the Chinese Foreign Ministry, December 16, 1955, FO 371/115200, TNA.

74. Memorandum of Conversation, Robertson, Department of State Assistant Secretary of Far Eastern Affairs, and Ambassador Nehta of the Indian Embassy, January 20, 1956, box 1, Asian Communist Affairs, Subject Files 1953–56, 210.1, RG 59, Archives II.

75. Guangzhou waishichu bao huide guiguo liuxuesheng he huaqiao qingkuang deng, May 8, 1956, 111–00235–02(1), MOFA Beijing.

76. April 30 Returnees, Guangzhou huaqiao shiwuju guanyu jiedai Meizhou guiqiao de baogao, Telegram to MOFA, OCAC, May 29, 1956, 111–00241–02(1), MOFA Beijing. In a tragic bit of foreshadowing, one 1956 returnee in this file mentioned rumors of famine and rice shortages that deterred returnees.

77. April 7 Returnees, Guangzhou huaqiao shiwuju guanyu jiedai Meizhou guiqiao de baogao, Telegram to MOFA, OCAC, May 29, 1956, 111–00241–02(1), MOFA Beijing.

78. W. Allyn Rickett and Adele Rickett, *Prisoners of Liberation: Four Years in a Chinese Communist Prison* (Garden City, NY: Anchor Press, 1973), 322–28. Only Allyn was released during the talks; Adele had been released earlier in the year.

79. In some cases, Chinese repatriates writing to MOFA or the *People's Daily* upon their return to China referenced these interviews as proof that the U.S. government made it very difficult for Chinese to return to the PRC. See Wo yi guiguo de liuxuesheng fanying Meiguo kouliu liuxuesheng de qingkuang, 11/15/53–2/12/54, 111–00052–04, MOFA Beijing.

80. Memorandum to Leland W. Williams from Edward Shaughnessy, District Director INS New York, May 11, 1956, "Redefector Program," 56364/10.1, RG 85, NARA.

81. The copy of the letter in the file is dated May 3, 1956. Report of Investigation, Redefector Activity, Chinese, January 7, 1957, 56364/80.9.1, RG 85, NARA.

82. "Communist China Lures and Coerces Overseas Students to Return to Mainland," *Chinese American Weekly*, May 31, 1956, 56364/10.1, RG 85, NARA.

83. "Chen Nengkuan zai Meiguo shi zenyang shou pohai de," *Renmin Ribao*, January 3, 1956; "Zai weixie he pohai de qifen xia liu Mei xuesheng bei po shenqing Meiguo ji," *Renmin Ribao*, January 9, 1956.

84. No. 188, Chen Shulian Fusizhang tong Yin shiguan Xinge canzan tanhua jiyao, December 8, 1955, 105–00062–05, MOFA Beijing.

85. Telegram 1298 from the Foreign Office to Peking, September 24, 1955, FO 371/115119, TNA.

86. Letter to C. T. Crowe from H. A. Graves, November 30, 1955, FO 371/115164, TNA.

87. At the time, the Indian Embassy suspected that the PRC's request that it investigate was not really about Liu's right of return, but instead intended to counter a U.S. request that the UK Embassy in Beijing investigate the case of Dr. Bradshaw, an American imprisoned in China. Telegram 23 from Beijing to the Foreign Office, January 10, 1956, FO 371/120979, TNA.

88. Mei Misuli zhouli yiyuan yuanzhang Huokete tan qiansong Liu Yongming wenti, December 31, 1955, 405.21/0096, MOFA Taipei.

89. Fei zhikong Meiguo zuzhi yi qiaosheng li Mei, December 31, 1955, 405.21/0096, MOFA Taipei.

90. Telegram 82 to SSC of Colonies from Hong Kong, February 1, 1956, FO 371/120979, TNA; Letter from P. G. F. Dalton, Hong Kong, to C. D. W. O'Neill, British Embassy, Beijing, February 9, 1956, FO 371/120979, TNA.

91. Telegram 89, to SSC from Hong Kong, February 3, 1956, FO, TNA; 371/120979, Telegram 99 from Peking to Foreign Office, February 4, 1956, FO 371/120979, TNA.

92. New China News Agency, "Liu Yung-ming Comes Back from Hong Kong," February 7, 1956, FO 371/120979, TNA; Letter from P .G. F. Dalton, Hong Kong, to C. D. W. O'Neill, British Embassy, Beijing, February 9, 1956, FO 371/120979, TNA.

93. Telegram 966 from Peking to the Foreign Office, October 19, 1955, FO 371/115199, TNA; Telegram, *Wai fa xi* 383 *hao*, from MOFA, October 29, 1955, 111–00061–05, MOFA Beijing.

94. Wenjian zonghao 165, Chen Shulian Fusizhang tong Yin shiguan Xinge canzan tanhua jiyao, November 22, 1955, 105–00062–04, MOFA Beijing.

95. Telegram 1020 from Beijing to the Foreign Office, November 8, 1955, FO 371/115200, TNA; Outward Telegram from the Commonwealth Relations Office no. 244, December 15, 1955, FO 371/115200, TNA.

96. Letter to C. T. Crowe from O'Neill, November 10, 1955, FO 371/115200, TNA.

97. Letter from O'Neill to W. D. Allen, Foreign Office, December 28, 1955, FO 371/120979, TNA.

98. Letter from H. Graves to W. D. Allen, March 9, 1956, FO 371/120979, TNA.

99. Chinese in U.S. Prisons, Memorandum from Clough to McConaughy, Chinese Affairs, May 23, 1956, box 1, Asian Communist Affairs, 1953–56, RG 59, Archives II.

100. MOFA Telegram 2722, June 1, 1956, 462.7/0001, MOFA Taipei.

101. Chinese in American Prisons, Memorandum of Conversation, June 1, 1956, box 1, Asian Communist Affairs, 1953–56, RG 59, Archives II.

102. "Taipei Unhappy at U.S. Move on Chinese in Jail; India Role in Red Blackmail Resented," *Chinese News*, June 5, 1956, 5, 462.7/0001, MOFA Taipei.

103. MOFA Incoming Telegram 2782 from Sino Embassy Washington, June 4, 1956, 462.7/0001, MOFA Taipei.

104. Chinese in American Prisons, Memorandum of Conversation, June 20, 1956, box 1, Asian Communist Affairs, 1953–56, RG 59, Archives II.

105. Telegram 3116 from Sinoembassy DC, June 20, 1956, 426.7/0001, MOFA Taipei.

106. Telegram 3335–36 from Sinoembassy DC, July 2, 1956, 426.7/0001, MOFA Taipei.

107. Memorandum of Conversation, June 13, 1956, 210.2, box 1, Asian Communist Affairs, 1953–56, RG 59, Archives II; Telegram 4990 from Sinoembassy DC, September 13, 1956, 426.7/0001, MOFA Taipei.

108. Foreign Service Despatch no. 1466, May 24 ,1956, 233 Americans in China 1956–57, General File, box 1, Hong Kong Classified General Records, RG 84, Archives II.

109. Letter to C. T. Crowe from O'Neill, November 21, 1956, FO 371/121017, TNA.

110. Ibid.; Memorandum from American Consul General in Hong Kong, December 18, 1961, 233 Americans in China, 1959–60–61, box 1, Hong Kong Classified General Records, RG 84, Archives II.

111. Telegram to JFK from Julius K. Kremski, January 27, 1961, CO 50–2 People's Republic of China, Central Subject Files, box 45, JFK Library. "Quickly" is relative, of course. Father Walter M. Ciszek was released from a Soviet prison in 1963 after a detention of twenty-three years. Memorandum for Mr. Ralph A. Dungan, April 20, 1963, folder ND 19–3, White House Central Subject Files, box 638, JFK Library.

112. Letter to Mrs. Redmond from Ralph A. Dungan, March 10, 1961, folder ND 19–3, White House Central Subject Files, box 638, JFK Library.

113. CIA Office of Current Intelligence, the Signs of Chinese Communist Friendliness, July 17, 1961, China General 7/15/61–7/24/61, NSF, box 22, JFK Library.

114. Yafeng Xia, "Negotiating at Cross-Purposes: Sino-American Ambassadorial Talks, 1961–68," *Diplomacy & Statecraft* 16 (2005): 297–329.

115. CIA Report, April 19, 1963, Rumors being circulated by Soviet official regarding Chinese possession of atomic capability, China Cables 3/63–5/63, box 26, NSF, JFK Library.

8. Visa Diplomacy

1. As the transitional period between the heady activist days of the late 1940s and the "terrorist" era beginning in the 1970s, not to mention long predating the later emergence of a political opposition party to the KMT that actively supported the notion of independence, the 1960s get a bit buried in the historiography of the Taiwan independence movement. The work of Mei-ling T. Wang is an exception: see Mei-ling T. Wang, *The Dust That Never Settles: The Taiwan Independence Campaign and U.S.-China Relations* (Lanham, MD: University Press of America, 1999). Other works on the independence movement broadly include Chen Jiahong, *Haiwai Taidu Yundong Shi* (Taipei: Qianwei Chubanshe, 1998) and *Taiwan Duli Yundong Shi* (Taipei: Yushan Chubanshe, 2006); Stephane Corcuff, ed., *Memories of the Future: National Identity Issues and the Search for a New Taiwan* (New York: M. E. Sharpe, 2002); A. James Gregor and Maria Hsia Chang, "The Taiwan Independence Movement: The Failure of Political Persuasion," *Political Communication and Persuasion* 2.4 (1985): 363–91; and Joseph Martin, *Terrorism and the Taiwan Independence Movement* (Taipei: Institute on Contemporary China, 1985). Student activism also gets left out of many scholarly treatments of the diplomatic relationship between the two countries. The exception are works that focus explicitly on Taiwan, like Nancy Bernkopf Tucker, *Taiwan, Hong Kong, and the United States, 1945–1992: Uncertain Friendships* (New York: Twayne Publishers, 1994); Steven Phillips, "Building a Taiwanese Republic: The Independence Movement, 1945–Present," in *Dangerous Strait: The U.S.-Taiwan-China Crisis*, ed. Nancy Bernkopf Tucker (New York: Columbia University Press, 2005), 44–69; Paul H. Tai, ed., *United States, China, and Taiwan: Bridges for a New Millennium* (Carbondale: Southern Illinois University Press, 1999). Others do not mention it at all—for example, John Garver, *The Sino-American Alliance: Nationalist China and American Cold War Strategy in Asia* (Armonk, NY: M. E. Sharpe, 1997).

2. Wang, *Dust That Never Settles*, 149–50.

3. Ibid., 128.

4. Tucker, *Taiwan, Hong Kong, and the United States*, 75–77, 114–16.

5. Wang, *Dust That Never Settles*, 173; Phillips, "Building a Taiwanese Republic," 52. George Kerr's account of these events is slightly different; he places Thomas in Taiwan and Joshua in Shanghai during the 228 Incident.

6. Phillips, "Building a Taiwanese Republic," 53.

7. Chen Yi-shen (interviewer), *Haiwai Taidu Yundong Xiangguan renwu koushu shi* (Taipei: Academia Sinica Institute of Modern History, 2009), 83.

8. Phillips, "Building a Taiwanese Republic," 54.

9. Wang, *Dust That Never Settles*, 187.

10. Chen Yi-shen, *Haiwai Taidu*, 85, 91.

11. "Exile Is Fighting for Free Taiwan:'Provisional Regime' Head in Japan Rejects Rule by Chiang or Peiping," *New York Times*, March 5, 1961.

12. Chen Yi-shen, *Haiwai Taidu*, 135–6.

13. Phillips, "Building a Taiwanese Republic," 54.

14. Chen Yi-shen, *Haiwai Taidu*, 138.

15. "The Thomas Liao Case," Chen Cheng Visit 7/31/61 Briefing Books, National Security Files (NSF), box 26, JFK Library.

16. Memorandum to JFK from McGeorge Bundy, the Secretary of State on Liao and the Generalissimo, June 26, 1961, China General 6/13/61–6/27/61, NSF, box 22, JFK Library.

17. Memorandum to McGeorge Bundy from Robert W. Komer, June 23, 1961, China General 6/13/61–6/27/61, NSF, box 22, JFK Library.

18. Memorandum for JFK from McGeorge Bundy, July 7, 1961, China General 6/25/61–7/7/61, NSF, box 22, JKF Library.

19. State to Taipei, June 30, 1961, China Cables 2/61–8/61, NSF, box 25, JFK Library.

20. Taipei to State, July 2, 1961, China Cables 2/61–8/61, NSF, box 25, JFK Library.

21. Memorandum for JFK from McGeorge Bundy, July 7, 1961, China General 6/25/61–7/7/61, NSF, box 22, JKF Library.

22. Letter to Chiang Kai-shek from John F. Kennedy, July 11, 1961, China General 7/8/61–7/14/61, NSF, box 22, JFK Library.

23. "The Thomas Liao Case," Chen Cheng Visit 7/31/61 Briefing Books, box 26, NSF, JFK Library.

24. Briefing Papers for Ch'en Ch'eng Visit, Robert W. Komer, n.d., China (Taiwan and Offshore Islands) 1961–63 [folder 1 of 3], Papers of Robert W. Komer, box 411, JFK Library.

25. Memorandum of Conversation, August 1, 1961, United States–China Relations, China General 8/11/61–8/23/61, NSF, box 22, JFK Library.

26. "U.S. Barred Chiang Foe in Deal to Let Outer Mongolia into UN," *New York Times*, October 30, 1961.

27. Secret memorandum, July 25, 1961, China General 7/25/61–7/27/61, NSF, box 22, JFK Library.

28. Memorandum for Dean Rusk from McGeorge Bundy, March 27, 1962, Visa Case of Thomas W.I. Liao, China General 1/62–3/62, NSF, box 22A, JFK Library.

29. Phillips, "Building a Taiwanese Republic," 53.

30. Dwight D. Eisenhower, "Special Message to the Congress on Immigration," March 17, 1960, online by Gerhard Peters and John T. Woolley, *The American Presidency Project*, http://www.presidency.ucsb.edu/ws/?pid=12160.

31. I-Fen Cheng, *Citizens of Asian America: Democracy and Race during the Cold War* (New York: NYU Press, 2013), 150.

32. Peter Schrag, *Not Fit for Our Society: Immigration and Nativism in America* (Berkeley: University of California Press, 2010), 163.

33. Peter Kwong and Dušanka Miščević have referred to these groups—all overwhelmingly anticommunist by background and inclination—as the "good Chinese" and the "uptown Chinese," to distinguish them from the longtime resident Cantonese, who were largely working class and more inclined toward leftist views. Peter Kwong and Dušanka Miščević, *Chinese America: The Untold Story of America's Oldest New Community* (New York: New Press, 2005), 232.

34. Letter to Charles Frankel from Walter McConaughy, November 13, 1967, EDU: Brain Drain, 1968–69, box 7, Asian Communist Affairs, 1961–73, RG 59, Archives II.

35. Memo to Harry Thayer from John A. Lacey, February 13, 1968, EDU: Brain Drain, 1968–69, box 7, Asian Communist Affairs, 1961–73, RG 59, Archives II.

36. Pei-te Lien, "Ethnic Homeland and Chinese Americans," in *Chinese Transnational Networks*, ed. Tan Chee-Beng (London: Routledge, 2007), 111.

37. Letter to Yu Zhenhai from Xia Liping, March 20, 1967, 406/0013 Taidu Zouqing, MOFA Taipei.

38. Letter to Xia Liping from Yu Zhenhai, n.d., 406/0013 Taidu Zouqing, MOFA Taipei.

39. Letter from Richard Wang, titled "U.S. Needs New Allies," transmitted to Taipei in cable 00630, May 5, 1967, 406/0013 Taidu Zouqing, MOFA Taipei. Other memos reference asking for a "huiguo shu," which moves beyond explanation and asks for repentance.

40. Memo for Wellington Koo from Yu Zhenhai, May 17, 1967, 406/0013 Taidu Zouqing, MOFA Taipei.

41. Fangzhi wei "Taidu" huodong fang'an, August 25, 1967, 406/0013 Taidu zouqing, MOFA Taipei.

42. Hongshan Li, *U.S.-China Educational Exchange: State, Society, and Intercultural Relations, 1905–1950* (New Brunswick, NJ: Rutgers University Press, 2007), 139.

43. Memorandum 5583 from Yu Zhenhai, October 13, 1967, 406/0013 Taidu Zouqing, MOFA Taipei.

44. Letter from Vernon J. Hazlett to Wei-min Lee, December 29, 1967, 406/0014, Taidu Zouqing, MOFA Taipei.

45. Joy Su, "Activists Have Their Own Take on History," *Taipei Times*, December 14, 2003.

46. In Chinese, *Quan Mei Taiwan Duli Lianmeng*. Him Mark Lai has a useful summary of the developing organizations in *Chinese American Transnational Politics*, ed. Madeline Hsu (Urbana: University of Illinois Press, 2010), 40.

47. Message number 1741, March 30, 1967, 406/0013 Taidu Zuoqing , MOFA Taipei.

48. "Formosa for Formosans," *Oklahoma Daily*, December 16, 1966, 406/0013 Taidu Zuoqing, MOFA Taipei.

49. Letter to Rusk from Francis W. Chang, January 5, 1968, POL 23—Organizations (Taiwan Independence Movement 1968–69), box 5, Bureau East Asian and Pacific Affairs, Office of the Country Director for the Republic of China, subject files of the office of ROC Affairs, 1951–75 (EA—ROC, 1951–75), RG 59, Archives II.

50. Lung-chu Chen to Mbekeani, October 8, 1970, 633/90048 Lianheguo Dahui 25 Jie, MOFA Taiwan.

51. Facts Leading to the Arrest of Peng Ming-min, Hsieh Chung-mi, and Wei Ting-chao, n.d., 406/0096 Peng Mingmin deng beibu, MOFA Taipei.

52. Letter to Harold Kahn, November 27, 1964, Letter to Esther Morrison, December 2, 1964, Letter to M. A. Teitelbaum, January 22, 1965, all from James C. Thomson Jr., Penfolda, White House Name File, Lyndon B. Johnson Library, Austin, TX.

53. Telegram from Washington to Taipei, no. 512, March 10, 1965, 406/0096 Peng Mingmin deng beibu, MOFA Taipei.

54. Douglas Mendel, *The Politics of Formosan Nationalism* (Berkeley: University of California, 1970).

55. Letter to Public Affairs Officer, Embassy of the Republic of China from Douglas H. Mendel Jr., April 7, 1965, 406/0096 Peng Mingmin deng beibu, MOFA Taipei.

56. Guomindang Central Committee to Minister of Foreign Affairs, June 29, 1968, 406/0097 Peng Mingmin deng beibu, MOFA Taipei.

57. Peng Ming-min, *A Taste of Freedom: Memoirs of a Formosan Independence Leader* (New York: Holt, Rinehart, and Winston, 1972), 211–13.

58. The Presbyterian church had close ties to the independence movement almost from the beginning; many of the most prominent independence advocates in the United States grew up in Presbyterian churches in southern Taiwan. Milo Thornberry, *Fireproof Moth: A Missionary in Taiwan's White Terror* (Mechanicsburg, PA: Sunbury Press, 2011), 114–24.

59. A cover story of sorts got some press in February 1970. It claimed he traveled to Hong Kong by fishing boat, and unnamed friends there supplied him with travel documents. "U.S. Wary of Chiang Foe," *Chicago Daily News*, February 19, 1970, 406/0098 Peng Mingmin deng beibu, MOFA Taipei.

60. "Taiwan: The Exile," *Newsweek*, February 16, 1970, 42 in 406/0098 Peng Mingmin deng beibu, MOFA Taipei.

61. Chinese Embassy to Secretary of State, January 29, 1970, 406/0098 Peng Mingmin deng beibu, MOFA Taipei.

62. Washington to MOFA, 739, January 29, 1970, 406/0098 Peng Mingmin deng beibu, MOFA Taipei.

63. "U.S. Wary of Chiang Foe," *Chicago Daily News*, February 19, 1970, 406/0098 Peng Mingmin deng beibu, MOFA Taipei.

64. Memorandum to Henry Kissinger from John H. Holdridge, January 28, 1970, Ex Im [1969–70], box 1, White House Central Subject Files, Richard M. Nixon Library, Yorba Linda, CA.

65. Memorandum to Brown from Shoesmith, January 26, 1970, Peng Ming-min: Potential Visa Applicant? Pol 29 Peng Ming-min, 1970, box 9, EA—ROC, 1951–75, RG 59, Archives II.

66. Memorandum from the President's Deputy Assistant for National Security Affairs (Haig) to the President's Assistant for National Security Affairs (Kissinger), October 5, 1970, *FRUS 1969–76*, vol. 17, China, 1969–72, http://history.state.gov/historicaldocuments/frus1969–76v17/d91. In the Liao case, it was the National Security advisers who made the case against the visa, while State fought in favor of it.

67. Letter to Kissinger from Peng, January 23, 1970, Ex Im [1969–70], box 1, White House Central Subject Files, Nixon Library.

68. Memorandum to Kissinger from Holdridge, February 4, 1970, Ex Im [1969–70], box 1, White House Central Subject Files, Nixon Library.

69. Memorandum to Green from Shoesmith, February 5, 1970, Possible Visa Application by Professor Peng Ming-min, box 9, EA—ROC, 1951–75, RG 59, Archives II.

70. Memorandum to file, from Shoesmith, April 29, 1970, Pol 29 Peng Ming-min 1970, box 9, EA—ROC, 1951–75, RG 59, Archives II.

71. Memorandum to Henry Kissinger from John H. Holdridge, January 28, 1970, Ex Im [1969–70], box 1, White House Central Subject Files, Nixon Library.

72. Memorandum to Secretary of State from Green, June 13, 1970, Pol 29 Peng Ming-min 1970, box 9, EA—ROC, 1951–75, RG 59, Archives II.

73. Peng Ming-min, *Taste of Freedom*, 230.

74. Letter to Kissinger from Reischauer, August 17, 1970, Gen Im/M [1969–70], box 5, White House Central Subject Files, Nixon Library.

75. Letter to Kissinger from Barnett, August 13, 1970, Gen Im/M [1969–70], box 5, White House Central Subject Files, Nixon Library.

76. See, for example, Washington to MOFA no. 7111, August 13, 1970, 406/0098 Peng Mingmin deng beibu, MOFA Taipei. Peng gave lectures in London and Canada that Chinese consulates then dissected and reported on to Washington and back to Taipei.

77. Memorandum to Green from Ambassador Brown, August 21, 1970, Reconsideration of the Peng Ming-min Case—Weekend Reading, Pol 29(d) Peng Ming-min August-October 1970, box 9, EA—ROC, 1951–75, RG 59, Archives II.

78. Washington to MOFA no. 8428, September 16, 1970, 406/0098 Peng Mingmin deng beibu, MOFA Taipei.

79. Telegram from MOFA to Washington no. 295, September 21, 1970, 406/0098 Peng Mingmin deng beibu, MOFA Taipei.

80. Peng Ming-min, *Taste of Freedom*, 247.

81. Jerome Alan Cohen, "Peng Case Deserves More Publicity," October 18, 1970, *Boston Globe*, 406/0098 Peng Mingmin deng beibu, MOFA Taipei.

82. Memorandum for Henry Kissinger from Winston Lord, Memcon of your conversations with Chou En-lai, July 29, 1971, National Security Archive, http://www2.gwu.edu/~nsarchiv/NSAEBB/NSAEBB66/ch-34.pdf.

83. Memorandum of Conversation, February 24, 1972, National Security Archive, http://www2.gwu.edu/~nsarchiv/NSAEBB/NSAEBB106/NZ-3.pdf.

84. Conversation among President Nixon, his Assistant for National Security Affairs (Kissinger), and his Chief of Staff (Haldeman), March 13, 1972, *FRUS 1969–76*, vol. 17, *China*, http://history.state.gov/historicaldocuments/frus1969–76v17/d212.

Conclusion

1. Nancy Bernkopf Tucker, *Taiwan, Hong Kong, and the United States, 1945–1992: Uncertain Friendships* (New York: Twayne Publishers, 1994), 97.

2. Memo to Green from Lindsey Grant, April 20, 1964, Talking Points on Communist China, Sino-United States Relations, box 1, Asian Communist Affairs, 1961–73, RG 59, Archives II.

3. Memo to Green from Cunningham, November 16, 1964, Talking Points on Communist China, Sino-United States Relations, box 1, Asian Communist Affairs, 1961–73, RG 59, Archives II.

4. Michael Lumbers, "'Staying Out of This China Muddle': The Johnson Administration's Response to the Cultural Revolution," *Diplomatic History* 31.2 (April 2007): 263.

5. On the factional divisions in MOFA see Stephen Fitzgerald, *China and the Overseas Chinese: A Study of Peking's Changing Policy, 1949–1970* (Cambridge: Cambridge University Press, 1972), 162–83; Theresa Chong Carino, *China and the Overseas Chinese in Southeast Asia* (Quezon City: New Day Publishers, 1985); Melvin Gurtov, "The Foreign Ministry and Foreign Affairs in the Chinese Cultural Revolution," in *The Cultural Revolution in China*, ed. Thomas W. Robinson (Berkeley: University of California Press, 1971), 313–66.

6. Hedrick Smith, "Effect on Overseas Chinese," *New York Times*, January 19, 1967, 2; also "To Its Millions Overseas, China Remains a Dominant, if Uninviting, Presence," *New York Times*, April 16, 1967, 17. In this last piece, an Indonesian Chinese businessman complained that "the publicity given to the Cultural Revolution in China has made the situation worse by giving the impression that the Chinese want to overrun the world."

7. Memorandum for Mr. Rostow, December 2, 1968, China (A) vol. 13 7/68–12/68 [1 of 2], box 242, National Security Files, Country File, LBJ Library.

8. Tucker, *Taiwan, Hong Kong, and the United States*, 95–96. Kennedy proved especially wary of any talk of Taiwan-based exiles staging a successful uprising on the mainland after the failure at the Bay of Pigs.

9. Letter to Alfred Le S. Jenkins from David L. Osborn, August 25, 1970, POL 17–8 Contacts with Chicoms—L. P. Sung, box 6, Asian Communist Affairs, 1961–73, RG 59, Archives II.

10. Travel between the United States and Communist China, n.d., Travel to Communist China, 1958–59, box 3, Asian Communist Affairs, 1961–73, RG 59, Archives II.

11. Snow was allowed to enter to interview Mao in 1960. Memo for McGeorge Bundy from William Burbeck, April 26, 1963, China General 4/63–6/63, box 24, NSF, JFK Library; Press Guidance: Travel of Dr. and Mrs. Rosen to Communist China, n.d., Travel Controls (General) October–December 1964, box 3, Asian Communist Affairs, 1961–73, RG 59, Archives II.

12. In 1957, a group of American students at Moscow's "Festival of Youth and Students" received an invitation from Beijing to visit China. Before they left for Asia, the U.S. Embassy warned them that crossing the border could result in forfeiting their passports and prosecution under the Trading with the Enemy Act. "U.S. Warns Group Not to Go to China," *New York Times*, August 14, 1957.

13. Ellen C. Collier, United States Policy toward Communist China in the 1970s: A Brief Review of Background and Alternatives, October 24, 1969, Congressional Research Service, ProQuest Congressional.

14. Lumbers, "'Staying Out of This China Muddle,'" 272.

15. Memorandum to Bundy from Jacobson, January 5, 1966, Sino-United States Relations F-1 January–April 1966, box 1, Asian Communist Affairs, 1961–73, RG 59, Archives II.

16. Draft memorandum to Bundy from Jacobson, Entry of ChiCom Scholars into United States, n.d., Travel Controls (General) January–August 1966, box 2, Asian Communist Affairs, 1961–73, RG 59, Archives II.

17. Yafeng Xia, "Negotiating at Cross Purposes: Sino-American Ambassadorial Talks, 1961–68," *Diplomacy & Statecraft* 16 (2005): 317.

18. Press Guidance: Travel of Dr. and Mrs. Rosen to Communist China, n.d., Travel Controls (General), October–December 1964, box 3, Asian Communist Affairs, 1961–73, RG 59, Archives II.

19. "The Strange Tale of American Attempts to Leap the Wall of China," *New York Times*, April 18, 1971.

20. Memorandum to McGeorge Bundy from James C. Thomson Jr., December 31, 1965, Travel Restrictions Vol. 1, box 50, NSF Subject Files, LBJ Library.

21. Memorandum to Secretary of State from Berger, Removal of Passport Restriction for Travel to Communist China, n.d., Travel Controls F-3, September–December 1966, box 2, Asian Communist Affairs, 1961–73, RG 59, Archives II.

22. *United States v. Laub et al.*, 385 U.S. 475 (1967); *Lynd v. Rusk*, 389 F. 2d 940 (1967).

23. U.S. Policy toward Communist China, Policy Planning Council, December 1968, box 50, NSF Subject Files, LBJ Library.

24. Memorandum to Henry Kissinger re Changes in Regulations Relating to China, n.d., POL—U.S./Communist China Policy, 1969, box 5, EA—ROC, 1951–75, RG 59, Archives II.

25. Editorial Note, *FRUS 1969–76*, vol. 1, *Foundations of Foreign Policy, 1969–72*, Document 33, 97–98.

26. Memorandum to Towery from Kent Crane, December 20, 1971, ChiCom Propaganda Tactics in the United States, POL 11 Nationalism—Overseas Chinese, box 10, EA—ROC, 1951–75, RG 59, Archives II.

27. "Peking Gains Favor with Chinese in the United States," *New York Times*, February 22, 1971.

28. Memorandum to Henry Kissinger from John H. Holdridge, April 20, 1971, Ex FG 11 4/1/71–4/30/71, box 4, White House Central Files, Nixon Library.

29. "U.S. and China: Ping . . . Pong . . . A New Approach to Diplomacy," *New York Times*, April 11, 1971.

30. "The Strange Tale of American Attempts to Leap the Wall of China," *New York Times*, April 18, 1971.

31. Letter to Nixon from Carl McIntire, National Chairman, United States March for Victory, August 3, 1971, EX RE 21 Tennis 1/1/71, box 10, White House Central Subject Files, Nixon Library.

32. Memorandum of Conversation, April 23, 1971, Chou En-lai Invitation to Senator Mansfield, POL 17–8, Contacts with Communist Representatives China 1971, box 6, Asian Communist Affairs, 1961–73, RG 59, Archives II.

33. A. M. Halpern, "China in the Postwar World," *China Quarterly* 21 (January–March 1965): 32.

34. Tucker, *Taiwan, Hong Kong, and the United States*, 3.

Index